RUTH SCURR

Ruth Scurr is an historian, biographer and literary critic. She teaches history and politics at Cambridge University, where she is a Lecturer and Fellow of Gonville & Caius College. Her first book, *Fatal Purity: Robespierre and the French Revolution* won the Franco-British Society Literary Prize, was longlisted for the Samuel Johnson Prize, short-listed for the Duff Cooper Prize and was listed among the 100 Best Books of the Decade in *The Times*. She reviews regularly for the *Times Literary Supplement*, *The Telegraph* and the *Wall Street Journal* and is a Fellow of the Royal Society of Literature.

ALSO BY RUTH SCURR

Fatal Purity: Robespierre and
the French Revolution

RUTH SCURR

John Aubrey

My Own Life

VINTAGE

For M. F. R.

1 3 5 7 9 10 8 6 4 2

Vintage
20 Vauxhall Bridge Road,
London SW1V 2SA

Vintage is part of the Penguin Random House
group of companies whose addresses can be
found at global.penguinrandomhouse.com.

Penguin
Random House
UK

Copyright © Ruth Scurr 2015

Ruth Scurr has asserted her right to be identified
as the author of this Work in accordance with
the Copyright, Designs and Patents Act 1988

First published in Vintage in 2016
First published in hardback by Chatto & Windus in 2015

www.vintage-books.co.uk

A CIP catalogue record for this book
is available from the British Library

ISBN 9780099490630

Typeset by Palimpsest Book Production Ltd, Falkirk, Stirlingshire

Printed and bound by Clays Ltd, St Ives plc

Penguin Random House is committed to a sustainable future
for our business, our readers and our planet. This book is made
from Forest Stewardship Council® certified paper.

MIX
Paper from
responsible sources
FSC
www.fsc.org   FSC® C018179

Contents

Contents

Dramatis Personae

Kings, Queens and Lord Protectors in Aubrey's lifetime

Charles I (1600–49), King of England, Scotland and Ireland from 27 March 1625 until his execution on 30 January 1649.

Henrietta Maria of France (1609–69), Queen Consort of England, Scotland and Ireland as the wife of Charles I, and mother of the future kings Charles II and James II.

Oliver Cromwell (1599–1658), Lord Protector of the Commonwealth of England, Scotland and Ireland from 16 December 1653 until his death on 3 September 1658.

Richard Cromwell (1626–1712), son of Oliver; Lord Protector of the Commonwealth of England, Scotland and Ireland from 3 September 1658 until he resigned on 25 May 1659.

Charles II (1630–85), son of Charles I, restored as King of England, Scotland and Ireland on 29 May 1660 until his death on 6 February 1685.

James II (1633–1701), King of England and Ireland, and James VII of Scotland, from 6 February 1685 until his deposition in the Glorious Revolution of 1688.

William III (1650–1702) of Orange and Mary II (1662–94), co-regents over England, Scotland and Ireland after the Glorious Revolution of 1688. William was James II's nephew and Mary was his Protestant daughter.

Aubrey's relations

Richard Aubrey (1603–52), father.

Deborah Aubrey (1610–86), née Lyte, mother.

Isaac Lyte (1576–1660), maternal grandfather.

Israel Browne (1578–1662), of Winterbourne Bassett, maternal grandmother.

Thomas Lyte (1531–1627), of Easton Pierse, Kington St Michael, maternal great-grandfather.

Rachel Danvers (d.1656), paternal grandmother; her first husband was Aubrey's paternal grandfather, John Aubrey of Burleton, Hereford (1578–1616); her second was Aubrey's godfather, John Whitson, Alderman of Bristol (1557–1629).

William Aubrey (c.1529–95), Regius professor, paternal great-grandfather.

William Aubrey (1643–1707), brother.

Thomas Aubrey (1645–81), brother.

Sir John Danvers of Chelsea (1588–1655), 'The Regicide', Aubrey's kinsman (third cousin once removed), MP for Oxford University and Malmesbury, Colonel for Parliament, member of Cromwell's Council of State and signatory of Charles I's death warrant. His first wife was a widow, Magdalen Herbert, mother of the poet George Herbert.

Sir John Aubrey (c.1606–79), 1st Baronet, uncle.

Sir John Aubrey (c.1650–1700), 2nd Baronet, Aubrey's cousin and patron; invited Aubrey to stay in his homes at Borstall (near Brill in Buckinghamshire) and Llanthrithyd (in the Vale of Glamorgan, Wales).

Elizabeth Freeman (1642–1720), Aubrey's cousin, married to Ralph Freeman, Esq. of Abspenden, Hertfordshire, daughter of Sir John Aubrey, 1st Baronet, sister of Sir John Aubrey, 2nd Baronet.

Aubrey's women

Miss Jane Codrington, whom Aubrey hoped to marry. Codrington was a common family name in the vicinity of the Wiltshire and Gloucestershire border. She married another.

Miss Mary Wiseman, whom Aubrey loved at first sight in April 1651.

Miss Katherine Ryves (d.1657), whom Aubrey sought to marry; she died, depriving him of the opportunity. Daughter of George Ryves of Blandford. In her will she left Aubrey £350 and a mourning ring to his mother.

At least one whore from whom Aubrey caught venereal disease in 1657.

Miss Joan Sumner (1636–71), an unusually litigious lady, whom Aubrey sought to marry, before she took him to court.

An unidentified rumoured mistress.

Mrs Jane Smyth (b.1649), the young and ailing mistress and partner of Aubrey's good friend Edmund Wylde. Aubrey was deeply fond of them both.

Lady Dorothy Long, née Leech, the wife, then widow, of Sir James Long, a loyal friend of Aubrey's in his old age.

Aubrey's contemporaries, many of them friends, some also patrons

Mr Elias Ashmole (1617–92), antiquary interested in astrology and alchemy; acquired the Tradescant Collection of rarities and donated them, together with his own, to Oxford University on the condition the Ashmolean Museum was built to house them. His third wife was Mr William Dugdale's daughter.

Dr George Bathurst (d.1645), son of George Bathurst (1579–1656) and Elizabeth Villiers (Dr Ralph Kettell's step-daughter). Brother of Ralph Bathurst. Fellow of Trinity College, Oxford (1631).

Mr Ralph Bathurst (1620–1704), Fellow of Trinity College, Oxford (1640), and President from 1664 until his death. Medically trained,

ordained (1644); pursued chemical researches after 1648 with Thomas
Willis and John Lydall. Fellow of the Royal Society (1663).

Mr John Birkenhead (1617–79), journalist, poet, satirist. In Oxford
during the Civil War he established the *Mercurius Aulicus*, the weekly
'intelligencer' of the King's party, England's first official newsbook
(1643–5). Under the Restoration he became Licenser of the Press
(1660–3). MP for Wilton (1661), knighted (1662). Fellow of the Royal
Society (1663).

Hon. Robert Boyle (1627–92), scientist, son of 1st Earl of Cork, Fellow
of the Royal Society (1660); best remembered for Boyle's Law, stating
that the pressure and volume of a gas have an inverse relationship
when temperature is constant.

Viscount William Brouncker (1620–84), 2nd Viscount Brouncker of
Lyons, mathematician, Fellow of the Royal Society (1660) and 1st
President (1663).

Sir Thomas Browne (1605–82), writer and scientist, author of *Religio
Medici* (1643) and *Hydriotaphia, Urn-Burial, or, A Discourse of the
Sepulchral Urns Lately Found in Norfolk* (1658).

Mr William Browne (d.1669), Fellow of Trinity College, Oxford,
Aubrey's tutor, afterwards vicar of Farnham.

Mr Thomas Bushell (*c*.1594–1674), mining engineer, mint master,
speculator. Creator of the grotto at Enstone that captured Aubrey's
imagination. Held Lundy Island for Charles I during the Civil War.

Dr Walter Charleton (1620–1707), physician and natural philosopher,
Physician in Ordinary to Charles I (1643), antiquary, author of *Chorea
gigantum, or, The Most Famous Antiquity of Great Britain, Vulgarly
Called Stone-heng . . . Restored to the Danes* (1663). Fellow of the Royal
Society (1663).

Dr William Chillingworth (1602–44), theologian, studied at Trinity
College, Oxford, friend of Thomas Hobbes. Converted to Roman
Catholicism (1629), soon returned to the Anglican Church. Royalist.

Mr Henry Coley (1633–1704), astrologer and mathematician, Mr
William Lilly's adopted son and amanuensis.

Mr Jan Amos Comenius (1592–1670), Czech philosopher and educationist, visited England in 1641, where Samuel Hartlib, his host, did much to spread his educational ideas.

Mr Samuel Cooper (*c*.1607–72), painter, miniaturist. Lived in King Street, Covent Garden (1642), and Henrietta Street, Covent Garden (1650), painted Oliver Cromwell and Charles II; appointed the King's Limner (or portraitist) in 1663.

Mr Edward Davenant (1596–1679), vicar of Gillingham, Dorset, then of Poulshot Parsonage, near Devizes, until the Civil War, mathematician, taught Aubrey algebra.

Sir Kenelm Digby (1603–65), courtier, diplomat, natural philosopher, alchemist, author, Roman Catholic. Married Venetia Stanley.

Mr William Dobson (1611–46), portrait painter, patronised by Anthony Van Dyck. Moved to Oxford with Charles I's court in 1643, became Serjeant Painter to the king.

Mr William Dugdale (1605–86), antiquary, herald, the first English medieval historian, author of *Monasticon Anglicanum* (1655–73) and *Antiquities of Warwickshire* (1656).

Sir George Ent (1603–89), friend and colleague of William Harvey, Fellow of the Royal Society (1663), demonstrated anatomy. Knighted by Charles II in 1665.

Mr George Ent (d.1679), son of Sir George Ent. Fellow of the Royal Society (1677). Aubrey's travelling companion in France.

Mr Anthony Ettrick (1622–1703), friend of Aubrey from Trinity College, Oxford and Middle Temple. They travelled together to Ireland in 1660. Lawyer and Recorder of Poole (1662–82).

Mr John Evelyn (1620–1706), diarist, Fellow of the Royal Society (1663), naturalist, annotated Aubrey's natural history of Wiltshire and Surrey manuscripts.

Lord Thomas Fairfax of Cameron (1612–71), Parliamentarian army officer, made commander-in-chief of the New Model Army, which he led to victory at the Battle of Naseby (1645).

Mr William Faithorne (c.1616–91), engraver and portraitist who drew Aubrey.

Dr John Fell (1625–86), Dean of Christ Church (1660), Vice Chancellor of Oxford University (1666–9), Thomas Willis's brother-in-law, disciplinarian. Persuaded Edward Sheldon to permit the Sheldonian Theatre to be used as a printing house (1669). Bishop of Oxford (1676) and uniquely allowed to hold this role while continuing as Dean of Christ Church.

Dr Thomas Gale (1635–1702), antiquary and classical scholar, Regius Professor of Greek at Cambridge (1666), High Master of St Paul's School, London (1672), Fellow of the Royal Society (1677).

Mr Thomas Gore (1632–84), lord of the manor at Alderton, antiquary who wrote on heraldry. Aubrey calls him 'The Cuckold of Alderton'.

Mr Edmund Halley (1656–1742), astronomer, educated at St Paul's School under Thomas Gale; best remembered for discovering a comet.

Father Harcourt, William Barrow (c.1609–79), Jesuit priest, ordained 1641, served as missioner in London for 35 years. A victim of the Popish Plot; evaded arrest until 7 May 1679, then imprisoned, tried and condemned to death.

Mr James Harrington (1611–77), political theorist, moderate republican, Groom of the Bedchamber to Charles I during his imprisonments at Holmby and Carisbrooke, founder of the Rota Club, author of *Oceana* (1656), imprisoned after the Restoration.

Mr Samuel Hartlib (c.1596–c.1662), Polish merchant, intelligencier.

Dr William Harvey (1578–1657), discovered the circulation of the blood.

Philip Herbert, 4th Earl of Pembroke (1584–1650), patron of Anthony Van Dyck, entertained Charles I at Wilton House every summer, renowned huntsman.

Philip Herbert, 5th Earl of Pembroke (1621–69), son of Philip Herbert, 4th Earl of Pembroke and Susan de Vere.

Philip Herbert, 7th Earl of Pembroke, (1653–83), unruly huntsman who kept a menagerie of animals at Wilton House.

Thomas Herbert, 8th Earl of Pembroke, (1656–1733), Fellow of the Royal Society (1685) and President (1689), dedicatee of Aubrey's natural history of Wiltshire.

Mr Thomas Hobbes (1588–1679), philosopher and political theorist, born in Malmesbury, subject of Aubrey's longest biography.

Dr William Holder (1616–98), clergyman and music theorist. Fellow of the Royal Society (1663).

Wenceslaus Hollar (1607–77), etcher, born in Prague, patronised by Thomas Howard, 2nd Earl of Arundel, worked as an illustrator for the printer John Ogilby and the antiquary and herald Sir William Dugdale. Converted to Roman Catholicism. Made a map of London before the Great Fire (1666).

Mr Robert Hooke (1635–1703), natural philosopher, assistant in Oxford to the chemist Thomas Willis, then to Robert Boyle. Fellow of the Royal Society (1663), Curator of Experiments (1662). Moved into Gresham College to lecture on the history of nature and art (1664) and became Professor of Geometry. Author of *Micrographia, or, Some physiological descriptions of minute bodies made by magnifying glasses, with observations and inquiries thereupon* (1665). Made an Official Surveyor for rebuilding London after the Great Fire.

Sir John Hoskyns (1634–1705), MP for Hereford (1685), Fellow of the Royal Society (1663); President (1682–3) and Secretary (1685–7).

Sir Charles Howard (1630–1713), landowner and natural philosopher, inherited the estate at Deepdene, near Dorking, Surrey, where he created an elaborate Italianate garden. Fellow of the Royal Society (1663).

Lord Henry Howard, 6th Duke of Norfolk (1628–84), second son of Henry Howard, 15th Earl of Arundel, and Lady Elizabeth Stuart. He succeeded his brother Thomas Howard, 5th Duke of Norfolk, in 1677. After the Restoration, he was summoned to the House of Lords in his own right, as the 5th Duke was insane. Fellow of the Royal Society (1666).

Lord Thomas Howard (Maltravers), 14th Earl of Arundel, 4th Earl of Surrey, and 1st Earl of Norfolk (1585–1646), art collector and politician. Grandfather of Lord Henry Howard, 6th Duke of Norfolk.

Henry Hyde, 2nd Earl of Clarendon (1638–1709), politician, eldest son of Edward Hyde (1st Earl of Clarendon). MP for Lyme Regis in the Convention Parliament and Commissioner of Trade (1660), attended the Middle Temple, Knight of the Shire for the county of Wiltshire during the Cavalier Parliament until the death of his father (1674), when he became 2nd Earl of Clarendon. Lord Lieutenant of Ireland (1685), supporter of James II, lived in seclusion under William and Mary.

Mr George Johnson (1632–83), at Blandford School with Aubrey; lawyer, granted a reversion of the Mastership of the Rolls (1667), but died before the incumbent holder of the post so was unable to appoint Aubrey to one of the lucrative secretary positions as he had promised.

Mr Inigo Jones (1573–1652), architect, Surveyor General of the King's Works (1615), and stage designer who collaborated with Ben Jonson. He attributed Stonehenge to the Romans.

Dr Ralph Kettell (1563–1643), Fellow and President (1599) of Trinity College, Oxford; over 80 years old when Aubrey was a student.

Mr Robert Latimer (c.1570–1634), rector of Leigh-de-la-Mere, school-teacher who taught Thomas Hobbes and much later Aubrey.

Mr Edward Lhwyd (1660–1709), succeeded Robert Plot as keeper of the Ashmolean Museum. Fellow of the Royal Society (1708).

Mr William Lilly (1602–81), astrologer. His first almanac was printed in 1644.

Dr John Locke (1632–1704), philosopher and physician. Fellow of the Royal Society (1668).

Mr Francis Lodwick (1619–94), linguistics scholar, corresponded about the 'Universal Character', author of A Common Writing (1647), The Ground-Work or Foundation Laid . . . for the Framing of a New Perfect Language (1652), which helped inspire John Wilkins's An Essay towards a Real Character (1668), and a proposal for a phonetic alphabet, in which related sounds were denoted by related symbols, which appeared in the Royal Society's Philosophical Transactions (1686). Fellow of the Royal Society (1681).

Mr David Loggan (1632–94), artist and engraver, born in Poland, settled
in London after 1656, left London because of the plague in 1665
and moved to Nuffield, Oxfordshire. Drew portraits of Aubrey,
Anthony Wood, Elias Ashmole and others. Appointed engraver to
Oxford University (1669), lived on Holywell Street. His *Oxonia
illustrata* (1675), a set of bird's-eye views of all the colleges, academic
halls, and university buildings, together with a map, was intended
to accompany Anthony Wood's *Historia Et Antiquitates Univ. Oxon.*
(1674).

Sir James Long (1617–92), unsuccessful commander of Royalist cavalry
during the Civil War. Aubrey's close friend and informant on natural
history. Fellow of the Royal Society (1663).

Mr Christopher Love (1618–51), Presbyterian minister executed for
plotting against the Commonwealth.

Mr John Lydall (1625–57), Fellow of Trinity College, Oxford.

Mr Thomas Mariett (d.1691), friend of Aubrey from Trinity College,
Oxford, and Middle Temple; landowner in the Midlands and High
Sheriff of Warwickshire.

General George Monck (1608–70), 1st Duke of Albemarle, army officer
and naval officer, commander under the Commonwealth (1650–3),
commander-in-chief of all forces in Scotland (1654–5), champion of
the English Parliament when it was purged by the English army
after the fall of the Protectorate (1659–60). Brought his army from
Scotland to London to guard Parliament; the City of London gave
him command of its militia.

Sir Isaac Newton (1642–1727), natural philosopher and mathematician,
Fellow of Trinity College, Cambridge (1668), Lucasian Professor of
Mathematics (1669), collector of alchemical books, corresponded
with Robert Boyle about alchemy. Author of *Philosophiae Naturalis
Principia Mathematica (Mathematical Principles of Natural Philosophy)*
(1687), Fellow of the Royal Society (1672), quarrelled with Robert
Hooke; became President (1703) after Hooke's death.

Lord Norris of Rycote (1655–93), James Bertie, made 1st Earl of
Abingdon in 1682. One of the peers who invited William of Orange

to become King of England. His first wife's mother was the daughter of Aubrey's kinsman Sir John Danvers of West Lavington in Wiltshire. Aubrey's patron.

Mr Titus Oates (1649–1705), informer, chaplain to the Protestants in the household of a Catholic nobleman, Henry Howard, Earl of Norwich and future 6th Duke of Norfolk (1676). Converted to Catholicism. Summoned before the House of Commons in October 1678 and questioned about the Popish Plot. Tried for perjury (1685). Released from prison after the deposition of James II.

Mr John Ogilby (1600–76), translator, printer, the King's Cosmographer.

Mr Henry Oldenburg (c.1619–77), German theologian, natural philosopher and scientific correspondent, Fellow of the Royal Society (1663) and First Secretary (1663); began the scientific journal *Philosophical Transactions*.

Mr Andrew Paschall (c.1631–96), Fellow of Queens' College, Cambridge (1653), rector of Chedzoy, Somerset (1662); Chancellor (1689) and Prebend (1690) of Wells. Participated in the search for a Universal Language together with Aubrey, Lodwick, Hooke, Ray and Pigott.

Mr William Penn (1644–1718), Quaker, founder of Pennsylvania. Fellow of the Royal Society (1681)

Colonel John Penruddock (1619–55), Royalist, fought for the King in the Civil War, seized Salisbury (1655), proclaimed Charles II king; defeated at South Molton, tried, condemned, beheaded at Exeter (16 May 1655).

Dr William Petty (1623–87), economist, friend of Hobbes, Fellow of the Royal Society (1660). Aubrey says he was the 'inventor of political arithmetic'.

Mr Fabian Philips (1601–90), lawyer of Middle Temple, London.

Mr Thomas Pigott (1657–86), Fellow of Wadham College, Oxford, Fellow of the Royal Society (1679).

Dr Robert Plot (1640–96), first curator of the Ashmolean Museum, Professor of Chemistry at Oxford (1683), author of *Natural History of Oxfordshire* (1677) and *Staffordshire* (1686), Historiographer Royal (1688). Fellow of the Royal Society (1677).

Mr Francis Potter (1594–1678), author of *An Interpretation of the Number 666* (1642), rector of Kilmington (1628–78), Fellow of the Royal Society (1663), instrument maker, experimentalist.

Mr William Radford (1623–73), friend of Aubrey's from Trinity College, Oxford.

Mr John Ray (1627–1705), Fellow of Trinity College, Cambridge (1649–62), naturalist. Presbyterian views caused him to retire to Black Notley, Essex. Fellow of the Royal Society (1667).

James Scott, Duke of Monmouth (1649–85), Charles II's illegitimate son by Lucy Walters. Captain General (1670), deprived of office (1679), banished (1684) for plotting against his father, landed at Lyme Regis to invade England (1685), defeated at Sedgemoor and beheaded.

Mr John Selden (1584–1654), jurist, antiquary, orientalist, active in Parliament's attempts to curb royal authority; retired from public affairs after the execution of Charles I.

Mr Ralph Sheldon (1623–84), of Weston in Warwickshire, Royalist, antiquary. Compiled a 'Catalogue of the nobility of England since the Norman Conquest', had a fine library at Weston, which Anthony Wood catalogued, and a cabinet of curiosities. Roman Catholic.

Sir Charles Snell (*c*.1617–51), of Kington St Michael, Aubrey's neighbour.

Mr Fabian Stedman (1640–1713), leading figure in campanology and bell-ringing who introduced the idea of change ringing.

Mr Thomas Tanner (1674–1735), antiquary, born at Market Lavenham in Wiltshire, Anthony Wood's literary executor.

Mr Israel Tonge (1621–80), Church of England clergyman and informer in the Popish Plot together with Titus Oates. Schoolmaster whose experimental methods impressed Aubrey.

Nicholas Tufton, 3rd Earl of Thanet (1631–79), Royalist, imprisoned 1655 and 1656–8 on suspicion of plotting against the Commonwealth.

Sir Anthony Van Dyck (1599–1641), painter and etcher, born in Antwerp, made three extended visits to England.

Sir John Vaughan, 3rd Earl of Carbery (1639–1713), politician and colonial governor. Knighted at Charles II's coronation (1661) and became MP for the borough of Carmarthen in the same year. Became his father's heir upon his elder brother's death (1667) and claimed the courtesy title Lord Vaughan. Appointed Governor of Jamaica (1674); intended to run Jamaica's government with the English Parliament as a model. Fellow of the Royal Society (1685) and President (1686).

Mr Edmund Waller (1606–87), poet, member of the Long Parliament, exiled (1644). Knew Hobbes in France and planned to translate *De Cive* into English. MP for Hastings after the Restoration. Fellow of the Royal Society (1663).

Sir William Waller (c.1598–1668), Parliamentarian army officer, occupied Malmesbury during the Civil War and razed the church at Westport.

Dr John Wallis (1616–1703), mathematician, cryptographer, Savilian Professor of Geometry at Oxford (1649), participant in experimental philosophy group leading to the foundation of the Royal Society, Fellow of the Royal Society (1663).

Mr Seth Ward (1617–89), astronomer, Bishop of Exeter and Salisbury, Fellow Commoner at Wadham College, Oxford (1650), friend of John Wilkins. Interested in the search for a Universal Language. Fellow of the Royal Society (1663).

Mr Christopher Wase (c.1625–90), Fellow of King's College, Cambridge, ejected for Royalist sympathies. Tutor to William Herbert, later 6th Earl of Pembroke, to whom he dedicated his translation of *Cygneticon* (1654). Headmaster of Dedham and Tonbridge schools, appointed Superior Bedell of Civil Law at Oxford (1671). Author of *Considerations Concerning the Free Schools, as Settled in England* (1678).

Mr John Wilkins (1614–72), promoter of experimental philosophy in England, established groups in Oxford and London from which the

Royal Society developed. Warden of Wadham College (1648–59). Fellow of the Royal Society (1663).

Dr Thomas Willis (1621–75), physician, chemist, natural philosopher, member of the Experimental Philosophy Club in Oxford (1650), which operated a chemical laboratory in Wadham College, sponsored by the college's president, John Wilkins. Collaborated with Robert Boyle. Fellow of the Royal Society (1663).

Mr Anthony Wood (1632–95), antiquary and historian of Oxford University, author of *Historia Et Antiquitates Univ. Oxon.* (1674) and *Athenae Oxonienses* (1691–2); Aubrey collected biographical notes for him. Expelled from the university for printing a libel on the Earl of Clarendon (Edward Hyde).

Mr Edward (Ned) Wood (d.1655), Aubrey's friend at Trinity College, Oxford, elder brother of Anthony Wood.

Sir Christopher Wren (1632–1723), scientist, architect, mathematician, designer of St Paul's and other churches and buildings after the Great Fire. Fellow of the Royal Society (1663) and President (1680–2).

Mr Edmund Wylde (1616–96), sat in Long Parliament and supported Parliamentary cause. Fellow of the Royal Society (1663). Aubrey's patron.

List of Illustrations

Unless stated, all illustrations are drawn by John Aubrey, and reproduced from his papers, held at the Bodleian Library, Oxford.

JOHN AUBREY

Engraved by C.E. Wagstaff, from a Drawing by Faithorne in the Ashmolean Museum.

JOHN AUBREY.

England's Collector

John Aubrey loved England. He was born a gentleman in Wiltshire in 1626. He grew up heir to the house he first drew breath in, surrounded by rolling green fields and falcon-frequented skies. From an early age, he saw his England slipping away and committed himself to preserving for posterity what remained of it – in stories, books, monuments and buildings. Aubrey was wonderfully imaginative. By posterity he meant us: people of the future, who would hear his voice through his writing and be grateful for the information he bequeathed. Throughout Aubrey's lifetime, the English were losing assuredness of their identity to a degree not to be repeated till the late twentieth century. When he was a child, Elizabethan times, which ended with the Queen's death in 1603, were within living memory. The disruption caused by the dissolution of the monasteries, initiated by Henry VIII in 1536, could still be felt a hundred years later when Aubrey went to school and noticed schoolbooks covered in old manuscript parchment from lost religious libraries. Aubrey lived through England's Civil War, which began while he was a student at Oxford. He was twenty-two when Charles I was executed. He saw Oliver Cromwell's rise to power as Lord Protector of the Commonwealth of England, and his son Richard Cromwell's brief succession. He experienced the Restoration of Charles II, the short reign of James II, who was deposed in 1688, and the Glorious Revolution that brought William of Orange and his wife Mary (daughter of James II) to the throne. Aubrey died in 1697, ten years before England and Scotland joined their parliaments to create the United Kingdom of Great Britain.

Throughout these constitutional crises and regime changes, Aubrey looked back to Ancient Britain. He worked out that the megaliths at Stonehenge, which he had known since childhood, were neither

Roman nor Danish, as his contemporaries thought. He offered as a 'probability' his theory that Druids erected Stonehenge. It is now known that the stone temples pre-dated the Druids by thousands of years, but in his time, Aubrey was closer to the truth than anyone else. He admired the civilising force of the Romans. He drew a direct parallel between the Roman occupiers of Britain and the English settlers of North America. He supposed that the Ancient Britons – with their iron tools, Druid priests and stone temples amidst the wolves and oak trees – were 'two or three degrees less savage' than the American tribes that the English adventurers and settlers of his own time encountered. The Romans, as Aubrey understood them, were great improvers: they brought into England architecture, skill in husbandry, and elm trees; they conquered most of the island, as far as Hadrian's Wall, and established the Ancient Roman province of Britannia. He thought that after the Roman Britons left and were succeeded by the Saxons, England was engulfed in a mist of ignorance for 600 years.

Aubrey exemplifies an English sensibility to be proud of – charming, self-deprecating, moderate in all matters political and religious, learned but never ponderous. In the aftermath of the Second World War, the biographer and novelist Anthony Powell, himself a great chronicler of England, found in Aubrey's work 'as striking a record of Englishmen and English ways as has ever been written'. Powell, who was as inter-ested in genealogy and ancestry as Aubrey was, might have emphasised that the Aubrey family was of Welsh, not English provenance. But Aubrey himself was quintessentially English. His sensibility was English; his sense of humour was undeniably English; his identity was deeply rooted in north Wiltshire and the West Country. The historical and scientific interests that enthused him as a student in Oxford and after-wards were not parochial; through his reading and correspondence he was connected to wide European and Scandinavian circles of scholar-ship. But ultimately Aubrey's intellectual pursuits arose from his love of particular places and people – predominantly English places and people. Looking back on his long life, he explained: 'I was inclined by my genius from childhood to the love of antiquities: and my Fate dropt me in a countrey most suitable for such enquiries.' If fate had dropped Aubrey into Greece or Italy, his enquiries into antiquities would have been more conventional. He longed to visit those countries, as many of his countrymen did on their Grand Tours. He considered emigrating to America, where his friend William Penn was prepared to grant him 600 acres in Pennsylvania, but nothing came of it. Aubrey's mother prevailed on him not to leave England, and aside from frequent visits to Wales, a trip to Ireland and an unsuccessful sojourn in France, he never did.

Aubrey understood antiquities within the framework established by the intellectual giant of the previous generation, Francis Bacon, Baron Verulam and Viscount of St Albans, who died the year Aubrey was born. Philosopher, statesman, scientist and author, Bacon set the foundations for the advancement of learning through experiment and observation. He divided human understanding into three parts: history, poetry and philosophy. History was then subdivided into religious, political and natural history; antiquities were a further subdivision defined as 'the remnants of history'. Antiquities, according to Bacon, are like the pieces of splintered wood that survive a shipwreck; they are what is rescued 'when industrious persons, by an exact and scrupulous diligence and observation, out of monuments, names, words, proverbs, traditions, private records and evidences, fragments of stories, passages of books that concern not story, and the like, do save and recover somewhat from the deluge of time'. Aubrey frequently likened his own activities to rescues after shipwreck.

Aubrey collected natural and antiquarian remarks: notes on nature, scientific phenomena, architecture, inscriptions, stories and anecdotes. He also collected artefacts: books, manuscripts, paintings, old coins and other rarities. He was unusually modest for a man of his social standing, upbringing and education, though keen to assert his gentlemanly status. He did not presume to know what use posterity might make of the remnants of the past he managed to salvage. He was concerned with accuracy like a scrupulous modern-day investigative journalist, but insistent that controversial components of his work should not be cited until long after his death. His notes are full of gaps where it was not possible to remember or find a particular piece of information. The imperative word *quaere*, meaning enquire or query, recurs like a refrain through his work. He saw himself more as collector than writer: a collector of fragments of fact that would otherwise be lost because no one else would trouble themselves to write them down and pass them on to the next generation. In childhood, Aubrey

collected stories from the older people he met. As a student, he started
to collect books. His first recorded act of antiquarianism was to
commission drawings of the ruins of Osney Abbey in Oxford. Later
the ruins were razed to the ground; without Aubrey, there would be
no contemporary record of what they looked like.

One of the drawings Aubrey commissioned of Osney Abbey was
engraved for William Dugdale's *Monasticon Anglicanum*, which strove to
restore Anglican and Royalist England after 1650 when the episcopacy
and the Book of Common Prayer were abolished under the
Commonwealth. During this time of rupture, antiquarianism gained
new urgency. Rescuing or remembering the material remains of lost or
shattered worlds became compelling for many who lived through the
English Civil War. Aubrey records that his antiquarianism was strongly
influenced by Sir Thomas Browne's *Hydriotaphia, Urn-Burial, or, A
Discourse of the Sepulchral Urns Lately Found in Norfolk*, a wide-ranging
meditation on commemorating the dead. Browne's book was published
in 1658, when the Church of England's 'Order for the Burial of the
Dead' had been banned for over a decade. Reflecting on the ancient
practice of burying cremated remains in pottery jars, Browne indirectly
criticised the Puritan prohibition of funeral rites. After the Restoration
of Charles II, Browne continued his antiquarian work, explaining to
Aubrey that he had made a record of all the remaining brass inscriptions
in Norwich Cathedral, lest they be lost to oblivion. Aubrey shared
Browne's conserving passion for the past. William Camden (1551–1623),
antiquary and topographer of an earlier generation, was another important formative influence. Camden produced the first chorographical
study (or systematic description and mapping of particular regions) of
Britain and Ireland, and the first history of Queen Elizabeth's reign. He
wrote at a time when it was not yet fashionable to talk about 'Britain',
a time before the union of the crowns of England and Scotland. Aubrey's
grandfather remembered Camden, in pursuit of information for his
county-by-county historical survey *Britannia* (1586), coming to visit the
church at Yatton Keynell in Wiltshire when he was a schoolboy. Aubrey
was destined to pursue related topographical and antiquarian work, but
unlike Camden, he wrote in English, not Latin.

Aubrey's book-collecting connected his antiquarianism to his enthusiasm for the advancement of learning. He was conscious of living
through a revolution in print culture, bookselling and journalism.

Alongside his excitement at new opportunities for disseminating information, Aubrey also valued what was being displaced: a rich oral tradition of folklore and old wives' tales. It was more important to him to make a home in his manuscripts for stories and facts that would otherwise be lost than to limit himself to producing printed books. Looking back, he wrote:

> Before Printing, Old-wives Tales were ingeniouse: and since Printing came in fashion, till a little before the Civil-warres, the ordinary sort of People were not taught to reade: now-a-dayes Books are common, and most of the poor people understand letters: and the many good Bookes and variety of Turnes of Affaires, have putt all the old Fables out of dores: and the divine art of Printing and Gunpowder have frighted away Robin-good-fellow and the Fayries.

In Aubrey's time, most books were sold in London, at booksellers' shops or stalls clustered around St Paul's churchyard. From here the book trade spread out to towns with printing presses: Oxford, Cambridge, York, Ipswich, Exeter, Edinburgh, Glasgow, Aberdeen, St Andrews. Chapmen or carriers transported books to dealers in the provinces. Distribution became easier after the introduction of the postal service in 1635. Paper in England was more expensive than in the rest of Europe because it had to be imported; there was no successful manufacture of white paper for printing in England until the eighteenth century. When it was sold, it was counted into quires (24 or 25 sheets) or reams (20 quires, so 480 or 500 sheets). Publication of books was funded by an undertaker, usually a bookseller, occasionally an author or printer. It was the financial backer who owned the copyright in this period. Stationers' Hall, where an undertaker could register ownership of a book after having agreed to finance it, was close to St Paul's. For the booming book trade, the Great Fire of London of 1666 – known as the Memorable, General or Great Conflagration in Aubrey's time – was a catastrophe.

Aubrey records that among the many publications burnt in the Great Fire were early issues of the *Philosophical Transactions of the Royal Society*. He became a Fellow of the Society in 1662, when it was granted a charter of incorporation, two years after it had been founded in London as a club devoted to the pursuit of scientific research. From its earliest days, the Royal Society received donations of physical objects of scientific or natural curiosity – a bird of paradise, a piece of elephant's skin, an ostrich egg – and formed a 'repository' to house such objects. Aubrey was a frequent attender of the weekly meetings at which discussion and experiment took place. While he was not one of the foremost intellects of the Society – where he coincided with Isaac Newton, Robert Hooke and Robert Boyle among others – he did make pioneering contributions to archaeology and architecture: he discovered a circle of holes named after him at Stonehenge; he was the first to date systematically buildings by the design of their windows. He saw that just as shells or insects could be collected and ordered, examples of handwriting from the past might be chronologically classified. During the Great Plague of 1665–6, many Fellows fled London and neglected to pay their membership fees. After the Great Fire, the Royal Society needed to rescue its finances and reinvigorate its activities. In this it succeeded triumphantly. As a proud and loyal member, Aubrey played his part in the advancement of learning, even though his own finances were increasingly under strain.

From childhood, Aubrey had looked forward to inheriting a comfortable income from the landed estates acquired by previous generations of his family in Hereford and south Wales. He had a refined temperament to match his privileged lot in life. Gregarious and good at making and keeping friends, he was also sensitive, self-contained and sometimes solitary. He received a gentleman's education at Blandford School, Dorset, at Trinity College, Oxford, and at the Middle Temple, London. He was fascinated by the present as well as the past – by the arts of drawing and painting and the advancement of scientific and mathematical knowledge. He might have become a scholar – he had passion and intellect enough – but even in more settled times, the world would have doubtless distracted him. He strongly resisted ordination, which was the usual career path of dons at that time. In his thirties, after his father died, it became clear that Aubrey's inheritance was encumbered by debt. Suddenly far from as secure as he had expected to be, he started to collect observations of Wiltshire, the English county he knew and loved best. His concerns about the material basis of his own life resonated with his passion for preserving antiquities that would otherwise be lost or destroyed.

Soon after the Restoration, around the time of the founding of the Royal Society, Aubrey showed Charles II the ancient stone circles at Avebury and secured protection for the monument from local people foraging for building material for new homes. He noted wryly the similarity between his name and the monument's, and considered himself its discoverer. Through his wide circle of scholarly friends, he was commissioned to undertake a survey of Surrey. He set off on horseback to make notes on the old buildings, inscriptions and any natural curiosities he encountered on his journey. Other ideas for collections occurred to him: styles of architecture, handwriting and clothing; lists of old place names; an assemblage of folklore. These collections were compiled in notebooks, or on scraps of paper, cross-referenced, revised, corrected over time. Aubrey's work was fundamentally inclusive and cumulative. Always reluctant to let the practicalities of publication curtail or limit his manuscripts, he published only one short book, about occult phenomena – *Miscellanies: A Collection of Hermetick Philosophy* (1696) – towards the end of his lifetime. In old age, when the debts he had inherited and those he had incurred living without regular employment had crushed him into bankruptcy, Aubrey began to panic, not about pain or death, but about the future of his precious collections. What should he do with all the piles of paper, the wealth of information, it had been his life's work to assemble? His antiquities rescued from the deluge of time were as vulnerable as the fragile boats the Ancient Britons sailed on the River Avon – baskets of twigs covered with ox skin called coracles or curricles – still used, Aubrey noted, by poor people in Wales in his time.

Fortunately for Aubrey – and for us – he had like-minded friends more worldly than he was. Elias Ashmole was a collector of markedly different temperament and circumstance: self-made, obsessive, ruthless and rich. He promised to give his own important collection of antiquarian artefacts to Oxford University, on the condition that the university erected a new building to house his donation. The Ashmolean Museum opened in 1683 and Aubrey contributed many rare objects to it. At the end of his life, he decided there was no better place for his paper collections, among them his most renowned gift to posterity: the compilation of biographical information entitled *Brief Lives*. It was this collection specifically that Anthony Powell thought such a striking record of Englishmen and their ways. The *Brief Lives* are mostly lives of seventeenth-century men: eminent writers, philosophers, mathematicians, scientists, doctors, astrologers, soldiers, sailors, lawyers, dignitaries of the state and the Church of England. There are a few female lives too: some commanding their own biography, others married to or fathered by famous men, outstandingly beautiful, or simply 'wondrous wanton'. And there are many more unnamed women, caught between the lines – mothers, sisters, wives, daughters, mistresses, whores. They are lives lived amidst the intense social turmoil of civil war, the Great Plague and the Great Fire. They encompass discoveries that changed the future, such as the circulation of blood, and magical spells and folklore from the distant past.

Agnostic and afraid of fanaticism, Aubrey tended always towards tolerance and open-mindedness in his religious and political views. He had both royalist and republican friends. He was close to Protestants, Presbyterians and Roman Catholics. He was captivated by exciting new science and its challenge to more orthodox temperaments. If he believed securely in anything, it was astrology. He collected birth charts for his biographical subjects whenever he could, consulted astrologers about his own life and remained convinced that astrology was a serious science, as did Ashmole and many of their contemporaries. There was a huge popular market for astrological almanacs at this time and beyond. About himself Aubrey concluded: 'His life is more remarqueable in an astrologicall respect then for any advancement of learning, having from his birth (till of late yeares) been labouring under a crowd of ill directions.' Modest and self-deprecating as he was, he felt completely confident of making an important and original contribution in one respect: he knew he was inventing a new form of biography. He cursed the classical tradition of high-style panegyrics and selective eulogies: 'Pox take your orators and poets, they spoile lives & histories.' A Life, he insisted, is a small history in which detail and minutiae are all. Contemporaries criticised him for being 'too minute' or trivial, but Aubrey was convinced that 'a hundred yeare hence that minutenesse will be gratefull'. He was right: the fine details he recorded are widely appreciated and the exemplary biographies so dominant in his time are now more a hindrance than a help to modern biographers. The words 'according to Aubrey', or 'Aubrey says', resound down the centuries to the present day, where they still appear in the introductions to new books on Hobbes, Milton, Jonson, Boyle, Harvey, Hooke, Newton, Wren and other luminaries. His idea was to get at the truth: 'the naked and plaine trueth, which is here exposed so bare that the very pudenda are not covered, and affords many passages that would raise a blush in a young virgin's cheekes'. An example is the Life of the brilliant, erudite jurist John Selden, who, Aubrey accurately notes, 'got more by his Prick than ever he had donne by his practise'. Aubrey heard this from one of the many people discussing the fortune Selden inherited from the widowed Countess of Kent. Aubrey is subtle, his prose florid but precise. He wrote in private, speaking freely to posterity, and has unfairly been characterised as a gossip. When he relates an anecdote, salacious or otherwise, he is careful to indicate its source, sceptically if necessary, and never to stray beyond the story into general inferences about the person concerned. In his book *John Aubrey and His Friends* (1948), Anthony Powell contrasted Aubrey's scrupulous regard for the truth with the opportunism of a much later biographical innovator, Lytton Strachey. Strachey, like Aubrey, changed the way biographies were written, liberating the genre from pious expectations and infusing it with the kind of irreverence and wit Aubrey would have enjoyed. But Powell found Strachey lacking where Aubrey was not:

In *Elizabeth and Essex*, Lytton Strachey writes of Francis Bacon: 'an old man, disgraced, shattered, alone, on Highgate Hill, stuffing a dead fowl with snow'. The story of stuffing the hen with snow is Aubrey's . . . Bacon was certainly an old man at the time of the incident; he was 'disgraced', he may have been 'shattered'; no doubt at times he was 'alone'; but Aubrey's story of stuffing the fowl on Highgate Hill shows Bacon, accompanied by the King's Physician, conducting a serious experiment to test the preservative properties of snow; and, on becoming indisposed, finding accommodation in the house of the Earl of Arundel. If Aubrey's story suggests anything, it is that Bacon's intellectual faculties were anything but 'shattered' and that he was not 'alone'. This is a trifling instance, though it illustrates how a fragment of a 'Life', combined with juxtaposition of epithets, may be used to convey an oblique hint; a method, incidentally, never employed by Aubrey himself.

It is remarkable that Aubrey resisted employing the method for which Powell rebukes Strachey. It is one of the tricks of the trade for working up the oblique hints, the small brushstrokes that accumulate gradually to become a finished portrait by the biography's end. But Aubrey never did this. He stayed strictly within the frame of the story, anecdote or incident he found revealing of a Life. He made no attempt to interpret definitively, still less judge or account for, the Lives he wrote. He set out more modestly to record about each of them some things that were true. He was especially concerned to capture the small and incidental details that would otherwise be lost.

I first encountered Aubrey through Anthony Powell's edition of *Brief Lives* in the library of my school in Slough: 'a very dirty place', according to Aubrey, who once passed through the town on a visit to Eton. *Brief Lives* is an evocative title, full of drama and poignancy – I did not know then anyone who had died, still less died young. I first wanted to write about Aubrey when I lived in the Wiltshire village of Wylye in my early twenties. Aubrey's places – Stonehenge, Wilton House, Salisbury Plain, the rivers and meadows and undulating hills – seemed still touched by his presence. He is one of the finest English prose writers there has ever been. Like all great writers, he lives on in the words he arranged on paper, no matter how scrappy or fragmentary or difficult to decipher the pages in his archive are. He lives on too in the places he loved and wrote about.

It is hard to turn the tables and write a biography of England's first great biographer. Aubrey was a mild-mannered man who did not impose himself strongly on his subjects. Instead he captured them for posterity, without presuming to know what posterity would make of them. He was a listener. Among the manuscripts and letters that he deposited in the Ashmolean Museum towards the end of his life were some scant autobiographical jottings, 'to be interponed as a sheet of wast-paper only in the binding of a Booke'. Aubrey's idea that his record of his own life might serve as endpapers to a book about something or someone else is typically self-effacing. He was, we can be sure, wonderful company. He pursued a wide range of historical and scientific interests and knew or corresponded with a large number of people – many of them cleverer, more confident or flamboyant than he was himself. He was in high demand as friend, guest, intellectual or literary collaborator, informant and recorder. Though impecunious, he survived well in a culture of hospitality, where it was important for the wealthy to fill their homes with interesting guests. When he could no longer afford to maintain his own household, he was welcomed into the homes of wealthier friends for weeks on end, paying only with his time. He knew the price was high and would mean that much of his work would be left incomplete, 'on the loom', at his death. Aubrey saw himself as a resource for honing other people's talents; he doubted the power of his mind, doubted even the quality of his distinctive prose, and claimed gratitude to others as his own greatest virtue. In describing himself, he echoed the words of the poet Horace – 'I perform the function of a whetstone, which can make the iron sharp though is itself unable to cut.'

The chaotic and fragmentary nature of Aubrey's work, punctuated as it is by gaps into which he hoped information would be inserted later by himself or others, is matched by the fragmentary record of his life. Aside from his few pages of autobiographical notes, the main sources for Aubrey's life are the remains of his correspondence, which are necessarily uneven and often oblique. Sometimes it is possible to tell exactly where Aubrey was and what he was doing on a particular date. Sometimes weeks, even months, go by where he cannot be traced. His relationships, especially the most intimate, flash past, illuminated only instantaneously, like a dark landscape beneath a clouded sky when the moon breaks through fleetingly. Unlike Samuel Pepys, John Evelyn and other celebrated men of the seventeenth century, Aubrey did not leave a diary. If he wrote one – regularly, intermittently or occasionally – it has disappeared. When I was searching for a biographical form that would suit the remnants of his life, I realised that he would all but vanish inside a conventional biography, crowded out by his friends, acquaintances and their multitudinous interests. Aubrey lived through fascinating times and has long been valued for what can be seen through him; there is no shortage of scholars who appreciate the use that can be made of him. But the biographer has other purposes: to get as close to her subject and his sensibility as possible; to produce a portrait that captures at least something of what that person was like. In the pencil portrait of Aubrey that survives, he looks like an unremarkable seventeenth-century gentleman, his bland face square between the curtains of a heavy wig. A portrait in words – one that does him more justice – is what I determined to write.

Biography is an art form open to constant experiment. Aubrey is not my first biographical subject. I wrote first about a vehement Frenchman, Maximilien Robespierre, whose life was caught up in revolution and violent change. Afterwards, Aubrey's sensibility – treasuring the past, rescuing what he could from the forces of destruction and the passage of time – seemed more attractive than ever. I was led back to Aubrey by a deep fascination with how and why we tell the stories of earlier lives. What is the nature of the relationship between biographers and their subjects? Do we honour or betray the dead when we write about them? When Lytton Strachey mocked 'tombstone' biographies and offered instead his impertinent *Eminent Victorians*, he liberated future generations of biographers. Instead of forcing lives into conventional books, it is possible to find a form – or invent one – to suit the life in question. After much experiment, trial and error, I decided to write Aubrey's life as a diary. I was inspired by the vivid sense of self that emerges from the diaries of Pepys, Evelyn and Hooke. I thought: if only we had Aubrey's diary, his modesty, self-effacement, attention to others would not be such a problem. No one gets crowded out of his or her own diary. Hooke kept an obsessive diary from 1672 to 1683: it is the memorandum book of a secretive man in a perpetual hurry. Pepys kept his diary for a decade – from 1660 until 1669 – and wrote in shorthand, probably not intending it to be read by anyone beside himself. The diary I have created for Aubrey is closer to Evelyn's. Evelyn's diary covered almost his entire life and included a retrospective account of his European Grand Tour, to which he added explanations of significant events with the benefit of hindsight. It was written in longhand, with a self-conscious air of moral contrivance, to be read later by family and close friends. In Aubrey's case, moral contrivance is completely out of the question. Never, in writing the lives of others, did he moralise or sermonise about the evidence he had assembled. Unlike his friend Evelyn, he was not constrained by religious dogma on how to live.

In constructing Aubrey's diary, I have used as many as possible of his own words. It is a diary based on the historical evidence; a diary that shows him living vividly, day by day, month by month, year by year, but with necessary gaps when nothing is known about where he was or what he was doing. I have not invented scenes or relationships for him as a novelist would, but neither have I followed the conventions of traditional biography. When he is silent, I do not speculate about where he was or what he was doing or thinking. When he speaks, I have modernised his words and spellings and indicated the original sources in endnotes. I have added words of my own to explain events or interactions that would otherwise be obscure and to frame or offset the charm of Aubrey's own turns of phrase. All dates have been modernised to the Gregorian calendar. When the year, but not the precise month or day, of a piece of evidence is known, I have arranged it with other entries, sometimes clustering themes or events that fit together. There are three distinct kinds of entry in the diary I have conjured for Aubrey: discursive descriptions of events and conversations within specific months or years based on his writing and correspondence; shorter notes about personal events that occurred on particular days; and entries providing brief accounts of public events which begin 'On this day'.

Aubrey's approach to his own and other lives was imaginative and empirical in equal measure. In imagining his diary by collating the evidence, I have echoed the idea of antiquities – the searching after remnants – that meant so much to him. I have collected the fragmentary remains of his life – from manuscripts, letters and books, his own and other people's – and arranged them carefully in chronological order. I have done so playingly (a word he used of his own writing) but with purpose. Ultimately, my aim has been to write a book in which he is still alive.

PART I

Wiltshire

I was born about sun rising in my maternal grandfather's bedchamber on 12 March 1626, St Gregory's Day, very sickly, likely to die. I was christened before Morning Prayer. My father was nearly twenty-two years old, my mother only fifteen and a half. She has cried through the night and given birth to three more babies since, but they have all died.

My mother's father, Isaac Lyte, is a man of the old time: he wears a doublet and hose and carries a dagger, as men did in the reign of Queen Elizabeth. He is a living history. We live with him at Easton

Pierse, a hamlet in the parish of Kington St Michael, in the hundred of Malmesbury, in the county of Wiltshire.

My grandfather tells me that our family sold the manor house and farm at Easton Pierse to the Snell family in 1575, the year before he was born. The house we live in now was built the year following, on the brow of the hill, above the brook, facing south-east. It has a great hall and parlour and a tall, carved chimney stack. In the parlour chimney is carved: 'T. L. 1576', my great-grandfather Thomas Lyte's initials and the year our house was built.

 On the chimney in my grand- father's chamber, where I first drew breath, there are two escutcheons. The first for my grandfather: 'Isaac Lyte natus 1576'. The second for my grandmother, Israel Lyte, whose family name before she married was Browne.

. . .

At home I am often alone. I watch the joiners, carpenters and stone-masons when they are hard at work rebuilding the manor house next door. Sometimes they give me scraps of their materials and lend me their tools. I fancy myself an engineer. I wish I lived near Bristol like my father's mother. In a city I would be able to visit the watchmakers and locksmiths and learn their trades instead of learning grammar. I can understand grammar easily, but struggle to remember it. I like to dream. I like to think about the past.

. . .

I like to ask the old men and women for stories. When I was smaller, old Jack Sydenham, the Snell family's servant, would swing me high in his arms. He lives at Kington St Michael, near the old priory across the brook. He tells me that long ago the old priory was full of women: nuns, widows, grave single women, and young maids, learning physic, writing, drawing, etc. In memory of those women, the meadow is called Nymph Hay. They used to spin there in the morning with their rocks and spinning wheels. On Fridays there was a market at the crossroads for the nuns to buy their fish, eggs and butter. There is no market now. My grandfather remembers that in his grandmother's time the tablecloth would be spread all day with food and drink to offer to pilgrims and other travellers passing by. But since the dissolution of the monasteries and religious houses, no one comes.

. . .

I lie on the bank of the brook and dig idly in the blue clay. I count and name the plant types: calver-keys, hare parsley, wild vetch, maiden's honesty, polypodium, foxgloves, wild vine, bayle, cowslip, primrose, adder's tongue and others whose names I do not know. It seems to me a kind of ingratitude not to care about the plants that grow round about our dwellings, since we see them every day and they nourish us.

. . .

The north part of Wiltshire between Chippenham and Malmesbury is stiff clay; the parish of Kington St Michael especially. Wormwood grows plentiful, as does woodwax and sorrel, an abundance of sower herbs and brook lime. It is an excellent place for plants. Our soil is very good for oaks and witch hazel trees.

The stones at Easton Pierse are full of small cockles, no bigger than silver halfpennies. The stones at Kington St Michael and Draycot Cerne are also cockley, but the cockles of Draycot are bigger.

. . .

I am so bored, so alone. My imagination is like a mirror of pure crystal water, which the least wind does disorder and unsmooth. So noise, etc., stirs me. I have been told that I was late to learn to speak. I still stutter on certain words.

. . .

When I was learning to read, I found a flint as big as my fist in the west field by our house: it was a kind of liver colour. Such coloured flints are rare.

. . .

I love to read. My nurse, Kath Bushell of Ford, taught me my letters from an old hornbook. The letters were black and purple and difficult to recognise. The parish clerk of Kington St Michael first taught me to read. His aged father was clerk before him and wore a black gown every day with the sleeves pinned behind, which was fashionable in Queen Elizabeth's time.

I started school in the church at Yatton Keynell: the parish next to Kington St Michael, where my mother was born. My grandfather went to the same school. There used to be a fair and spreading yew tree in the churchyard there; we boys delighted in its shade and loved to sit under it to learn our grammar; it furnished us with scoops and nutcrackers. But it was lopped to make money from its branches and died; the dead trunk stands there still.

There is another remarkable tree in our parish: a great oak at Rydens. It was struck by lightning, not in a straight but in a spiral line, which wound one and a half times round the tree, as a hop twists about the pole. The scar in the bark looks like it was made with a gouge.

. . .

Mr William Stumpe is the rector at Yatton Keynell: he is the great-grandson of a great clothier from Malmesbury who purchased the site of the abbey and some of its neighbouring lands. Mr Stumpe has inherited several manuscripts that came from Malmesbury Abbey. He says that when he brews a barrel of special ale he stops the bunghole, under the clay, with a sheet of manuscript and, according to him, nothing works so well: my eyes prick with tears at the thought. Even before I could read, I loved to look at the parchment pages that covered the books of the older boys.

. . .

I have moved to Mr Latimer's school at Leigh Delamere, which is in the next parish and better. Manuscripts are used to cover books at my new school too. Now I can decipher some of them. My grandfather says that in his time all music books, account books, copybooks, etc. were covered with pages of antiquity, and the glovers at Malmesbury even used them to wrap their gloves for sale. He says that over the last century, a world of rarities has perished hereabouts. Before that, they were safe in the libraries of Malmesbury Abbey, Broad Stock Priory, Stan Leigh Abbey, Farleigh Abbey, Bath Abbey and Cirencester Abbey. All these old buildings are within twelve miles of my home. But when the great change – the Dissolution – came, the religious houses were emptied, the occupants all turned out in the road, and their manuscripts went flying around like butterflies through the air. A hundred years later, it seems to me that they are still on the wing. I would net them if I could. It hurts my eyes and heart to see fragile painted pages used to line pastry dishes, to bung up bottles, to cover schoolbooks, or make templates beneath a tailor's scissors.

. . .

My fine box top has been stolen from me. At the age of eight I have learnt what theft is. I know that I am lucky not to have learnt before now.

. . .

In Latin lessons I have learnt the first declension without a book and it has made my head ache, or perhaps the heat of the weather we are having this May is to blame.

. . .

My most distinguished ancestor, my paternal great-grandfather William Aubrey, was a fine statesman and a Doctor of Law. He argued against the execution of Mary, Queen of Scots but Queen Elizabeth forgave him and called him her 'little doctor'. He lived at Kew, a mile from Dr Dee, the learned alchemist, who lived at Mortlake. When she was a child, my grandmother often saw them together. In the house of Dr Dee, I have heard, they used to distil eggshells and other revolting ingredients: menstrual blood, human hair, clouts, chalk, shit and clay. The children were frightened because they thought Dr Dee was a conjuror of evil spirits.

I do not think I would have been frightened of him.

. . .

My nurse, Kath, presses her cool hand to my forehead. I have been lying in bed all day. I was riding my pretty horse back from school when I had a premonition I would fall: a briar swept against my face; the horse bolted. I cannot remember them carrying me home. My body woke to vomit. Nothing, I think, is broken. It is just the ague come upon me again. The ague is my earliest memory; since

I was about three or four years old, it has come regularly: my stomach wringing itself into knots, like a rancid wet sack, trying to turn inside out. Moments before, when I know it will happen, I scrabble at the sheets. I need to vomit; I need it to be over; I need it not to begin. There is pain. There is blood. There is bile. There is nothing left inside me. I fall back, my body slack around the tight little ball below my ribs. I had measles too, but that was nothing: I was hardly sick.

Kath knows the history of England in ballad from the Norman Conquest down to the reign of the present King. She learnt it when she was young, sitting up late by the fireside, where fabulous stories of the olden days are passed from grandmother to mother to daughter: stories of sprights and the walking of ghosts. Many women cannot read. Kath can, but she still loves the old songs and all the frightening fables she learnt the same way. She believes in spirits, ghosts and fairies; so, sometimes, do I.

. . .

I am newly recovered from a violent fever that almost carried me off. But now there is fluid running from a lesion in my head that will not stop.

. . .

It is venison season. As I arrived at school today, I overheard a tall stranger ask about me of my teacher Mr Latimer, who still wears a dudgeon with a knife and bodkin in the old-fashioned style. The stranger was our Malmesbury philosopher, Mr Thomas Hobbes, returning to visit the man who had been his teacher too. Mr Hobbes is over forty but has no streaks of grey in his crow-black hair. He was born in Malmesbury, his father was the vicar of Westport, the parish outside the West Gate of the town, and his brother Edmund, a glover, lives here still.

When he looked up at me on my little horse, there was kindness in his bright eyes that are hazel colour. When he laughs, his eyes almost disappear. He told me that we boys are lucky to have Mr Latimer, who is a fine Grecian, the first in Wiltshire since the Reformation. When Mr Hobbes was a boy, some years older than I am now, but not many, Mr Latimer encouraged him to translate

Euripides's *Medea* from Greek to Latin iambics. He did it and presented the manuscript to Mr Latimer, who must still have it somewhere. Whenever we leave the class to go for a pee, Mr Latimer gives us a Latin word and we have to give it back to him upon returning. It is a good teaching method, by which he gives us a store of words without us noticing.

Mr Hobbes went to Oxford at fourteen in the year 1603. His uncle, another glover, paid. Malmesbury is good for gloves and glovers. Mr Hobbes, who is tutor to the young Earl of Devonshire, will leave for a tour of Europe in a matter of weeks, but when he is back I hope we will know each other well for a long time.

Riding home, I felt happy. I have invited Mr Hobbes to meet my family tomorrow. He says he will come. He will stay in Malmesbury for a week or so. Something has happened to me and more will happen to me. This meeting seems an end to my loneliness. Mr Hobbes's kind words were still in my mind this evening as I turned into Bery Lane, where there were two women in conversation beside a laburnum bush, one old, one young. They turned their backs. Malmesbury is good for witches too. They like the mud.

Here are some of the bad things witches can do: twist trees; tear and turn up oaks by the roots; raise tempests; wreck ships; tumble steeples; blast plants; cause whirlwinds and hurricanes; dwindle away young children; bind spirits and imaginations; make men impotent and women miscarry.

. . .

I rode over to the old stones at Stonehenge today. I go often and know them well. About two or three miles from Andover is a village called Sarsden: Caesar's dene on Caesar's plains (also known as Salisbury Plain). The Sarsden stones peep above the ground a yard or more high. Those that lie exposed to the weather are so hard that no tool can touch them. They take a good polish. As for their colour, some are a kind of dirty red, towards porphyry; some perfect white; some dusky white; some blue, like deep blue marl; some an olive greenish colour; but generally they are whitish. Stonehenge – that stupendous antiquity – is framed from these stones.

Sir Philip Sidney, one of Queen Elizabeth's courtiers, wrote verses about Stonehenge almost a hundred years ago:

> Near Wilton sweet, huge heaps of stones are found,
> But so confused, that neither any eye
> Can count them just, nor reason try
> What force brought them to so unlikely ground.

But it must be possible to count and number the stones. I will do so one day.

. . .

My honoured teacher, old Mr Latimer, has died. There will be an inscription for him on a stone under the communion table in the church of Leigh Delamere.

. . .

I love the music of the tabor and pipe that is played especially on Sundays, holy days, christenings and feasts.

. . .

Anno 1635

Above alderman and woollen draper Mr Singleton's parlour fireplace, in his house near the steeple in Gloucester, there is a moving screen, a thing of marvels. One long strip of paper, the length of the room at least, pasted together from printed pages, and rolled like cloth, tight at each end on a tall pin. The pins are secured either side of the chimneypiece, and if you stand at one end and turn, you see the figures from Sir Philip Sidney's funeral procession march by all in order, a glow beneath their feet.

First come thirty-two poor men, one for every year of Sidney's life. Next come the band, playing but softly on their flutes and drums; the standard bearer, with lowered and trailing flag; trumpeters, corporals, officers of his horse; statesmen, gentlemen, servants, friends. It took fourteen to carry the body of the soldier, courtier, poet in its leaden coffin below its velvet drape, to its resting place in St Paul's Cathedral. Sidney died after the Battle of Zutphen from a bullet-torn thigh, almost fifty years ago. At his funeral, on 16 February 1587, Queen Elizabeth and her nation mourned.

Today I watched Sidney's funeral on the screen while my father talked of business in Alderman Singleton's study. I know something of Sidney already. I have heard my great-uncle tell stories of how, out hunting on Salisbury Plain, he would stop suddenly to make notes for his *Arcadia* in a pocket book; I like the idea that the muses visited Sidney on horseback. I wonder what it would be like to be visited by muses?

In the parlour I turned the pin to make the figures walk forwards and back, over and over, so I could study their faces and clothes more carefully. The figure of Daniel Bachelar caught my eye, a boy like me, Sidney's page, perched on a great horse caparisoned with golden cloth. I have heard people say that when Sidney lay dying, Daniel sang him verses from *Arcadia*:

> Since nature's works be good, and death doth serve
> As nature's work, why should we fear to die?
> Since fear is vain, but when it may preserve,
> Why should we fear that which we cannot fly?
>
> Fear is more pain than is the pain it fears,
> Disarming human minds of native might;
> While each conceit an ugly figure bears,
> Which were not ill, well viewed in reason's light.

But I am not brave like Sidney. I am frightened of death.

When my father's business was done today, I rode my own small horse home beside him. I love but scarcely know my father. He was born for hawking, whereas I know already that I am made for books and drawing. What I desired to do today was to sketch the contours of the countryside from Gloucester to Cirencester and back home to Easton Pierse, taking note of all the old buildings that we passed on our way. But it would have angered my father to wait for me on his tall horse, treading a muddy impatient circle. So I will save my drawing for the long empty days in our parlour, where there is no moving screen to distract me. I wish I could see and turn that screen again. I will always remember it.

. . .

My grandmother, Rachel Danvers, was widowed in 1616, when my father was about thirteen years old. Afterwards, she married Alderman Whitson of Bristol. She was his fourth wife and they had no children of their own. Alderman Whitson was a good stepfather to my father. He taught him to hawk. He cut down woods my father had inherited and never gave him any compensation, but did him plenty of good too. My father says his stepfather lived nobly: he was the most popular magistrate in the city; always chosen as a Member of Parliament. Alderman Whitson was my godfather, but he died when I was about three years old, so I do not remember him. He was pitched from his horse and hit his head on a nail that stood on its head outside a smith's shop. Seventy-six poor old men and women followed his coffin: one for every year of his age. He was the colonel of the trained band, who came to his funeral with black ribbons on their pikes and black cloth on their drums.

. . .

Since Alderman Whitson's death, my grandmother lives outside Bristol, at Burnett in the parish of Compton Dando, about two miles from Keynsham. About four miles from Burnett is Stanton Drew, where I go whenever I am staying with my grandmother because there is a monument of ancient stones behind the manor house there, which the people round about call the Wedding: it is far bigger than Stonehenge. The story (which I do not believe) is that on her way to be married, a bride and the company she was with were all turned into these stones, which are grouped together, hard as marble and nine or ten feet high. One is called the bride's stone, another the parson's stone, another the cook's. The stones are a dirty reddish colour and take a good polish. I cannot help wondering how they really came to be there, and why.

. . .

When we are not at Easton Pierse in north Wiltshire, we live at Broad Chalke farm in south Wiltshire, close to the River Ebble. Here the bells of Broad Chalke church ring agreeably alongside the music of the running river. Just a short walk across the valley from our farm there is Wilton House, where Sir Philip Sidney and his beloved sister Mary, Countess of Pembroke, lived in their time. Our families are distantly connected. I have not tried to count the many volumes in the grand library at Wilton. There are a great many Italian books, books of poetry and polity and history. There is Sidney's translation of the whole Book of Psalms into English verse, bound in crimson velvet and gilt. There is a manuscript of a Latin poem from Julius Caesar's time. There are books of coats of arms and genealogies and histories of the English nobility: all well painted and written.

I have seen a book in Wilton library on hunting, hawking and heraldry, written in verse by Dame Juliana Berners, a nun from Henry VIII's time, keen on field sports and fishing – who was perhaps the first woman to write a book in English. The book was printed in the time of Edward IV. Dame Juliana Berners says in her book that a hoby is a priest's hawk and a merlin is a lady's hawk, so it seems that in those olden days priests and ladies kept hawks too. When my father and I go hawking together his birds land on my gloved and outstretched arm.

. . .

I wander in the parklands at Wilton, imagining myself in Sidney's *Arcadia*. I have fallen in love with the house, the grounds, and the beautiful old paintings in the long gallery. I have been shown them so many times by old servants and friends of this noble family that I am a good nomenclator of these pictures – I could make a portrait in words to set alongside each of them.

Here is the 1st Earl of Pembroke, William Herbert.

The last time I was staying with my grandmother near Bristol, she told me the story of black Will Herbert, who was a mad fighting young fellow. Once when he was arrested in Bristol he killed one of the sheriffs, then escaped via Back Street, through the great gate into the marsh, and so to France. Afterwards, the city gate was walled up, leaving just a little door and turnstile for foot passengers. Will Herbert joined the army in France, and fought so well that favours were heaped on him. At the dissolution of the monasteries, Henry VIII gave him Wilton and its surrounding lands. He was much envied: a stranger and an upstart in our county. Toward the end of his life, he had a little reddish picked-nose dog (not of the prettiest), which loved him; when the Earl died, the dog would not leave his body, but pined away, starving himself to death. There is a picture of the dog in the gallery at Wilton that hangs below the picture of Will.

Here is Mary, Countess of Pembroke.

She was Sir Philip Sidney's sister; married to Henry, the eldest son of Will Herbert, Earl of Pembroke. That subtle old Earl predicted that his witty daughter-in-law would horn his son, told him so, and advised him to keep her in the country and not to let her frequent the court. She had a pretty sharp-oval face. Her hair was of a reddish yellow. She was very salacious. For example: each spring, she had the stallions brought close to a part of the house where she had a special place to stand and watch them mounting their mares. She had many lovers who mounted her, including Cecil, the crooked-back Earl of Salisbury. This is her epitaph:

> Underneath this sable hearse
> Lies the subject of all verse:
> Sydney's sister, Pembroke's mother.
> Death! Ere thou kill'st such another
> Faire and wise and learn'd as she,
> Time will throw a dart at thee.

Here is Sir Philip Sidney, Mary's brother.

Not only an excellent wit, but extremely beautiful, he is said to have much resembled his sister. His hair was not red; it was a dark amber colour. Perhaps it was not masculine enough; and yet he was a person of great courage. He was the reviver of poetry in those dark times. He bought Queen Elizabeth a bejewelled whip as a sign of his submission (which she had come to doubt).

In one of the pictures of Sir Philip Sidney are these verses:

> Who gives himselfe may well his picture give,
> Els were it vain, since both short time doe live.

In Mary's time, Wilton was like a college: full of learned, scholarly people. She collected the library. She was a great chemist and set up a laboratory alongside the library. She talked of her experiments with her brother, and he in turn described them to Dr Dee. Philip dedicated his *Arcadia* to her, declaring: 'Now it is done only for you, only to you.' They loved each other so much that people wondered if they slept together. These siblings, one auburn-headed, the other amber, who live so vividly in my imagination, are not even ghosts in the garden now; or if they are, I cannot see them. I walked sombrely on the terraces at dusk this evening, trying to catch sight of them. But

they are gone, and their fair bodies laid to rest: hers (I think) in
Salisbury Cathedral beside her first husband, Henry, Earl of Pembroke;
and his in St Paul's. I shudder to think of it:

> England, Netherlands, the Heavens and the Arts
> Of . . . Sydney hath made . . . parts;
> . . . for who could suppose,
> That one heap of stones could Sydney enclose.

. . .

The situation of Wilton House is incomparably noble. King Charles
loves it above all places and comes here every summer. He prompted
the present Earl, Philip, 4th Earl of Pembroke, to make the magnificent
garden and grotto, and to extend the side of the house that fronts the
garden, with two stately pavilions at each end, all 'al Italiano'. His
Majesty intended to have his own architect, Mr Inigo Jones, do it. But
Mr Jones was too busy with His Majesty's buildings at Greenwich, so
recommended another architect, Monsieur Solomon de Caus, a
Gascoigne, who performed it very well; but not without the advice
of Mr Jones.

There is a picture of King Charles at Wilton, which Sir Anthony
Van Dyck copied from Whitehall. The King is on horseback, with his
French riding master on foot, under an arch, all life-sized. Next to it
is a picture of the famous white racehorse Peacock, also life-size and
by Van Dyck.

Peacock has run the four-miles course in five minutes and a little
more. He used to be owned by Sir Thomas Thynne of Longleat and
valued at 1,000 li. Philip, Earl of Pembroke, gave 5 li. just to have a
sight of him. Now, at last, his lordship owns him (I think he was given
to his lordship as a gift). Peacock is a bastard barb. He is the most
beautiful horse ever seen in this age, and is as fleet as he is handsome.

Philip, Earl of Pembroke, is a great patron to Van Dyck and has
more of his paintings than anyone in the world.

. . .

I have been shown the armoury at Wilton. It is a very long room – full
of weapons. The collection is as great as the manner in which it was
obtained. During the Italian war, when Queen Mary was on the throne,

there was a victory at the Battle of St Quentin, in Picardy, in 1557. At that battle, William, 1st Earl of Pembroke, was General, Sir George Penruddock of Compton Chamberlain was Major General, and my great-grandfather, William Aubrey, was Judge Advocate. The spoils collected were arms enough for sixteen thousand men on horse and foot.

. . .

On the south down of the farm at Broad Chalke, there is a little barrow called Gawen's-barrow. I sit there sometimes, thinking of how the barrow must have been named for the Knight Gawain, nephew to King Arthur, whose exquisite manners are commemorated in Chaucer's 'Squire's Tale':

> That Gawain with his old curteisye . . .

. . .

Anno 1638

This autumn, Broad Chalke is sickly and feverish; I walked through the churchyard earlier today and saw three open graves.

. . .

My father has a pin, or web, in his eye, like a pearl, or a humour coming out of his head. The learned men of Salisbury could do him no good, but a good-wife of Broad Chalke, a poor woman named Holly, has cured him these past few days.

. . .

Mr Peyton is now vicar of Broad Chalke, and I have made friends with his wife's brother, Theophilus Woodenoth, who was at Eton and then a scholar at King's College, Cambridge, and is now come to stay at the vicarage. He talks to me about books, old English proverbs, and answers my questions about antiquities. He has advised me to read Lord Bacon's essays, which I have found among my mother's books. Mr Woodenoth is writing a book of his own, a little manual called *Good Thoughts in Bad Times*.

. . .

I am now a boarder at Blandford School in Dorsetshire: the most eminent school for the education of gentlemen in the West of England. Here books are covered with old parchments and leases, never with manuscripts, so far as I have seen. But there were no abbeys or convents for men in these parts before the Dissolution, so far fewer manuscripts flew around afterwards.

. . .

My health is improving. I am excelling at Latin and Greek: am the best among my peers. I have been lent a copy of Cooper's Dictionary – *Thesaurus Linguae Romanae et Britannicae*, printed in London in 1584 and dedicated to Robert Dudley, Earl of Leicester, and the Chancellor of Oxford – which is new to me. I am reading all the Terence parts first, then will move on to Cicero.

Reading Ovid's *Metamorphoses*, translated into English by Sandys, leads me to understand the Latin better and is a wonderful help to my imagination.

I find Tully's *Offices* too dry.

I prefer Lord Bacon's *Essays* for an introduction to morals, excellences of style, hints and transitions. My mother has told me that Lord Bacon used to visit her kinsman, Sir John Danvers, at Chelsea and delight in his garden. Sir John helped Lord Bacon with his *History of Henry VII*, with more honesty and better judgement than any scholar.

Lord Bacon has argued that antiquities are 'remnants of History, which have escaped the shipwreck of time'. I am drawn irresistibly to the past. Old objects and stories delight me.

. . .

I have found as much roguery at Blandford School as there is said to be at Newgate Prison. I know now the wickedness of boys. The ones who are stronger than me mock and abuse me, so I must make a friendship with one of them to protect me from the others.

. . .

A terrible day. The master flexed his cane and looked away. I have seen it before: that hard look of anticipation, so deep, it is almost behind his eyes; the quick flick of his tongue across thin lips. It has happened before, happened so often already that I know there is nothing to hope

for in catching his gaze or holding it. There is only endurance, and
pain. He tells me to bare my buttocks and bend over the chair. I go
to another place in my head: the bank of the brook at Easton Pierse,
or the tree-lined riverbank at Broad Chalke, where I count the flowers
and arrange their names in alphabetical order. I hear the cane hiss
through the air, high above his head, before the burning begins, one
stroke after another: *hic, haec, hoc; hic, haec, hoc.* The cane cuts as
precisely as the Latin declensions. I do not, I will not, cry out. I am
not in this scene; I am somewhere else, with the soothing sound of
water running by. He beats me then about the head for insolence. *Hic,*
haec, hoc: more brutal blows, less precisely aimed, but still the same
rhythm. It is the grammar and rhetoric of violence. A language I will
not learn, though the whole school seems to speak it. My face is running
now with tears, blood and snot. *Hic, haec, hoc;* I wonder will my wits
ever recover, or has something been smashed inside me that cannot
be mended? My speech falters and my stammer will be worse in the
morning. I will fall asleep thinking nothing.

. . .

Saturday. A play-day. Now that we are old enough, we boys are let out
of school on Saturday afternoons to walk round Blandford in pairs, or
larger groups. I have made friends with Sir Walter Raleigh's grand-
nephews, Walter and Tom. I take them with me to visit old Mr Harding
the glass painter's workshop and furnaces again. I am fascinated by
the ancient craft and by the furnaces. I like the gentleness of laying
one thin coat of dilute colour across another, slowly and carefully, until
the colour is perfect. Like a limner, or painter of manuscripts, a heavy
hand makes the paint go on too thick, then it cracks and the effect is
spoiled. This is how I would rather learn: slowly, gently. Inventive
children (I know this is true of me) tend not to be tenacious. It is better
to let the knowledge sink in slowly, calmly. If a child's mind is parchment, or glass to be painted on, thick, vehement strokes – the harsh
hic, haec, hoc of the master's cane – will tear or smash it to pieces.

. . .

Sir Walter Raleigh is remembered with misgivings among our friends
and neighbours in Easton Pierse because he all but ruined Sir Charles
Snell by getting him to invest in the *Angel Gabriel*: a ship destined for

Guyana. The ship cost Snell the manor of Yatton Keynell, the farm at Easton Pierse, Thornhill and the church lease of Bishop's Canning. Raleigh's grand-nephews are clever, proud, quarrelsome boys with tunable (but small) voices, who play their parts well on the viol. They tell me that their great-uncle had mapped out an apparatus for the second part of his *History of the World*, but when his publisher complained about the sales of the first part, he burnt it in disgruntlement, saying, 'If I am not worthy of the world, the world is not worthy of my works.' How I wish he had not done that! Now no one will know what would have been in the second volume of his book.

. . .

I have heard my grandfather Lyte say that Sir Walter Raleigh was the first to bring tobacco into England and make it the fashion. In north Wiltshire, my grandfather remembers a silver pipe being handed round the table from man to man. Ordinary people smoked through a walnut shell and straw. Tobacco was sold for its weight in silver, so when our old yeomen neighbours went to Malmesbury or Chippenham market, they kept their biggest shillings to place in the scales against the tobacco. Sir Walter Raleigh smoked a pipe of tobacco before he went to the scaffold. Some people thought this scandalous, but I think it was well and properly done to settle his spirits. My grandfather remembers when apothecaries sold sack in their shops.

. . .

Sometimes, on holy days or play-days, we boys go to tread the maze at Pimpherne, which is near Blandford.

. . .

Sauntering through Blandford today, dreaming of seeing the sea, the harbours and the rocks I have read about in books, I met a man weeping on the bowling green. He spoke English with a strong German accent. He sat upon the grass and rocked himself, like a nurse rocks an inconsolable infant. I sat down beside him and he told me he had been driven from his estate and country by the wars that rage there. Before the wars came, he had as good an estate as any Englishman. Now he is forced to maintain himself by surveying the land. He told me it is good to have a little learning for no one knows to what shifts and straits he might be brought. The German was not an old man, my father's age, perhaps. I thought of Easton Pierse and the farm at Broad Chalke. I wondered how I would live, if I had to, without them, and in my mind's eye I saw them suddenly ravaged by flames and blackened with soot. Would I earn my bread by painting then, or be employed to survey the land like this poor man?

. . .

Anno 1639

Monday after Easter: my uncle Anthony Browne's bay nag threw me today. She ran away with me and gave me a very dangerous fall. Just before, I had an impulse of the briar under which I rode that tickled the nag at the upper end of Bery Lane. *Deo gratias!*

. . .

Anno 1640

13 April
On this day the King summoned Parliament for the first time since 1629.

. . .

5 May
The King dismissed Parliament after only three weeks.

. . .

3 November
The King recalled Parliament, hoping it would pass financial bills.

. . .

7 November
There was a debate in the newly convened Parliament in which preaching in support of absolute monarchy was attacked.

. . .

Fearing that he might be called to account for his argument that sovereignty must be absolute, Mr Hobbes has fled to France.

. . .

Anno 1641

15 February
On this day Parliament passed the Dissolution Act. This means that
the King can no longer rule without Parliament, which from henceforth must meet for a least one fifty-day session every three years.

PART II

Oxford

Anno 1642

May

Mr Hobbes encouraged me to come to Oxford and I am here now, in Trinity College. I have matriculated; I have written my name in the buttery book and paid my 3d caution money. I study logic and ethics. I lie in bed some mornings in my chamber, looking at the canonised saint in one of the windows: Gregory the Great. I was born on St Gregory's Day, 12 March 1626, so am glad to have this window. The painting is as good as any I saw in old Mr Harding's workshop. I cannot tell who the saint in the second window in my chamber is because it was broken before I got here: perhaps the students who slept in this chamber before me were less careful than I am; cared less for glass and other precious things. It is spring, and summer is coming. In my study window, there is a crucifix. I think of Mr Hobbes, and the stories he has told me of his student days in Magdalen Hall. He says he used to rise very early to catch birds at his college window. First he tied leaden weights to pieces of string, then dipped them in birdlime, then baited them with cheese-parings. Jackdaws would spy the parings from high in the sky, as far away even as Osney Abbey, and swoop for the bait. The string, lime and weight would pinion their wings, holding them fast and netted. Perhaps Mr Hobbes cooked and ate them, or let them go, remarking to himself on the wonderful eyesight that could see cheese-parings from that great distance up in the air.

. . .

All this time I am falling deeper and deeper in love with books. Here in Trinity, Dr Ralph Bathurst has an excellent collection: well chosen and broad-ranging. He lets me turn them over and peruse them, for which I am truly grateful. Many of the currish fellows will not let their pupils touch their precious books: they are like churlish trade masters – carpenters, for example – who make money from taking on apprentices but never teach them the mysteries of the trade.

. . .

In London, I get lost among the piles of books for sale in St Paul's churchyard; most of them are sold in sheets, but some are already bound. I pick up one after another without any idea where to begin: the books that are bound all look alike. How to tell which will be worth buying with my spare money? I come away empty-handed, overwhelmed, as though the books have become trees again and I am wandering blind in a forest. Back in Dr Bathurst's library, I can explore more calmly; I am starting to find my way.

. . .

Because I am busy and happy, the summer has come quicker than ever before. This morning, I attended a rhetoric lecture in hall. Dr Ralph Kettell, the President of Trinity, often attends our lectures and exercises with an hourglass. He has been president since 1598 – the second president since the foundation of our college in 1555 – and is now almost eighty years old, with sharp grey eyes, white hair and a fresh ruddy complexion. He is over six foot tall, gigantic and terrible in his russet cloth gown, surplice and hood. He drags one foot – his right foot – so we hear him coming before he rounds the corner, like a rattlesnake.

'Turds! Tarrarags!' These are his names for the worst kind of boys. 'Rascal-Jacks! Blindcinques! Scobberlotchers! Get to your books and lessons, good-for-nothing idlers!' Such are his names for the boys that do no harm but do no work either, idling around the college grove with their hands in their pockets and telling the number of trees, etc. The President is a man of great charity. When he notices diligent boys with little money, whose friends have more, he is wont to drop money in at their windows at night. By day he walks up and down the college, peeping in at the keyholes to see if we boys follow our books or not. We mock him but we love him. 'Seneca writes as a boar does piss: by jerks,' he tells us. Our college has the best beer in Oxford, since

Dr Kettell observed that colleges with small beer force their students out into town to comfort their stomachs. At Trinity we have no cause to drink outside our own college and have the fewest drunkards. He tells us to keep our bodies chaste and holy.

This morning we were listening to a lecture in the hall when there was a knock at the door and Dr Kettell was called away on college business. A raucous murmur rose, higher and higher pitched, before falling straight down, like a hawk to its prey, when the door opened again and an armed man entered. Jack Dowch, a boy in front of me, whom I have never liked, raised his arm to point at Dr Kettell's hourglass. The man smirked and smashed it with the butt of his rifle. There was silence. War is coming. The King and his Parliament cannot agree. Dr Kettell returned and the lecture continued as if nothing had happened. I heard nothing. I stared at the light refracted through the broken glass on the floor. I hoped Dr Kettell would not drag his foot through it. Lots of the young scholars are training instead of attending lectures; in New College gardens there are two squadrons taking shape, one wielding pikes, the other halberts; there are roadblocks and trenches between the colleges. Oxford is becoming a garrison town. My father is summoning me home. I do not wish to go.

. . .

In Dr Ralph Kettell's dining room hangs a picture he commissioned of the late Thomas Allen (1542–1632), who was educated here at Trinity College and became a Fellow before retiring to Gloucester Hall. In those dark times, astrologer, mathematician and conjuror were accounted the same things, and the vulgar verily believed Thomas Allen was a conjuror. He had a great many mathematical instruments and glasses in his room, which confirmed the ignorant in their opinion, and his servant used to frighten freshmen and simple people by telling them he had seen spirits coming up Thomas Allen's stairs like bees. I was told this before I came up to Trinity by an old man in Kington St Michael, who was at Oxford over seventy years ago. Looking at Allen's picture today, it seems to me he was a handsome, sanguine man of excellent habit and body. I have been told he had a wide circle of acquaintance that he visited in the long vacation. Once at Holm Lacy, staying with Mr John Scudamore, he left his watch in his chamber window (watches were rare then). The maid came in to make the bed and hearing a thing in a case cry 'Tick,

tick, tick,' concluded it must be the devil. She picked up the watch with fire tongs and flung it out the window into the moat to drown out the devil. But the watch was saved when the string caught on a sprig of elder that grew up from the moat (confirming in her mind that it was indeed the devil). So good old Allen got his watch back again. He is buried in Trinity College Chapel, but I cannot tell where exactly, as there is no stone with his name over him.

. . .

May Day

I went with friends to join the celebrations in the nearby village of Woodstock, where I was saddened to see many hawthorn trees dug out of the park and set down in the street. There was dancing, feasting and merriment, but it seemed to me a pity so many fair white hawthorns were spoiled for one day's disport.

. . .

Today I heard the story of the death of Dr George Webb, one of the King's Protestant chaplains in Ireland, from his nephew, who was his archdeacon and with him in Limerick. Dr Webb died just days before the city, which had been under siege from the Irish army since the rebellion last year, fell earlier this month. After the Irish soldiers took possession of the town, they dug up Dr Webb's body. I must confess, I do not like the zeal in the Canon Law that does not let the bodies of heretics rest in peace. It is inhumane.

. . .

Whitsun

This morning, I saw the master cook of Exeter College and his assistants ride out on horseback in silk doublets to 'fetch in the Fly' (the spirit of cookery) from Bartholemews, or Bullington-green. They drank well before they left. They will ride out again at Michaelmas to carry the Fly away.

. . .

At St John's College there is a servitor named Shakston, a tall, thin, pale fellow, who eats spiders with as much greediness as nuts, saying they comfort his stomach.

August

There has been a brush between the Earl of Northampton and Lord Brooke (his rebel neighbour), near Banbury. Last month, Parliament granted Lord Brooke six guns to strengthen Warwick Castle, but when he rode out to collect them from Banbury, the Earl of Northampton leading forces loyal to the King prevented him and captured the rebel guns.

. . .

My friends rode out with me today to Woodstock Manor, where I was excited to visit Rosamund's Bower, built, it is said, in the twelfth century. My nurse Kath used to sing me the story of how Henry II had the bower built for his lover Rosamund de Clifford, so they could be safely together, without fear of his wife, Elinor of Aquitaine, finding them. But Elinor, suspecting her husband, rode furiously across the land, and came upon his spurs at Woodstock Manor. There was a tiny ball of silken thread caught on one of them, which the enraged queen followed until she came upon the lovers at the heart of the labyrinthine bower.

> Yea, Rosamund, fair Rosamund,
>   her name was called so,
> To whom dame Elinor our Queen
>   was known a deadly foe,
> The King therefore for her defence
>   against the furious Queen
> At Woodstock builded such a Bower
>   the like was never seen.
>
> Most curiously that Bower was built,
>   of Stone and Timber strong,
> A hundred and fifty dores,
>   did to this Bower belong,
> And they so cunningly contriv'd
>   with turnings round about
> That none but with a clew of thread,
>   could enter in, or out.

Now the place is full of ruined walls, five or six feet high, which
must once have formed the intricate bower. One freestone vault is
still in place, leading underground to Combe church, which is almost
a mile distant. I think there must originally have been more vaults.
Meadows surround what is left, and beyond them clouds above the
woods, that give a very lovely melancholy prospect. In the high park
there are stag-headed oak trees that have not borne leaf for over a
hundred years. They are of great antiquity, which, for me, makes
them worthy of veneration. Looking at the crumbling walls of the
bower, I began to think that it might once have been like the labyrinth
Daedelus built to contain the Minotaur on Crete. I thought of
Rosamund running through the vaults trying in vain to escape the
angry Queen. I have seen a picture of Rosamund in Sir Laurence
Washington's house near Malmesbury. I am not sure when the picture
was painted, maybe around the time of Henry VI. Rosamund is
depicted with deep red hair, inclining towards chestnut brown. Her
eyes like those of a viper, but somewhat small; her skin fair, clear,
delicate, warm. An oval face with arched eyebrows, but imbued with
too much pride for my liking. I prefer sweeter looks.

I intended to sketch the remains of the bower today, but my
friends were rowdy and impatient, urging me to come away. When
I can, I will return to sketch more carefully. I would like to find the
gatehouse window too, where it is said Princess Elizabeth, imprisoned by her sister in Woodstock Manor, scratched into the glass:
'Much suspected, of me; Little proved can be, Quoth Elizabeth,
Prisoner.' I noticed the stately gilded statue in the courtyard, and
the great hall, with pillars like a church. It seems a place of ill omen
for monarchs.

. . .

Today Dr Kettell greatly embarrassed my friend Anthony Ettrick. The
President had heard how Ettrick and others frightened a poor young
freshman of Magdalen Hall by conjuring. So he announced: 'Mr Ettrick
will conjure up a jackanapes to be his great-grandfather.' Anthony
was born at Berford in the parish of Wimburne Minster, Dorset, on
15 November 1622. His mother always says he is a Sunday's bird.

. . .

Dr Kettell upbraided the Fellows today: 'Oh! You are gallant gentlemen and learned men, who snort and fart at your poor president. I am old and blind but who was it brought you in to be Fellows from poor rascal-jacks and servitors? Was it not your president? And yet none of your friends were ever so grateful as to present me with so much as a wrought nightcap . . . Ah! But I cry you mercy! I remember indeed that one of your mothers once sent me a gammon of bacon!'

. . .

By order of the Parliament, the Lord Viscount Saye and Sele is visiting all the college chapels to search out new signs of Popery. In Trinity we have two painted altars on the far side of the screen that are in danger: one dedicated to St Katherine, on the right as you enter the chapel; and one dedicated to the Saviour coming down from the Cross, on the left. My friends and I are fond of them both. To save them Dr Kettell told the Lord Viscount Saye and Sele, 'Truly, my lord, we regard them no more than a dirty dish-clout.' His lordship seemed convinced, so for now, at least, these fresh and lively paintings will not be coloured over. There is good Gothic painting in the windows of the chapel, a figure in every column: St Cuthbert, St Leonard, St Oswald, etc. I have taken careful note of all the escutcheons in the college glass. Above the door of the screen in the chapel there is an ancient little organ, whose pipes are in the bursary. We sing the psalms on Sundays, holy days and the eves of holy days, and one of the scholars sings the gospel for the day in the hall at the end of dinner, ending: *tu autem Domine miserere nostri*. The President sings in a shrill high treble and one young Fellow, John Hoskyns, who has an even higher voice, plays the wag and makes him strain even further up.

. . .

Oxford is now held by the Parliament's soldiers.

. . .

Today I visited Abingdon and much admired its market cross from the time of Henry VI. I think it must be one of the finest in England. It is admirable Gothic architecture, with fine figures in the niches, after the fashion of the cross in Bristol High Street, but more curiously worked.

. . .

How now Bellona thunders! And as a clear sky is sometimes suddenly overstretched with dismal cloud and thunder, so England's serene peace is shattered by the factions of these times. I think of Homer's *Odyssey*.

. . .

13 September
On this day there was a considerable fight at Babell Hill (between Sherborne and Yeovil). Sherborne Castle is besieged by the Parliament's soldiers.

. . .

I have regretfully obeyed my father and am back at Broad Chalke. He is afraid of the trouble that has come to Oxford: the war without an enemy, the gathering storm over England, threatening to rend the country apart, like a great oak struck by lightning. I lie, listless, in my chamber, reading. I am sad and alone again as I was in childhood. I miss my friends and all the books in Oxford. The books I have with me here are getting damp and rotten in the heavy Wiltshire air. My books in my closet at Easton Pierse were never touched by mouldiness, but here at Broad Chalke they get so covered in hoary mould that I cannot tell what colour the leather used to be. The downs of Wiltshire can be covered with mists even when the vales are clear and the sky serene.

. . .

I visit Salisbury often. Outside the Close, as you come into the town from Harnham Bridge, opposite the hospital, there is a hop yard, with a fair high stone wall round it, and the ruins of an old pigeon house. This was once the Collegium de Valle Scholarum, College de Vaux. It took its name from the Vaux family. It was a *magister scholarum*, in the manner of a university, but never an endowed college; now it is in ruins.

. . .

The eldest son of Mr William Stumpe, rector of Yatton Keynell, the parish in which my mother was born and where I first went to school, has received a commission as a foot captain in the army of King

Charles. This man, named Thomas, has already led a strange life of wondrous adventure. He was a boy of daring spirit; he would climb towers and trees most dangerously; would even walk on the battlements of the tower at Malmesbury. He could never have been a scholar, so aged about sixteen he went on a voyage with his uncle, Thomas Ivy, to Guyana, in 1632 or 1633. When the ship put in, four or five of them straggled too far into the country, and in the interim the wind served, and the sails were hoist, and the stragglers were left behind. It was not long before the wild people seized on them and stripped them, and knocked the brains out of those that had beards and ate them; but the queen of the wild people saved Thomas Stumpe and one other boy. Thomas threw himself into the river to drown, but could not sink (he is very full-chested). The other youth shortly died. Thomas lived with the tribe until 1636 or 1637.

He says there is incomparable fruit in Guyana, and that it may be termed the paradise of the world. He says that the spondyles of the backbones of the huge serpents there are used to sit on, as our women sit upon butts. He says he taught them to build hovels, and to thatch and wattle. I never heard of any man that lived so long among those savages. Then one day, a Portuguese ship came sailing by; he swam to it and they took him up and made use of him as a sea-boy. As they sailed near Cornwall he stole out of a porthole and swam to shore and begged his way back to his father in Wiltshire. When he came home, nobody knew him, except Jo Harris the carpenter, until at last he recounted so many accurate memories and circumstances that his family welcomed him back.

. . .

Francis Potter, a reclusive, monkish man whom I have never met, even though he used to live in Trinity College and his brother Hannibal whom I know well still does, has a book with the booksellers called *An Interpretation of the Number 666*. It is said the idea for it came to him seventeen years ago as he climbed and counted the stairs to his college room. He has extracted 25 as the nearest square root to the Number of the Beast and contrasted it with 12: the square root of 144, the number of the Church. Potter, whom I would love to meet, argues that 25 is a fatal and unfortunate number. In the Book of Revelation he has found many instances of the number 12; in the Roman Church he has found many instances of 25. There were 12 Apostles, but 25 cardinals in the Church of Rome. There were 12 Commandments in the Apostles' Creed, but 25 Articles of the Roman faith, published by Pius IV after the Council of Trent. The High Altar in St Peter's Church in Rome is surmounted by a gilded cross, 25 hands high, and the High Altar itself is an exact cube 25 x 25 feet. Christ began to do his father's work when he was 12 years old; but priests, deacons and subdeacons of the Roman Church reach vocational maturity at 25. The Church's main holidays, including Christmas, are held on the 25th of the month. As I lie awake at night in Broad Chalke, reading, missing Oxford, wishing I could return there, I imagine Potter waking in a cold sweat, terrified of being brought before the Pope in Rome and condemned to death for his ideas. Thoughts of the Antichrist fill my mind as the rising sun throws a lattice of intersecting lines across the bedroom floor. Those who talk of politics say a universal darkness is gathering. The King and his Parliament are irreconcilably at odds. Chaos will break over England.

. . .

I have met and become friends with the divine and mathematician Edward Davenant, vicar of Gillingham in Dorset. He is of great diligence in study and well versed in all kinds of learning. He tells me he has no esteem for astrology at all. He is helping me learn algebra; his daughters are already algebrists.

. . .

23 October

On this day the Battle of Edgehill was fought in southern Warwickshire: the war is begun. Neither the King's nor the Parliament's army triumphed. The result is inconclusive and the King has resumed his march on London, but is thwarted in arriving there.

. . .

Anno 1643

February

I have revolted against my father. With much ado, I have overridden his fearful anxiety and am once again in Oxford, where King Charles has entered the city like Apollo and taken it back from the Parliament's soldiers. As I rode back here I saw perhaps a dozen soldiers, belonging to the King's garrison in Abingdon, keeping watch near the barrow on Cutchinlow Hill. They stood guard in a great pit so that if the enemy comes, only their heads will be shot at. Oxford is crowded with soldiers. The King resides in Christ Church and his Queen in Merton College. A special path has been laid through the grounds of Corpus Christi for them to visit each other. Sometimes the visits are secret, sometimes ceremonial. The court has been shrunken in scale and mapped on to Oxford and the King's army is billeted here: he is gathering his forces. There are already several thousand foot soldiers and three troops of horses, but more keep coming. The city is too small to cope. It is overfull, disease-ridden, people in the street are hungry and dying. All the colleges have become barracks; Magdalen Hall is an arsenal; where once was the corn market men make bullets, so grain is stored now in the Academic Schools and those that labour there produce military uniforms not arguments or scholarship; Oxford Castle is a prison; Osney Abbey a powder mill.

. . .

Osney Abbey is a ruin in Oxford, just south of the Botley Road. A woman named Edith Forne lies in her tomb there dreaming of magpies. When she was alive, she asked a friar to interpret her dream, and he told her the magpies were souls in purgatory needing a church to rest in. She urged her wealthy husband to found Osney, which he did in 1129, and now she rests there herself, surrounded by a picture of her dream of the birds. Osney's Bell, Great Tom, was taken to nearby Christ Church during the dissolution of the monasteries. Much furniture went too, and the abbey fell into disuse. Almost a hundred years later, I can see the ruin cannot stand much longer. There is a great arch hanging unsupported on one side, waiting to crash down on crumbling walls below. The birds, truly, have come to nest here now. The exposed ledges, the roofless rooms, the always open windows are home to hundreds, maybe thousands, of restless, crying birds. I squint against the sun to try and name them: magpies, as in Edith Forne's dream; jackdaws like the ones Mr Hobbes baited. The ruins should be drawn for future generations before they disappear further. I could do it myself, but not well enough. Osney and posterity deserve better. I will find someone skilled to do it.

. . .

I am made much of by the scholars. This city suits me well. I studied
my reflection in my looking glass today. I am almost seventeen years
old and must by now be fully grown: of middling height with a quick
look about me. My clothes are smart: black velvet, a plush-gippe and
silver shoulder belt. I cut a sparkish figure in the town.

. . .

Tonight I watched the King dine in Christ Church. Old Tom rings out
the hour. The meal was of mutton and veal (boiled and roasted), capons,
hens (with eggs), partridges, pheasants, cocks, larks, beef, mallards, pig,
salmon, sea flounder, venison, conies and teales, with baked tart and
Pippins to follow. I heard the King tell of a time when he was hawking
in Scotland:
'I rode into the quarry and came across a covey of partridges falling
upon the hawk. I swear upon the Book 'tis true. When I came to my
chamber, I told this story to my tutor; said he, "That covey was
London."'
The gentlemen of the court rushed to tell him it will not happen:
London and its Parliament will not fall upon him; the natural order
will stand, not be overturned. But I have heard another story, more
peculiar. When the King's bust in marble, carved by Bernini, from a
drawing by Van Dyck, was carried on a barge up the Thames in the
open air, a strange bird, of a kind the bargemen had never seen before,
swooped down and dropped what looked like a drop of blood upon
it. It left a stain that could not be wiped away. There was a seam in
the middle of the forehead, which is a very ill sign in metoposcopy,
which predicts a person's character and destiny from the lines on his
forehead.

. . .

Many of the courtiers have brought their wives and families to Oxford.
Suddenly the city is full of beautiful women. Lady Isabella Thynne,
daughter of the Earl of Holland, aged about nineteen, is staying in
Balliol College with her husband, Sir James Thynne. She comes often
to visit her intimate friend, fine Mistress Fanshawe, who is staying at
Trinity with her husband, John Fanshawe the poet. These two young

women came to chapel this morning, half-dressed, like angels. For a frolic, they tried to visit the President's lodgings, but old Ralph Kettell could see they meant to make fun of him and said to Mistress Fanshawe: 'Madam, your husband and father I bred up here, and I knew your grandfather; I know you to be a gentlewoman, I will not say you are a whore; but get you gone for a very woman.' These dissolute times, the lively courtiers, the soldiers and their rough ways, grieve the President. He has taken to standing by the gate into the college and observing the persons who come to walk in our grove: it has become like Hyde Park in London.

I have heard Lady Isabella play the lute in our grove – which she does outstandingly. She is most beautiful, humble, charitable, etc., and cannot refuse or subdue anyone. One might say of her as Tacitus said of Agrippina: *Cuncta alia illi adfuere, praeter animum honestum* (All other things are present in her, except an honest mind). Mr Edmund Waller adores her and celebrates her in verse:

> Of My Lady Isabella Playing on the Lute
> Such moving sounds, from such a careless touch,
> So unconcern'd her self, and we so much!
> What Art is this, that with so little Pains
> Transports us thus, and o'er our Spirits reigns! . . .

. . .

I have seen Dr William Harvey come to Trinity College to visit my friend Ralph Bathurst's brother George, who is a Fellow here too. I feel too shy, too unimportant, to press for an acquaintance with the famous doctor.

Dr William Harvey was at the Battle of Edgehill with the King last October. When the fighting began, he was given charge of the Prince of Wales and the Duke of York, aged twelve and ten. He took them to sit under a nearby hedge, produced a book from his pocket and began reading to them. Soon afterwards, a bullet from a great gun grazed the ground nearby, so they moved further off.

I have heard another story about the Battle of Edgehill: terrifying and miraculous. Sir Adrian Scrope was seriously wounded and left for dead, his body stripped like the other corpses. It was cold, clear weather and there was a frost that night which staunched his bleeding. He woke around midnight among the corpses and pulled one of them on top of him to keep warm. I pray that I never lie on a battlefield.

After the Battle of Edgehill, Dr Harvey followed the King to Oxford. Here he keeps busy, tending the King's health, and pursuing his own researches.

In George Bathurst's rooms there is a hen laying eggs, which he and Dr Harvey dissect. They are repeating Aristotle's experiments, hoping to see the progress and way of generation. Their interest is in the interior of the egg and the first beginnings of the chick, which can be seen, like a little cloud, by removing the shell and placing the egg into warm clear water. In the midst of the cloud is a tiny point of blood, as small as the point of a needle, which beats.

. . .

I hope I can find someone to draw the ruins of Osney Abbey before they fall down. I have sought out William Dobson, the court painter, in his rooms on the High Street almost opposite St Mary's Church. Dobson is a painter of genius, but poor. He became court painter just last year after Van Dyck died, at a time when everything was changing. His father was a St Albans man who helped Lord Bacon build his magnificent Verulam House, within the bounds of the old Roman city walls: a talented man, but a lover of many women, who left his son to make his own way in the world. In his studio today I saw a wonderful work in progress: a sumptuous portrait of the Prince of Wales, commemorating his participation in the Battle of Edgehill. The Prince's figure dominates the canvas, seeming too big to fit upon it, as he tramples underfoot the head of Medusa and the horrors of war. It is hard to reconcile Dobson's splendid portrait with Harvey's story of the young princes being read to under a hedge as the fighting began. Dobson has a new wife called Judith who has accompanied him to Oxford. Her flesh is luminous and her face very sweet and pretty. There was a cast of her hands on a pedestal in that chaos of canvas and paint that I coveted. Dobson is probably too occupied to draw Osney Abbey for me himself, but he says his friend and assistant Mr Hesketh will do it for twenty shillings.

. . .

Robert Greville (Lord Brooke), married to the daughter of the Earl of Bedford, was killed this month on 2 March at the siege of Lichfield. The story is that he was armed head to foot, but his lower face and neck were exposed because his bevor was open.

. . .

April

Camp fever is raging in Oxford. I have fallen sick with smallpox: it will unpolish my complexion. My father is summoning me home again, for fear I cannot recover in this disease-racked city. But I am bedridden and cannot leave, nor do I wish to. I know what a lonely life awaits me in the country, far from books, far from ingenious conversation. Whereas here I lie, a scurvy antiquary, entertained by my faithful friends at least. Mr William Radford, in his third year here at Trinity, comes to see me every day for several hours, saving me from melancholy. Dr Ralph Kettell, who cannot be reconciled to long hair, or hairy scalps as he calls them, once cut off Will's hair with the bread knife from the buttery hatch when we were all eating in hall. He sang:

And was not Grim the collier finely trimm'd? Tonedi, Tonedi.

Then he turned to our friend John Lydall and asked: 'Mr Lydall, how do you decline *tondeo*? *Tondeo, tondes, tonedi*?' As to periwigs, Dr Kettell believes them to be the scalps of hanged men, cut off after death.

Will brings me stories of our other Trinity friends: Tom Mariett and Ned Wood especially. Tom Mariett is from Whitchurch in Warwickshire: a passionate supporter of the King. Ned's family live in the old stone house, Postmaster's Hall, opposite Merton College; his father died early this year, his older brother is fighting for the King. Today Will told me how Ned's younger brother Anthony, six or seven years ago, was playing in the street outside their house when the university carrier rode over him on a horse named Mutton and bruised his head badly. Ned's family were worried for a while that Anthony had been damaged and made slow by the accident, but he has grown into a clever boy, as interested as I am in antiquities. I hope we meet when the pox has passed.

. . .

Smallpox is periodical. There was smallpox in Sherborne during 1626 (the year of my birth), and during the year 1634, and it has been back again since Michaelmas last year. Such facts and observations in the great towns should be recorded, but few care for these things.

. . .

I am not there to see or mourn it, but I have heard of the demolition of the Malmesbury church, St Mary Westport. That church was very pretty, consisting of a nave and two aisles, and it had a very tall spire, with five tunable bells, which will be melted down now the church is nothing but rubble on the ground. Sir William Waller, who fought before in Germany, commanded it in the Parliament's cause. He approached from Tetbury on 21 March, crossed Newton River by Stanes Bridge, occupied Westport and laid siege to Malmesbury, declaring it the best naturally defended place he ever saw inland. And it is true: Malmesbury, where the Bristol Avon and Tetbury Avon almost meet, where the Bristol Road and Oxford Road cross, is surrounded by steep hills, almost cliffs. Westport, outside the old town walls, is a weakness in those defences granted by nature. Waller entered through Westport, then pulled down the church, lest others follow him and lay siege that way. I think it sacrilege to disarrange those stones. When there is thunder and lightning, it is customary in Malmesbury, to ring St Adelm's bell at the abbey. I have heard it said that this ringing of the bell exceedingly disturbs spirits. I imagine many spirits walk abroad now that soldiers occupy the town.

. . .

Sir William Waller's soldiers have broken the head of the handsome Gothic monument of King Athelstan in Malmesbury Abbey. I think the monument is workmanship from the time of the Conquest. On the figure's left hand, I remember, a carved falconer's glove, with a knob or tassel to put under his girdle, as is still used in falconry. King Athelstan deserves a shrine of gold for bringing in the statute of trial by a jury of twelve men. Instead, Waller's soldiers have broken the head of his monument to pieces.

. . .

My kinsman, Major Morgan of Wells, has been lying for almost a month under my father's roof at Broad Chalke. He was marching west with the King's army when fever overtook him at Salisbury. They took him to my father's house in secret to recover. I have heard that there is a sparrow that comes to the window of his garret every day and pecks, always at the same lozenge of glass, knocking the lead beside it, over and over, in the same place. Two of my father's servants have observed this sparrow. I predict that when my kinsman leaves to re-join the King's forces, the bird will cease to visit.

. . .

I have become a brother at the age of seventeen. My mother, in these troubled times, has given birth to a new baby boy named William.

PART III

War

My father's caution has prevailed. I am come home again to a sad country life. I recovered from the smallpox after the end of Trinity Week (Trinity Sunday was 4 June) and my father sent for me. Here I converse with none but servants and rustics and quartered soldiers, to my great grief. Horace's Odes come to mind: *Odi profanum vulgus et arceo* (I hate the profane rabble and steer clear of them). I am scarcely acquainted with my father. I am in the prime of my youth and I am without the benefit of ingenious conversation, and have hardly any good books. I am almost a consumptive. I have carried some books from Oxford home with me: Thomas Browne's *Religio Medici*, printed last year, has opened my understanding. And I have Sir Kenelm Digby's 'Observations on Religio Medici', printed this year, to keep my thoughts company.

. . .

July

Dr Ralph Kettell has died. He was a good man and a good president of Trinity College. He was over eighty years old, but I believe would have lived well for longer without these wars. He might even have made a century. The wars grieved him deeply. He was used to being in charge of Trinity absolutely. It was hard for him to bear the affronts and disrespect of the soldiers garrisoned at the college.

. . .

I have met a soldier garrisoned near Broad Chalke who is the brother of John Birkenhead, who set up the newsbook *Mercurius Aulicus* in Oxford after the Battle of Edgehill.

. . .

August

My grandfather Isaac Lyte has a precious document in his keeping. It is a copy of the entertainments for the visit of Queen Henrietta Maria in August 1636 to Thomas Bushell's hermitage and grotto at Enston in Oxfordshire entitled: *The Severall Speeches and Songs, at the present-ment of Mr Bushell's Rock to the Queenes Most Excellent Majesty.* It was given to my grandfather by Old Jack Sydenham, the servant who worked for our neighbours in Easton Pierse, who fed my youthful fancy with stories of the olden days. He once also worked for Mr Bushell. From Old Jack, I have heard many stories of Mr Bushell, who, as a young man, waited on the Lord Chancellor Bacon. Like Mr Hobbes, Mr Bushell was one of Lord Bacon's amanuenses. After Lord Bacon died in 1626, Mr Bushell married and went to live at Enston, where he built a marvellous grotto.

. . .

3 August

I went to visit Mr Bushell today and he showed me his famous grotto, dug into the hillside, where rocks hang down like pendants, as they do at Wookey Hole in Somerset (which is not far from Lytes Carey, where my grandfather grew up). Before the wars, Queen Henrietta Maria gave her name to Mr Bushell's pleasure palace. It is surrounded by beautiful walks. A decade ago, when Mr Bushell was designing his gardens, he decided that he was advanced enough in years to mean he could not plant his hedges in the usual way and wait for them to grow, or he would hardly live to enjoy them. He sent his workmen all over the country, searching for white-thorn, plum trees and so on that had already reached fifteen or twenty feet. He transplanted them in the month of October, before All Saints Day, and they did very well. I have never seen better hedges. This story fits with the Somerset proverb:

> For Apples, Peares, Hawthornes Quickset, Oakes
> Set them at All-hollowtyde and command them to grow
> Set them after Candlemas and entreat them to grow.

Mr Bushell demonstrated his device for simu-
lating rain and causing a rainbow at the grotto's
entrance. I made a drawing of the little pond
opposite the grotto: there stood Neptune on a
scallop shell, with his trident in his hand, aiming
at a duck that swam perpetually round, chased
by a spaniel. The statue is of wood and about
three quarters of a yard high. It looks very
pretty.

. . .

September

Since before these wars began, Mr Bushell has been minting money
for the King. He had huge medals of twenty shillings and ten shillings
struck in silver and handed them out to the King's soldiers on the eve
of the Battle of Edgehill. When the King came to Oxford he moved
his mint there from Shrewsbury, and Mr Bushell became joint warden
of it with Sir William Pankhurst, warden of the Tower mint. Since
July, when Bristol was taken for the King, Mr Bushell has been erecting
another mint in the castle there.

In this time of civil war, he has swathed his grotto at Enstone in
soft black woollen cloth. His bed has black curtains, and hangs from
four ropes wrapped around with more of the black cloth, instead of
bedposts. When Queen Henrietta Maria came to Oxford this month
to join the King, I hear that she brought with her (I think, unless
someone gave it to her in Oxford) an Egyptian mummy that she
presented to Mr Bushell. He has placed it in the grotto that bears the
Queen's name, but I fear that is too damp a place and the mummy
will grow mouldy. Something so old and rare should not be ruined.

. . .

My friend and tutor William Browne writes with news from Oxford.
Like me he was educated at Blandford School and was a great help
when I arrived at Trinity College. He tells me that since the Battle of
Newbury, all goes well in the north. Legates from the pontiffs of Ireland
are said to be approaching the King and seeking conditions of peace.
The garrison of Abingdon will create trouble for that of Oxford. The
soldiers in Reading, Henley and St Albans are said to be converging,

and it is reported that envoys from London are coming to Oxford to seek terms from the King. How I wish I were back in Oxford.

. . .

Dr Hannibal Potter (brother of the monkish Francis) will be the next President of Trinity. It is rumoured that he has not been lawfully elected, but forced upon the Fellows by the Bishop of Winton. Dr William Chillingworth was a competitor for the presidency, but he has been inconsolable since the death of his friend Dr Lucius Cary, Viscount Falkland, at the Battle of Newbury.

According to William Browne, when William Chillingworth was a student at Trinity College, he did not study much, but when he did, he did much in a little time. He delighted in Sextus Empiricus and would walk often in the College Grove contemplating, and there he would meet some cod's-head or other, and dispute with him and baffle him. I think disputing was something of an epidemic then, but now it has fallen out of fashion and is considered unmannerly and boyish.

. . .

William Browne says that whilst they are safe in Oxford, anxiety rises by the day. Sir William Waller and his Parliamentarian forces still elude the King's army, and the Parliamentarian garrison of Poole remains strong. But at least well-munitioned Bristol Castle has been captured, along with Nantwich, and Oliver Cromwell, one of the leaders of the Parliament's forces, has suffered a defeat in Lincolnshire. The King is summoning the Great Council to meet in Oxford, and it is said Prince Rupert has been made commander-in-chief.

. . .

There has been an explosion at Osney Abbey, where they are making gunpowder for the King. I thank heaven that I had the remains of the abbey drawn before this happened. I was fearful the ruins would collapse from neglect, but war has helped them on their way.

. . .

Some time before Bristol Castle was captured, Mr Bushell got away. He is now on Lundy Island, in the mouth of the Bristol Channel, which is still loyal to the King.

. . .

Anno 1644

January

The King has set up a new Parliament in Oxford for the conduct of the war. He has summoned the members from London to assemble in Christ Church Hall. Most of the House of Lords and about a third of the House of Commons have heeded his summons.

. . .

Anthony Hungerford, Member of Parliament for Malmesbury, obeyed the King's summons to attend the Oxford Parliament in December. As a consequence, the London Parliament has fined him, disabled him and appointed a new member for Malmesbury: Sir John Danvers, my honoured kinsman on my mother's side.

. . .

March

Sir Francis Dodington has blown up part of Wardour Castle in Dorset, the seat of Lord Henry Arundel, whose father died in Oxford of battle wounds last year. Edmund Ludlow's garrison of Parliamentarian forces held Wardour Castle this past year, but soldiers loyal to the King, led by Dodington and Arundel, laid siege last December. Now it is surrendered, damaged irreparably, to its rightful owner. It will never be used as a fortress again.

I rode over to see the ruins of Wardour Castle the day after the explosion. The mortar it was built with is so good that one of the little towers reclining on one side still hangs together and has not fallen to pieces.

. . .

Anno 1645

January

Parliament directed the Committee of Both Kingdoms, which oversees the conduct of the war, to review its forces. The result is the establishment of a new-modelled army, under the command of Sir Thomas Fairfax.

. . .

The King's forces have garrisoned Faringdon House. All the small towns on the main roads through Berkshire – Wallingford, Abingdon, Faringdon, Wantage, Newbury, Hungerford, etc. – have seen either the King's soldiers or the Parliament's riding in with their troops.

. . .

The Parliament's soldiers are destroying the ancient monuments, which they consider idolatrous.

. . .

2 May

On this day Dr George Bathurst, brother of my friend Dr Ralph Bathurst, was killed in the Battle of Faringdon fighting for the King. He was one of thirteen sons and like a step-grandson to Ralph Kettell.

. . .

Mr William Browne writes to me from Oxford. He believes it a mistake to suppose that the University can preserve its privileges if the State perishes.

The King's soldiers have been defeated at Abingdon this month, despite the King's instructions that it be held at all costs. Oxford is threatened now. My friends there are afraid.

. . .

14 June

On this day, in a battle at Naseby, the King's army was all but destroyed by the Parliament's new-modelled army.

. . .

The fine high steeple at Calne, which stood upon four pillars in the middle of the church, has collapsed. One of the pillars was faulty, and the churchwardens were dilatory, as is usual in such cases. Mr Chivers of that parish foresaw this but he could not prevent it, and brought down Mr Inigo Jones to survey the steeple. This was in about 1639 or 1640: he gave him 30 li. out of his own purse for his pains. Mr Jones would have underbuilt the steeple for 100 li. But it fell down on Saturday, and brought the chancel with it too; the parish will be charged 1,000 li. to make a new heavy tower. I fear the same fate will

befall our steeple at Kington St Michael. It is impossible to persuade
the parishioners to go out of their own way to invest in such repairs
before it is too late.

When I was a boy I was told that
the figures in the south aisle window
of Kington St Michael church were
King Ethelred and his Queen. Since
then I have looked in the Legier
Book of Glastonbury and found that
they gave the manor of Kington and
Langley to the abbey, so I think what
I was told must be true since it was
a common fashion in those days to
place in the windows the effigies of
pious benefactors to inspire others.

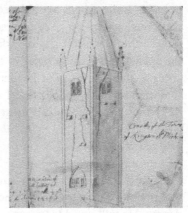

. . .

There is a church in Salisbury – St Edmund's – that had curious painted
glass windows, especially in the chancel. One of the windows (I think
the east window) was of such exquisite work that Gondamar, the
Spanish ambassador, offered to buy it for some hundreds of pounds.
In another of the windows there was a picture of God the Father,
like an old man, which gave offence to Mr Henry Shervill when he
was recorder of the city in 1631. Out of zeal he clambered on one of
the pews to be able to reach high enough to break the window, but
fell down and broke his own leg. For this he was brought into the
Star Chamber and heavily fined, which, I think, ruined him. But what
Mr Shervill left undone, the soldier vandals have seen through: there
is not a piece of glass painting left now.

. . .

I am once more a brother! My mother – who is now aged thirty-five
– has given birth to another baby boy, this one named Thomas.

. . .

September
My friend William Browne writes from Oxford and tells me my gown
has been mouldering in a box, so he will convert it into a divine's

gown for himself. I am glad this friend of mine has need of my gown. But I regret that beloved item was ever abandoned by me, who could have been a scholar, who still wishes to be. I left that gown behind because I thought I would return to my studies. Circumstance conspires against me. Yet I persevere. Mr Browne has promised to replace the gown if I go to Oxford to take my degree. But he says the soldier spoils the scholar in that town, and I would do better by going to the University of Leyden, which is cheaper and safer. He has sent me two of the books that I asked for, but not my Tacitus, which he cannot find. He thinks I must have locked it in my trunk, which I left in Oxford.

. . .

William Browne has another suggestion for my future: that I move to London, if my father will not let me go to Oxford to take my degree. He will not. Mr Browne asks whether my mother and grand-father will intervene on my behalf and not let my father 'stop all good notions'. But my father's anxiety has blocked my path my whole life. London would be as cheap as Oxford. One way or another, I am plotting my escape from sequestered rural life.

. . .

Anno 1646

January

My father had to go to Falstone House near Wilton to hand over more money to the Parliamentarian committee that sits there, raising funds by force for its bad but prospering cause. He has already paid 7 li. in North Wiltshire, and now for our Broad Chalke farm and other property in Herefordshire must pay 33 li. in sixty fat sheep and 60 li. in money. I have been to Herefordshire myself recently, to review our holdings. There I glimpsed the father of the famous courtesan Bess Broughton, who is one of the 5th Earl of Dorset's mistresses and among the greatest beauties of her age. Bess's father, old Mr Broughton, an octogenarian, seemed to me the most handsome, well-limbed, straight old man that I have ever seen. He has a good wit and a graceful elocution. Small wonder that his daughter is so beautiful. There is a ballad sung about her:

From the watch at twelve a clock
And from Bess Broughton's button'd smock,
Libera nos, Domine.

Old Mr Broughton brought in the husbandry of soap ashes. When he was living at Bristol, where much soap is made, and the haven there seemed likely to be choked up with it, he undertook an experiment to see if soap ash, like compost, improves the soil. He duly improved his land near the city in this way. My grandmother remembers Bess's mother (who was her neighbour) and I have heard her say she was as great as her husband.

. . .

They have started watering the meadows about Marlborough and Hungerford, and Mr John Bayly, of Bishop's Down, near Salisbury, is making great improvements by watering near St Thomas's Bridge. This practice is as old as the Romans. Virgil alludes to it in his *Bucolica*: '*Claudite jam rivos, pueri, sat prata biberunt*' ('Stop the currents now, young men, the meadows have drunk enough'). The improvement of watering meadows began at Wylye, in about 1635, and it was around that time – when I was about nine years old – that I remember the same practice introduced at Broad Chalke.

There are otters in the River Wylye, and perhaps in other rivers too. The otter is our English beaver.

. . .

April
To my great pride and joy, I have been admitted to Middle Temple, where I hope I will be able to make new friends and study the law. I intend to divide my time from this day forth between London and Oxford. No more secluded rural life for me!

The Middle Temple gardens run alongside the River Thames. There are fewer buildings on the bankside opposite.

. . .

But alas! Despite my good intentions, my father's sickness and business do not permit me to settle to my studies.

. . .

The war goes badly. There is little food and no cheer in Oxford. Mr Dobson is running out of painterly materials that cannot be sent for or fetched from London. The war has reduced the thick impasto of his earlier canvases to thin skim paint. Even so, he works with what he has. There is a new portrait of the King in his studio, nearly finished. It is done almost entirely in black and brown. The King wears military dress: his proud head and shoulders fill the canvas, ready to do battle, yet there is anxiety, sadness about his dark eyes. He seems much older than when he first came triumphantly into the city like Apollo; his face narrower, his hair thinner, his lips pressed tight together; a stubborn and a frightened man.

. . .

24 June
On this day Oxford surrendered.

. . .

Sir Thomas Fairfax, Lord General of the Parliament's army, has set a good guard of soldiers to preserve and protect the Bodleian Library. It is said that during their garrison of the town, the King's army did much damage to the library, embezzling the books and cutting off the chains that hold them in place. Lord Fairfax is a lover of learning, who will take care that our noble library is not further destroyed.

. . .

While the King had his court at Oxford, after the Battle of Edgehill, John Birkenhead, a Fellow of All Souls, wrote up the news wittily enough in his newsbook *Mercurius Aulicus*. Now that Oxford has surrendered, he will stop.

. . .

Many of the King's party, some already known to me, have come to London. I love not their debauches. I have friends who are not debauched, but even so their conversation is not improving: I find it unfit for the muses.

. . .

I have heard that Dr William Harvey has come to London to live with his brother Eliab, who is a rich merchant with a country house at Roehampton. I hope I will make his acquaintance before long.

. . .

July
Lundy Island, where Mr Bushell has been commandant for the King, has finally surrendered.

. . .

October
The painter William Dobson has died, aged just thirty-five. Like other supporters of the King who have left Oxford now the Parliamentarians have it, he came to live in London recently. But he was soon imprisoned for debt and died in poverty. I must see Judith, his sweet-faced widow, soon.

. . .

My honoured neighbour, Sir Charles Snell, has told me of an interesting sepulchre called Hubbaslow (or Barrow Hill) on the road from Chippenham to Bristol, and has shown me a reference to it in the first edition of Stow's *Chronicle*. I will see it.

. . .

November
To my great joy, I am returned to Trinity College, Oxford. The Fellows make much of me, and I am again amidst their learned conversation, books and music: ingenious youths, as rosebuds, imbibe the morning dew.

. . .

The Parliamentarian Visitation – which has been sent to Oxford to reform and regulate the University – came to Trinity today. Hannibal Potter, Pro-Vice Chancellor at the moment, as well as President of Trinity, does his best to protect the antiquities and elude the Visitors. Last month, Dr Potter was summoned to appear before the Visitors but he declined to attend. Now he has been called before a parliamentary committee of Lords and Commons in London, but still refuses to go.

. . .

I went to visit the ruins of Eynsham Abbey – the Benedictine monastery that was dissolved in 1538 – and greatly admired the two high towers at the west end. The ruins set my thoughts working to make out their magnificence in former times.

. . .

Dr William Petty teaches anatomy at Brasenose College and keeps a partially pickled dead body for this purpose. He brought the body to Oxford from Reading by water. He is beloved by all the scholars, especially Ralph Bathurst of Trinity College (brother of Dr George Bathurst, who was killed in the Battle of Faringdon), John Wilkins (astronomer and natural philosopher), Seth Ward (mathematician), Thomas Willis (royal physician), etc. Together they pursue experimental philosophy.

. . .

Ralph Bathurst says the poet Ben Jonson was a Warwickshire man (though others dispute this). Jonson came to Trinity College with an Exhibition after a benefactor overheard him reciting Greek verse from Homer as he worked on the wall between Lincoln's Inn and Chancery Lane alongside his stepfather, a bricklayer.

. . .

My Trinity friends, Thomas Mariett, William Radford and Ned Wood, have had a frolic on foot from Oxford to London. Never having been to Windsor before, they passed through it and visited Mr John Hales, Fellow of Eton College, general scholar and poet, who has a noble library of books. When the court was at Windsor, the learned courtiers much delighted in his company, but the Parliamentarian Visitation of 1642 ejected Mr Hales from his position as Canon of Windsor. My friends presented themselves to him as scholars, so he treated them well and gave them ten shillings.

. . .

I went to visit William Stumpe, out of curiosity to see his manuscripts (I remember seeing some of them in my childhood); but by now they are mostly lost. I have never forgotten how he used to abuse them,

lining the corks of ale bottles with precious pages. His sons are gunners
and soldiers who follow their father in their disrespect for manuscripts
and scour their guns with them. But Mr Stumpe showed me several
old deeds granted by the Lords Abbots, with their scales annexed,
which I suppose his son Captain Thomas Stumpe of Malmesbury – he
who had adventures as a boy in Guyana – will inherit.

. . .

Despite all the disruptions and distractions of this troubled time, I am
continuing my studies at Middle Temple. This evening we were finishing
our common meal when Sir John Maynard came in from Westminster
Hall, weary with the business of the day and hungry. He sat down by
Mr Bennett Hoskyns, son of the poet Serjeant Hoskyns, and some others
who were discussing the meaning of the text: 'For a just man one would
dare to die: but for a good man one would willingly die.' They asked
Sir John what the difference is between a just man and a good man. He
said it was all very well for those who had eaten to begin on such a
discourse, but he was hungry. Then, after a couple of mouthfuls, he
said: 'I'll tell you the difference presently: Serjeant Rolle is a just man
and Matthew Hale is a good man.' That is all he said before returning
to his food. There could not be a better elucidation of that text. Serjeant
Rolle is just, but naturally penurious (and his wife makes him worse).
Whereas Matthew Hale is not only just, but charitable, open-handed,
and no sounder of his own trumpet, as hypocrites are.

. . .

James Harrington and Thomas Herbert have been appointed to His
Majesty's Bedchamber at Holmeby House, by order of the Parliament.
I am told that Mr Harrington passionately loves the King, and they
often dispute together about government, but the King will not hear
talk of a Commonwealth. I hope to meet Mr Harrington: he was a
gentleman commoner at Trinity College before my time.

. . .

Anno 1647

May
'How it comes to pass, I know not; but by ancient and modern

example it is evident, that no great accident befalls a city or prince but it is presaged by divination or prodigy, or astrology, or some way or other.' This is from Book I, Chapter LVI of Machiavelli's *Discourses*, and I believe it true. On the first day of this month of May, my mother saw a sign of dire things to come when she went outside to read the time on our horizontal dial at Broad Chalke. It was a very clear sunny day, but from just before eleven until twelve, two circles appeared in the sky: a rainbow and a reversed rainbow, its bow turned down and the two ends standing upwards. The sun was caught inside the intersecting circles. My mother was the first to see it. She ran back into the house and told all the servants, who went outside and saw it too. The vicar and his family also saw it, and others who were hunting on the Downs.

. . .

3 June
On this day a young officer in the Parliament's new-modelled army, Cornet George Joyce, carried King Charles prisoner from Holmeby House. My mother saw a portent of this terrible news last month.

. . .

Anno 1648

6 January
On this day Dr Hannibal Potter was formally removed from the Presidency of Trinity College, but he refuses to leave his lodgings.

. . .

February
I am at Broad Chalke. My friend Mr John Lydall writes to me from Oxford. He hopes to be able to send me some *Aurum Fulminans* – or exploding gold – as soon as our chemist (Dr Thomas Willis) has prepared it. It is extremely susceptible to friction when heated and might have medicinal uses, as well as being helpful in our investigations into the nature of combustion. *Aurum Fulminans* is one of the few explosives not compounded with nitre.

Mr Lydall has not yet received my books, but expects them daily. His caution money is 3 li. Mr Ralph Bathurst and my other Trinity

College friends send me their love via Mr Lydall: how much I miss their company.

. . .

March
Mr Lydall has done as I asked and delivered my two pairs of sheets and pillow-bed to the carrier: but my towel is still at the laundress's in Oxford. Mr Bathurst has sent me a catalogue of the writers of the Saracen history. My friends assure me that they are as unhappy as I am that I am deprived of their company and the comforts of my study. They recognise me as one born for the honour and preservation of learning. How I miss them.

. . .

April
In regard of the recent contempt of Fellows, officers and members of the University of Oxford towards the authority of Parliament, all who will not submit to it shall be removed from their positions in colleges and halls, and the Parliamentarian Visitors will appoint others to their places.

It is difficult to evade the simple question: 'Do you submit to the authority of Parliament in this Visitation?'

. . .

Hannibal Potter has escaped a violent ejection from his lodgings by fleeing in advance. He was found guilty of contempt of the Parliament and will be replaced by a Puritan.

. . .

27 May
On this day Parliament passed an Ordinance enabling the Committee for the University of Oxford to send for convicted malignants and to destroy superstitious relics.

. . .

June
My good friend William Radford has been removed from his Fellowship at Trinity by the Parliamentarian Visitors.

. . .

John Wilkins, whose father was an Oxford goldsmith, has been made Warden of Wadham College by the Parliamentarian Visitors.

. . .

The south front of Wilton House has burnt down while the rooms were being aired. Philip, Earl of Pembroke, will rebuild it, from designs by Mr John Webb, who is married to Inigo Jones's niece. Mr Inigo Jones is now too old to come himself to Wilton.

. . .

At Morecomb-bottome, in the parish of Broad Chalke, on the north side of the river, it has been observed time out of mind that when the water breaks out there, it foretells a dear year of corn. It has happened again this year.

. . .

The walls of the church at Broad Chalke, and of the buttery at the farm there, shoot out nitre and a beautiful red, it is lighter than scarlet, an oriental horseflesh colour.

. . .

The River Thames runs through Wiltshire on its journey to Oxford. The source of the river is in Gloucestershire, near Cubberley, where there are several springs. Through Wiltshire it visits Cricklade, a market town, and gives its name to Isey, a nearby village, where its overflowings make a most glorious verdure in the spring season.

. . .

Clay abounds in Wiltshire and particularly about Malmesbury, Kington St Michael, Allington, Easton Pierse, Draycot Cerne, Yatton Keynell, Minty and Bradon Forest. At Minty, and at a place called Woburn, in the parish of Hankerton, there is the very good absorbent clay called fuller's earth. Last week I took up a handful of the fuller's earth at Minty Common, at the place called the Gogges: it was as black as black polished marble; but, having carried it in my pocket five or six days, I find it has become grey.

I believe the name Malmesbury comes from Malme, which signifies mud or clay. Some say it comes from the name of the first religious man who settled here – Maidulf – hence Maidulphi Urbs, that is Maidulph's City, but such an etymology seems forced to me. This is a place of mud.

. . .

December

Since Christmas Eve, my father has been dangerously ill. My mother is more anxious than ever. In these empty days it is a relief to get out of the house to hunt with friends who live close by: Lord Charles Seymour and Colonel John Penruddock, who was at Blandford School six or seven years before me. Two of John's younger brothers have been killed fighting for the King, and his father, Sir John Penruddock, like mine, is ill.

. . .

We set off with the hounds this morning from the Grey Wethers, which are stones as hard as or harder than marble that lie scattered across the Downs around Marlborough. In some places these stones are sown so thick that travellers in the twilight at a distance take them for flocks of sheep (wethers): hence their name. We headed north through countryside I do not know and it seemed to me we were passing through the place where the Giants fought with great stones against the Gods as described by Hesiod. Then, to my astonishment, we came upon megaliths in a village called Avebury to rival the ones I have known since childhood at Stonehenge. I had not previously heard of these Avebury stones, so when the sight of them burst upon me I reined back my horse and dismounted in wonder. The rest of the hunt passed on, but I stayed marvelling at the bank and ditch and strange stone circles. I tried to picture how they must have looked in olden times. I think Druids erected the circles, and they were complete long ago. I was lost to the present, until suddenly I heard the hounds again and hastened off to overtake them. We rode on to Kennett where there was a good dinner. I will return to draw those stones. It seems to me that Avebury excels Stonehenge as a cathedral does a parish church.

. . .

Anno 1649

Epiphany

On this day, at last, I met Francis Potter. He is the brother of Hannibal, who was our president at Trinity until the Parliamentarian Visitors ejected him recently, and the author of *An Interpretation of the Number 666*. Francis is like a monk, quite long-faced, with clear pale skin and grey eyes. He was at Trinity when I first went to Oxford, together with his brother, but we never met. Since then, he has succeeded his father as parson of Kilmington in Somerset. Like me, he was much given to drawing and painting when a boy, and of a very tender constitution in his younger years. He says that when he was beginning to be sick, he would breathe strongly to emit the noxious vapours.

Mr Potter says that the idea of moving blood from one body to another came to him ten years ago from reading Ovid. He is haunted by the barbarous Medea, mixing her witch's brew: roots, juices, flowers, seeds, stones, the screech owl's flesh and its ill-boding wings. He sees her, hair all unbound and blown about as she dances round, throwing more ingredients into the gruesome mix: the head of an old crow, the scaly skins of small snakes. Medea slit her lover's father's throat. She drained the blood of old Aeson and replaced it with her youth-giving medicine. Aeson's hair turned black again, colour came to his cheeks, his flesh plumped up behind his skin and his wrinkles disappeared.

Mr Potter says he will try moving blood between chickens. He is brooding on the quills or tubes that might allow the transfer from one bird to another to take place. He intends to make a little bag, perhaps from the craw of a pullet, to catch the blood when it comes down the tube, and hold it there until it can be transfused into another bird. He is wondering how it might be possible to fix the quill to the bag so it will not let the blood seep out and spoil the experiment. I have promised to help him.

Mr Potter does many experiments. He showed me bees' thighs under a microscope. He gave me a copper quadrant and a silver one, and showed me that the best way of making an arch is with a parabola and chain. This he demonstrated by taking the girdle from his cassock and holding it against a wall. He has a pretty square garden with the finest box-hedges I have ever seen. They are planted on a mount at the centre of the garden, and cut to look like fortifications, with high pillars of box standing out, looking very stately both summer and winter. It troubles me that a man of Mr Potter's gifts should lie mouldering away in a place like Kilmington, where he has no one to discuss his ideas with. He is like an old carrying pail growing moss in an orchard. Mr Hobbes has often said to me that such isolation is a great setback, even to the deepest-thinking of men.

. . .

These are the peaks in Wiltshire: Clay-hill, near Warminster; the Castle-hill at Mere, and Knoll-hill, near Kilmington, which is half in Wiltshire, and half in Somersetshire; all of them seem to have been raised (like great blisters) by earthquakes. Mr Potter takes great delight in Knoll-hill. We climbed it together today. It gives an admirable prospect every way; and from the summit you can see the Fosse Way between Cirencester and Gloucester, which is forty miles away. And you can see the Isle of Wight, Salisbury steeple, the Severn Sea, etc. It would make an admirable station for someone intending to draft a geographical description of Wiltshire or Somerset.

. . .

Mr Potter tells me stories of his great Trinity friend Sir Henry Blount, who travelled to the Levant. Sir Henry was pretty wild when young and especially addicted to common wenches. He appears in Henry Nevill's satirical pamphlet, *The Parliament of Ladies* (1647), responsible for spreading the dangerous doctrine that it is far cheaper and safer to lie with common wenches than with ladies of quality. He is gentleman pensioner to the King and was with him at the Battle of Edgehill, and afterwards in Oxford. When he returned to London, he walked into Westminster Hall with his sword by his side. The Parliamentarians all stared at him; they knew he was a Cavalier who had fought with the King. He was called before the House of Commons, where he insisted he was only doing his duty, so they acquitted him.

. . .

January

The trial of the King has ended and his fate is decided. The court has decreed: 'That the King, for the crimes contained in the charge, should be carried back to the place from whence he came, and thence to the place of execution, where his head should be severed from his body.' My kinsman Sir John Danvers has been serving on the committee that tried the King and will now be one of those that signs the death warrant.

Mr Emanuel Decretz, Serjeant Painter to the King, tells me that the bed of state erected in Westminster Abbey for the King's father's funeral was designed by Inigo Jones from plaster of Paris and white calico: it was very handsome and cheap, showing as well as if the caryatids which bore up the canopy had been cut from white marble. The present King must expect a lesser funeral.

. . .

30 January

On this day, the King was executed. It was bitter cold, so he wore two heavy shirts, lest he should shiver and seem afraid. The executioner was masked, so no one could tell his name.

On the scaffold, the King declared: 'I go from a corruptible to an incorruptible crown; where no disturbance can be, no disturbance in the world.' It is said that James Harrington and Thomas Herbert were with him on the platform and that before he died, the King gave them watches. And it is said that while he was a prisoner in Carisbrooke Castle, and on the eve of his execution, the King recited Pamela's Prayer from Sir Philip Sidney's *Arcadia*: 'Look upon my misery with Thine eye of mercy and let Thine infinite power vouchsafe to limit out some proportion of deliverance unto me.'

I read these lines in the library at Wilton. I walked on the terrace there, when I was a boy, hoping to see the ghost of Sir Philip Sidney or his sister Mary. The world since then is changed utterly. His Majesty loved Wilton above all places; now he is dispatched to a place outside of time. We who remain behind must weather the disturbance of the world. The King is dead.

PART IV

Learning

January

Until very recently, it was held a strange presumption for a man to attempt an innovation in learning, and not to be good manners to be more knowing than his neighbours and forefathers. Even to attempt an improvement in husbandry, though it succeeded with profit, was looked upon with an ill eye and it was once held a sin to scrutinise the ways of nature.

In our present times I know many who are concerned with the advancement of learning. At Oxford there is a new club for the pursuit of experimental philosophy estabished by Mr John Wilkins, Warden of Wadham College. My honoured friend Mr John Lydall has promised he will write to me about their experiments and discoveries. In this way I hope to follow their progress even though I am not in Oxford.

. . .

Since the Parliamentarian Visitation of Oxford, and the replacement of many Fellows, the mathematician John Wallis has been made Savilian Professor of Geometry. It was he who deciphered the King's letters after they were seized at the Battle of Naseby. Soon afterwards they were printed as a book, *The King's Cabinet Opened*.

. . .

At Hullavington there has been a strange wind, which not only flattened the corn and grass as though a huge roller had been drawn over them, but also flattened the quickset hedges in two or three fields. It was a hurricane.

. . .

Old good-wife Dew of Broad Chalke has died, aged 103. She told me
she was, I think, sixteen years old when King Edward VI was in this
county, and that he lost his courtiers, or rather, his courtiers lost him,
out hunting, and found him again in Falston Lane.

. . .

7 February

I attended the baptism of my godson, John Sloper. His father is vicar
of Broad Chalke.

. . .

17 March

On this day Parliament abolished kingship.

It is rumoured that Parliament intends to purge Oxford again. No
favours will be granted to those who refuse to recognise Parliament's
authority. They will be removed from their positions in the University.

. . .

April

Mr Lydall and I have been corresponding about the adventurers into
new plantations. He tells me that his brother, who is at Corpus College,
will travel to Barbados on the next ship. He wishes our friend Mr
Etterick would travel with him.

. . .

19 May

On this day Parliament passed an Act declaring England to be a
Commonwealth and free state. The House of Commons is now the
supreme authority in the land.

. . .

July

Parliament will govern the sales of the lands of the late King and of
Queen Henrietta Maria and Prince Charles. The lands have been vested
with trustees and the profits from them are to be used to pay off
army arrears.

. . .

September

Mr Lydall has written from Oxford to say he will gladly exchange information with me on the discoveries or experiments we make in our respective studies. He has given me an account of the motions of the moon to explain the cause of the hunter's moon at this time of year. Earlier this year I recommended to him a book called *Sciographia, or the Art of Shadows*, by Mr John Wells, published in 1635, and he says it has helped him to make a reflecting sundial in his room.

. . .

Anno 1650

April

On the last day of this month, my mother has fallen from her horse and broken her arm. I have been paying suit to Miss Jane Codrington, but now I must cease advancing my marriage prospects and visit my mother.

. . .

I have been hunting with William, Lord Herbert of Cardiff, who is the grandson of Philip, 4th Earl of Pembroke: the greatest hunter in living memory. I have become interested in the history of hunting in this nation. The Roman governors had not, I think, the leisure for it. The Saxons were never at rest, and the barons' wars, and those of York and Lancaster, took up the time since the Conquest. But under King James and King Charles, during times of serene calm and peace, hunting reached the greatest height it ever has in England. Good cheer was then much in use, but to be wiser than one's neighbours was considered scandalous and to be envied at. The nobility and gentry were, in that soft peace, damnable proud and insolent. Old Serjeant Latham lived then and wrote his books on falconry, which were printed in 1614 and 1618.

In the stables at Wilton, before the civil wars, there were horses fit for all seasons of the Earl's stag hunting, foxhunting, brook hawking and land hawking, plus horses for at least half a dozen coaches. In total, there were probably no less than a hundred horses. His lordship had all sorts of hounds for several disports: great hounds to harbour the stags and small bulldogs to break the backs of the stags; fox-hounds, finders, harriers and others; the choicest tumblers in England. When they returned from their sport, the ladies would come out to see the hawks flying at their highest.

Since the civil war many of the forests and parks have been sold and converted into ploughed fields and the glory of English hunting has breathed its last.

My friend Mr Christopher Wase comes hunting with us sometimes. He is at Wilton House teaching William Herbert Latin. He is translating Gratius the Faliscian's heroic poem *Cynegeticon*, and will dedicate it to the memory of Philip, 4th Earl of Pembroke, who died this year: a lasting monument for that great hunter.

. . .

Sir Charles Snell, of Kington St Michael, who is my honoured friend and neighbour, has as good a pack of hounds for the hare as any in England: handsome, deep-mouthed, good and suited to each other admirably well.

. . .

The Wiltshire greyhounds are the best in England; my father and I have had as good as any in our time. They are generally of a fallow colour, or black; but Mr Button's, of Sherborne in Gloucestershire, are some white and some black. Gratius, in his *Cynegeticon*, advises:

> And chuse the grayhound py'd with black and white,
> He runs more swift than thought, or winged flight;
> But courseth yet in view, not hunts in traile,
> In which the quick Petronians never faile.

. . .

Michaelmas

I have been to Verulam (St Albans) to see the Roman remains.

There you can see, in a few places, the remains of the old city wall. Magnanimous Lord Bacon – Lord Chancellor and Baron of Verulam – was minded to have it made a city again, and planned for it to be rebuilt with great uniformity, but Fortune denied him this. Within the bounds of the walls of the old city is Verulam House, about half a mile from St Albans, which his lordship built: the most ingeniously contrived little pile that ever I have seen.

I approached the house from the entrance gate on to the highway: viewed from there, the sides of the house mirror one another. On the east side there were five, or maybe seven, windows, bay windows, I think, of the kind his lordship describes in his essay *Of Building*. This house cost nine or ten thousand pounds to build. There are good chimneypieces, the rooms very lofty and all very well wainscoted. There are two bathing rooms, where his lordship used to retire in the afternoon. All the chimney tunnels run into the middle of the house and there are seats round about them. The kitchen, larder, cellars, etc. are underground. In the middle of the house is a delicate wooden staircase, curiously carved, a pretty figure on the posts of every interstice: a grave divine with his book and spectacles, a mendicant friar, etc. – never the same thing twice. The doors of the upper storey are painted dark umber, and decorated with the figures of the Gods of the Gentiles: Apollo, Jupiter with his thunderbolt, bigger than life-size and done by an excellent hand. The heightening is of hatchings of gold, which make a glorious show when the sun shines on them. The top of the house is well leaded, and looking out from the leads there is a lovely prospect to the ponds, opposite the east side of the house, and the stately walk of trees that leads to Gorhambery House. The view over that long walk of trees, whose tops afford a most pleasant variegated verdure, reminded me of tapestry works in Irish-stitch.

I felt myself a marvelling stranger in this house. When I had at last finished looking at the entertaining view from the top balcony, I turned to return into the room, and was mighty surprised to see another prospect of ponds, walks and countryside through the house. The servant who was showing me around had quietly closed a mirrored door behind me, so thus was I gratefully deceived by a looking glass. This was his lordship's summer-house – he says in his essay *Of Building* that one should have seats, like clothes, for summer and winter: 'Lucullus answered Pompey well, who, when he saw his stately galleries and rooms so large and lightsome in one of his houses, said, "Surely an excellent place for summer, but how do you in winter?" Lucullus answered, "Why, do you not think me as wise as some fowl are, that ever change their abode towards the winter?"'

The ponds are now overgrown with flagges and rushes, but in his lordship's time they were filled with clear water, through which coloured pebbles arranged in the shapes of fishes, etc. could be seen. If a poor person brought his lordship half a dozen pebbles of curious colour, he would give them a shilling, so interested was he in perfecting his four acres of fish-ponds. In the middle of the middlemost pond, on the island, is a curious banqueting house of Roman architecture, paved with black and white marble, covered with Cornish slate, and neatly wainscoted.

Then I went a further mile to Gorhambery to see Lord Bacon's winter-house and park. The way ascends easily, inclining no more than a desk. Three parallel walks run between the two houses: through the middle one, three coaches may pass abreast, two through each of the wing-walks. Stately trees of similar growth and height line the walks: elms, chestnuts, beeches, hornbeams, Spanish ash, cervice-trees, etc. Their leaves form the variegated verdure pattern I saw from the balcony. At this time of year, the colour of their leaves is most varied.

Gorhambery House is large, well built, and Gothic; I think his lordship's father, Sir Nicholas Bacon, built it. His lordship added a grand portico, which fronts the garden to the south. Inside every arch of this portico are emblematical pictures. One of the most striking is a ship tossed in a storm, with the motto: *Alter erit tum Tiphys* (there will be another Tiphys). Above the portico is a stately gallery, all its windows are painted: each pane of glass with several figures of beast, bird or flower. The gallery is hung with pictures of King James, his lordship, and other illustrious figures of their time. These figures, like the Gods on the doors at Verulam House, are done larger than life-size in umber and gold. The roof is semi-cylindrical and painted, by the same hand and in the same manner, with heads and busts of Greek and Roman emperors and heroes.

The garden is large and was no doubt rarely planted and kept in his lordship's time. There is a handsome door that opens out into an oak wood, where the trees are very great and shady. Beneath them his lordship planted fine specimens of flower, such as peonies and tulips: some are still there. Beyond the oak wood is a coppice-wood where there are walks cut straight as lines, and it was here that his lordship meditated, attended by Mr Bushell or Mr Hobbes or another of his secretaries, to whom he would dictate his thoughts.

Where once there was a paradise, there is now a large ploughed field. The little resting houses of Roman architecture that his lordship had built at good viewing places along the well-designed woodland walks still stand, but are defaced, as though barbarians made a conquest here.

If I close my eyes, I can think myself back to a time when this place was a sanctuary for pheasants, partridges and birds of various kinds and countries. I can hear his lordship drive his open coach through the rain to receive the benefits of irrigation, the nitre in the air and the universal spirit of the world. 'I do not look about me, I look above me,' he was wont to say.

Mr Hobbes told me that the cause of his lordship's death was conducting an experiment on Highgate Hill. He was taking the air in a coach with Dr Witherborne (a Scotsman and physician to the King) when snow lay on the ground. It occurred to his lordship that flesh might be preserved in snow as well as in salt. These two went into a poor woman's house at the bottom of Highgate Hill, bought a hen and had her kill it, then stuffed the body with snow. The snow so chilled his lordship that immediately he fell extremely ill, and could not return to his lodgings, but was taken instead to the Earl of Arundel's house at Highgate. There he was put in a good bed warmed with a pan, but the bed was damp as no one had been in it for about a year, this gave his lordship such a cold that he died within two or three days.

. . .

My friend John Lydall writes to tell me what Mr Hawes has told him about the ghosts that plagued the parliamentary committee for selling the King's lands, when it sat at Woodstock Manor recently. The committee members who stayed over night to try and finish measuring the parklands were pelted out of their chambers in the manor by stones thrown through the windows. Their candles were continuously put out, as fast as they could light them; and one man who drew his sword to defend his candle was cudgelled with his own scabbard. He fell sick and the others were forced to move out of the manor.

. . .

December
There has been a remarkable occurrence at Oxford. Earlier this month, Nan Green, a servant maid, was hanged in the castle for murdering her bastard child. After suffering the law, she was cut down and carried away for some of the young physicians to practise anatomy on. But while she

was lying on the dissecting table, Dr William Petty, assisted by Mr Ralph Bathurst, among others, found life in her, so revived her. Now the young poets of the University are versifying about this great wonder.

. . .

I have helped my friend Mr Potter with his attempt to move blood between chickens in Kilmington.

. . .

I have acquired a copy of Lord Bacon's *Historia Naturalis Et Experimentalis De Ventis*.

. . .

Dr William Petty has been elected Professor of Music at Gresham College.

. . .

There has been smallpox in Sherborne for a year now, since last Michaelmas.

. . .

Anno 1651

February

Mr Lydall is leaving Oxford and has made arrangements for those possessions of mine that are still there in boxes to be looked after by other friends. He has recommended some books in answer to my Quaere: how is it possible to find the latitude of a place by a quadrant in the dark without sun or stars?

. . .

I have acquired a copy of Lord Bacon's *Remaines*, first printed in 1648.

. . .

March

My friend Mr Francis Potter is coming to stay with me in Broad Chalke and while he is here I will take him to Wilton House to visit the Earl of Pembroke and show off his design for a clock operated by bellows rather than cogs, which he invented when he was still a student at Trinity College. I have tried to find out from my kinsman Sir John Danvers how Mr Potter might obtain a patent for his invention.

. . .

Sir John Danvers's house at Chelsea is very elegant and ingenious. As you sit at dinner in the hall you are entertained by two delightful vistas: one southward over the Thames and towards Surrey; the other northward into a curious garden. Over the hall is a stately room of the same dimensions, which has the same prospect, where there is an excellent organ, which I have heard the organist and composer Christopher Gibbons play. The house is vaulted, which meliorates the sound. I have never heard better harmony than in that room.

Lord Bacon came often to visit Sir John Danvers at Chelsea. Sir John told me that after his lordship wrote the *History of Henry VII*, he sent a copy of the manuscript to him, desiring his opinion of it before it was printed. Sir John said: 'Your lordship knows that I am no scholar.' ''Tis no matter,' Lord Bacon replied, 'I know what a scholar can say; I would know what *you* can say.' Sir John read it and gave his opinion, for which Lord Bacon was grateful. 'Why,' he said, 'a scholar would never have told me this.' I am sorry that I have forgotten what it was Sir John misliked in the manuscript.

. . .

April

Mr Potter is greatly obliged to me for letting him have John Wilkins's book, *Mathematical Magick*, which interests him very much. The book contains accounts of strange phenomena and happenings, e.g. water round the moon and the magnetic attraction of bodies. Mr Potter has discussed with me the earth's magnetism and motion. His idea is that if there were loose parts round the moon they would fall to the centre of the earth. He wonders if the interior of the moon may be inhabited, though not the exterior. He doubts the opinion expressed in the book that the higher from the earth bodies go the lighter they are, losing their gravity the more distant they are from the earth's centre.

Mr Potter considers that flight is impracticable because materials could not stand the strain – the weight being so great and the material too fragile in proportion to motive power (he compares a flea and an ape). But given materials of sufficient strength he says he can imagine the possibility of flight. He is interested too in the possibility of submarine navigation and has a conception of how it could be done, providing the water under the surface is calm (he envisages a pipe from the surface to the boat, aided by bellows). He has also sent me a pencil sketch of an ingenious cart with legs.

. . .

I have fallen in love – at first sight – with the incomparable good-conditioned gentlewoman Miss Mary Wiseman.

I am like Virgil's Dido, wounded by love:

> Sick with desire, and seeking him she loves,
> From street to street the raving Dido roves.
> So when the watchful shepherd, from the blind,
> Wounds with a random shaft the careless hind,
> Distracted with her pain she flies the woods,
> Bounds o'er the lawn, and seeks the silent floods,
> With fruitless care; for still the fatal dart
> Sticks in her side, and rankles in her heart.

. . .

May

Mr Lydall tells me that Dr Petty has discovered how to set a field of corn by means of a sowing and harrowing engine; that Mr Christopher Wren of Wadham College has invented a means of weighing grains, scruples, drams and ounces with the same weight, and also an engine for double writing. Mr Lydall now has of a copy of Athanasius Kircher's *Ars magna lucis et umbrae*, on experiments in geometry and illusion, and if he finds in it secrets worth imparting he will share them with me.

Here are some of the most interesting problems Mr Lydall is thinking about:

– How by means of a cylinder to make any image appear hanging in the air.
– How to draw pictures on a cone, so that at one set distance they

shall appear in true proportion, and at all others deformed.
- How by the use of many plain glasses reflecting light in the same place to burn anything at a distance.
- How to make a statue like Memnon's, in the Theban Necropolis, which, when heated by the sun, shall breathe and send forth a sound.

. . .

August
My friend from Trinity College, Anthony Ettrick, has married Anne Davenant, one of the great mathematician Edward Davenant's daughters. She is a notable algebrist. I know this from when her father taught me.

. . .

23 August
On this day, after dinner, I saw Mr Christopher Love beheaded on Tower Hill for plotting against the Commonwealth. I have never seen a person beheaded before, and hope never to again. The sky was as clear and delicate as any I have seen, but shortly after Mr Love's suffering and execution it began to thicken, the clouds gathered black and dismal, and since then there have been terrible claps of thunder through the night, the greatest I have ever heard. I believe this is an omen: such a tempest tonight as one might think the machine of the world is dissolving. His poor wife – now widow – is pregnant with their fifth child.

. . .

The bookseller Mr Crooke at the Green Dragon in St Paul's Churchyard has printed Mr Hobbes's *Leviathan: or the Matter, Forme and Power of a Commonwealth Ecclesiastical and Civil*. Mr Hobbes wrote the book in exile in France where he has been for over a decade now. From the printing press in London, *Leviathan* has flown forth to neighbouring regions, passionately attacking those who fail to see that the monarch – not the parliament under him – is the absolute representative of his people. Since the execution of the King, there has been talk of a free state in England and praise for the benefits of republicanism. But Mr Hobbes will have none of it. He is hostile to the English and Scottish

rebels and an ardent defender of monarchy. He is as hostile to the
Presbyterian clergy as he is to the Church of Rome, which both
pretend that the Kingdom of God is of this world. Mr Hobbes insists
that religion cannot have a power distinct from that of the civil state.
He is opposed to what he calls religious 'enthusiasm'.

. . .

My friend Dr William Petty knows Mr Hobbes. They met in Paris a
few years ago, studying anatomy. Dr Petty has drawn the illustrative
schemes for Mr Hobbes's treatise on optics. When he was a boy, his
greatest delight was to watch the artificers – smiths, watchmakers,
carpenters, joiners, etc.

Since the printing of *Leviathan*, Mr Hobbes has lost the protection
of the King's supporters in France, who are angered by his arguments
against religion. He will come back to England before the end of the
year.

. . .

15 November
My friend Anthony Ettrick's son was born today.

. . .

At last I have met Dr Harvey, whom I admired from a distance when
I was a student and heard so much about from mutual friends. He is
an old man now and a critic of the Commonwealth. He lives here in
London with his brother Eliab and they drink coffee together. He has
given me advice about my longed-for tour of Italy: what to see, whom
to visit, what to read. He recommends Aristotle, Cicero and Avicenna
particularly. He has very bad handwriting. Dr Harvey grieves for his
papers that were destroyed in Whitehall at the start of the rebellion
against the King: papers concerning dissections of frogs, toads and
other animals, and a book he had written about insects. He says, 'Man
is but a great mischievous baboon.'

I have met Mr James Harrington recently too, through one of my
cousins. He is of middling stature, a well-trussed man, strong and thick,
well set, sanguine, quick-hot-fiery hazel eyes, thick, moist curled hair.

Mr Harrington was an acquaintance of Sir Walter Raleigh's, whose
grand-nephews I knew at school. He told me an amusing story about

the famous courtier. Being invited to dinner with some great person, where his son was to go with him, Sir Walter said to his son: 'Thou art such a quarrelsome, affronting creature, that I am ashamed to have such a bear in my company.' Master Walt promised his father he would behave himself. So away they went, and young Master Walt was very demure at least until halfway through the dinner. Then he said: 'I, this morning, went to a whore. I was very eager of her, kissed and embraced her, and went to enjoy her, when she thrust me from her, and vowed I should not, "For", she said, "your father lay with me but an hour ago."' Sir Walter, being so strangely surprised and put out of countenance at so great a table, fetched his son a damned blow over the face. His son, rude as he was, would not strike his father, so struck the face of the gentleman that sat next to him and said: 'Box about, 'twill come to my father anon.' It is now a common proverb.

. . .

Anno 1652

March

I have been to see Mr Hobbes. He has returned to London from Paris. He lives for the most part in Fetter Lane, where he is finishing his book *De Corpore* in Latin. In cold weather he wears a black velvet coat lined with fur, and all year round he wears boots of Spanish leather, laced or tied along the side with black ribbons. He enjoys the company and learned conversation of Mr John Selden, Dr William Harvey, etc.

. . .

A coffee house has opened, the first in London, in St Michael's Alley in Cornhill, opposite the church. Mr Hodges, who trades in Turkish merchandise, encouraged his coachman, Mr Bowman, to set it up and promote the virtues of the coffee drink. It will prevent drowsiness and make one fit for business, but should not be drunk after supper as then it will prevent sleep.

It was Mr Mudiford who first introduced the practice of coffee to London about two years ago. This worthy gentleman deserves the respect of the whole nation! Chaco-lati, or chocolate, was first brought out of Spain by Sir Arthur Hopton who was ambassador there in about 1647. My lady Browne, wife of Sir Richard Browne, was the first English

lady who brought it into common use after residing with the French
King in whose house Sir Arthur Hopton lived after he was recalled from
Spain.

. . .

August
Dr William Petty has been recommended to Parliament for appointment as one of the surveyors of Ireland. My good friend Edmund
Wylde of Glazeley Hall, Salop, MP for Droitwich, helped secure this
employment for Dr Petty, even though he was not previously acquainted
with him. Mr Wylde is a great promoter of talented good men on
grounds of merit alone. The survey of Ireland will be exact and comprehensive and Dr Petty will make use of ordinary fellows, foot soldiers
perhaps, to circumambulate with their box and needles and take measurements even without understanding what they are doing.

. . .

Sir Charles Cavendish died earlier this year of scurvey. During his
lifetime he collected (in Italy, France, etc.) enough manuscript mathematical books to fill a hogshead. He intended to have them printed.
His executor, an attorney of Clifford's Inn, died soon afterwards, and
left his wife executrix. She has sold Sir Charles Cavendish's incomparable collection by weight as waste paper to the paste-board makers.
This is a caution to all those who have good manuscripts to take care
to see them printed in their lifetimes.

. . .

October
The London physician Mr Samuel Bave has examined my father and
finds he is an utter wreck: almost all his organs are diseased and his
ailments are like a many-headed hydra. Even so, Mr Bave will persevere
trying to cure him.

. . .

21 October
On this day my father died. Three (or maybe four) days ago – grief
disorders my memory – I lay perfectly awake in my bed at nine o'clock
in the morning and heard three distinct knocks on the bedhead, as

though with a ruler or ferula. I believe this was an omen warning of his death.

. . .

26 October
We buried my father today in the south-east chancel of Kington St Michael church.

. . .

November
My friend Mr Potter sends his condolences upon the death of my father. He promises to find the time to prepare the crooked pipe we will need for the experiment we have been planning on the anatomy of veins. When he has done so, I will go and visit him in Kilmington, or else he will come to me. I remember how the witch Medea's rejuvenation of old Aeson got Mr Potter thinking about the circulation of the blood. If only the physicians could have succeeded as Medea did. If only they could have rejuvenated my father.

I will go to London soon and find lodgings there.

. . .

At Wilton House, the Earl of Pembroke introduced me to the poet Sir John Denham. He was much beloved by the late King, who valued him for his ingenuity. I remember when Sir John's *Cooper's Hill* was printed at Oxford in 1643 after the Battle of Edgehill, on brown paper, for they could get nothing else at that troubled time. Later in the war, before the execution of the King, Sir John got the two young dukes out of London and conveyed them to the Prince of Wales and Queen Mother in France. He came back to England this year and since he is in some straits, financial, etc., the Earl of Pembroke is kindly entertaining him in London and Wilton. Sir John is translating Virgil's *Aeneid*, and also burlesquing it.

. . .

December
I am lodging at the Rainbow-Stationer in Fleet Street near the Middle Temple.

Today I went for the first time to the intelligencer Mr Hartlib's house, in Charing Cross, over against Angel Yard. I sought him out on my own initiative because he has a large number of ingenious correspondents in this country and beyond (he was born in Poland around 1600, but has lived most of his life in London). He has collected a wealth of information about books, manuscripts and inventions, which he disseminates widely. Three years ago, the Parliament voted Mr Hartlib a pension of 100 li. a year for the advancement of arts and learning.

We discussed my friend Mr Potter, the 666 divine, and I explained how I keep trying to get him to communicate and publish his experiments and inventions, but not prevailing. I told Mr Hartlib how I have talked to the Earl of Pembroke and my kinsman Sir John Danvers about trying to patent Mr Potter's invention of a watch without any wheels. We discussed his other inventions too, including a threshing machine, which Mr Hartlib thinks might undo the poor.

Then we talked about our mutual acquaintance Mr Boyle, who is very tall (about six feet high) and straight. His greatest delight is chemistry. He is charitable to ingenious men in need, and many foreign chemists have had proof of his generosity, for he spares no expense in collecting rare secrets.

Mr Boyle speaks Latin very well, and I have heard him say that when he was young he learnt it from Cooper's dictionary, just as I did. Cooper's dictionary was first published in 1584 and dedicated to Robert Dudley, Earl of Leicester. Cooper was married to a shrewish woman who resented him sitting up late at night compiling his dictionary. When it was half done she got into his study, threw the manuscript in the fire and burnt it. But Cooper had such a zeal for the advancement of learning that he began the dictionary again and bequeathed us that most useful work.

Mr Boyle says that after seeing the antiquities and architecture of Rome, he esteems none anywhere else. How much I desire to see them too!

. . .

I returned to Eynsham Abbey today. The twin towers I remember from my last visit have been demolished.

. . .

Anno 1653

February

Following my father's death, a weight of trouble has fallen on my head. I am his heir but there is much to do before my inheritance can be obtained.

Despite these troubles, I have been to Oxford, where I saw my friend Mr John Lydall and had great entertainment. But he cannot find my box of books, so I must wait until Mr Ralph Bathurst is back in Oxford. He will be able to find it for me, I hope. I miss my books and desire to have them with me again.

Mr Lydall says he will attempt to answer my questions about navigation. He recommends to me Bernhardus Varenius's *Geographia Generalis*, which is a thick book printed in 1650.

. . .

Mr Lydall has sent me some more advice on the literature of navigation, but he says he has never seen the book I asked about: 'The Seaman's Grammar'. Instead he mentions 'The Mariner's Dictionary' (though this does not touch on the more scholastic or geometrical parts of navigation), Wright's 'Errors of Navigation'; and a treatise by Richard Norwood, the mathematician, on sailing.

. . .

March

Mr Samuel Hartlib has written to me at Broad Chalke from his house near Charing Cross entreating me to give him an account of worthy and excellent Mr Potter's life and experiments. I shall happily give him the details of Mr Potter's inventions concerning bees, crossbows, a machine for double writing, and a new pair of compasses. And I will also describe Mr Potter's interest in a common language.

Mr Hartlib has a manuscript of Lord Bacon's that was never printed which he has offered to show me. He urges me to view the remainder of Lord Bacon's manuscripts if I can. And he tells me that if I travel to Italy next month he will improve my opportunities and arrange introductions for me. How much I desire to go.

. . .

Mr Potter was to come to see me and my mother this week, but he has been delayed. So far he has failed to make the crooked pipe we need for our experiment on the anatomy of veins, and must try another way. He urges me not to go to Italy in these troubled times when we are at war with the Dutch. He hopes my mother will persuade me to stay at home!

. . .

April

I am trying to find friends who will come with me to Italy. Mr Lydall would do it if only he could be confident that his constitution – crazy and sickly of late – would not break down. Mr Bathurst cannot do it. I do not know if I will have time to go and see my friends in Oxford before I leave.

. . .

Dr Harvey has prescribed me a purge to prevent an impostumation.

. . .

My father's will has been proved. He has left me the farm at Broad Chalke, a manor at Burleton in Herefordshire, which he inherited from his own father, and some other smaller properties at Brecon and at Monmouth near the Welsh border. There are small bequests to charity and servants, but there are also debts of 1,800 li. and my brothers' portions of 500 li. each to be paid from the estate. I do not know how much will be left for me after these debts and portions are paid. Also my entails in the properties at Brecon and Monmouth may be disputed and difficult to secure.

I hope I can erect a little inscription in white marble to the memory of my father. I would like it to be an ell (or cubit) tall, or more.

. . .

My friend Anthony Ettrick of the Middle Temple, a very judicious gentleman, has been observing the witch trial of Anne Bodenham at Salisbury, and is not satisfied. He tells me the crowd of spectators made such a noise that the judge, Chief Baron Wild, could not hear the prisoner, nor the prisoner the judge. Words were handed from one to another by Mr Chandler, and sometimes not truly reported. It is now decided that Anne Bodenham is guilty and she will be hanged.

She was once the servant of John Lambe, the astrologer and conjuror who was stoned to death by an unruly crowd in London in 1628. At her trial it was rumoured that Anne Bodenham could summon the devil and turn herself into a dog, lion, bear, etc.

. . .

Mr Potter's brother Hannibal, who slanders him and accuses him of folly, is holding up all his experiments, so he has not yet sent me the full account of them, which I promised to obtain for Mr Hartlib. Mr Potter tells me he can have replicas of the screw compasses made for me if I find them useful, will gladly make me a quadrant, and he thanks me for my *Thaumaturgia Mathematica*. But still he does not send me what I need for Mr Hartlib. Instead, he preaches me a severe religious lesson, urging me to mark my infirmities and keep God ever in mind, condemns his brother for pride, foolishness and neglect of his duties, and bemoans his own misery and penury. No man, he says, will stir for him, except possibly me.

. . .

June

Mr Lydall urges me to be in Oxford for the summer degree ceremony that will begin on the morning of Saturday 9 July and end on the night of Monday 11 July. He tells me to arrive on the Friday to be sure to be there in time to hear Mr Ralph Bathurst present some of his work on anatomy.

Following my questions about anatomy, Mr Lydall has recommended books by Bartholemus and Johannes Riolanus, but he still has not found anyone willing to accompany me on my journey to Italy. Neither Mr Bathurst nor Dr Willis will come with me.

. . .

October

Mr Potter has written to me explaining in more detail his ideas for moving blood between two living animals (he has been corresponding with Dr Harvey on the subject). He imagines it can be done by means of a little bellows which must have two flexible pipes made of some small animal's windpipe, one of which must be inserted into the vein of one arm, the other into the other arm from which the blood will come.

. . .

16 December

On this day Oliver Cromwell was installed as Lord Protector of
England, Scotland and Ireland.

. . .

At Kington St Michael, at Sir Charles Snell's after dark, we walked
out into the court full of very thick mist. We saw our shadows
projected on to the fog as though against a wall by the light of lanterns,
about thirty or forty foot away. I am told that people who go bird-
bating on winter nights have seen such things too, but rarely.

. . .

As you ride between Cricklade and Highworth in Wiltshire you find
roundish stones, as big as or bigger than one's head, which I think
they call brain-stones because nature has worked on the outside like
the ventricles of the brain: these are petrified sea-mushrooms.

. . .

Captain Stokes, in his *Wiltshire Rant*, recites the strangest extravagan-
cies of religion ever heard of since the time of the Gnostics. I think
that the rich wet soil makes the Wiltshire people hypochondriac. The
astrologers and historians write that the ascendant at Oxford is
Capricorn, whose lord is Saturn, a religious planet, and patron of
religious men. If this is so, then surely the same influence runs through
north Wiltshire, the vale of Gloucestershire, and Somersetshire. In all
changes of religions these people are more zealous than others; in the
time of the Roman Catholic religion there were more and better
churches and religious houses founded in Wiltshire than in any other
part of England; and now they are the greatest fanatics, even to the
point of spiritual madness.

. . .

More Roman money has been found at Sherston during ploughing
this year. I now have a piece of silver from the time of Constantine
the Great from there.

. . .

Anno 1654

I am at Llantrithyd, Glamorganshire, staying with my kinsman and cousin Sir John Aubrey. Here I have begun to enter philosophical and antiquarian remarks into pocket memorandum books. This is a habit I mean to keep up, since I realise that if I do not keep careful notes, my observations will be lost. No one else will make these records in my place.

Sir John's estates have been sequestrated by the Parliament.

. . .

Today I rode from Llantrithyd to Caerleon, where Roman baths have been discovered. There I measured the altar stone and saved a Latin inscription from being pulverised into scouring powder by the local women. I am horrified by how much damage had been done to the remains in a single month through carelessness and ignorance.

I think I will send my copy of the inscription to Mr Hobbes's honoured friend Mr John Selden for safe keeping. Mr Selden, aside from being the most distinguished scholar of England's ancient laws and constitution, is a polymath: he is the most learned of men.

. . .

In Weekfield in the parish of Heddington the ground has been dug up deeper than it is when ploughed, and many Roman remains have been found: foundations of houses, hearths, a great deal of Roman coins, both silver and brass. I have a pint of them: some little copper pieces no bigger than a silver halfpence. Quaere: are they Roman denarii?

. . .

Mr Samuel Hartlib has given me a copy of his book, *The True and Ready Way to Learne the Latin Tongue*, printed this year. He is extremely interested in education and shares some of the ideas of the Puritan reformer Jan Amos Comenius. In Bohemia, Comenius was a minister of the Church of the Bohemian Brethren. He was exiled on account of his religion. When he came to London in 1641, he lived with Mr Hartlib for nine months. Previously, they had corresponded about Lord Bacon and his ideas for a reformed natural philosophy.

. . .

I am planning to leave England on a Grand Tour at last, and have made my will in preparation.

The draft of my will:

- To my loving grandfather, Mr Isaac Lyte, 50 li., and to my grandmother, 50 li.
- A decent inscription of white marble for my father and the like for myself (Mr Anthony Ettrick to write my epitaph).
- To Anthony Ettrick of Berford, Dorset, I bequeath 10 li. to buy a piece of plate, my sapphire ring, Sir Walter Raleigh's history and my copy of Philip Comineus's history.
- My executors will buy for Trinity College, Oxford, a college pot of the value of 10 li., with my arms inscribed on it; and I bequeath my honoured friends, Mr Ralph Bathurst of Trinity College and Mr John Lydall, 10 li. to spend on mathematical and philosophical books.
- I give to the library of Jesus College, Oxford, my Greek *Chrysostum*, Bede's two tomes, and all the rest of my books that are fit for a library, as Mr Anthony Ettrick or Mr John Lydall shall think fit, excepting those books that were my father's which I bequeath to my heir, my brother.
- I bequeath to John Davenant, Esq., of the Middle Temple, a ring of the value of 50s., with a stone in it.
- . . . to Mr William Hawes of Trinity College a ring of the like value.
- . . . to Mr John Lydall of the aforesaid college a ring of the like value.
- . . . to Mr Ralph Bathurst of Trinity College aforesaid a ring of the like value.
- . . . to Miss Mary Wiseman of Westminster, my best diamond ring and . . .

I wonder what else I might leave to Miss Mary Wiseman, whom I love.
. . .

November

Mr Potter has still not made my quadrant. He tells me he is either too busy, or else too filled with melancholy. He has returned the essay by Edmund Wingate about logarithms that I lent him last spring.

Mr Hobbes's friend, the great scholar of ancient English laws and jurist Mr John Selden, has died of dropsy, alas! Now I will need to find another place for the Roman inscription I copied near Caerleon. I had intended to give it to him for safe keeping.

. . .

14 December

Today I attended Mr Selden's funeral. He was magnificently buried in the Temple Church. All the Parliament men, the benchers and great officers, were invited to attend. All the judges were in mourning and an abundance of persons of quality.

Mr Hobbes told me that when Mr Selden was close to death, the minister, Mr Richard Johnson, Master of the Temple, attempted to see him. Mr Hobbes happened to be there and said, 'What, will you that have wrote like a man, now die like a woman?' So the minister was not let in.

My sadler, who has known the family a long time, tells me that in his lifetime Mr Selden got more by his prick than his practice (since he married the widow of the Earl of Kent and failed to distinguish himself at the Bar). He was wont to say: 'I'll keep myself warm and moist as long as I live; for I shall be cold and dry when I am dead.'

In his funeral oration today, Mr Richard Johnson quoted the saying: 'When a learned man dies, there dies a great deal of learning with him . . . If learning could have kept a man alive, our brother would not have died.'

Mr Selden meant to leave his books to the University of Oxford, but has not done so because recently he was disobliged by their refusal to lend him a manuscript. I do not know what will happen to the books now.

. . .

Anno 1655

January

Mr Hobbes's *De Corpore* is being printed. In it he argues that there are two parts of philosophy, natural and civil, concerned with two kinds of bodies, very different from one another.

. . .

22 January
On this day Oliver Cromwell, Lord Protector, dissolved the Parliament.

. . .

February
Meredith Lloyd, chemist, lawyer and antiquary, is living near me at the girdler's shop under the King's Head Tavern in Fleet Street. He has collected much information about Celtic languages and Welsh monuments.

. . .

I visited Mr Hartlib and told him that I am trying to write the life of Lord Bacon.

. . .

I have been to visit Mr John Hales at Eton. He was ejected from his Fellowship at Eton College five years ago, after refusing to swear the oath of loyalty to the Commonwealth. Since my Trinity friends went to see him in 1647, he has had to sell his library to maintain himself. He has kept only a few books for his private use, to wind up his last days withal.

Mr Hales is a pretty little man, sanguine, of cheerful countenance, very gentle and courteous. He received me with much humanity. He was wearing a violet-coloured cloth gown with buttons and loops and reading Thomas à Kempis. He is living now with a widow, Mrs Powney (I wish I had her Christian name), in her handsome dark old-fashioned house in Eton opposite the churchyard, next to the Christopher Inn. In the hall, after the old fashion, above the wainscot, there is painted cloth with godly sentences out of the Psalms, according to the pious customs of old times.

Mrs Powney was much against the sale of Mr Hales's books (which the bookseller Cornelius Bee bought for less than a third of their value) because she knew the library was his life and joy. She is a very good woman and a grateful spirit. Mr Hales helped set her and her husband up in the world when they were first married, so now she is helping him. She is primitively good and deserves to be remembered.

. . .

Slough, near Eton, is a very dirty place, and such a dirty place we call a slough, which is a Welsh word.

. . .

14 April
My honoured kinsman Sir John Danvers died at Chelsea today, aged seventy. He will be buried at Dauntsey.

. . .

I have learnt that my friend from student days, Ned Wood, has died of consumption. He was only twenty-eight.

. . .

Mr Inigo Jones's theories on the origins of Stonehenge have been posthumously published by his assistant Mr John Webb, but the monument has been framed to fit Mr Jones's hypothesis that it was a Roman temple. I do not think the evidence of the stones supports his argument.

I find it strange that Mr Camden in his *Britannia* does not notice that the stones at Stonehenge are Grey Wethers and come from a pit no more than fourteen miles away, where there are thousands of such stones to be drawn out of the earth. Some stones, not big enough for use at Stonehenge or Avebury, still lie on the brink of the pit.

I know Avebury well now because my honoured friend Sir James Long of Draycot spends a week or two every autumn hawking there, and sometimes I have had the happiness to accompany him.

The downs surrounding Avebury are romantic country: the prospects noble and vast. They are well stocked with flocks of sheep; the turf is rich and fragrant with thyme and basil; and the nut-brown shepherd-esses are worthy of attention too. We have had good sport there. Yet the flight of the falcon was a mere parenthesis to Sir James's witty discourse: the muses accompany him, along with his hawks and spaniels.

Ever since I came upon Avebury for the first time, in the empty days after Christmas 1648, when I was out hunting with Colonel John Penruddock, I have longed to understand better what those stones meant in their own time.

. . .

I asked Dr Harvey how flints are generated. He told me that the black of the flint is a natural vitrification of chalk, and added that flint is an excellent medicine for gallstones and the green sickness. In the stone-brash country of north Wiltshire, flints are very rare and only little ones can be found.

Dr Harvey's brother Eliab has bought Cockaine House, and this is where the doctor now lives and contemplates. He tells me he delights to be in the dark, where he can think best. Once he had a house at Combe in Surrey, with good air and prospects, where he had caves made in the earth, in which he delighted to meditate in summer.

During our late wars, after the arrest of the King, Dr Harvey's rooms were plundered and he lost many of his papers and unpublished manuscripts, which he had worked on for years, trying to understand the generation of insects. He says this loss is the greatest crucifixion he has experienced in his life. It seems nothing can be done to recover those papers.

Dr Harvey tells me that after his book on the circulation of the blood, *De Motu Cordis*, came out in 1628, his medical practice declined mightily, since the vulgar thought him crack-brained and all the physicians were against him and envied him. Many wrote against him, but after about twenty or thirty years his doctrine was received in all the universities of the world. In his book *De Corpore*, Mr Hobbes says that Dr Harvey is perhaps the only man 'that ever lived to see his own doctrine established in his lifetime'.

I have seen Dr Harvey ride on horseback to visit his patients, his man following on foot.

. . .

16 May

On this day Colonel Penruddock was beheaded at Exeter for leading an uprising against the Protectorate, which started out in Salisbury and headed west through Blandford and Yeovil proclaiming Prince Charles king. The Parliament's new-modelled army defeated Colonel Penruddock and his followers at South Molton in Devon. He was tried before Serjeant Glynne and condemned to death.

. . .

June

I had a fall at Epsom, and have broken one of my ribs. I fear it might cause an impostumation. I went there to evaporate water from the Epsom Spring, intending to analyse its mineral content.

The mineral waters at Epsom, Bath, Tonbridge and other places are of great importance for medical cures. If it were possible to discover more waters of this kind, that would be a great benefit to others and a financial benefit to myself.

. . .

I have evaporated water from Holy-well, in the parish of Chippenham. I found two sorts of sediment, perhaps by reason of the oblique hanging of the kettle: one a deep soot colour, the other the colour of cullom earth. The colour did not change when I infused powder of galles. I will try it with syrup of violets.

. . .

Hancock's well at Luckington is so extremely cold that in summer one cannot endure one's hand in it. It does much good to the eyes. It cures the itch, etc. By precipitation it yields a white sediment, inclining to yellow, like a kind of fine flour. I believe the water is much impregnated with nitre. In the lane that leads from there to Sapperton, the earth is very nitrous.

. . .

November

I have received Dr Harvey's bill for my purge to prevent an impostumation. This bill, and the recipe he sent me back in April 1653, is in his own handwriting, so I will preserve them both.

. . .

December

My friend Lord Nicholas Tufton has been imprisoned in the Tower on suspicion of plotting against Oliver Cromwell, Lord Protector.

. . .

I visited Sherborne House, Mrs Sadler's great house in Salisbury Close. The pitched causeway in the court was so neglected in the late troubles that it became overgrown and lost below weeds. Recently they intended to pave it, but discovered the old pavement when they dug down deep enough.

Mrs Sadler's niece Katherine Ryves lives with her in the great house. She would be a most eligible wife.

. . .

Anno 1656

January

As I requested, my honoured friend Mr Lydall has bought twelve apple and four pear trees for me from the Oxford gardener Ralph Austen, at 12d a piece. Now they must be brought to Easton Pierse and planted. Mr Austen has provided a list of the names of the trees and some directions on how they should be ordered. The courier told Mr Lydall he would not take them until next week, when he promises to get something in which they can be transported without harm.

Mr Lydall tells me that Mr Hobbes's *Elements of Philosophy* has been printed, and he will send me a copy.

. . .

I have been visiting my great friend Sir James Long, of Draycot Cerne, and his wife Dorothy – a most elegant beauty and wit – daughter to Sir Edmund Leech. Her ladyship has in her possession some copies of unpublished poems by Edmund Waller. She lent the originals to the Duchess of Beaufort before their friendship was broken. Mr Waller has no copies. Among these unpublished poems is one 'On the Lady Isabella Cutting Trees in Paper':

> Fair hand! That can on virgin paper write,
> Yet from the stain of ink preserve it white;
> Whose travel o'er that silver field does show
> Like track of leverets in morning snow.
> Love's image thus in purest minds is wrought,
> Without a spot or blemish to the thought.
> Strange that your fingers should the pencil foil,
> Without the help of colours or of oil!
> For though a painter boughs and leaves can make,
> 'Tis you alone can make them bend and shake;

> Whose breath salutes your new-created grove,
> Like southern winds and makes it gently move.
> Orpheus could make the forest dance, but you
> Can make the motion and the forest too.

I remember hearing Lady Isabella playing the lute in Trinity College gardens when I was a student. How beautiful she was!

Here at Draycot is a great deal of vitriol ore. Petrified periwinkles and also belemnites are frequently found in the ground. The water in the wells is vitriolate, and with powder of galles it turns a purple colour. It is not good for tucking or fulling mills because it tinges the cloth a little yellowish.

I have taken careful note of the coats of arms in the windows at Draycot House. The Longs were anciently Lords Lieutenant of Braden Forest and one was Chief Justice in Eire.

. . .

I have recommended Dr Willis's treatise *De Fermentatione* (printed this year) to Mr Hartlib, most highly. I went to see him at his house where he is confined now by kidney stones. His eyesight is failing too.

. . .

I have acquired a copy of Laurus's *Antiquae Urbis (Romae) Splendor* (1612), and inserted my bookplate into it.

. . .

Mr Harrington has published his *Commonwealth of Oceana*. His genius lies towards politics and democratic government. His main principle is that power depends on the balance of property (usually landed property). His book is well received in the coffee houses. Mr Hobbes says Henry Nevill has had a finger in that pie.

. . .

May

Mr Potter has suggested that I visit a certain ironmonger who sells pliers, hand-vices, and other such tools for goldsmiths and watchmakers. He says there I should be able to obtain for him the steel plate he needs to

try another way of making the screw compasses, which will be service-
able for circular divisions.

. . .

My friends Sir John Hoskyns, Mr Stafford Tyndale and I went to visit
a weaver in Pear-poole Lane today to see a loom for making stockings.
The machine was invented in the last century by William Lee, a poor
curate who had observed the pains his wife took knitting a pair of
stockings. Oliver Cromwell, Lord Protector, has made it a crime to
export the loom, to ensure it is known in no part of the world but
England.

. . .

I have started collecting natural remarks for the county of Wiltshire.
I do not think I will write of gardens, the pleasure of which was
unknown to our great-grandfathers, who were content with potherbs
and did chiefly mind their stables.

Henry Lyte, of Lytes Carey in Somersetshire, my honoured
ancestor, translated Rembert Dodoens's *Herbarium* into English and
dedicated it to Queen Elizabeth near the beginning of her reign. He
had a pretty good collection of plants for that age, and some of them
are still alive. In his edition of the *Herbarium*, he added some notes
about the Somerset plants and their habitats. He hoped to contribute
something to the renown of his country as well as to the health of
its people. And he was very interested in genealogy, thinking the
British to be of Trojan descent. His second book, also dedicated to
Queen Elizabeth, was *The Light of Britayne: A Recorde of the Honorable
Originall and Antiquitie of Britaine* (1588).

This ancestor of mine is an inspiration.

. . .

I have drawn from memory a model of Lord Bacon's Verulam House,
which will now be sold by the current owner, Sir Harbottle Grimston.
This view of the house is from the entrance into the gate from the
highway. I cannot remember if there were bay windows on the east
side, or whether there were five or seven windows on the east side,
but to the best of my remembrance there were five. I wish I had
measured the front and breadth of the house when I visited it.

My friend Lord Charles Seymour has commissioned a portrait of me.

. . .

A second coffee house has opened in London, set up by Mr Farr, a barber, at the Rainbow by Inner Temple Gate. Sir Henry Blount, of Trinity College, a great friend of Francis Potter's, now drinks nothing but water and coffee. He first discovered coffee when he was travelling in Turkey, but now he can drink it in London easily.

. . .

My tedious lawsuit over the entail in Brecknockshire and Monmouthshire has begun. The entail in question is a matter of 600 li. a year, but in order to prove my claim to it I must go to Chaldon in Surrey to search the parish register there for the record of the burial of my great-grandmother, Dr William Aubrey's widow, Wilgiford Williams. What legal and financial troubles I am embroiled in since my father's death!

But I am cheered in this tedious business by one of my counsels, Walter Rumsey, who is being exceedingly kind to me. He has invited me to stay with him at his house, where he has many fine things, both natural and antiquarian. He is an ingenious man with a philosophical head, very interested in grafting, inoculating, planting and ponds.

Mr Rumsey is much troubled by phlegm. He has a method for relieving it which is to tie a rag to the end of a fine tender sprig and pass it down his throat to the top of his stomach: he has also tried this with a whale bone and says it works wonderfully for fetching up the phlegm. But when I tried, I could not make the device go down my throat. Mr Rumsey recommends taking an eluctuary made from coffee powder, butter, olive oil and honey, before swallowing the instrument, which he calls a 'provang'. He thinks that coffee promotes vomiting and farting and that unless the fore-door and back door of the body are kept open it will be destroyed by undigested meat fermenting the whole moisture of a man's body. He is working on a treatise called *Organon Salutis: An Instrument to Cleanse the Stomach*.

. . .

As I rode from Brecknock to Radnor on the top of a mountain (I think not far from Payn's Castle), I saw a monument of stones like a sepulchre, but much bigger than that at Holyhead. The stones are great and rudely placed. It think people call it Arthur's Chairs, or some such name.

. . .

I visited Caerphilly Castle today. It seems to me the oldest and most entire piece of Roman architecture that I know of in this Island. I wonder it is so little taken notice of.

. . .

I went to Monmouth church today. There is a sash window with a very old escutcheon, as old as the church, belonging to the Sitsilt of Monmouthshire family, which is of great antiquity. The window was hanging a little dangerously. I fear it will fall and be spoiled.

. . .

September
My good friend Mr Edmund Wylde has a grievous quartan ague.

. . .

My amours with Mary Wiseman continue, but she seems likely to marry another. I have started to pay suit to Katherine Ryves too.

. . .

December
Veneris morbus: I have been sleeping with whores and am stricken now with one of their venereal diseases.

. . .

Anno 1657

26 June
On this day I attended the funeral of my honoured friend William Harvey, who died earlier this month. He was buried in the vault of the church of Hempstead, Essex, which his brother Eliab Harvey built. He is lapt in lead and on his breast in great letters: DR WILLIAM HARVEY. I helped to carry him into the vault.

In his will, he has left the house he was born in at Folkestone in Kent, a fair stone house that is now the post-house, to Caius College, Cambridge.

. . .

October
My honoured friend John Lydall, whose health was never strong, died suddenly on 12 October, at four in the morning, aged about thirty-two. He has been buried in Trinity College: his coat of arms was on his hearse. He was an outstanding tutor to the young.

He left the college one of his most valuable books, Claudius Mydorgius's *Sectiones Conicas*, and our friend Ralph Bathurst, in his capacity as college librarian, has entered Lydall's name in the book of college benefactors, and written this eulogy: 'No one was quicker or more acute in exploring the inner chambers of nature. No one was more the Lynceus (or sharp-sighted) in mathematics. No one erected more fruitfully the foundations of medicine by means of anatomy, botany, and chemistry.'

Our grief is overwhelming.

. . .

November
Katherine Ryves, of the Close, Sarum, Wiltshire, whom I was to marry, has died, to my great loss. She will be buried by her father and mother

at Blandford Forum. Her portion was more than 2,000 li. a year, and her husband would have been the guardian of her brother's portion too (worth another 1,000 li. a year). She has left me a bequest of 350 li. and a mourning ring for my mother. Her death is a terrible blow for us.

. . .

Dining at Hampton Court, I heard Oliver Cromwell, Lord Protector – who rules with kingly, and more than kingly, power – tell Lord Arundel of Wardour that he has been in all the counties of England and finds Devon husbandry the best.

. . .

Anno 1658

I have been thinking about the antiquary William Burton, who died last year. His posthumous commentaries on chorography showing the importance of Roman remains have been printed recently: *A Commentary on Antoninus his Itinerary, or Journies of the Roman Empire, so far as it concerneth Britain.* My friend Mr Hollar did the engravings. I am struck by these commentaries and minded to devote more time from this day forward to my own interest in chorography. William Burton left his manuscripts and collections to the Bodleian Library.

. . .

John Wilkins has been made Master of Trinity College, Cambridge. The experimental philosophical club he founded in Oxford sometimes meets in London now, at the Bull Head tavern in Cheapside. Mr Wilkins is a lusty, strong-grown, well-set, broad-shouldered person, who revived experimental philosophy in Oxford. Experimental philosophy is inspired by the teachings of Lord Bacon.

. . .

3 September

On this day Oliver Cromwell died of quartan ague. A short while ago a whale came into the River Thames and was taken at Greenwich. It is said Oliver was troubled at it. Perhaps he thought it a portent. Perhaps it was. Oliver's son Richard has been made the new Lord Protector.

. . .

There has been smallpox in Taunton all this year.

. . .

The experimental philosophical club that once met in Oxford, and has lately been meeting in the Bull Head and other London taverns, will now meet in William Ball's chamber in the Middle Temple and from henceforth there will be paper records of the discussions that take place.

. . .

December
The Lord Protector's Privy Council has called a Parliament to address the problem of the regime's debt, which is said to be two million li.

. . .

Anno 1659

21 February
On this day my honoured grandfather, Isaac Lyte of Easton Pierse, died. He will be buried in the church at Kington St Michael. Among his old books I have found one of the sermons of George Feriby (who was one of King James's chaplains), called *Life's Farewell*.

. . .

March
I attended a meeting to choose the Knights of the Shire, and some present expressed the wish that our county of Wiltshire, where there are many observable antiquities, should be surveyed in imitation of the antiquary Mr William Dugdale's *Illustration of Warwickshire*, which was printed three years ago.

Wiltshire is too great a task for one man, so Mr William Yorke (counsellor at law and lover of this kind of learning) advised a division of labour. He will cover the middle part of the county himself; I will undertake the north part, and collect notes on all the antiquities there. Three others will assist us. I hope this design does not just vanish into tobacco smoke.

In former days, the churches and great houses of this county so abounded with monuments and things remarkable that an antiquary would have been deterred from taking notes on them all. But now, like Pythagoras, who guessed the vastness of Hercules's stature from the length of his foot, there are just enough remains among the ruins to guess at what noble buildings were made by the piety, charity and magnanimity of our forefathers. I think my eyes and mind are no less affected by these stately ruins than they would have been by the buildings themselves.

. . .

Sir George Penruddock of Broad Chalke and I have made ourselves churchwardens of Broad Chalke church, for fear it will fall down from the niggardliness of the churchwardens of mean condition who have been looking after it until now. We will arrange for repairs of the building and intend to add a sixth bell.

. . .

Yesterday I visited Ely. I nearly broke my neck in the minster, where I had climbed on to a high ledge to better examine the cathedral's windows and stonework.

Today, riding at a gallop, my horse tumbled over and over, and yet (thank God) I was not hurt.

My stammer has been troublesome since these mishaps.

. . .

April

I have gone with Mr Hobbes's brother Edmund to visit the house where my friend the eminent philosopher of Malmesbury was born. I hope to prevent mistakes or doubts hereafter as to the birthplace of this famous man. So we went into the very chamber where his brother says Mr Hobbes was born, in their father's house in Westport, which points into (or faces) the horse fair,
the farthest house on the left as you go to Tedbury, leaving the church on your right. It is a firm house, stone-built and tiled: one room (with a buttery or the like within) and two chambers above. It was in the

innermost of these chambers that Mr Hobbes first drew breath on Good Friday 5 April 1588. It is said his mother took fright at the invasion of the Spanish Armada and went into labour early.

Mr Hobbes's horoscope is Taurus with a satellitium of five of the seven planets in it. It is a maxim of astrology that a person who has a satellitium in his ascendant becomes more eminent in his life than an ordinary person who does not. Oliver Cromwell had this, same as Mr Hobbes.

. . .

May

After less than nine months as Lord Protector, Richard Cromwell has fallen from power. He had no confidence in the army, and the army had none in him. Now one of the army's factions has undone him. He refused the army's demand to dissolve the recently elected Parliament, so troops assembled at St James's Palace to force his hand. The recent Parliament has been dissolved and the Parliament of 1648 has been recalled. The Parliament of 1648 is called the Rump Parliament because it is what was left after the Long Parliament was purged of all members hostile to putting the late King on trial for high treason.

. . .

25 May

On this day the Rump Parliament agreed to pay Richard Cromwell's debts and give him a pension in return for his resignation as Lord Protector.

. . .

I have made my will and settled my estate on trustees, and intend to leave the country to see the antiquities of Rome and Italy. When I return, I will marry, since I am now thirty-three years old and I must secure my fortune in this world.

. . .

July

Mr Stafford Tyndale has written to me from Alençon. He urges me
to join him in Paris. He says I should come abroad now while times
are favourable and travel cheap: it will be much cheaper and safer
to travel in company than alone. He says that if I allow myself just
200 li. a year I can live and travel like a prince in the company he
will introduce me to. Convinced I will have a rambling fit before I
die, he insists that if I do not take this opportunity I will never have
so good a one again. He sends his respects and services to my
mother.

. . .

My mother, to my inexpressible grief and ruin, has hindered my plan
to travel abroad. She simply forbids me to go, and I feel I cannot
disregard her wishes.

   Dis aliter visum (it seemed otherwise to the Gods).

. . .

I have sold the old manor of Burleton in Herefordshire, which I
inherited from my father, to Dr Willis for 1,200 li.

. . .

I have sold the smaller manor of Stretford, which I inherited from my
father, to Herbert Croft, Lord Bishop of Hereford. I sold it to pay
debts, but in part I am glad to be free of another property: ownership
comes accompanied by weighty responsibilities that keep me from
my studies.

. . .

I am taking a course of lessons with the Danish mathematician Nicolas
Mercator, but truly my life is dominated by debts and lawsuits – *opus
et usus* – borrowing of money and perpetual riding. I have no time to
settle to my studies.

. . .

I am sharing lodgings in London with my friend Tom Mariett, of
Whitchurch in Warwickshire. He is in correspondence with Prince
Charles in exile and I have seen letters in the Prince's own hand in

our rooms. Tom and Colonel Edward Massey are tampering daily with General Monck, commander-in-chief of the Parliamentary forces, to see if he will be instrumental in bringing the Prince back to England, but they cannot find any inclination or propensity to this purpose in General Monck. Late every night in bed I hear an account of all these transactions. Sometimes I think I should commit these accounts to writing while they are still fresh in my memory.

. . .

Michaelmas

I am an auditor, or listener, at Mr Harrington's new Rota Club, which is a coffee club that meets every night in the Turk's Head in the New Palace Yard, at one Mr Miles's house next to the stairs. Here there is an oval table with a hole cut in one side for Mr Miles to stand and serve the coffee. These meetings are a forum for exchanging republican views, and the discourses I have listened to at them are the most ingenious and smart that I have ever heard, or expect to hear.

After the meetings we often repair to the Rhenish-wine house.

At our meetings we have a formal balloting box and we ballot about how things should be carried by tentamens or experiment. The room is crammed full every evening, as full as it can be, with gentlemen diverting themselves with philosophical or political discussions.

My Trinity College friend Sir John Hoskyns is a member of the Rota Club, as is the learned Dr William Petty. Dr Petty troubles Mr Harrington with his arithmetical proportions and ability to reduce politics to numbers. It seems that every day in the coffee house, Mr Harrington's *Commonwealth of Oceana* and Henry Nevill's discourses make new proselytes.

Mr Harrington recently printed a little pamphlet called *Divers Modells of Popular Government*, and now another called *The Rota*. His doctrine is being taken up, the more because there seems to be no possibility of restoring the monarchy. And yet the greater part of the Parliament's men hate Mr Harrington's design for allocating political office through rotation by balloting. The Parliament's men are cursed tyrants in love with the power they would lose if Mr Harrington's method of rotation came in. The model provides that a third of the senate should be replaced every year by ballot, so that it will be completely renewed every nine years, and no magistrate

should continue in office more than three years. There is nothing
invented that is more fair and impartial than choosing by ballot. The
pride of senators appointed for life is insufferable and they can grind
anyone incurring their ill will to powder. They are hated by the army
and their country: their names and natures will stink for years to
come.

. . .

I have often heard Mr Harrington speak of the late King at the Rota
meetings, with the greatest zeal and passion imaginable. Mr Harrington
was so grief-stricken by the King's execution that he contracted a
disease: never did anything touch him so closely.

PART V

Restoration

3 February
On this day General Monck entered London, around 1 p.m., with none opposing him.

. . .

9 February
General Monck's forces, on the Rump Parliament's orders, pulled down the city gates and burnt them. This action will make him odious to the people of London.

. . .

11 February
General Monck has apologised for the destruction of the city gates.

. . .

The Rump Parliament invited General Monck to the House, where a chair was set for him, but he would not sit down, out of modesty. They invited him to a great dinner, at which Members of Parliament stayed until the early hours of the morning, but suspecting treachery, General Monck did not attend.

. . .

Someone anonymous has written these words on the door of the House of Commons:

Till it be understood
What is under Monck's hood
The citizens putt in their hornes.
Untill the ten days are out
The Speaker haz the gowt,
And the Rump, they sitt upon thornes.

. . .

Threadneedle Street was crammed all day long with multitudes crying:
'A free Parliament! A free Parliament!' The air was ringing with the
crowds' clamours. Around seven or eight in the evening, General
Monck, after being nearly knocked from his horse, addressed them
thus: 'Pray be quiet, yee shall have a free Parliament!' Then a loud
holler went up and all the bells in the city were rung, and bonfires
were lit in celebration. I saw little gibbets set up and roasted rumps
of mutton and very good rumps of beef. In the streets the people
drank to Prince Charles's health, even on their knees.

. . .

The news has spread to Salisbury, and on to Broad Chalke, where
they made a great bonfire on the top of the hill. From there the news
travelled to Shaftesbury and Blandford, and so to Land's End: perhaps
this is what it has been like all over England.

. . .

My bedfellow Tom Mariett insists that General Monck did not intend
the restoration of the monarchy when he first came from Scotland
to England, or to London, any more than his horse did! But shortly
after finding himself at a loss, and made odious to the city by the
Parliament's ordering him to pull down the gates and burn them, he
made up his mind in favour of Prince Charles becoming King.

. . .

The members of the Long Parliament who were purged in 1648 on
account of their hostility to putting King Charles on trial have been
readmitted under General Monck's protection. So the Rump Parliament
is no more and the Long Parliament is restored.

. . .

Mr Harrington's Rota Club has met for what I think will turn out to be the last time. Ever since General Monck's coming in, debate on republican government and the Commonwealth has ceased abruptly. Whereas before those airy models of government were so hotly debated at the Turk's Head, now those debates have fallen silent. Soon it will be treason to hold such meetings. At the breaking up of his club, Mr Harrington says, 'Well, the King will come in. Let him come in and call a Parliament of the greatest Cavaliers in England, so they be men of estates, and let them sit but seven years, and they will all turn Commonwealth men.'

. . .

16 March
On this day the Long Parliament called for free elections and its own dissolution.

. . .

Mr Milton's impassioned work *The Ready and Easy Way to Establish a Free Commonwealth* has been printed but the people have turned strongly against republicanism. Mr Milton is a spare man, of middling stature, scarcely as tall as I am.

. . .

Samuel Pordage, whom I know well since he is head steward of the lands of the Earl of Pembroke, has given me his translation into English of Seneca's *Troades* (*The Trojan Women*).

. . .

I borrowed money from Captain Stumpe of Malmesbury. I will repay the bond.

. . .

Earlier this month I bought – by fortunate accident – a curious Turkey, or turquoise, stone ring. It is not of fine blue rock, but greenish. Today I noticed that it has become nubilated, or cloudy, at north and south. It is a much more curious ring than I knew it to be when I bought it.

. . .

April

The aurora of our soon to be gracious sovereign has arrived. In exile, the King in waiting has issued the Declaration of Breda, in which he makes certain promises with regard to reclaiming the crown of England:

- A full pardon to all who appeal to him within forty days, excepting only those who signed his father's death warrant.
- Liberty to tender consciences in religious affairs, unless national peace is threatened.
- Settlement of army pay arrears; and all disputes arising from property deals since 1649 to be resolved by the new Parliament.

. . .

25 April

On this day the Convention, which General Monck summoned to solve the constitutional crisis, assembled for the first time. The first thing put to question was 'Whether Charles Stuart should be sent for or no?' No one voted against, and the cries of 'Yea, yea' resounded, so England will have a king again. This is the dawn of the coming of our soon to be gracious sovereign.

. . .

May

The Convention has proclaimed Charles II the rightful king since the execution of his father on 30 January 1649.

. . .

As the morning grows lighter and lighter and more glorious until it is perfect day, so now does the joy of the people. Maypoles, which were banned in hypocritical times, have been set up again at crossroads. At the Strand, near Drury Lane, the tallest maypole ever seen was erected with help from seamen.

. . .

25 May

On this day the King landed at Dover. He was met by General Monck and cheering crowds. To the thunder of a five-round salute from the ship's guns, answered by the cannon of Dover Castle, Charles climbed down from his ship and into a barge. When he stepped ashore, around three o'clock, he knelt and thanked God. General Monck was the first to greet him, then they processed up the beach with a canopy of state held above their heads.

. . .

Last month, I wrote to Mr Hobbes (who has been in Derbyshire this spring) and advised him to return to London in readiness for the King's arrival in the city. He has heeded my advice. In 1647, Mr Hobbes taught His Majesty mathematics in Paris. This would be a fine time for the King to renew his grace and favour to his former tutor! I have an idea as to how a meeting might occur. If Mr Hobbes were to agree to have his portrait painted by Mr Samuel Cooper, the prince of limners, of whom the King has heard much abroad, they might meet most conveniently in the artist's studio. Mr Cooper lives between Covent Garden and the Strand on Henrietta Street, which is very broad and pleasant.

. . .

Today is King Charles's thirtieth birthday, and he has celebrated by making his entry into London.

This fine song (composed by William Yokeney back in 1646 or 1647) was sung to a lively brisk tune:

> What if the King should come to the city,
> Would he be then received I trow?
> Would the Parliament treat him with rigor or pity?
> Some doe think yea, but most doe think no, &c.

Most were wrong! The King has been received with rapture in the city.

. . .

At Rye, at Stansteds-bury, in the marsh ground, oak trees have been found standing upright underground.

. . .

Mr Hobbes tells me the King noticed him at the gate of Little Salisbury House today. Passing in his carriage through the Strand, the King recognised Mr Hobbes, raised his hat very kindly to him and asked how he did.

. . .

The King and Mr Hobbes met again today at Mr Samuel Cooper's studio, as I hoped they might. The King is a great lover of painting. Mr Cooper will paint portraits of both the King and Mr Hobbes, and the King has ordered that Mr Hobbes be freely admitted to his presence from now on.

. . .

I have heard that in Malmesbury, on the day of the return of the King and his birthday, there was such rejoicing, so many volleys of shot and cannon fired in celebration by the inhabitants of the hundred, that the noise thoroughly shook the abbey church. One of the pillars of the tower and two parts above it fell down that night.

. . .

July
My turquoise ring has changed again. Now the cloudy spot in the north of the ring has entirely vanished and the one in the south has lessened.

. . .

29 August
On this day the Parliament passed An Act of Free and General Pardon, Indemnity and Oblivion, asking the King to pardon everyone involved in the death of his father, except those who officiated at his execution. The Interregnum will be legally forgot. Blind Mr Milton will be released from prison. He was arrested recently and there have been burnings of his books.

. . .

October
My turquoise ring has become cloudy again in the north and a little speck has appeared in the middle.

. . .

December
I am one of the signatories to proposals for a Royal Society for experimental philosophy, scientific experiment and discussion in London. The proposals will formalise an association of ingenious minds that has existed for a good number of years already.

My most honoured and obliging friend Sir Robert Moray will try and obtain a Royal Charter for the new society. He has the King's ear as much as anyone and is indefatigable in his undertakings.

. . .

Anno 1661

30 January
On this day, the twelfth anniversary of the execution of the late King, the exhumed bodies of Oliver Cromwell, Henry Ireton and John Bradshaw were hanged on the gallows at Tyburn Hill. Henry Ireton was Cromwell's son-in-law; he died of fever in 1651. John Bradshaw was president of the court that condemned Charles I to death and it was he who read the sentence against the King. He died in 1659.

My servant saw the decomposed bodies taken down and buried under the gallows. Only Cromwell's body was wrapped in serecloth. Ireton's hands were rotted off but his body was not putrefied. Worms ran up and down the holes in Bradshaw's body too.

. . .

The astrologer Mr William Lilly has claimed that George Joyce was the masked executioner who condemned Charles I to death, so there is a warrant out for his arrest.

. . .

February
My mysterious turquoise ring has changed again. Now there is a cloudy spot on the west side that seems to be approaching the cloudy spot on the east side.

. . .

24 February

My honoured grandmother, Israel Lyte of Easton Pierse, has died. I am planning to place a memorial plaque to her in the church at Kington St Michael where my grandfather is buried.

. . .

I have been to visit Old Sarum, which went to rack after the building close by of Salisbury Cathedral in the thirteenth century. In the time of Edward VI, the great house of the Earl of Pembroke at Wilton was built from the ruins of Old Sarum. I found the remains of some of the walls of the great gate on the south side, and on the north side there were some remains of the bottom of a tower, but the incrustation of freestone was almost all gone. I saw a fellow picking at what little was left.

. . .

The cloudy spot in the north of my turquoise ring is now encircled with a halo. The ring is a rarity. I will show it to Mr Robert Boyle, who is interested in movement within stones and the hardening and softening of them by time. His book, *The History of Fluidity and Firmness*, will be printed this year.

. . .

Since the return of the King, my cousin Sir John Aubrey of Llantrithyd has been created baronet.

. . .

Mr Hobbes has had printed *Dialogus Physicus, sive de Natura Aeris*, in which he attacks the ideas of Mr Boyle and others in the Royal Society for experimental researches. Mr Hobbes complains that the new society is not beginning from the principles and method he set down in his book *De Corpore*.

. . .

April

Sir John Hoskyns writes to tell me of his visits to see the great collections of pictures and statues in Paris which, though he had read about them, greatly exceed his expectations. What would I not give to go to France to see those collections for myself? Sir John hopes to be in

Venice for the ceremony of the Doge wedding the sea: the best sight in Venice all year.

. . .

I discussed the lace the King wore for his coronation, which took place on the 23rd of this month, with William Dobson's sweet-faced widow Judith. His Majesty was crowned at the very conjunction of the sun and Mercury, Mercury being then *in corde solis*. As he was at dinner in Westminster Hall afterwards, it thundered and lightned extremely. The cannons and the thunder played together.

. . .

My friend, the prodigiously talented Mr Wenceslaus Hollar, has moved from Holburn to new lodgings without St Clements Inn. He tells me that when I call on him I should ask for 'the Frenchman Limner', for his neighbours know not his name perfectly. Mr Hollar was born in Prague, not France. He lived in England before our wars in the household of Thomas Howard, Earl of Arundel. During our wars he moved to Antwerp, but came back to London about ten years ago.

Before the wars, Mr Hollar married Margaret Tracy, a servant of the Countess of Arundel. She died in 1653, leaving their two small children: a daughter who is one of the greatest beauties I have ever seen, and a son who is an ingenious youth that draws delicately, like his father.

Mr Hollar is very short-sighted. When he sketches his landscapes, he uses a glass to help his sight. His work is so closely drawn that the curiosity of it cannot be judged without using a magnifying glass.

. . .

May

Sir John Hoskyns writes to tell me he has spent two days in Venice, where he saw the ceremony of the Doge's wedding of the sea and in the evening the Corso, which he says is like Hyde Park on water. He says the fine folk of Venice have fat faces and low noses, but are still handsome and well complexioned, either naturally or by art. But he is still convinced that Rome is the beauty of the world. He plans to visit Padua too. How much I wish I could go with him. I have asked him to try and find a book by Scarnolii for me while he is in Italy, but he claims it is exceeding scarce. He asks me in return to obtain copies of Mr Hobbes's books for him before the hangman burns them. Mr Hobbes is suspected of atheism and heresy.

. . .

June

My cousin James Whitney, once a Fellow of Brasenose College, and afterwards vicar of the Wiltshire parish of Donhead St Andrews, tells me that during the Visitation of Oxford under Edward VI, mathematical books were burnt for conjuring books, and if the Greek professor had not happened to come along in time, the Greek Testament would have been thrown into the fire for a conjuring book too. Mr Whitney gave me his copy of Sebastian Münster's *Rudimenta Mathematica*.

. . .

From north Wales, my friend and fellow antiquary Anthony Ettrick and I have crossed into Ireland, where we are travelling on horseback, observing this unhappy island. I find I am a quick draughtsman and can sketch the landscape in symbols as we pass through it.

This kingdom is in a very great distemper and has need of Mr Hobbes's advice to settle it. The animosities between the English and the Irish are very great and before long, I am confident, will break into war.

The natives seem to scorn industry and luxury, contenting themselves only with necessities. On holidays we have seen whole parishes of the wild Irish running from hedge to hedge wren-hunting.

My friend William Petty conducted a survey of Ireland and in payment was granted great estates here by the Commonwealth government, but since the Restoration of the King he has had to return them to their former owners.

. . .

In Dublin we met Mr Stoughton, who has climbed Mount Pico in the Azores. He told us that they carried with them to the summit claret wine, strong waters and canary wine. The claret and strong waters turned, or curdled, at the top of the Pico like whey. But the canary wine did not. He said that the Pico can be seen from a distance of forty leagues at sea.

. . .

Today we saw a manuscript in Saxon characters in which the Magi are described as Druids.

. . .

On our way back from Ireland, through the waters of St George's Channel, Anthony Ettrick and I seemed likely to be shipwrecked at Holy-head, but in the end we came to no harm. Deo Gratias!

. . .

August

I am newly returned into Wiltshire and have deferred my journey into Derbyshire until I have word that Mr Hobbes is there. I will talk to him about Ireland and how it might be settled.

Mr Tyndale writes with advice about the journey I might make next to Portugal. And he tells me he has seen my mistress again recently – just in passing in the street – looking prettier than she did when we all met together at Samuel Cooper's and in the garden last spring.

. . .

I am delighted with the picture of Mr Hobbes that I commissioned from Mr Samuel Cooper: it is one of the best pieces Mr Cooper has ever done. Mr Cooper is an ingenious man of great humanity. A week on Monday, I shall see Mr Hobbes's brother and we shall drink his health together.

. . .

When I ask myself what I have accomplished in my life thus far, my efforts add up to truly nothing; only umbrages! I am proud of the fact I had drawings done of the ruins of Osney Abbey when I was a student, and I have saved and collected some antiquities, things that were neglected or forgotten and would have sunk without trace if I had not cared for them. But I have been a whetstone to other people's achievements. Nothing more.

My friend Mr Wencelaus Hollar has engraved one of the drawings I commissioned of Osney Abbey for inclusion in the second volume

Insignes hujusce Fabricæ Ruinas,
quas, Antiquitatis ævo plurimum suspexit
Meliofferdidus junctim Oxoniensis: décriptas
adeoque conservando asserit, prout astroplaus
Belli Civili suadibus è medio tollerentur, ne-
dumiar cievnit. Posteris quas redivivas.
L. D. C. Q.
Johannes Albericus
de Cham Pierre
in Agro Wilts Arm.

Prospectus Ruinarum Abbatiæ de OSNEY, juxta Oxon:

of Mr Dugdale's *Monasticon Anglicanum*, printed this year. The first volume was printed in 1655. In these books, Mr Dugdale is compiling the history of the ancient abbeys, monasteries, hospitals and collegiate churches in England and Wales. He also includes some French, Irish and Scottish monasteries formerly relating to England. Alongside the drawing of Osney Abbey I am proud to see my coat of arms together with an explanation of how I commissioned the drawing when I was a student in Oxford.

. . .

My friend William Petty has been knighted.

. . .

December
Mr Harrington has been interrogated and imprisoned in the Tower for conspiracy. He is a gentleman of high spirit and hot head. I fear for his reason.

. . .

My friend Mr Edmund Wylde has a dangerous fever.

. . .

Mr Samuel Cooper has been commissioned to draw the King's profile for the new milled coinage: Mr Cooper prefers sketching at night and by candlelight.

. . .

Anno 1662

March
Mr Hartlib has died. After the Restoration of the King, he lost his pension, and his petition to Parliament concerning his penury went unanswered.

. . .

May
Sir John Hoskyns writes to me of Mr Hobbes. He tells me Mr Hobbes has written another book, *Problemata Physica*, and dedicated it to the King. He hopes that Mr Hobbes will not provoke the mathematician

Lord Brouncker, who has found favour with the King and been made the Queen's chancellor.

The King has granted Mr Hobbes a pension of 100 li., and he is often at court, where his irascible nature has earned him the name 'the Bear': 'Here comes my Bear to be baited,' the King is wont to say.

. . .

Mr Hobbes has silenced his detractors, Dr Wallis especially, and put a stop to malicious doubts about his loyalty to the King by printing a new pamphlet, *Mr Hobbes Considered in His Loyalty, Religion, Reputation and Manners*. Here he explains that he wrote and published his *Leviathan* on behalf of the faithful subjects of His Majesty, who took his part in the war, or otherwise did their utmost to defend His Majesty's right and person against the rebels. After His Majesty's defeat, these subjects, having no other means of protection, nor (for the most part) of subsistence, were forced to compound with the new masters and promise obedience to save their lives and fortunes. *Leviathan* affirms that they did this lawfully: they had done all they could be obliged to do in defence of His Majesty and were consequently at liberty to seek the safety of their lives and livelihoods without treachery. I am myself one of these people.

Mr Hobbes says that were it not for the laws, many men would have no more scruples about killing a man than he or I do about killing a little bird. In his *Leviathan* he says that men will never be obedient and good subjects until his doctrine is taught in schools, and he attacks the ecclesiastics and universities.

. . .

Mr Tyndale complains that he misses me greatly in London and declares that my absence makes him feel low and fretful. The Queen has been very ill. He tells me that our friend Sir John Hoskyns has a severe fever. For all these reasons I must return to the city as soon as I can.

. . .

June
Parliament has passed a new Licensing Act, which requires books on most subjects to be licensed by the Archbishop of Canterbury or the Bishop of London.

. . .

July
The Royal Society has received its charter from the King. It will now be permitted to print books. The professors at Gresham College in Bishopsgate have generously offered rooms for the new society's meetings. There is a great hall for elections and a separate room for the ordinary meetings every Wednesday.

. . .

November
On Mr Boyle's recommendation, Mr Hooke has been elected the Royal Society's Curator of Experiments.

Mr Hooke is of but middling stature, something crooked, pale-faced, but his head is large and his eye full, popping and grey. He has a delicate head of brown hair and an excellent moist curl. He seems a very temperate man.

. . .

Sir William Petty presented a treatise on shipbuilding to the Royal Society, but the President, Lord Brouncker, confiscated it, claiming it is too great an Arcanum of State to be commonly perused!

. . .

December
Dr Walter Charleton has proposed me as a candidate for election to the Royal Society. He is a learned, melancholy man and Physician in Ordinary to the King.

. . .

Anno 1663

7 January
On this day I have been elected to the Royal Society.

. . .

21 January
To my great joy, I have been admitted, formally, to the Royal Society. Our meetings include experiments. Today I proposed to the learned company Mr Potter's idea of moving blood between chickens. But it

was considered absurd and impossible: a blemish on the Society's reputation to experiment with such an idea. This embarrassed me very much and brought a hot blush to my cheeks. My stammer started up and was the worst it has been in years.

. . .

The minister of Avebury claims that the huge stones may be broken wherever you please without any great trouble. This is how: they make a fire on that line of the stone where they would have it crack; and, after the stone is well heated, draw over a line with cold water and immediately give a smart knock with a smith's sledgehammer, and the stone will break like collets at the glasshouse. I hope this breaking of the ancient stones can be stopped.

. . .

4 March

Today I attended my second Royal Society meeting. My stammer was less bad this time. Mr Hooke presented his proposals for experiments on the resistance of air to bodies moved through it. He was appointed curator of these experiments, which will begin with a pendulum sealed up in a glass.

I presented the Society with my friend Francis Potter's scheme for a cart with legs instead of wheels. The Society asked Mr Hooke to consider it and report back at the next meeting.

I have proposed Mr Potter as a member of the Royal Society.

. . .

18 March

Mr Hooke's report on Mr Potter's cart with legs was read before the Society today. A copy of the report, with a few alterations and corrections suggested at the meeting, will be sent to Mr Potter. Mr Hooke will also draw up a full description of the cart and a scheme for building it. Mr Potter has been elected a member of the Royal Society, to my immense delight.

I mentioned before that learned company today that I have been told that the Duke of Orleans had a way of producing animals from the putrefaction of vegetables. This gave rise to a return to the discussion on equivocal generation that took place back in October 1662, before I was a member of the Royal Society. A number of the Fellows have been charged with experiments in this regard. Mr John Evelyn will put several pieces of flesh and some blood in a closed vessel that cannot be fly-blown and see what is produced.

. . .

Mr Potter will come in person to the Royal Society after Easter, and in the meantime send me forty shillings so I can pay his admittance for him.

. . .

6 May
Today I described to the Royal Society my observation that holly berries, after lying five or six hours in the bottom of a vessel of water, will rise and swim up to the middle, which is thought to be due to a kind of fermentation and swelling that means the berries increase in size. The Royal Society decided this experiment should be tried again in the winter.

I also described my observation that grains of wheat will sink in water with an air bubble attached to them. When the bubble breaks, the grains rise again, then sink a second time to the bottom and do not rise again.

Quaere: if a bladder filled with smoke will be carried up into the air, and if so, perhaps several such bladders might draw a man up into the air to a certain height?

. . .

13 May
The new charter of the Royal Society was read before its council, which met for the first time today. It has been decided that discussion of who should be received and admitted into the Royal Society will be kept secret.

. . .

June
When I was about two thirds of the way down Dundery Hill, on my way from Bristol to Wells, I saw a thin mist rise out of the ditch on the right-hand side of the highway. When I came nearer to the place, I could not discern the mist, so I retraced my steps and saw it again from a distance. Then I noticed that there was some flower or weed growing

in the ditch from which the vapour came. My nose was affected with
a smell that I knew, but it did not come immediately to mind. My
groom, who is dull of understanding, but whose senses are very quick,
caught up with me and I asked him what he could smell. He answered
that he smelt the smell of the canals that come from the baths at Bath.

. . .

At Crudwell, near the manor house, is a fine spring in the street called
Bery-well. Labourers say it quenches their thirst better than other
waters. To my taste it seems to have *aliquantulum aciditatis*, and is
perhaps vitriolate. The town is called after this well; perhaps it is called
Crudwell because of the water turning milk into cruds.

. . .

July
Mr Walter Charleton has presented the Royal Society with a plan of
the stone antiquities at Avebury, near Marlborough, suggesting that it
would be worth digging there under a certain triangular stone, where
a monument to some Danish king might be found. I have been asked,
together with my friend Sir James Long, to make further enquiries
into this.

. . .

September
Sir Kenelm Digby says that Dr Dee (whom my great-grandfather knew
well) diligently observed the weather for seven years, and as a result
developed such skill in predicting the weather that he was accounted
a witch.

. . .

I have found, I think, a place for the free school at Malmesbury that
Mr Hobbes intends to establish. The land is in Bradon Forest, worth
about 25 li. per annum, and in His Majesty's gift.

I have also found Mr Hobbes a house in London, but he hesitates
to take it lest his pension should cease in this time of austerity when
the court is reducing its expenses. He is at Chatsworth for the time
being and will make no decisions until he comes to London himself.

. . .

The rivulet that runs through Chalke rises at a place called Naule, belonging to Broad Chalke farm, where a great many springs issue out of the chalky ground. It makes a kind of lake covering about three acres, where there are two-foot-long trout, the best in England. The water is good for washing and brewing. I tried putting crawfish in it, but they did not live, the water is too cold for them. When horses from north Wiltshire, or other horses from further afield, come to drink in the Chalke River, it is so cold and tort that they sniff and snort, I suppose because it is very heavily impregnated with nitre.

. . .

In the presence of the King, Walter Charleton and the President of the Royal Society, William Brouncker discussed my view that Avebury excels Stonehenge as much as a cathedral does a parish church. His Majesty expressed surprise than none of our chorographers have yet taken any notice of Avebury, and he has issued a Royal Command that Stonehenge and Avebury be investigated. Mr Charleton will arrange to take me into His Majesty's presence to discuss this.

. . .

In his book *Chorea Gigantum*, published this year, Mr Charleton argues that Stonehenge was the work of the Danes. The stones are so exceeding old that books do not reach them. They savour of an antique rudeness.

I think Mr Charleton is wrong. His book shows a great deal of learning in a very good style, but as to his hypothesis that the Danes built Stonehenge, that cannot be right: it is a gross mistake. In the thirteenth century, the historian Matthew Paris expressly affirmed that Stonehenge was the place where the Saxons' treachery massacred the Britons, which was four or five hundred years before the conquest of the Danes. I think Simeon of Durham and Henry of Huntingdon said the same thing in the twelfth century.

Mr Charleton writes in his book, 'Many things are well worthy our knowledge, that cannot yet deserve our belief; and even fictions some-times have accidentally given light to long obscured writers.'

. . .

Today I met His Majesty. Into the King's presence I took with me a draft of Avebury done only from memory, but well enough resembling it, I think. He was very pleased with it. He gave me his hand to kiss and commanded me to wait on him at Marlborough when he travels to Bath with the Queen in about a fortnight's time.

. . .

October

On their progress to Bath, His Majesty and the Duke of York left the Queen and diverted to Avebury where I showed them that stupendous antiquity. I thought my stammer would start up through nervousness, but it disappeared when I saw how delighted by the monument the royal visitors were. The stones there are pitched on end, bigger than those at Stonehenge, but rude and unhewn, just as they were when they were drawn out of the earth.

Afterwards, as we were leaving, the King cast his eye on Silbury Hill, about a mile away, and said he desired to see it. I climbed to the top with him; Mr Charleton and the Duke of York came too. At the top, the King saw his kingdom from a new prospect. After we descended he proceeded to the entertainment and dinner at Lacock; then on that evening to Bath. The gentry and common people of those parts received the royal party with great acclamations of joy.

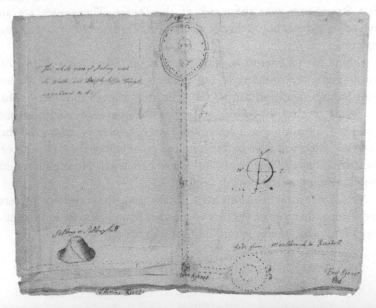

His Majesty has commanded me to write a description of Avebury and present it to him, and the Duke of York has commanded me to provide an account of the Old Camps and Barrows on the Plains. I will attempt to do both.

His Majesty also commanded me to dig at the bottom of the stones, to see if I could find any human bones, but I will not do it.

. . .

I have returned to Stonehenge and discovered some new holes.

I noticed too, but not for the first time, that the high stones are so deeply honeycombed that the starlings use them as nests. Whether these holes in the high-up stones are natural or artificial I cannot tell. In Wales, starlings are called Adar y Drudwy (meaning Birds of the Druids). Perhaps the Druids made these holes on purpose for their loquacious birds to nest in. This calls to my mind Pliny's description of the starling in his time that could speak Greek.

While I think it very probable that Stonehenge already existed long before the Romans became masters of Britain, they would have been

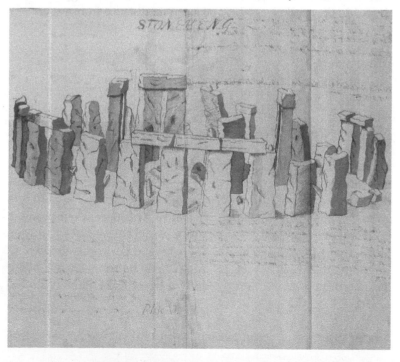

delighted with the stateliness and grandeur of it, and (considering
the dryness of its situation) would have found it suitable for urn-
burial. There are about forty-five barrows near Stonehenge. It must
have taken a great deal of time to collect so many thousand loads
of earth, and soldiers have better things to do, so I do not think these
barrows were for burying the dead slain in battles. When Christianity
became the settled religion, the temples that had been dedicated to
the heathen gods were converted to Christian use and worship.

The monument is still being damaged. Ever since I can remember,
the locals have been picking at it. One large stone was carried away to
make a bridge; and it is generally believed, by those living close by, that
powder from these stones tipped down wells will drive away the toads
that infest them. The source of this belief seems to be that no magpie,
toad or snake has ever been seen at Stonehenge. But this is no surprise.
Birds of weak flight will not fly beyond their power of reaching cover,
for fear of their enemies, the hawks and ravens, and there is no cover
within a mile and a half of Stonehenge. Snakes and adders love cover
too, so avoid Stonehenge for the same reason as the magpies. As for
the toads, they will not go beyond a certain distance from water.

. . .

11 November
Mr Francis Potter was admitted to the Royal Society today.

. . .

30 November
St Andrew's Day: the day of the General Meeting of the Royal
Society. Today at our meeting I remarked to Sir William Petty that
it seems not well to me that we have pitched upon the feast day of
the patron saint of Scotland. I would have thought it better to
choose the feast of St George, or that of St Isidore, the canonised
philosopher. 'No,' said Sir William, 'I would rather have had it on
St Thomas's Day, for he would not believe in the resurrection until
he had seen and put his fingers into the nail holes in Christ's body.'
This according to the motto *Nullius in verba* (take nobody's word
for it).

. . .

December

Sir George Ent has shown the Royal Society a table top made of
fossilised wood that was sent to him from Rome by the renowned
collector of rarities Cassiano dal Pozzo. Sir George Ent met Cassiano
dal Pozzo when he was in Rome with Dr William Harvey in 1636. Mr
Evelyn visited him too, when he was on his Grand Tour in 1644.
Cassiano dal Pozzo stayed in touch with Sir George Ent; he sent him
examples of petrified wood and they carried on a lively correspondence and exchange of books, until Cassiano dal Pozzo's death six years
ago. I wish I could have visited Cassiano dal Pozzo's paper museum
myself and seen the two sets of drawings – things human and things
divine – into which I have heard it was divided. There would have
been many things in those collections of stupendous interest to a
scurvy antiquary such as I am.

. . .

Anno 1664

January

I am lovesick. I left Sir John Hoskyns's house abruptly, and claimed
to be beset by melancholy, but I do not think he believed me. He
urges me to divert my mind – to return to the city to meet him next
Wednesday and enjoy ingenious company. He says I should let her
go, and will do well enough without her. But I am lovesick and can
think of nothing else besides my beloved.

. . .

March

I have been elected to the Royal Society's new Georgical Committee.
The committee has thirty-two members and will collect information
on the history of gardening and agriculture in England, Scotland and
Ireland. We will draft a set of questions and send them out to knowl-
edgeable people in different regions. I will seek to obtain reports from
Wiltshire and Dorset.

. . .

May

At the Royal Society I mentioned my desire to talk to Mr Jonas Moore about the astronomical tables of Mr Jeremiah Horrox. Mr Horrox died suddenly in 1641 as our wars were beginning, aged just twenty-two. He was the first to demonstrate that the moon moves round the earth in an elliptical orbit. His achievements must not be lost from the records of the advancement of science.

I have described to the learned Fellows a new way of brewing good and lasting beer with ginger but without hops. I have promised to bring some bottles of this beer to a future meeting for them to taste. . . .

My friend Lord Nicholas Tufton, who was twice imprisoned in the Tower during the Commonwealth, has succeeded to the peerage and become the 3rd Earl of Thanet. He is a kind patron to me.

PART VI

Stone, Water, Fire

June

My friend Mr George Ent and I are travelling together. After a rough crossing, we landed at Calais.

We have been exchanging stories of our schooling. George Ent tells me he was once kicked by his schoolmaster down seven or eight flights of stairs, landing on his head. He was lucky not to break his neck! The day before, he had shaled one of his teeth, so he wrote to his father, Sir George Ent, to describe the treatment he had endured, enclosing the tooth and claiming he had lost it falling down the stairs. Sir George arrived the next day and took him away. Afterwards he went to my Trinity friend William Radford's school at Richmond. William Radford is an honest sequestered gentleman and has become an excellent schoolmaster since he was excluded from his Oxford Fellowship by the Parliamentarian Visitors.

I intend to travel on to Orleans by way of Paris.

. . .

I have reached Paris and have a plan to see next the Loire, Brittany and the country around Geneva. I am staying with M de Houlle, in the churchyard of Saint-Julien-Le-Pauvre, at the sign of the golden rock, in front of the fountain of Saint-Séverin, near the Châtelet. I have written a letter to Mr Hobbes, who told me much about Paris before I came here.

. . .

The shopkeepers here in France count with counters, which is the best way. Counters were anciently used in England too.

. . .

August
I have reached Orleans, but here am suffering a terrible attack of piles.

. . .

About a mile from Saumur on the road to Doué-la-Fontaine is an ancient monument near the highway called Pierre Couverte. The perpendicular stones are at least four foot high from the ground.

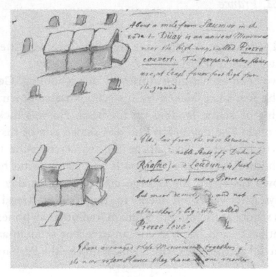

. . .

Not far from the road between the noble seat of the Duke of Rhône and Loudon is another monument like Pierre Couverte, but more demolished and not altogether so big. It is called Pierre Levée.

. . .

October
I have paid for my passage from Dieppe and will return to England.

. . .

I am back in England.

I hear that Mr Hooke's position as the Royal Society's Curator of Experiments has been confirmed for life, and that he has been chosen as Professor of Geometry at Gresham College. This is excellent news, since his head lies much more to geometry than arithmetic.

I have seen Mr Hobbes and encouraged him to write about the Law. I said I think it a pity that he who has such a clear reason and working head has never taken into consideration the learning of the laws. At first he said he did not think he was likely to live long enough for such a difficult task – he is now seventy-six years – but I presented him with Lord Bacon's *Elements of the Law*, to inspire him. He was pleased with the book and is reading it.

. . .

I have seen Mr Hobbes again and he showed me two clear paralogisms in Lord Bacon's *Elements of the Law*, one of them on the second page, but whether or not he will write his own treatise on law I cannot tell.

Mr Hobbes always has very few books in his chamber. I have never seen more than half a dozen there when I visit him. Homer and Virgil are commonly on his table, sometimes Xenophon. He has described to me how he works. He sets about thinking and researching one thing at a time (sometimes for a week or fortnight). He rises about seven, has his breakfast of bread and butter, then takes a walk meditating until ten. In the afternoon he writes down his thoughts.

. . .

My friend Mr George Ent, who is still in Paris, writes to say he might have found a suitable French-speaking boy servant for me named Robert, to replace the one I brought back from Paris myself, who is no good. He will send me a copy of Andrea Palladio's *I quattro libri dell'architettura* (*The Four Books of Architecture*), which was first published in Venice in 1570, as soon as he can. Book I was published in English last year.

. . .

I have made a survey of Avebury with a plane table (helped exceedingly by my neighbour Sir James Long). The plane table provides a solid, level surface on which to make drawings.

. . .

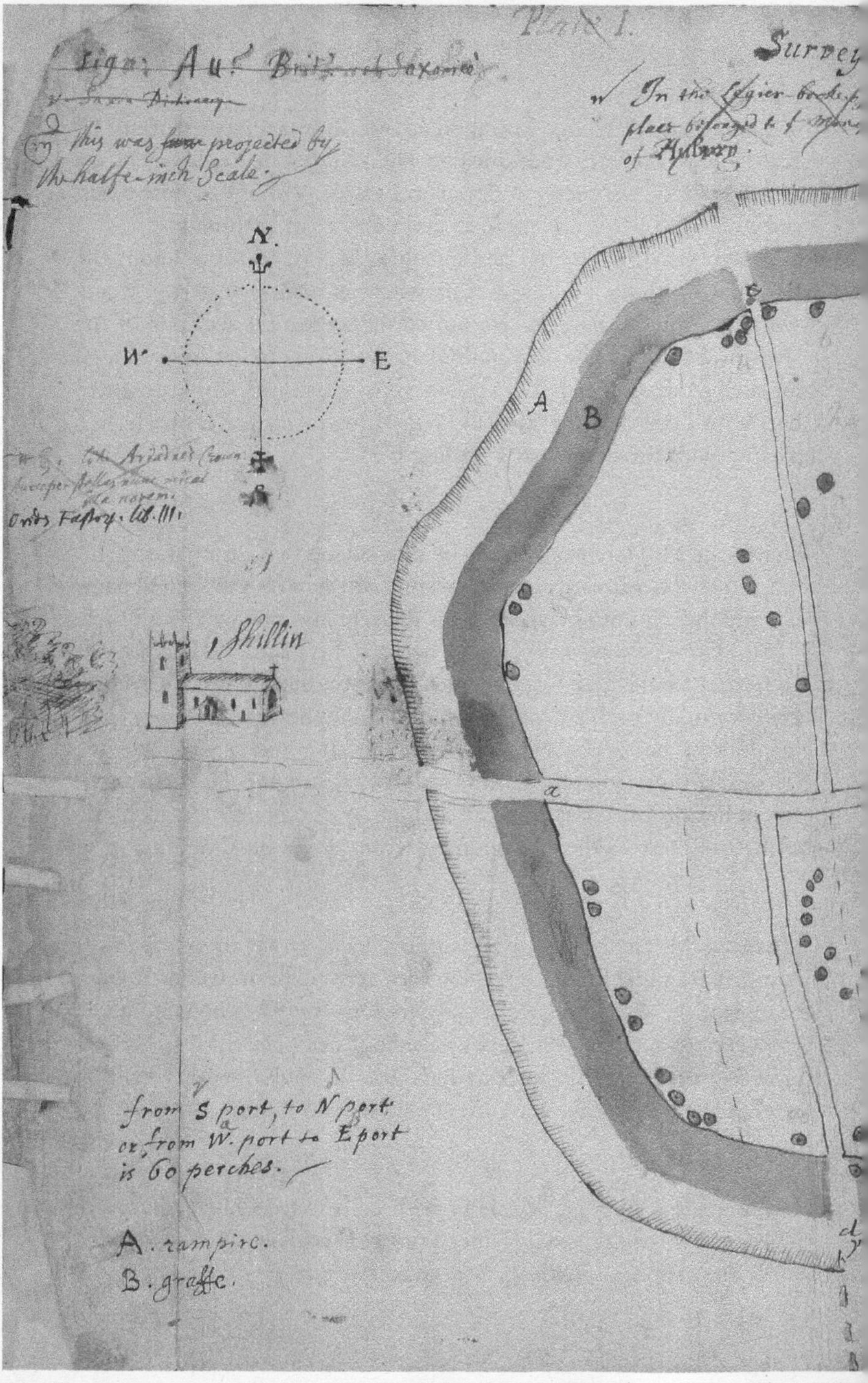

Figu: Aul. Brit: ... Saxonicæ

... this was ... projected by
the halfe-inch Scale.

Plate I.

In the elder bookes
place belonged to ... of Hulborn.

N.

W — E

S

Ovid: Fastor: lib. III.

Shillin

A
B

a

from S port, to N port
or from W. port to E port
is 60 perches.

A. rampire.
B. graffe.

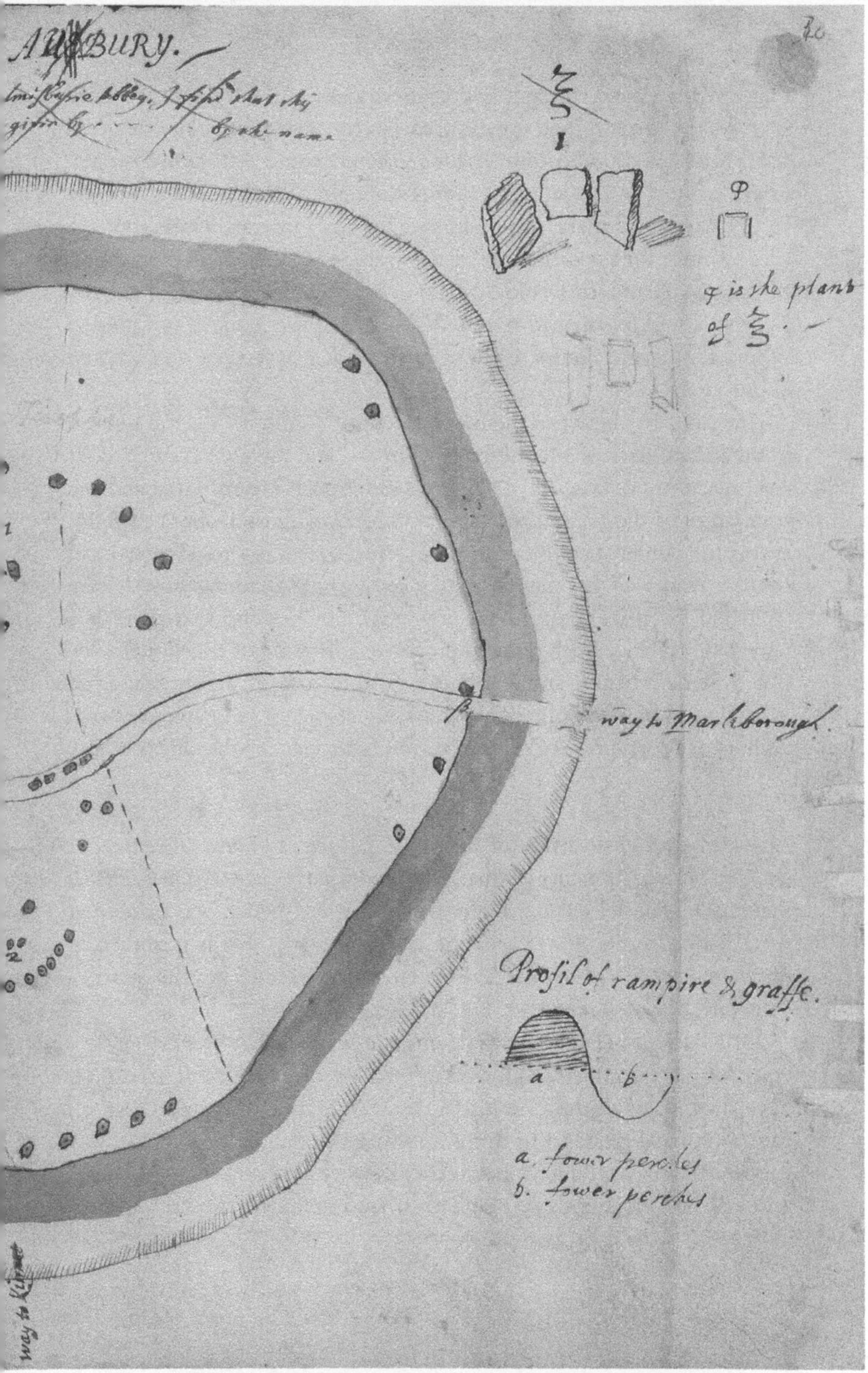

AVEBURY.

this fabric holloy, & hold that his
gifts by ... broke name.

N / S
l

$\frac{N}{S}$ is the plant
of $\frac{N}{S}$.

way to Marlborough

Profil of rampire & graffe.

a .... b

a. fower perches
b. fower perches

way to Kinnet

I have written upon the spot about the stones at Avebury, because there is no way to retrieve their meaning except through comparative antiquities. History is good however made (*Historia quoquo modo facta bona est*). I have written, as I rode, at a gallop. I hope the faithfulness and novelty of my words will make some amends for any incorrectness in style.

The hinge for my discourse on Avebury is Mr Camden's description of Kerrig y Druid (or Druid-Stones) in his *Britannia*, published in 1586. I wish I could journey to north Wales to see the stones Mr Camden writes about, and compare them with what I have seen and written about at Avebury.

The similarity between the name 'Avebury' – 'Aubury' (as it is written in the ledger book of Malmesbury Abbey) – and my own 'Aubrey' does not escape my notice. 'Au' or 'Aub' in old French means white and is a translation of the Latin *albus*. The whiteness of the soil about Avebury seems to countenance this etymology. But here in my mind's eye I can see the reader of my diary smiling to himself, thinking how I have stretched the place name to be my own, not heeding that there is a letter's difference, which quite alters the signification of the words. I see my reader's scornful smile. I must obviate it with arguments from etymology. I hope no one could think me so vain! I have a conceit that 'Aubury' is a corruption of Albury (meaning old-bury, or the old borough).

. . .

I have made a close study of Walter Charleton's *Chorea Gigantum, or the Most Famous Antiquity of Great Britain, Vulgarly Called STONE-HENG, Standing on Salisbury Plain, Restored to the Danes*, which was printed at the Anchor in the New Exchange last year (1663). He is mistaken in his claim that the stones are 'unhewen as they came from the quarry'. They are hewn!

Mr Charleton claims that Stonehenge was built by the Danes as a court of election. He imagines that persons of honourable condition gave their votes in the election of their king, standing in a circle on the columns of stones. But this is a monstrous height for the grandees to stand! They would have needed to be very sober, have good heads, and not be vertiginous to stand on those upended stones! I cannot believe Mr Charleton is right.

. . .

I went back to Stanton Drew to see the stone monument there that I knew as a child. The stones stand in plough land. The corn was ripe and ready for harvest at this time of year, so I could not measure the stones properly as I wished. The villagers break them with sledges because they encumber their fertile land. The stones have been diminishing fast these past few years. I must stop this if I can.

The diameter of the stone circle is about ninety paces. I could not find any trench surrounding it, as at Avebury and Stonehenge.

. . .

Southward from Avebury, in the ploughed field near Kynnet, stand three huge upright stones perpendicularly, like the stones at Avebury. They are called the Devil's Coytes.

. . .

I have been to visit Mr Thomas Bushell at his house in Lambeth. He is about seventy now, but looks hardly sixty and is still a handsome proper gentleman. He has a perfect healthy constitution: fresh, ruddy face and hawk nose. He is a temperate man. He always had the art of running in debt, but money troubles oppress him now. He has never been repaid for the money he spent in the King's cause during our late wars, and he has been in flight from his creditors ever since.

How well I remember my visit to his grotto at Enstone in 1643. I hear the Earl of Rochester has the statue of Neptune that used to be there now, and that he looks after it very well. I should ask old Jack Sydenham, who was once Mr Bushell's servant, for the collection of remarks of several parts of England that Mr Bushell prepared. They may help my own collection.

. . .

6 November

The weather today has been terrible: very stormy.

I missed seeing my friend Mr Tyndale, who has been in London these past few days. He did not realise I was here until the day before he had to leave, and I was remiss in not contacting him. He had letters and a box to deliver to me, which he wishes me to pass on to his sister.

. . .

December

This Christmas I have seen again at Wilton, in Mr Hinton's private garden, blossoms on the thorn bush that he grew from a bud of the Glastonbury Thorn, before it was cut down and burnt by Parliamentarian soldiers in the civil war.

Men say that the Glastonbury Thorn grew when Joseph of Arimathea visited Glastonbury with the Holy Grail and thrust his staff into Wearyall Hill. The tree flowered twice a year: in winter as well as in spring. Before it was destroyed, one of its budding branches was sent to the monarch each Christmas.

The bush in Mr Hinton's garden gives out enough blossoms to fill a flowerpot, and I have sent some to my mother as a present. In this small way I keep memory of the ancient custom alive.

. . .

Monday after Christmas

My horse almost killed me, and I have lacerated my testicle, which is likely to be fatal! My stammer has been terrible since.

. . .

My testicle is healing.

. . .

The widow of the Oxford mathematical instrument maker, Christopher Brookes, has given me a copy of the pamphlet he printed in 1649, 'A new quadrant of more natural ease and manifold performance than any other heretofore extant'.

. . .

Anno 1665

Candlemas Eve

Looking on a serene sky this evening, I suddenly noticed a nubecula, much brighter than any part of the *via lacteal*, and about five times as big as Sirius. I shall show it to my neighbour Sir James Long tomorrow night. When the moon shines not too bright, it is very easily seen. It lies almost in the right line, between the bright star of the little dog and the constellation of Cancer.

. . .

15 February
Mr Samuel Pepys, proposed at the last meeting, was unanimously elected and admitted as a Fellow of the Royal Society today.

. . .

March
Sir John Hoskyns has been offered some three or four of the late Mr William Dobson's paintings for sale by Mr Gander, which he knows I might be interested in buying. One of them is of the clerk of the Oxford Parliament, good, but somewhat defaced. He says if I will pay 10 li. the portraits can be reserved for me until I go and see them and agree a price, or else have my deposit returned.

. . .

The poet Sir John Denham has married for the second time. His wife, Margaret Brookes, is a beautiful young lady, but Sir John is ancient and limping.

. . .

4 March
On this day England declared war on the Netherlands. The cause is mercantile competition.

. . .

June
I have been to see young Lord Rochester, currently imprisoned in the Tower, for attempting to abduct the heiress Elizabeth Malet. Sometimes his actions are extravagant, but he is generally civil enough. He reads all manner of books and is a wonderful satirist.

. . .

The Royal Society has suspended its Wednesday meetings because so many members have left London fearful of the plague.

. . .

August

Mr Wenceslaus Hollar has now finished engraving the portrait of Mr Hobbes I lent him. He has shown it to some of his acquaintances, and it is a very good likeness. The printer demurs at taking it, so Mr Hollar feels all his labour lies dead within him, but he has made a dozen copies for me.

. . .

There is plague in London.

In Mr Camden's *Britannia* there is a remarkable astrological observation, namely, that when Saturn is in Capricornus, a great plague is a certainty in London. Mr Camden, who died in 1623, observed this in his own time, as had others before him. This year, 1665, Saturn is so positioned, as it was during the London plague of 1625.

. . .

November

I have made my first address to Joan Sumner, whom I hope I shall marry and thereby rescue my finances. She is thirty years old and comes from a family of clothiers who live near mine, at Sutton Benger and Seend, which are both close to Kington St Michael.

. . .

Anno 1666

I am at Seend. I came here for the revel and to wait on Joan Sumner, hoping for marriage: our alliance will bring me the money I need to rescue my finances and her family will be glad of a connection to mine. Meanwhile, I have discovered chalybeate waters in her brother's well: heavily impregnated with iron ore, and potentially of great medicinal value (more so, I suspect, even than the waters at Bath, which is only about ten miles away).

I discovered the waters when I was taking the air this afternoon, around 3 p.m. It had been raining all morning, until about 12 or 1 o'clock, so the sand had been washed away from the ore. By 3 p.m. the sun was out and I was surprised to see so many spangles in the light reflected by the clean ore. I examined some of the stones and went to talk to the smith in the town (George Newton), an ingenious man and clock-maker, who tells me he has melted some of this ore in his forge.

I sent my servant Robert Wiseman to Devizes for some powder of galles and when I infused a little in the ore-rich water, it immediately became as black as ink – so black that I could write visible letters with it. I have also tried evaporating it and it yields a sediment that is umber-like.

I have instructed my servant, ingenious Robert Wiseman, to try water from all the wells in the village with powder of galles.

. . .

Joan told me the story today of a poor pregnant woman who drowned herself in the River Avon. The body was brought into the church at Sutton Benger, where Joan saw it and noticed it seemed to be producing a cold sweat. She wiped the sweat away several times and pressed to have the body cut open to find out if the child was still alive inside.

. . .

Joan has given me a recipe to stop dogs barking which, she tells me, thieves used to use. It involves mixing boar's fat and cumin seeds in a horn.

. . .

March

I am at Easton Pierse. I have finished transcribing Mr Pell's *Idea of Mathematics* and will send it to Mr Boyle, who has been waiting for it. I have been so long perplexed with the unpleasant affairs of this earthen world that I have not been able to give as much time as I would like to the life of the mind. Mr Boyle has been expecting discoveries and fine things from me, but for now he will be sorely disappointed.

In about a month, I hope to send him observations of my mysterious Turkey, or turquoise, ring, along with some other rustic observations I have been collecting. My collections are various. I do not disdain to learn from ignorant old women.

. . .

Meetings of the Royal Society at Gresham College had ceased until recently on account of the plague sweeping over London, but they have been resumed.

. . .

April

I have taken out a licence at Salisbury for my marriage to Joan.

. . .

Mr Faithorne is drawing my portrait in graphite and chalk. I cannot say if it makes me look younger than my forty years, but my clothes at least are elegant.

. . .

My good friend and fellow antiquary Mr Elias Ashmole has at last finished cataloguing the Bodleian Library's collection of Roman coins – a very laborious task, which he began in 1658 at the request of the Bodleian librarian Mr Thomas Barlowe.

. . .

I have shown my mysterious ring to Mr Boyle and told him how I have observed over many months that the cloudy spots in the stone move very slowly from one side to the other. He asked if he could borrow the ring so he can observe it himself. I readily assented. A young man in his employment will make careful drawings of the spots in the ring every two or three weeks. Afterwards it will be possible to compare the drawings and indisputably observe the motion of the spots. Mr Boyle says he has heard that a turquoise stone may lose its lustre upon the sickness or death of the person that wears it. He is reluctant to admit strange things as truth, but not forward in rejecting them as possibilities.

I promised Mr Boyle that I would make careful observations of another stone, an agate, which belongs to a friend of mine. The agate has a cloudy spot in it that seems to move from one side to another. Mr Boyle is collecting observations of this kind.

. . .

All my business and affairs are suddenly running kim kam! There are treacheries and enmities in abundance against me. Joan Sumner is now claiming that she never agreed to marry me. She complains that I have claimed to be richer than I am and accuses me of concealing the fact that there is a mortgage on my house at Easton Pierse. My mother and I had hoped to borrow 100 li. from her, but that will not be possible now, and who knows what worse will befall. Joan says she will pursue me through the courts. She imagines I have conspired to defraud her of her dowry. But I was willing to settle my beloved Easton Pierse on her and any sons we might have brought into the world. She was to bring 2,000 li. as her portion to the marriage. Our settlement was sealed and I sincerely expected our marriage to be solemnised soon after.

. . .

May
General Monck, now General at Sea, has set sail against the Dutch.

. . .

September
Fire has blazed in London for four days: the part of the city inside the old Roman wall is charred and ruined. Fortunately, the Great Conflagration did not reach Westminster or the King's palace in Whitehall, but thousands of people have lost their homes. They roam the streets like beggars.

. . .

October
Mr Hobbes is disturbed because he has learnt that some of the bishops have moved in Parliament to have him burnt as a heretic. He tells me he has burnt some of his papers.

The Parliamentary Committee is considering a 'Bill against Atheism Prophaneness and Swearing'. It has been empowered to consider books that tend against the 'Essence or Attributes of God', and in particular Mr Hobbes's *Leviathan*.

. . .

November
Following the Great Conflagration, the City of London must be rebuilt. Mr Hooke has been chosen as one of the two surveyors of the City. The other is the glass painter Mr John Oliver. Since the Guild Hall is in ruins from the fire, the city's officials and clerks have moved to Gresham College. This means the Royal Society can no longer meet at Gresham College every Wednesday. We will meet instead at Arundel House in the Strand, the home of Lord Henry Howard.

. . .

At a meeting of the Royal Society, Mr Oldenburg, Lord Henry Howard and others reported on their visits to the ruins of St Paul's to see the preserved body of Bishop Braybrook, the Bishop of London, who died in 1404. The Bishop's body, like many others, has been disturbed by the Great Conflagration: when the roof of St Paul's fell in, the lead coffins below fell through the floor and broke open. Workmen clearing the rubble have put the bodies in the Convocation House and are charging people twopence a person to view them. I will go myself.

. . .

I saw Bishop Braybrook's body. It was like a preserved fish: uncorrupted except for the ears and pudenda, or genitals. It was dry and stiff and would stand on end. It was never embalmed. His belly and stomach were untouched, except for a hole on one side made by the falling debris. I could put my hand in the hole and could see his dried lungs.

I could not find Sir Philip Sidney's body. It was buried somewhere without regard and his coffin sold for rubbish.

. . .

I spoke to some of the labourers clearing the rubbish in St Faith's Church, which was ruined by the collapse of St Paul's. They tell me that when they took up the leaden coffin of William Herbert, Earl of Pembroke, whose sumptuous monument was among those tumbled into the church, the stink was so great that they took a week to scour themselves of it.

. . .

A little before the Great Conflagration, somebody made a hole in the lead coffin of Dean Colet, which lay above the ground beneath his statue. I remember my friend Mr Wylde and Ralph Greatrex, the mathematical instrument maker, decided to probe the Dean's body through the hole with a piece of iron curtain rod that happened to be near by. They found the body lay in liquor, like boiled brawn. The liquor was clear and insipid: they both tasted it. Mr Wylde said it had something of the taste of iron, but that might have been on account of the iron rod. This was a strange and rare way of conserving a corpse. Perhaps it was a pickle, as for beef. There was no ill smell.

. . .

At a meeting of the Royal Society I volunteered to recommend the observation of tides to the Deputy Governor of Chepstow in Monmouthshire. The Society's secretary will procure the printed papers with the relevant enquiries and tables. Sir Robert Moray then proposed that directions for seamen and enquiries about tides be separately printed, and the instruments mentioned in the printed papers be made available, at the Society's expense. He hopes to obtain an order from the Duke of York to Trinity House, which has care of maintaining lighthouses and other aids to navigation in British waters, to ensure that the captain of every ship takes with him on his voyages a copy of this book, and makes observations accordingly and notes them down in a journal. Upon return, a copy of the captain's journal should be given to Trinity House and to the Royal Society. The Fellows approved these proposals.

Mr Hoskyns then suggested that it would be a good idea to include in the printed book an instruction to the captain to fetch up different sorts of earth from the bottom of the sea. Mr Hooke is considering the design of an instrument that would be easy to use for this purpose.

Lord Henry Howard intends to bring before the Royal Society his account of the management of agriculture in Surrey and Berkshire.

. . .

14 November
I have been chosen by ballot (along with four other Fellows) to serve on the committee that examines and audits the Royal Society's accounts. The others are Dr Christopher Merret, Mr William Harrington, Dr Walter Pope and Mr John King. We meet next Wednesday at Dr Pope's lodgings before the next meeting of the Society.

. . .

Blood has been moved between two dogs for the first time. Before the Society, Mr King and Mr Thomas Coxe successfully performed the experiment on a small bulldog and a spaniel. The bulldog bled to death as its blood was transferred into the spaniel, which emitted as much of its own blood as was needed to make room for that of the bulldog.

No one takes any notice now of the fact that Mr Potter first thought of moving blood between animals. He and I tried it on chickens sixteen years ago: if only we had succeeded.

. . .

The band of my turquoise ring has broken. I fear that if I have the stone set again, the heat will destroy its peculiarity. I have told Mr Boyle I am unwilling to have it meddled with.

. . .

21 November

Today at the Royal Society I was given the printed enquiries (from nos. 17 and 18 of the *Philosophical Transactions*) on the observations of tides, which I will now take to the Deputy Governor of Chepstow.

In the Great Conflagration, all the unsold copies of the *Philosophical Transactions* were burnt in St Faith's Church, near St Paul's, where they were being stored. The booksellers in St Paul's Churchyard lost their stock of books too. After the fire, volume no. 17 of the *Philosophical Transactions* was printed free of charge, and no. 18 was printed in Duck Lane.

At the meeting today, I was also given a grain of wheat, taken from a batch produced in Surrey, said to shoot up like a rush, not a hollow straw. I am one of five Fellows involved in this plant trial. We will all plant our grains of wheat and compare our results.

. . .

30 November

At the Royal Society's anniversary election meeting, we presented our report as examiners of the Society's accounts.

My lord Brouncker, Mr Wylde, Dr Charleton and I rode in a coach together on our way to the meeting at Gresham College. At the corner of Holborn Bridge, we saw a cellar of coals that had been opened by the labourers (who are digging the rubbish and new foundations of the city). The coals were burning and had been burning ever since the Great Conflagration.

. . .

Anno 1667

January

Lady Denham died on the 6th of this month; it is rumoured that she was murdered by means of poison in her cup of chocolate. After her marriage to Sir John two years ago, the Duke of York fell deeply in love with her, which occasioned a distemper of madness in Sir John. This madness first appeared when he went from London to see the famous freestone quarries at Portland in Dorset, but when he got within a mile of his destination, turned back to London again and he did not see them. He went to Hounslow and demanded rents of lands he had sold years ago. He went to the King and told him he was the Holy Ghost. There are others at court who might have poisoned Lady Denham's drinking chocolate. Some think the Duchess of York did it out of jealousy, but others think it was the Countess of Rochester. Lady Denham had no children.

. . .

March

My friend Edward Davenant has written to tell me that he has now given up his mathematical studies because his age is calling him to serious thoughts of another world. He is seventy-one this year. I am hoping to get him to print his work, lest it be lost, and have introduced him to John Collins of the Royal Society who may help him in this.

. . .

Since the Great Conflagration last year, all the ruins in London are overgrown with herbs, especially one with a yellow flower. On the south side of St Paul's Church it grew as thick as could be, even on the very top of the tower. The herbalists call it *Ericolevis Neapolitana*: small bank cresses of Naples.

Many Roman remains have been discovered among the ruins of London. Christopher Wren, digging deep to lay the foundation of Bow church tower, came to the Roman way which now lies nineteen feet under Cheapside: they know it to be the Roman way by the gravel mixed with Roman brick-bats and potsherds and baked earth such as urns. Dr Wren believes it firm enough to act as the foundation of the tower.

. . .

June

At the Royal Society, before a large audience, we tested bottles of
water I had carried up from Seend. It did not turn black, after so long
a journey, but went a deep dark claret colour. The physicians present
were all wonderfully surprised and urged me to recommend the water
to the doctors of Bath. They think that in the treatment of some
ailments, it would be better to begin with the waters at Seend and
end with those of Bath (and in other cases vice versa).

. . .

I have written to several doctors in Bath, but to no purpose. I have
now discovered that what the London doctors told me is true: the
Bath doctors are in agreement about the quality of the Seend water,
but they do not care to have their customers leave Bath. I shall make
known the discovery myself by inserting it into Mr William Lilly's
almanac.

. . .

Joan Sumner's brother John tells me floods of people have started
coming to Seend to take the waters I discovered there. The village
cannot accommodate them all, so there are plans to build new guest-
houses before next summer. Sumner (whose well is the best) hopes
the trade will be worth 200 li. per annum to him.

My discovery has been mentioned by Dr Nehemiah Grew in his
History of the Repository of the Royal Society. There is iron ore in
the water, which was not noticed before.

. . .

31 July

On this day the Treaty of Breda has secured peace between England
and the Netherlands.

. . .

I have promised my old friend Mr Hobbes that I will publish his life:
nobody else knows so many particulars of his life as I do. I have known
him since I was eight years old. If it please God that I prosper in the

world, I will arrange for an exact map of Malmesbury, showing the place of Mr Hobbes's birth. I would have Mr Hollar draw a map of the town with the names of the rivers that embrace it – the Avon and Newnton Water – together with the prospect, the abbey church and King Athelstan's monument. In the abbey church, where the choir was, now grass grows, where anciently were buried kings and great men.

. . .

August

In Oxford, I browsed the booksellers' stalls, including Edward Forest's, opposite All Souls College. Afterwards I met Anthony Wood: the younger brother of my deceased Trinity College friend Ned Wood. We drank at Mother Web's and in the Mermaid Tavern, where Mr Wood spent 3s. 8d. He aims to be a despiser of riches, to live independently and frugally, and not to be afraid to die. His income is around 40 li. per annum. He supplements this by cataloguing libraries and occasionally selling a manuscript. He is at work on an historical survey of the city of Oxford, including its university, colleges, monasteries and parish churches. I offered to assist him with his researches.

We talked of Mr Hobbes, my honoured friend, whose life I have promised to write. And we talked of poor Ned. It is already twelve years since he died of consumption: he was a promising scholar and had been elected a proctor of the University just weeks before his death. His brother is lastingly proud of the fact that Ned was freely elected, not imposed on the University by the Parliamentarian Visitor. He has edited five of Ned's sermons.

Mr Wood was in the Bodleian quad last year when, by order of the King, John Milton's works were burnt because they defended the execution of the late King. Mr Wood tells me he saw scholars of all degrees and qualities standing around the flames and humming while the books were burning.

He recently met and became friends with Mr William Dugdale, at work in the records in the Tower of London, gathering material for a third volume of his *Monasticon*. Mr Wood has promised to send Mr Dugdale documents to help him.

This summer, Mr Wood has been perusing the rent rolls, etc. in

Christ Church treasury. He says there are many evidences there that belonged to Osney Abbey and innumerable writings and rolls which belonged to the priories and nunneries that Cardinal Wolsey dissolved when he set about founding his college in Oxford. But the Cardinal died before the task was completed, so the lands of the dissolved religious houses came under the King's protection. He gave much away before the college was finally settled three years later in 1532; and for this reason, Christ Church cares little for those ancient documents that lie around in the damp and at the mercy of the rats. I will share with Mr Wood my own notes on the history of Christ Church, Trinity College and Osney Abbey.

I do not remember such hot weather as we have had this summer. Mr Wood says Oxford saw no rain from 30 June to 27 July, and none after that until 9 August. Several scholars have gone mad with heat and strong drink.

. . .

November

I have received a letter from Mr Wood in Oxford, asking me for details of Dr John Hoskyns's time at New College – his birth, death, burial and the books he wrote – and for some details of other Oxford men including John Owen, the epigrammatist, and Sir Kenelm Digby. But I am leaving for London and am too plagued by my lawsuit to reply.

. . .

December

At a meeting of the Royal Society today, I was delighted to present Mr Francis Potter's device for measuring time through an air-strainer. Mr Potter's clock is powered by bellows, not cogs. Mr Hooke has been asked to consider and comment on it at a subsequent meeting. Mr Wylde said he had heard of a similar approach to measuring time (from Sir Edward Lake, via Mr Smethwick). We are both to present the Society with descriptions of these instruments.

. . .

12 December

Today, before the Royal Society, Mr Hooke reported on the method for measuring time through air that Mr Wylde and I introduced at the last meeting. He said that though the invention is ingenious and new, it will not be suitable for pocket watches, nor as accurate and useful as the pendulum. The obstacle, in his view, is the unevenness of air, caused by the various degrees of its rarefaction and condensation, as well as its dryness and moisture.

. . .

I was arrested in Chancery Lane at Mrs Joan Sumner's suit. I have been released, but there will be a trial at Sarum between us this coming year. How much I regret that I ever involved myself with that woman. I hoped she would restore my finances, but now she seems likely to ruin me.

. . .

Anno 1668

January

I am at last within reach of leisure to assist Mr Wood. I will leave Broad Chalke and go to Oxford as soon as I can.

. . .

In Oxford, I have spent the evening with Mr Wood at the Crown Tavern. My French servant Robert Wiseman (Robinet Prudhomme) lit Mr Wood's way home and was extravagantly rewarded with sixpence.

. . .

24 February

Early this morning my trial against Joan Sumner was heard at Sarum. I won and was awarded 600 li. damages, though there was devilish opposition against me. I fear this will not be the end of the matter, as Joan seems intent upon continuing to pursue me through the courts. I have discovered that I am not the only man she has treated thus. On 10 July 1665, a few months before I made my first address to her in an ill hour, there was a marriage licence taken out at Salisbury between Joan and one Samuel Gayford.

. . .

7 April

I read a paper on Wiltshire springs to the Royal Society.

9 April

I went today to Sir William Davenant the Poet Laureate's funeral. He died two days ago. Mr Hobbes knew him well and they were in France together during the late wars. He wrote more than twenty plays, besides his *Gondibert* and *Madagascar*. His coffin was of walnut wood: Sir John Denham declared it the finest he has ever seen. Davenant's body was carried in a hearse from the playhouse to Westminster Abbey, where he was received at the great West Door by the choir and choristers, who sang the church service: 'I am the Resurrection', etc. His grave is in the south cross aisle and on it is written (in imitation of Ben Jonson): 'O rare Sir Will. Davenant.'

When Sir William Davenant became Poet Laureate in 1638, after Ben Jonson's death in 1637, Thomas May was also a candidate.

Thomas May translated the poet Lucan's *Pharsalia* (1626), which made him in love with the Roman republic. The odour stuck to him. His *Breverie of the History of the Parliament of England* was printed in 1650, the year he died from choking when tying his cap. Thomas May compared the Long Parliament to the history of Rome, even while admitting that the affairs of Rome were of such transcendent greatness that they admit of no comparison to states before or after. My friend Edmund Wylde knew Thomas May when he was young, and says he was thoroughly debauched, but I do not by any means take notice of this, for we have all been young. I must find out where his monument is.

. . .

I have seen Mr Hobbes. He is writing a tract on the law of heresy.

. . .

The Council of the Royal Society has licensed the printing of John Wilkins's *Essay towards a Real Character and a Philosophical Language.*

. . .

23 April

Today I brought before the Royal Society some mineral water from Milson in Wiltshire. Despite being carried eighty miles or so, the water kept its strength so well that when a little powder of galles was added to it and stirred in, the water became a dark red colour. The remainder of the water has been sent to Mr Merret for further examination.

. . .

I have decided to make a map of the remains of the Roman camps in Britain. Lord Bacon urged active men to become writers and after all the travelling that I have done on horseback through Wiltshire and south Wales, I am sure I can consider myself an active observer whose inspections of ancient monuments must be worth writing down. When I ride through the downs and see the numerous barrows – those beds of honour where now so many heroes lie buried in oblivion – they speak to me of the death and slaughter that once raged upon this soil, where so many thousands fell in terrible battles. I will trace the route the victorious Roman eagle took through ancient Britain and map the sites of those Imperial camps, now given over to sheep and the plough.

. . .

27 April
Exploring the sky with a telescope I noticed a cloudy star, which appeared to be about the size of Venus and resembled a dim planet, lying in a right line and near the midway between Cancer and the Head of Hydra.

. . .

May
The Royal Society has established a committee to examine, consider and report on Mr Wilkins's *Essay Towards a Real Character and a Philosophical Language*, published this year. A Real Character, as opposed to a notional, nominal or verbal one, has a shape that embodies the structure of the language, lexically, grammatically, or both. Mr Wilkins is developing ideas about Real Characters in Lord Bacon's *Of the Advancement and Proficience of Learning*, which was translated from Latin into English in 1640.

. . .

When I was a boy, I used to hear from my grandmother the story of how Queen Elizabeth loved my great-grandfather, Dr William Aubrey, even though he voted against the execution of Mary, Queen of Scots.

Mr Wood has asked me to help him by consulting Thuanus's *Annals* for honourable mention of my great-grandfather Dr William Aubrey, who is also mentioned in the Life of Mary, Queen of Scots. Thuanus was a president of the Parlement of Paris and the author of a history of his own times from 1546 to 1608.

. . .

I have a mind to make a kind of pilgrimage this summer to see some Druidish monuments in Caernarvonshire, and will go via Weston on my way. The Royal Society has requested that Mr Wood make a list of all the treatises that Lord Bacon wrote.

I have been told that in the library of the Royal Society there is a book that would be of help to Mr Wood in compiling his history of Oxford, it being a collection of several writers of both universities and of the nation.

. . .

6 July
By malicious contrivance I was arrested today, in connection with my proposed marriage to Mrs Joan Sumner, but was retained for less than two hours. I was meant to go to Winton for a retrial tomorrow, but the date has been put back now.

. . .

My servant Robert hopes to get employment in Oxford: it is the place he loves and he hopes to make a better livelihood there than I can now offer him in my straitened and beleaguered circumstances. I hope Mr Wood will help him when opportunity arises.

. . .

My lawsuit continues, to my great dismay and financial ruin.

I am collecting my letters from The Lamb in Katherine Street in Salisbury.

. . .

I have been to see the Coway Stakes in the Thames, opposite Cowe-way, on the right bank of the river between Sunbury and Shepperton. It is said this is the place where Julius Caesar crossed the river. According to the local people, three of the stakes are visible on a clear day when the water is low. Venerable Bede says the stakes could be seen in his day (at least 500 years ago). The fishermen still avoid casting their nets here. But this summer the Lord Mayor's Water Ballif had one of the stakes taken up because it hindered the barges and was likely to split them. If I can I will ask the Water Ballif for a sight of this antiquity.

. . .

November

As soon as my lawsuit will give me leave, I will lengthen my life a little by reviving my spirit in Oxford. Joan Sumner is an unusually litigious woman: she insists I intended to defraud her and is demanding a retrial, but my defence is that I was sincerely prepared to marry her and still am, despite all the legal troubles she has brought down upon my head.

. . .

The great poet Dr Abraham Cowley died at the end of July last year (1667). His will is a testament to true and lasting charity. He has settled his estate so that so much every year is to be paid for poor prisoners cast into gaol by cruel creditors for some debt or other. I have been told this by Mr Dunning of London, a scrivener who is acquainted with Dr Cowley's brother. I do not think this benefaction is mentioned in the Life of Cowley that has been printed along with his collected works this year. It is certainly the best method of charity.

Sir John Denham has written some excellent verses on the death of Abraham Cowley (which prove that Sir John has fully recovered his wits since the fit of madness that overcame him before his wife died):

> His fancy and his judgement such,
> Each to the other seemed too much:
> His severe judgement giving law,
> His modest fancy kept in awe;
> As rigid husbands jealous are,
> When they believe their wives too fair.

. . .

Anno 1669

25 January

St Paul's Day: I hope Mr Wenceslaus Hollar will make more etchings of my several prospects of Osney Abbey. I fear that the one he made for Mr Dugdale's book might have melted in the Great Conflagration. Mr Hollar is expected back in England around Candlemas. He has gone on a journey to Tangier with Lord Henry Howard, grandson of the Earl of Arundel, to negotiate with Moulay Al Rashid, the Moroccan Sultan. Mr Hollar, who is His Majesty's Designer, will make drawings to show the King what his most remote colony looks like.

. . .

If Mr Wood needs any records at Rome searched, I think I can arrange this for him through the Jesuits I met in Paris. One of them has suggested to me that Mr Wood should first print his book in English, not Latin, because it will become more famous and sell better that way.

. . .

18 February

I brought my drawing of the cloudy star I discovered last year before the Royal Society and it was entered into the Register Book.

. . .

5 March

Early this morning, between eight and nine o'clock, my retrial was heard at Winton. With much ado I got a verdict of damages of 300 li. in my favour. This is half the amount I was awarded in my first trial at Sarum, but it is still something to set against what I must now pay my lawyer.

. . .

23 March

Sir John Denham was buried today in Westminster Abbey, in the south cross aisle, near Sir Geoffrey Chaucer's monument.

. . .

Because of my financial troubles, I am in as much affliction as a mortal can be, and it seems I will never be at peace until all has been lost and I wholly cast myself on God's Providence.

. . .

29 April

Today, I brought before the Royal Society Mr Potter's account of his experiments in moving blood between animals, which he wrote in 1652, to try and establish that he was the first to attempt this experiment. I helped him with an experiment to move blood between chickens as early as 1649.

. . .

In Mr Samuel Cooper's studio, which I visited today, I had an interesting conversation with Dr Hugh Crescy of Merton College, a great acquaintance of Lord Lucius Cary, Viscount Falkland. Dr Crescy says he was the first to bring Socinus's books into England, and Lord Cary borrowed them from him soon afterwards. Before the civil war, Lord Cary lived at Tew, about twelve miles from Oxford, and the best wits of the University visited him there, so his house, in that peaceable time, was like a college, full of learned men, including my great friend Mr Hobbes. I have heard Mr Hobbes say that Lord Cary was like a lusty fighting fellow that drove his enemies before him, but would often give his own party smart back-blows.

Lord Cary adhered to the King when the civil wars began, and after the Battle of Edgehill he became Principal Secretary of State, together with Sir Edward Nicholas. Lord Cary died in 1643 at the Battle of Newbury, where he rode in between the two armies – the Parliament's army and the King's – like a madman, just as they were starting to engage. And so he threw his life away. Some say this was because he had given the King bad advice, but others say it was because his mistress at court, whom he loved above all creatures, had recently died, and this was the secret cause of him being so madly guilty of his own death.

. . .

June

I have sent Mr Edward Davenant Euclid's *Data*. Lately he has been working very hard at mathematics, especially on the problem of the doubling of the cube geometrically. But now he tells me he is so oppressed by other business that he has little time to think about mathematics.

. . .

July
Mr Wood has quarrelled with his sister-in-law and been thrown out of the house where he was born opposite Merton College. He is also slowly becoming deaf, which makes him more melancholy and retired than ever.

. . .

August
I have now but one horse fit to be ridden, otherwise I would send one to Oxford for Mr Wood so that he might come to stay with me in Wiltshire.

. . .

September
The work of making the River Avon navigable from Salisbury to Christ Church has commenced. Seth Ward, Bishop of Salisbury, dug the first spit of earth, and pushed the first wheelbarrow. His lordship has given at least a hundred pounds of his own money to finance the digging.

. . .

Seth Ward tells me that at Silchester in Hampshire, which was once a Roman city, it is possible to discern in the ground where corn is now grown signs of the old streets, passages and hearths. He saw this with Dr Wilkins (now Bishop of Chester) in the spring.

. . .

This searching after antiquities is a wearisome business, yet nobody else will do it.

. . .

At Bemarton, near Salisbury, is a paper mill, which is now over a hundred years old, and the first that was erected in the county of Wiltshire. The workmen there told me it was the second paper mill in England. I remember the paper mill at Longdeane, in the parish of Yatton Keynell, was built by Mr Wyld, a Bristol merchant, in 1635. It supplies Bristol with brown paper. No white paper is made in Wiltshire.

. . .

Mr Wood has been summoned by the Delegates of the University Press and told that they will give him 100 li. for his manuscript of *The History and Antiquities of the University of Oxford*, on the condition that he allows the book to be translated into Latin, under the supervision of Dr Fell, Dean of Christ Church. But I am certain it would bring more fame and sell better in English.

Dr Fell made another (more helpful) suggestion: that Mr Wood should begin to compile short biographies of all the writers and bishops who have attended Oxford University. I would be more than willing to help him in this.

A new idea for a treatise on education has come into my head.

. . .

October

I am in Broad Chalke. Before I left London I left a cloak in the warehouse of the carrier Mr Wood uses. The carrier's wife has since sent me a cloak, but it is a much shorter one, not mine. I hope Mr Wood can speak to the carrier's wife about this for me, but I am sorry to trouble him about so mean a business. I am going to Easton Pierse next week.

. . .

I have heard that my Oxford tutor, Mr William Browne, has died, aged fifty-one or two. About eight years ago he was made vicar of Farnham in Surrey. He died of smallpox, infected by burying a corpse that had died of the disease.

. . .

Anno 1670

January

I have presented the Royal Society with a portrait of Mr Hobbes by Jan Baptist Jaspers: an excellent painter and a good piece.

. . .

February
I was to see Mr James Harrington last Wednesday night, but he proved
unable to meet me. He lives in the Little Ambry in a fair house on
the left side, which looks into the Dean's yard in Westminster. There
is a pretty gallery in the upper storey where he commonly dines,
meditates and takes his tobacco.

I have a short poem by Mr Harrington in his handwriting:

On the State of Nature

The state of Nature never was so raw
But oaks bore acorns and there was a law
By which the spider and the silk worm span;
Each creature had her birth right, & must man
Be illegitimate! Have no child's part!
If reason had no wit, how came in Art?

He is wont to say, 'Right reason in contemplation is virtue in action,
et vice versa. To live according to nature is to live virtuously, but the
Divines will not have it so.' He also says that when the Divines would
have us be an inch above virtue, we fall an ell (an arm's length) below.

Mr Harrington suffers from the strangest sort of madness I have
ever found in anyone. He imagines his perspiration turns to flies, or
sometimes to bees. He has had a movable timber house built in Mr
Hart's garden (opposite St James's Park), to try an experiment to prove
this delusion. He turns the timber structure to face the sun, chases
all the flies and bees out of it, or kills them, then shuts the windows
tight. But inevitably he misses some concealed in crannies of the cloth
hangings and when they show themselves he cries out, 'Do not you
see that these come from me?' Aside from this, his discourse is rational.

. . .

My former servant, Robert, sends word from Rome where he is accompanying his new master, having visited Florence and Pisa and expecting
to proceed to Naples. He tells me that they have seen the great duke's
palace at Pisa, but not the jewels, and that the carnival is not taking
place, as the Cardinals have not yet elected the new Pope. It is one of

my most lasting sorrows that my mother interfered with my plans to visit Italy.

. . .

5 April

Easter Tuesday. I must now take leave of my beloved Easton Pierse, where I first drew breath in my grandfather's chamber. Cruel fate dictates that I cannot afford to keep the house in which I was born, the house that was my mother's inheritance. Four years ago, before my troubles with Joan Sumner began, I had an income of around 700 li. per annum from my estates, and I went around in sparkish garb with a servant and two horses. Now all my estates will soon be sold, my servant is gone, and I live in happy delitescency, free from responsibilities.

. . .

12 April

Today I made sketches of the prospects of Easton Pierse: the trees and the thin blue landscape that surround this house I love. The prospect from Easton Pierse is the best between Marsfield and Burford, and though all along that ridge of hills between those two towns are lovely prospects, none has so many breaks and good ground objects as the prospect from Easton Pierse.

Many of the old ways are lost, but some vestigia are left. Anciently there was a way from the gate at the brook below my house to Yatton Keynell, and another by the pound and manor house, leading northwards to Leigh Delamere and southwards to Allington, but there is no sign of it left now.

I remember how my grandfather told me that back at the beginning of the century, the land from Easton Pierse to Yatton Keynell was common land and the inhabitants of Yatton and Easton put cattle on it equally. Likewise, the land between Kington St Michael and Draycot Cerne was common field, where the plough maintained a world of labouring people. In my time, much has been enclosed, and every year more and more is taken in. Enclosures are for the private, not the public good. After it has been enclosed, a lone shepherd and his dog or a milk-maid can manage the land that used to employ several score labourers when it was worked as ploughed land. Ever since the Reformation, when the enclosures began, these parts have swarmed with poor people.

I have sketched my house at Easton Pierse and marked with a cross my grandfather's chamber where I was born. If it had been my fate to be a wealthy man I would have rebuilt my house in the grandest of styles. I would have added formal gardens in the Italian mode of the kind I have seen at Sir John Danvers's house in Chelsea and at his house in Lavington. It was Sir John who first taught us in England the way of Italian gardens. I would have erected a fountain like the one that I saw in Mr Bushell's grotto at Enstone: Neptune standing on a scallop shell, his trident aimed at a rotating duck, perpetually chased by a spaniel. I would have carved my initials on a low curved bridge across the stream. I would have remade my beloved home in the shape of the most beautiful houses and gardens I have visited in my unsettled life, tumbling up and down in the world. But fate has taken me on a different path and the house of my dreams is mere fantasy: a pretty sketch on paper.

I have collected together my drawings of Easton Pierse, my beloved house and its prospects, and designed a grand title page: Designatio de Easton Piers, by the unfortunate John Aubrey! Alas, I fear I will soon be an exile! I am mindful of Ovid's description of Daedalus, exiled on Crete: *tactusque loci natalis amore* (touched by love for his birthplace). I will make this one of the epigraphs for my book of drawings.

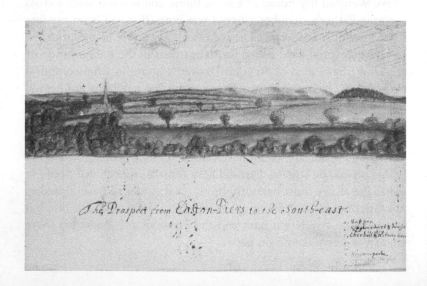

There is smallpox in Taunton again this year.

. . .

May
I saw Mr Wood today in London and told him the news that the Welsh antiquary Percy Enderbie, the author of *Cambria Triumphans*, died recently.

. . .

September
I am at Broad Chalke. I have received the astrological chart of my birth from Mr Thomas Flatman and it reveals no end of trouble. He has made the figure of my nativity and found it agreeing with all the misfortunes of my life. Part of my unhappiness has proceeded from Venus, love, and love affairs, altogether ineffectual so far, together with Saturn in my house of marriage.

. . .

My former servant, Robert, has left a hat and other keepsakes for me with Mr Browning's maidservant. He has other items to present to me when I can pay him for his services.

. . .

As Ovid tells us, families, and also places, have their fatalities: *Fors sua cuiq'loco est* (Ovid, *Fasti*, Lib. iv).

. . .

This year, not far from Cirencester, there came an apparition, which when asked if it be a good spirit or bad, returned no answer, but disappeared with a curious perfume and most melodious twang. My friend Mr William Lilly believes it was a fairy.

. . .

Mr Lodwick, my friend and Mr Hooke's, has sent me an essay he has
written on the Universal Character, which continues the search for
an artificial language he began as a young man when he published *A
Common Writing* (1647) aged just twenty-seven. In his new essay Mr
Lodwick seeks to describe all possible sounds using a new syllabic
notation (vowels are expressed as diacritics). Possible sounds and their
notations are presented in a table that allows certain syllables to be
placed, even if they are not used in a particular language. In this way,
he has invented a way of truly writing what is pronounced, or truly
pronouncing what is written. Mr Lodwick claims his system is
complete, rational and therefore universal. He hopes it will lead to
the construction of a philosophical language.

. . .

November

I think I have now done about three quarters of my perambulation
of Wiltshire. In the spring I hope I can do what remains to be done
in two or three weeks. I must hope to do it invisibly to avoid arrest
for my debts. I feel as though I am working under a divine impulse
to complete this task: nobody else will do it, and when it is done no
one hereabouts will value it: but I hope the next generation will be
less brutish.

I have sought out the Roman, British and Danish camps and the
highways. I have traced Offa's Dyke from Severn to Dee and Wednesdyke
and corrected Mr Camden's *Britannia* in some places, and his claim as
to where Boudicca's last battle was. I surveyed the camps and found
out the places of the battles by the barrows. Sir John Hoskyns and Dr
Ball say this work is the best I have done: but it is dry meat.

Between south Wales and the French sea, I have taken account of
the several kinds of earth and the natural observables in it, and the
nature of the plants, cattle and people living off each respective soil.

When I was a boy, my grandfather used to tell me the story of Mr
Camden's visit to the school at Yatton Keynell in the church there.
Mr Camden took particular notice of a little painted glass window in
the chancel, which has been dammed up with stones ever since I can
remember, presumably to spare the parson the cost of glazing it.

Also in Yatton Keynell, on the west side of the road, where it forms
a 'Y' shape, there is a little close called Stone-edge. From this name,

one might expect a stone monument, but if there was ever one there, time has defaced it. There is a great quarry of freestone nearby, which would be suitable for building such a monument. I am inclined to believe that in most counties of England there are, or have been, ruins of Druid temples.

Mr Samuel Butler told me that Mr Camden much studied the Welsh language and kept a Welsh servant to improve him in that language for the better understanding of our antiquities.

. . .

The Roman architecture flourished in Britain while the Roman government lasted, as appears by history, which makes mention of their stately temples, theatres, baths, etc., and Venerable Bede in his History tells us of a magnificent fountain built by the Romans at Carlisle in Scotland, that was remaining in his time. But time and northern incursions have left us only a few fragments of their grandeur. The excellent Roman architecture degenerated into what we call Gothic by the inundation of the Goths.

The Roman architecture came again into England with the Reformation. The first house then of that kind of building was Somerset House. Longleat in Wiltshire was built by Sir John Thynne, steward to the Duke of Somerset. The next house that I can find about London is the new Exchange, then the Banqueting House at Whitehall, by King James. In the time of King Charles I: Greenwich, Queenstreet, Lincoln Inn Fields. By now it has become the most common fashion.

. . .

30 November
Today I presented the Royal Society with an old printed book in the Ancient British language. It will be added to the Society's library.

. . .

15 December
Today I gave two more books to the Royal Society: *Grammatica Linguae: Cambro-Britanniae*, by Dr Davies; and *Heronis Ctesbii Belopoica: Telefactivia* by Bernardinum Baldum.

I have also presented the Society with a piece of Roman antiquity: a pot that was found in Weekfield, in the parish of Hedington in

Wiltshire in 1656. When it was found it was half full of Roman coins (silver and copper) from the time of Constantine. I explained to the learned Fellows that this was the site of a Roman colony and the foundations of many houses and much coin has been found there.

. . .

Anno 1671

January

Since the Great Conflagration of London, many of the inscriptions in the city's churches are not legible any more, but there is one for Inigo Jones that can still be read notwithstanding the fire. The inscription mentions that he built the banqueting house and portico at St Paul's. Originally, there was a bust of Inigo Jones too, on top of this monument, but Mr Marshall in Fetter Lane took it away to his house (I must see it).

I am pleased to hear that Mr Payne Fisher has gone round transcribing as many of the London inscriptions that remain legible since the fire as he can find.

. . .

Glass is becoming more common in England. I remember that before the civil wars, ordinary poor people had none. But now the poorest people on alms have it. This year, between Gloucester and Worcester, three new houses with glass are being built. Soon it will be all over the country.

. . .

February

I have been helping Mr Wood in his biographical researches and have discovered that Christopher Wren has played a trick on us by making himself a year younger than he really is. He has no reason to be ashamed of his age, given that he has made such admirable use of his time.

I have introduced Mr Wood to Mr Ralph Sheldon, another esteemed antiquary, who has devoted himself to study since he was widowed in 1663. He has a fine library and a cabinet of curiosities in his house at Weston in Warwickshire, and has been working on a catalogue of the nobility of England since the Norman Conquest. He is a Roman Catholic.

. . .

My friend Walter Charleton, physician to the present King and the late King, has warned me against too much credulity in astrology. He has fulfilled my request and sent me the double scheme of his unhappy nativity, which Lord Brouncker worked out for him. But he says he has no belief in astrology and does not believe his birth considerable enough to be registered by the stars. He has personal experience of the inaccuracy of Lord Brouncker's predictions: and thus he hopes to divert me from the rock upon which he has been shipwrecked.

. . .

Surely my stars impelled me to be an antiquary. I have the strangest luck at it: things seem just to drop into my mouth, as though I were a baby bird.

. . .

March

I have now completed the sale of that most lovely seat, my beloved Easton Pierse. I handed over possession of it today, and the farmland at Broad Chalke. I have lost 500 li. + 200 li. + goods + timber. I am absconded as a banished man.

There are places unlucky to possessors. Easton Pierse has had six owners since the reign of Henry VII (I myself have played a role in this), and one part of it, called Lyte's Kitchin, has been sold four times since 1630. The new owner is Mr Robert Sherwin.

It is certain that there are some houses lucky and some that are unlucky; for example, a handsome brick house on the south side of Clarkenwell churchyard has been so unlucky for at least these forty years that it is seldom tenanted; and now no one will venture to live there. Also a handsome house in Holbourne that looked into the fields: about six tenants, one after another, did not prosper there.

. . .

Would I find refuge from my troubles by entering a monastery?

Of late, I have begun to wish there had been no dissolution of the monasteries under Henry VIII and that his reformers had been more moderate. The Turks still have monasteries. Why were our reformers so severe? There should be receptacles and provision for contemplative men, if not five hundred at a time, at least one or two. I have been thinking recently what a pleasure it would have been to travel from monastery to monastery. In the Lutheran countries the reformers were more prudent: they did not destroy the monasteries, only altered the religion.

I leave the task of reconciling the differences of the Roman and English Churches to them that have nothing else to do and know not how to spend their pains better. For my part, after so many tossings and troubles in the world, I cannot think of a better place for a man to withdraw than that learned Society of Jesus where the Jesuits study what they have a mind to: music, heraldry, chemistry, etc. I have always reserved this as my *ultimum refugium*. I do not waste my time and thoughts on religious disagreements, but how I wish I could retire to a monastery to advance my work in peaceful surrounds.

PART VII

Work

Anno 1671

My chief virtue: gratitude.

. . .

Now that I have sold my house and have lost all the money I ever received, I find I have a strong impulse to finish my description of Wiltshire. I cannot rest until I have done it, though I live in fear of the catchpoll crocodiles pursuing me for the debts I inherited from my father. I am in constant danger of arrest and am shifting between the households of my generous friends who help me.

. . .

Providence, thank goodness, has raised me good friends in my time of need and impoverishment. My lord Nicholas, Earl of Thanet, has invited me to stay with him at Hothfield in Kent. Also, Sir Christopher Wren and Mr Edmund Wylde will help me if they can.

. . .

April

I am concerned to discover that some of my letters to Mr Wood have gone astray. Almost all my letters to Mr Wood contain information I have found to help him in his biographical researches. He sends me queries and I search for the answers to them. I long to see him for one whole day with the longing of a woman. If I were more at liberty, I could serve him more. I must find a way to send him the manuscripts of Sir Walter Raleigh's that I have collected.

I have now collected notes on half of Wiltshire, but I should go through and sort them, for I know nobody else will do it for me. My description of Wiltshire is two volumes in folio already. There is also Monumenta Druidum, my tract on Avebury and stone antiquities, to finish. And I must pursue some ideas that have occurred to me on the education of gentlemen.

. . .

In London I have received some astrological advice from my friend Mr Henry Coley, but he warns me to use my own judgement too in the coming months.

. . .

Henry Coley was born in Magdalen parish in Oxford on 18 October 1633. His father was a joiner, who lived close to where the Sheldonian Theatre has now been built on Broad Street. Henry works as a women's tailor in Grays Inn Lane. His book on astrology, *Clavis Astrologiae*, was published three years ago in 1669; it is a most ingenious discourse. He comes by his learning through the strong impulse of his genius – understands Latin and French – yet never learnt grammar. He became enamoured of astrology and grew proficient at it in a short time. He is working on a second edition of his book, in which he will compile an account of the whole science of astrology from the best authorities. He is as good a natured man as can be and more is to be expected of him every day.

. . .

Whitsuntide

I have sent Mr Wood Mr Hobbes's dates and a list of his writings. I have also written to him of Henry Coley, and of John Florio, whom King James made tutor in Italian and French to Prince Henry and Clerk of the Closet to Queen Anne.

. . .

John Florio was born in London at the beginning of Edward VI's reign (his father and mother having fled Italy for religious reasons). Under the persecutions of Queen Mary, the family returned to Italy, where he was educated. He came back to England under King James. He wrote two books on learning Italian, a dictionary, and a translation of Montaigne's *Essays*. He died of the plague at Fulham in 1625.

. . .

I find my stomach better ordered this past year. Previously it was so tender that I could never drink claret without sugar, and white wine would cause it to disgorge. I do not know what has made the difference.

If you dissolve sugar in some kind of waters (hard waters), you cannot boil it into sugar again. I had this for a truth from a sugar-baker of my acquaintance: a sober person.

It is a relief to me to spend less time on horseback. It seems to me that between the years 1649 and 1670, I was never off horseback, but even so, I managed to glean some observations on my travels, of which I have a collection, two quires of paper in folio and a dust basket full of papers, some of which are valuable.

. . .

A man's spirit rises and falls with his fortune: mine makes me lethargic of late.

. . .

June

I am interested in Mr Gadbury's Almanac for this year, and his proposals for the advancement of astrology. Mr friend Ralph Bathurst would laugh at this, but others take astrology as seriously as I do. I hope to contribute to the science by making a collection of the nativities of thirty distinguished men. I shall need to know the exact year, day, hour, if possible, of their birth, and the place.

Mr Gadbury assures me that the first printing in England was in Westminster Abbey. For this reason, the name 'Treasurer of the Chapel' is retained.

. . .

I think it might be said of antiquaries as of poets: they are born, not made. Mr Wood and I are driven by the same impulse towards antiq-uities. I would do some good in the world before I die, *ne videar inutilis esse servus* (lest I should seem a useless servant). The good I would do arises from my passion for the past.

. . .

I have never been riotous or prodigal, but sloth and carelessness are equivalent to all other vices. They have played their part in my troubles.

. . .

Mr Wood writes to tell me that he will mention me in his book. This brings me such joy. My name will live within his living work, to remain there for ever, like an unprofitable elder or yew tree growing on the ramparts of some noble structure. I will ask him to add the name of my beloved house at Easton Pierse, where I was born, which would still be mine, if that had pleased Heaven.

. . .

I am rumoured to be beyond the sea; at Salisbury they say I am in Italy, which is good. Perhaps it will prove prophetically true. I have often considered joining the Jesuits, or some such learned society, as my last refuge. I have no leaning towards the Roman Church but would welcome a living and an opportunity to study in peace.

. . .

October

Mr Thomas Gore has written to me to say he is sorry not to have been shown my collections of Wiltshire antiquities by my brother. He has asked me to look out for any newly printed heraldry books, so he can insert them into his catalogue ready for the press.

. . .

Sir John Hoskyns wishes I would accompany him on a journey through Wales where there are many natural and antiquarian beauties to be observed. He believes there are many solitary places waiting to be discovered, unheard of in the late civil war and no doubt of much natural curiosity. Also, he tells me that by using a pendulum he has discovered a universal standard measure.

. . .

I have asked my brother Tom to copy Bishop Jewell's epitaph at Sarum so I can send it to Mr Wood for his book. I wrote to my old acquaintance Seth Ward, Bishop of Sarum, with many apologies, not expecting he would trouble himself about such matters, but perhaps get his secretary, or chaplain, to help answer Mr Wood's questions. But Seth Ward sent me the devil of an answer and scorns the task. I am sure none of the cardinals would have treated me with such disdain. I have sent the questions on to others who might help in Devonshire and Cornwall.

Riches and honours are fine things at the age of twenty-five or thirty, but I vow to God I would not be Bishop of Sarum now for the trouble it would bring. My mother and I were left 700 li. per annum together by my father, and I would have been glad to keep it, or at least turn it over to my brothers. But never was a man so plagued by an estate. I have had more enjoyment since losing Easton Pierse and my land, than I had throughout the rest of the nineteen years since my father died.

. . .

Now that I have more leisure to write, I am making good progress with my notes for Mr Wood and my observations of antiquities. I have also nearly finished a comedy for the young playwright and poet Thomas Shadwell. His first play, *The Sullen Lovers*, was performed by the Duke's Company in 1668, when he was twenty-eight years old. Afterwards, I intend to provide him with another play, *The Country Revell*, which will be very satirical against some of the most mischievous enemies I have collected in my tumbling up and down in the world. Revels are fallen from fashion now, but they used to be a time for the elders and betters of the parish to sit and observe the pastimes of young men: wrestling, shooting, bowling and dancing.

I have drawn inspiration from a short poem printed at London: *The Shepherds Delight Both by Day and by Night*, describing the shepherds' simplicity and their felicity; their birth and their mirth; their lives and their wives; their health and their wealth; their ways and their plays; their diet and quiet. And how their damsels, they laugh and lie down, and to each pretty virgin they give a green gown. This poem was sung to a delightful tune at the Duke's Playhouse, before the King and the nobility.

I shall set my play amidst a revel on St Peter's Day, when there is a collection for the poor. I will take one of my characters – Sir Fastidious Overween – from the Earl of Oxford's secretary Gwyn: a better instance of a squeamish and disobliging, slighting, insolent, proud fellow cannot be found. No reason satisfies him, but he overweens, and cuts sour faces that would turn the milk in a fair lady's breast.

. . .

If I desired to be rich, I could be a prince and go to Maryland, one
of the finest countries in the world, with a climate like France. Lord
Baltimore's brother is his lieutenant there: a very good-natured gent.
There is plenty of everything there; land for 2,000 miles westward. I
could take a colony of rogues with me, another of ingenious artificers,
and I am sure I could fix things so I took five or six companions along
for ingenious conversation (which would be enough).

. . .

Mr Hobbes tells me that if he thought Magdalen Hall would accept
them, he would give them his works. I will ask Mr Wood to make
enquiries about this.

I have been told there is a Fellow at Merton who can conjure and
quieten troubled houses. I hope Mr Wood can find out more, for I
would love to be acquainted with such a person.

. . .

Before I leave England on my travels, I hope to go to Oxford to see
Mr Wood, but must do so incognito, like an invisible ghost, for fear
of creditors. Even my letters I must collect secretly: they come
addressed to my brother Thomas and care of the Lambe in Katherine
Street, Sarum, or else addressed to my brother William care of his
landlord in Kington St Michael.

. . .

A cabal of witches has been detected at Malmesbury. Sir James Long
of Draycot Cerne, my honoured friend and an absolute gentleman, has
examined them and committed them to Salisbury Gaol. I think seven
or eight of these old women will be hanged. Odd things have been
sworn against them: the strange manner of the dying of a local horse,
and flying in the air on a staff. Sir James has written up his examinations
fairly in a book that he has promised to give to the Royal Society.

Sir James and I will go hawking together again soon: he is a man
of exceptional charm. One time, when Oliver Cromwell was out
hawking on Hounslow Heath, he got talking to Sir James and fell in
love with his company, despite the fact that Sir James led the Royalist

charge on Chippenham in 1644 and chased the Parliamentarian soldiers along the road towards Malmesbury. Oliver Cromwell ordered Sir James to wear his sword and meet him again for hawking, which caused the strict Cavaliers to look at him with an evil eye. When we hawk together I am reminded of what a great historian and romancer Sir James is. His History and Causes of the Civil War is a wonderful book that should be printed. I am deeply fond of Sir James's wife Dorothy too.

. . .

Phantoms. Though I myself have never seen any such things, yet I will not conclude that there is no truth at all in reports of them. I believe that, extraordinarily, there have been such apparitions; but where one is true a hundred are figments. There is a lechery in lying and imposing on the credulous; and the imagination of fearful people tends towards admiration.

For example: not long after the Roman mosaics in the cave at Bathford (near Bath) were discovered in 1655, a ploughboy happened to fall asleep close to the mouth of the cave. A gentleman chanced to be sailing past in a boat on the River Avon, which runs close by, playing on his flajolet. The boy woke, believed the music to be coming from the cave, and ran away in lamentable fright: his fearful fancy made him believe that he saw spirits in the cave. Mr Skreen, in whose grounds the mosaics were discovered, told me that the locals believe the ploughboy and cannot be undeceived.

The mosaic, or *opus tesselatum* pavement, was made of small stones of several colours: white (hard chalk), blue (liasse) and red (fine brick). In the middle of the floor was a blue bird, not well proportioned, and in each of the four angles a sort of knot. This ground and the whole manor used to belong to the abbey of Bath. Underneath the floor there is water. The floor is supported by pillars of stone. On top of the pillars, plank stones were laid, and on top of them the mosaic. The water issued out of the earth a little below.

After the mosaic was discovered, so many people came to see it, from Bath especially, that Mr Skreen had to cover it up again to halt the damage that the visitors were doing to his grounds. Unfortunately, he did not do this soon enough to stop them tearing up all the best part of the mosaic before I managed to see it. But Mr Skreen's daughter-in-law showed me the tapestry she made, copying the whole

floor with her needle in gobelin-stitch. Mr Skreen says there is another
floor, adjacent to the one that has been destroyed, that is still
untouched.

. . .

This year I have begun transcribing notes on architecture that I have
been collecting for many years now. My idea is to write a Chronologia
of architecture. I have become very interested in how Roman architecture degenerated into Gothic, before gradually recovering its
antique purity.

I have noticed that the shape of the windows is often the surest
indicator of the age of a building, and I have been sketching pictures
in ink of different styles of windows in important or interesting buildings. Perhaps I can gather them into a short book and dedicate it to
my cousin Sir John Aubrey. I have drawn careful diagrams of the
different kinds of windows in the church at Kington St Michael. I
notice that the windows of the tower of Kington St Michael are of
the same kind as those in the church at Ifley, near Oxford. I must ask
Mr Wood to find out when the Ifley church was built.

I think it would be easy too to make a Chronologia of styles of
handwriting from the Norman Conquest to the present day: which
would be very useful to have.

I have sought advice on collecting statistics from Sir William Petty
and he has sent me some helpful directions.

. . .

December
Two trunks full of my books, which I left with Mr Fabian Stedman,
have been seized by his landlady for debts. I hope I can recover them.

. . .

I wish to go to Oxford, but am fearful of the fever, so common and
infectious. I have written to Mr Wood to ask if he believes there is
any danger, or might I risk a visit soon?

. . .

I have been sending Mr Wood many notes for his great book on
the history and antiquities of Oxford University, including some

40/

South and North windows
of ye S. & N. Aisles of
Westminster Abbey
tpe. Rich: II.d

information about Dr Thomas Muffet, of Trinity College, Cambridge, and Gonville Hall, the author of *De Insectis*, who lived and died at Wilton House and was physician to Mary, Countess of Pembroke, Sir Philip Sidney's sister. Quaere: Dr John Pell told me that *De Insectis* was begun by a friar. In about 1649, long after Dr Muffet's death, his book *Of Meates* was printed. I have it and must check the date of printing. I also have the Life of Sir Philip Sidney, written by Sir Fulke Greville.

. . .

Anno 1672

January

Mr Edward Bradsaw, my old acquaintance from the Middle Temple, a religious controversialist, was buried on the first day of this month, in the burying place for fanatics by the artillery ground in Moorfields. There were between 1,500 and 2,000 at his funeral. He died on 28 December in Tuttle Street, Westminster. He was forty-two years old and on parole from Newgate Prison, where he was serving a sentence of twenty-two weeks for refusing to take the Oath of Allegiance. I will go to visit his sorrowful widow as soon as I can. She intends to place an epitaph for him.

. . .

My lord the Earl of Thanet has thanked me for my thoughts on how lanterns might be better fixed to coaches. I have the idea that the lantern could be fixed to the end of the pole between the shafts, closer to the ground, but he argues that this will not work as the horses may break it, or it will be thrown against them on rugged ways. He insists the lantern must go on the top of the coach above the coach-man's head. He invites me to visit him in Hothfield and to make an inventory for him of all his land: the name, situation and boundary of every field. I could travel there by water and take a horse from Gravesend for the last part of the journey.

. . .

11 January

Mr Isaac Newton has been elected Fellow of the Royal Society.

. . .

To help Mr Wood, I have searched through the records of the Heralds'
Office from 1617 to 1642. The archive has been rehoused since the Great
Conflagration.

. . .

February
Sir John Hoskyns has written to me of phantoms – a fundamental of
the Tridentine creed: the sudden ataxies of the spirits that forerun
death – and stories of dreams predicting events. He tells of magic and
ominous appearances of lights in rooms and of ancient superstition.
He says the plant woad is a cure for cancer of the breast; and that he
has seen crystal spheres for sale.

. . .

March
I am going to Somerset tomorrow, to see my mother, now living at
Bridgwater, and a cousin at Wells. About half a mile from Bridgwater
is a place called Chief Chidley Mount, which was inhabited by the
Romans and where Roman coins have been found. Bridgwater sprang
out of the Roman ruins.

. . .

Mr John Evelyn has become secretary of the Royal Society.

. . .

6 April
On this day, England joined France in declaring war on the Dutch
Republic. The Parliament has little enthusiasm for this new war.

. . .

Mr Paschall has written to thank me for my persevering zeal in the
search for a philosophic language. He intends to send me more questions about the 'Universal Character'.

. . .

The headmaster of Brentwood School modelled his teaching method on the Comenius didactic, after Mr Paschall recommended it, and having done so, made that great educational foundation both famous and useful. Mr Paschall hopes to prevail on the new headmaster of Bridgwater School to adopt the same method (which involves substituting emulation and shame for the rod: inducements to learning, instead of punishments) and wishes the headmaster of Brentwood School would publish an account of his experience and success as an educator: he is an ingenious man. How much better my own schooling at Blandford would have been if the masters there had followed Comenius's methods.

I know of men aged forty or more who, whenever anything troubles them, dream they are back under the tyranny of their schoolmaster, so strong an impression does the horror of discipline leave.

. . .

May

I have been to Oxford to see Mr Wood, whom I have been longing to see. And now I will go to Essex, Norfolk, Cambridge, and finally to London: all in about ten days.

For his collection of short biographies of the writers and bishops who have attended Oxford University, Mr Wood's method is to find answers to these questions:

> Where was . . . born?
> What employment or preferment had he?
> What did he write?
> When and where was his death and burial?
> What, if any, was his epitaph?

I am doing my best to help him collect answers to these questions whenever possible.

Mr Wood is a candid historian who does not make himself a judge of men's merits or abilities, but instead takes great pains to record all his subjects' printed writings and unpublished manuscripts. I commend his minuteness, but would like to go even further toward recording the tiny details that shape lives.

. . .

My honoured friend, Samuel Cooper, His Majesty's limner, has died
after a sudden illness at the age of sixty-three. He is now buried in
the chancel of St Pancras Church in the next grave to Father Symonds,
the Jesuit. Their coffins touch.

Mr Cooper gave me the second picture he made of Mr Hobbes
(the King has the other), but like a fool, I did not take it away with
me. I left it in his studio because part of the garment was unfinished
in the picture. Now it is with Mr Cooper's widow, Christiana; when
I am next in London, I must remember to collect it.

. . .

Last night I was nearly killed by a drunkard in the street opposite
Grays Inn Gate – a gentleman I'd never seen before – but thank God
one of his companions hindered his thrust. Deo Gratias!

. . .

June
Mr Paschall tells me he is using Skinner's lexicon (1669), and would gladly
seek to obtain a collection of words peculiar to Devon and Cornwall.

. . .

Sir John Hoskyns has been extremely ill with noise and giddiness in
his head – sometimes shooting pain – and has written to me for advice
about cures and drugs. He tells me that Monmouth Castle is under
guard and being rebuilt. Henry Ludlow is using Monmouth as his
base for governing Wales, and has stationed his agent for military
affairs, Richard Jeffries, there.

. . .

August
I have discovered that without my knowledge, to help my failing
finances, my dear friend Sir Christopher Wren has suggested to Mr
John Ogilby (the King's Cosmographer) that I might help him
improve the maps he is compiling for his *History of England*. I was
intending to go to Kent, but shall wait now until Michaelmas to see
what comes of this possibility of employment. Mr Ogilby is writing
the history of all England and surveying the roads to this purpose.
It is true that such work suits my talents, but Mr Ogilby is a cunning

Scot, so I must deal warily with him, taking advice from my friends.

In his youth, Mr Ogilby was apprenticed to Mr Draper, who kept a dancing school in Grays Inn Lane. In a short time he so excelled at that profession that he set up on his own. He was chosen to perform an extraordinary part in one of the Duke of Buckingham's masques, but by the misfortune of a false step came to the ground, sprained a vein in his leg and was afterwards lame. Then he went to Ireland in the Lord Lieutenant's troop to teach dancing. There he wrote excellent verse and when he came back to England, in about 1648, he printed a translation of Virgil. After the Restoration he printed and published His Majesty's entertainment at his coronation. In 1665, his *Odysses* came out, then his history of China and his history of Japan. But he lost all he had in the Great Conflagration and had to begin in the world again worth 5 li. at best. Such is his invention and wit that when he was undone he could shift handsomely and in a short time he has gained a good estate again.

If anything comes of Sir Christopher Wren's suggestion, it will probably be February before I begin work for Mr Ogilby, then I will curry, or comb, over all England and Wales for about ten months. The King will give me protection and letters of introduction to assist my enquiries, etc.

Mr Ogilby's list of questions towards a description of Britannia has been discussed at several meetings of the Royal Society. I was present and so were Christopher Wren, John Hoskyns, Gregory King and Mr Ogilby himself. The list of queries has been extended to include a request to the nobility, gentry and all ingenious persons to communicate information on sea coasts, ports, harbours, havens, creeks, watchtowers, lighthouses, islands, shoals, etc.

. . .

The books I sent by carrier to Sir John Hoskyns have not arrived, nor has my letter.

Mr Hooke is ill. The Royal Society droops. My cousin Sir John Aubrey has been following a milk and buttermilk diet and recommends balsam pills. I wonder if Mr Hooke can be persuaded to try either of these cures. The buttermilk cure was recommended to Sir John by a beggar woman who cured the wasting disease of an old man who lives near him.

Mr Wood continues to demand much of me.

. . .

I have found out for Mr Wood that George Sandys, the foremost poet of his time, died in 1643, aged sixty-three, and is buried at Boxley Abbey. How much I loved his translations of Ovid when I was a boy.

. . .

Mr Thomas Browne tells me that there was once a Roman camp at Caster, near Yarmouth, where many Roman coins have been found, and one at Bennen near Burnham.

. . .

September
About a hundred brass inscriptions have been stolen from Norwich Cathedral.

. . .

I am staying with my lord the Earl of Thanet and his lady at Hothfield in Kent. My lord is a hypochondriac. I have recommended he drink white wine infused with ashen rinds, which has done my relations much good. But first he asks me to ask Mr Boyle, who recommended it, when, how much, and for how long he should take this medicine.

. . .

Sir John Hoskyns insists that there is vast room for researches into the anatomy of animals and plants: he has written to me about a boy who was bewitched into a bird and passed from branch to branch of several trees too remote for human locomotion. He has passed on other stories of magic in various parts of the world – haunted houses, charms and prophecies.

. . .

My lord the Earl of Thanet is sending a groom with a horse and my portmanteau to me. The groom will return by foot as a punishment for stopping all day recently at an alehouse and neglecting the horse in his charge.

. . .

October

I am at Hothfield still with my lord the Earl of Thanet. The ways are so bad, and the air so ill, that I stir not out of doors, but divert myself very pleasantly with algebra.

My thoughts keep returning to Sir Thomas Browne's book *Hydriotaphia, Urn-Burial, or a Discourse of the Sepulchral Urns lately found in Norfolk*, which was first published in 1658. Sir Thomas is now augmenting his book, and I discussed it with him when I was last in London.

Sir Thomas Browne writes:

> What Song the Syrens sang, or what name Achilles assumed when he hid himself among women, though puzzling Questions are not beyond all conjecture. What time the persons of these Ossuaries entered the famous Nations of the dead, and slept with Princes and Counsellours, might admit a wide solution. But who were the proprietaries of these bones, or what bodies these ashes made up, were a question above Antiquarianism.

. . .

I am still trying to help Mr Wood with his questions. I wish he had more impertinent scobberlotching agents (as Dr Kettell would have said) to help him as I do in advancing his antiquarian work.

I have in my possession the prospect of Woodstock House and Park; a description of Bushell's Grotto at Enstone and the songs he printed when the late King and Queen were so 'romancely' entertained there; and two other drafts of the ruins of Osney Abbey (one done by Mr Dobson himself, the other by his man Mr Hesketh, who was a priest). All these I will take to Oxford and give to him, as soon as I can.

. . .

Mr Hobbes has given the Royal Society a copy of his book *Lux Mathematica*, printed this year in London.

. . .

November

I have a great desire to see my honest brother Tom, who is now twenty-seven years old, well settled, married to a good discreet wife with about 800 or 1,000 li.

. . .

December
Sir John Hoskyns has written to me again of witchcraft, and of the Royal Society's experiments, and algebra. He recommends to me Lord Maidstone's collection of antiquities from Constantinople; and suggests that my proposed survey should begin with the west of England.

. . .

I hope to retrieve Dr Dee's papers in Kent. Sir Thomas Browne told me where they are lodged. I remember the stories my grandmother told me about seeing her grandfather with Dr Dee at his house in Mortlake. Sir William Aubrey and Dr Dee were great friends. When Dr Dee wrote his book *The Soveraignty of the Sea*, dedicated to Queen Elizabeth, he asked my ancestor to read it and give advice on it.

. . .

Today I went on a five-mile pilgrimage on foot in the frost to search the register at Mortlake, but even here I found no trace of Dr Dee. I asked and was told to enquire of old Goody Faldo, aged eighty but still a lusty woman. She knew Dr Dee – her mother tended him in his sickness and did his laundry – and she told me exactly where he lies buried in the church of Mortlake. His body is in the middle of the chancel, a little towards the south side, between two of Queen Elizabeth's servants. A marble stone was laid above him, but afterwards removed. Previously, when the children played in the church, they would use Dr Dee's gravestone as their base and run to it in their games. But while he was alive the children dreaded him because they thought he was a conjuror.

According to Goody Faldo, Dr Dee was tall and slender; he wore a long black gown, like an artist's gown, with hanging sleeves and slits without buttons or loops and tufts. She told me he kept a great many stilles for his experiments in alchemy, and that he could calm storms and use magic to recover hampers of stolen linen. It was from Dr Dee's practice of distilling eggshells that Ben Jonson had the hint for his play *The Alchemist*.

My friend and fellow antiquary Mr Elias Ashmole has a very good painting of Dr Dee, from his son Arthur Dee. It shows that Dr Dee had a very fair, clear complexion and a long beard as white as milk. Mr Ashmole has thought of writing Dr Dee's life. His deep interest in magic and astrology make him well suited to the task.

During our civil wars, Mr Ashmole held the post of Gentleman of the Ordnance in the garrison at Oxford, but spent most of his time studying at Brasenose College. He is a great friend of Mr William Lilly's: they are both devoted to astrological pursuits.

. . .

My friend Henry Coley, another astrologer, has written to tell me I am much missed in London and daily expected. He hopes I will not be away much longer.

. . .

I am back from Kent. I saw Mr Hooke today, who has been ill. On Christmas Eve he passed the worst night he has ever had: melancholy and giddy, with shooting pain in the left side of his head above the ear. Since then he has cut his hair very close to his head, and though still giddy, is starting to get better. His vision in one eye is distorted and he has strange dreams of riding and eating cream.

My friends at the Royal Society have found me a small employment. I am to maintain a correspondence with numerous ingenious virtuosi in several counties, and the Society will pay the expenses of the letters and something of an honorarium. The point is to gather intelligence of things natural or artificial or anything remarkable in philosophy or mathematics.

It has been decided that from now on the Royal Society will keep only mathematical and philosophical books in its library. I had donated to the Society's library a manuscript from around the time of Henry IV (namely Historia Roffensia), and have now agreed that it can be exchanged with Mr Wood in Oxford for some mathematical or philosophical books.

I think my former servant Robert could win favour with the Royal Society if he were to go twice a year to Paris to obtain books direct from the sellers there. It is so difficult to buy books and maps from Paris at a distance: either they are not to be got, or are five times as expensive when sent for.

. . .

Anno 1673

22 January

I dined yesterday (21st of this month) with my honoured friend Sir Christopher Wren, and tomorrow night my Lord Thanet will send a horse to carry me back to Kent. This evening I am dining with Mr Elias Ashmole.

Christopher Wren's sister, Susan, is married to William Holder, the composer and theorist of speech and music. She is a rare she-surgeon. Recently she has cured His Majesty's hand after he hurt it and it became swollen from the treatment of other surgeons. Before Susan Holder made a poultice to cure the wound, it pained him right up to his shoulder so extremely that he could not sleep and began to be feverish.

. . .

February

My account of Avebury commissioned by the King, Templa Druidum, and my Chorographia Antiquaria are with the philosopher Dr John Locke. He is six years younger than I am and grew up a mile or so from Stanton Drew, where he liked to play amongst the ancient stones, as I did too when I visited my grandmother who lived nearby. We meet sometimes at the Royal Society. I have encouraged Dr Locke to go and visit Mr Hobbes.

Dr Locke has become so interested in my work that he has offered to help meet the cost of printing it by interceding for me with his patron the Earl of Shaftesbury, but I must wait until the end of March to know what will happen between me and Mr Ogilby, whether he will employ me or not. I find him very inconstant. I had thought to begin my work for him by now. But whatever happens, I am determined to have my some of my own work printed by next mid-summer at the latest, so that Mr Wood can enroll my name in his book alongside the great authors of Trinity College.

I have succeeded in putting Mr Hobbes in correspondence with the Vice-President of Magdalen Hall and now he has got his works printed and bound for sending to his old college. He says he would have gladly done this before now, if he could have been sure his books would be welcomed. But they have been so decried by Dr Wallis and others of influence in the University that he has hesitated to donate copies of his books until now. The old gent is strangely vigorous in mind still and walks every morning to meditate. He has finished the treatise on law that I urged him to write eight or nine years ago. I am like a whetstone that can make things sharp, even if it cannot cut itself.

. . .

5 February
I read my paper on winds to a meeting of the Royal Society.

. . .

Mr Ashmole has shown me a learned letter that my great-grandfather Dr William Aubrey wrote to his cousin Dr John Dee, which was found in one of Dr Dee's manuscripts.

. . .

March
I would like to return to see Rosamund's bower again at Woodstock near Oxford. I have my drawings of it from when I went there as a student, before the war. My friend Edmund Wylde of the Royal Society tells me that there was once a nunnery near Cremer church, and a vault leading from Rosamund's bower. I have heard that two or three years ago, scholars dug up Rosamund's bones.

I have also heard that there is a spring near Woodstock in Oxford that turns earth crumblings into cockleshells. I have asked Mr Wood to investigate for me. I am making a collection of the natural miracles of England.

. . .

April
My books are in my trunk at Kington St Michael, but I dare not trust my brother William with the key, for then they would fly all about the country like butterflies. There are three views of Osney Abbey in that trunk (a fourth I gave to Mr William Dugdale for the second volume of his *Monasticon*, which was printed in 1661).

Mr Dugdale avows that at the time of his birth, on 12 September 1605, a swarm of bees came and settled under the window of the room in which he was born: an omen, as it were, of his laborious collections of antiquities. The third volume of his *Monasticon* will be printed this year.

. . .

I dined recently at Rumney Marsh with one Mr Goresuch who told me that at the old Gothic house near the park gate at Woodstock, which was the house of Sir Geoffrey Chaucer, there is a picture of him that has been passed down with the house from one owner to another. I must go and see it.

. . .

Easter

James, Duke of York – heir to the throne, the present King having no children born within wedlock – refused to receive the Eucharist in the Anglican Church this Eastertide. Nor will he swear the oath prescribed by the Parliament's new Test Act for addressing the dangers that may arise from Popish recusants. This is an open declaration of his allegiance to the Church of Rome. The King opposes his brother's conversion and has ensured that James's children, Mary and Anne, are raised as Protestants. Fear of Roman Catholic influence at court grows by the day. God preserve our country from a return to religious strife.

PART VIII

Surrey

Sir Lleuellin Jenkins and Sir Joseph Williamson have been sent as plenipotentiaries to Nemeghen. They set off under the opposition of Saturn and Mars, so if their ambassadoring comes to any good I will never trust to astrology again! They are to attend a congress in Cologne to try and end our war with the Dutch. The Swedes will act as mediators.

. . .

My spirit is dejected, but after this quartile aspect of Saturn and Mars, it will be better about Whitsuntide, for we are all governed by the planets just as the wheels and weights move the index of a clock. As soon as these ill aspects are over, and not before, I will treat with Mr Ogilby, who is a cunning Scot and must be held fast.

. . .

At last, Mr Ogilby has officially commissioned me to perform a survey of the County of Surrey. The licence, which he has signed, sealed and dated the 2nd of this month, requires, in His Majesty's name, all Justices of the Peace, mayors, bailiffs, parsons, vicars, churchwardens, high constables, constables and headborows – in other words all His Majesty's officers, ministers and subjects whatsoever – to aid and assist me in the conduct of my survey. I shall have free access to all public registers and other books, whereby the geographical and historical description of Surrey may be promoted or ascertained. I am delighted and will begin my perambulation of Surrey in about a fortnight. I

will take notice of the county's hundreds, parishes, villages and
hamlets; the cities, corporate towns, market towns and fair towns;
the houses of the nobility and gentry; castles, churches, chapels,
monasteries, hospitals, schools, colleges; forests, woods, groves; waters,
springs, baths; Roman ways, stations, coins and monuments, etc. And
I will be sure to note any obsolete or peculiar words and any old
customs I come across. In the meantime, I have some queries towards
a description of Britannia to send Mr Wood.

. . .

June

Alas, I must wait another week or so to set off for Surrey, because
my brother has lamed my good and handsome horse just as I need
it. So now I shall have to ride my brother's little nag. I have found a
new servant: a pretty youth to wait on me who can read and write
and loves ingenious things. I think he will do me good service on my
perambulation.

I am still not free of the malicious aspects of Saturn, which will
do me no good for two more years. I hope the delicate air and diversion of Surrey will cure my lassitude of spirit.

. . .

Dr Fell, Dean of Christ Church, is making trouble for Mr Wood in
Oxford and keeps trying to alter his book, for which I too have worked
so hard. *The History and Antiquities of the University of Oxford* (*Historia et
antiquitates universitatis oxoniensis*) will be published later this year in two
volumes by the University Press, where Dr Fell is very influential. An
undergraduate at Christ Church, Richard Peers, whom Mr Wood calls
'a sullen, dogged, clownish and perverse fellow', is translating the book
into Latin and making vexatious changes that very much peeve Mr Wood.

I have sent Mr Wood some notes towards a description of Britannia.

. . .

St John's Night

Two days ago, terrible flooding began. All the hay and grass on the
low ground is spoiled, and enormous damage has been done.

Tonight I was in danger of being run through with a sword at Mr
Burges's chamber in Middle Temple.

4 July

I was with my friend Sir Robert Moray for three hours this morning; he seemed well enough, but he has died suddenly this evening around 8 p.m. This morning he drank at least half a pint of water, as was his custom. He died in his lodging in the leaded pavilion in the garden at Whitehall. He had just one shilling in his pocket, but the King will bury him.

Robert Moray's death is a great loss, as I know he would have got some employment for me if I had needed it, if only he had lived. He was a good chemist and often assisted His Majesty in his chemical operations. He had the King's ear as much as anyone and was indefatigable in his undertakings. He had promised to send me an account of some of the stone temples in Scotland and what the common people called them, but now death has prevented him. He was a courtier who would do courtesies for friendship's sake. Mr Wood says he was an abhorrer of women, but this might be a gross mistake.

. . .

I leave for Surrey on Monday (the wet weather has hindered me so far).

I have decided not to include Southwark in my survey, since the great antiquary Mr Stowe carefully did it in folio (nine leaves) already. I will refer my readers to his work rather than repeat it.

I have decided to begin my own perambulation of the county in South Lambeth.

. . .

The celebrated River Thames washes its banks through the county of Surrey and divides it from Middlesex. The part of the Thames which lies between London Bridge and the Tower, as far as Blackwall, is generally called the Poole by the trading people; e.g. the orange-women, oyster-women, etc. say they bought things at the Poole, meaning this part of the Thames.

. . .

London Bridge was first built of wood and then, with thirty-three years of labour, finished with stone. There is a commonly received tradition that when this bridge was to be made, the River Thames was turned into Surrey by a channel drawn from somewhere towards Cuckold's Point (I think Venerable Bede's *Chronicle* mentions this). But making such a channel would have been a Herculean labour. It sounds more like old romance than true history.

. . .

It is generally agreed that the Tower of London was built by some of the Roman emperors. The great square tower (wherein is the magazine for gunpowder) is called Caesar's Tower. At the posterior gate of the Tower, before the Great Conflagration, I saw many Roman bricks. Since the fire there is only a piece or part of it remaining, but it is still possible to see some Roman bricks.

. . .

At South Lambeth the farthest house is the house where the botanist and collector John Tradescant the Younger lived and showed his collection of rarities and curiosities, which he inherited from his father, John Tradescant the Elder, who was royal gardener to the late King. After his father's death, John Tradescant the Younger was appointed Keeper of His Majesty's gardens in his place.

The Tradescants' garden at Lambeth was once stocked with choice plants, among them the rare Balm of Gilead tree. My friend Edmund Wylde had some layers of this tree, and grew it very well in Bedfordshire, until one hard winter the mice killed it. I have not heard of any other examples of it growing in England.

Very few rare plants remain here; there is only a very fair horse chestnut tree, some pine trees, sumach trees, Phylereas, etc. And at the entrance to the gate, over the bridge of the moat, are two vast ribs of a whale. Before John Tradescant the Younger died in 1662, people came to view his collection here and it was known as 'The Ark'.

The Tradescant collection was given to my friend Mr Ashmole by Deed of Gift in 1659.

. . .

In the ditches about South Lambeth, Our Lady's Thistle grows frequently. But on the journey between South Lambeth and Kingston towards the Thames side is the greatest abundance of Upright Blite, or All Feed, that ever I have seen.

. . .

East of Kingston on the rising of the hill stands the gallows, in dry gravelly ground, where they often find Roman urns.

. . .

All Saints' Church, Kingston-upon-Thames, is spacious and the steeple is leaded, wherein eight bells hang. Three of the Saxon kings were crowned here: Athelstan, Edwin and Eldred. The windows of the church are of several fashions, which is as much as to say they are of several ages, but most are of the time of King Richard II.

. . .

West of Kingston-upon-Thames, near Thames-side, is a spring that is cold in summer and warm in winter. It bubbles and is called Seething Well. The inhabitants wash their eyes in its water and drink it for health.

. . .

At Cobham there is a medicinal well that was discovered a few years ago by a countryman using the water in his food and giving it to his pigs. I am told that at the bottom of this well are stones like Bristol Diamonds.

. . .

At Norbury near Letherhed, Sir Richard Stidulph has 40,000 walnut trees. It is likely that there are more walnut trees in this county than there are in all England besides.

. . .

At Deepdene, Sir Charles Howard of Norfolk has contrived a long valley in the most pleasant and delightful solitude for house, gardens, orchards and boscages that I have seen in England. From the top of the hill and vineyard there is a prospect over Sussex, towards Kent, and so to the sea.

I have spent today drawing a careful plan of Deepdene, but it
deserves a poem! This place is a subject worthy of Mr Abraham
Cowley's Muse.

Sir Charles has shaped his valley in the form of a theatre with more
than six narrow walks on the sides, like rows of seats, one above the
other. They were made with a plough and are bordered by thyme
(there are twenty-one varieties in this garden), cherry trees and myrtles.
There are many orange trees and syringas too, which are in flower at
this time of year. The pit (or bottom of the valley) is full of rare
flowers and choice plants.

The gardens are tended by two pretty lads who wonderfully delight
in their occupation and the lovely solitude. It is as though they are
outside this troublesome world and live in the state of innocency.

There is a cave on the left-hand side of the hill, thirty-six paces
long, four broad and five yards high, and two thirds of the way up
the hill there is another subterranean walk through which there is a
vista over all of southern Surrey towards the sea.

There is a vineyard of about eight acres on the south side of the
hill. On the west side there is a little building, which Sir Charles uses
as a laboratory and oratory.

The house was not made for grandeur, but for retirement. It is a
noble hermitage: neat, elegant and suitable to the modesty and solitude
of its proprietor, who is a Christian philosopher, who lives up to those
of primitive times.

On the orders of Sir Charles, his steward, Mr Newman, gave me
a very civil entertainment. The pleasure of the garden, etc. was so
ravishing that I can never expect enjoyment beyond it, except in the
Kingdom of Heaven. It is an epitome of paradise; an imitation of the
Garden of Eden.

. . .

I have copied a draft of the River Mole from Sir Charles Howard's
map of the Manor of Dorking.

. . .

As I rode over Albury Down, I was wonderfully surprised by the
prodigious snails there, which are two or three times as big as our
common snails.

. . .

On Letherhed Down there is a perfect Roman way in the road from London to Dorking. I asked the shepherds if there are any traces of it on Bansted Downs, but they know not. The shepherds here use a half horn nailed to the end of a long staff, with which they can throw a stone a good way to keep their sheep within their bounds or from going into the corn. I have seen pictures of such staffs in some old hangings and at the front of the first edition of Sir Philip Sidney's *Arcadia*, but never saw the thing itself but on these downs.

. . .

In Albury Park there is a spring called Shirburn Spring which breaks out at the side of the hill, over which is built a handsome banqueting house, surrounded by trees, which yield a pleasant solemn shade. Below the house is a pond that entertains you with the reflection of the trees above. Albury was purchased by Sir Thomas Howard, Lord Marshall in 1638.

. . .

Today I went to find the place of the great mathematician Mr William Oughtred's burial in the chancel at Albury, on the north side near the cancelli. I had much ado to find the very place where the bones of this learned and good man lay. When I first asked his son Ben, who lodges with my cousin, where to look, he said his grief for his father was so great that he could not remember. But after he put on his considering cap (which is nothing like his father's), he did remember.

In the chancel there is no memorial to Mr Oughtred, which grieves me, so I will ask Mr John Evelyn to speak to our patron the Duke of Norfolk about bestowing a decent marble inscription to perpetuate his fame. He did honour to the English nation as a mathematician and was rector of this parish for many years. During his lifetime he was more famous abroad than at home; foreign mathematicians would travel to England to consult him. He died on 13 June 1660, aged eighty-eight. His great friend Ralph Greatrex said he died for joy at the coming-in of the King. 'And are you sure he is restored?' Mr Oughtred asked. 'Then give me a glass of sack to drink his sacred majesty's health.' Afterwards his spirits were on the wing to fly away.

I have questioned Ben closely about his father and whether he died a Roman Catholic. Ben insists not. It is true that when Mr Oughtred was sick, some came to tamper with him, but he was past understanding. Ben was by his bedside.

Ben remembers how his father talked much of the philosopher's stone. He remembers him using quicksilver, refined and strained, and gold, to try and make the stone. Mr Oughtred was an astrologer who foretold luckily. His wit was always working – I say the same of myself – and he would draw lines and diagrams in the dust.

. . .

I went to see the remains at Blackheath, where there is a toft (as the lawyers term it) of a Roman temple on a plain a stone's throw eastwards from the road to Cranley. Some of the Roman tiles here are of a pretty kind of moulding with eight angles and there are some lumps of stone with Roman mortar. Ben Oughtred says that forty years ago one might have seen the remains plainly which were as high as the top of the banks are now. I deduced from a piece of extant ground pinning that it was square, since it goes straight at an angle. But two years ago the wall was dug up for stone and brick, and now the remains are so mangled that I cannot tell what to make of them. I found some pieces of Roman tiles and brick on the heath, where there was a great deal of building in old times. The tradition of the old people hereabouts is that there was once a river that ran below the temple. And that is all I could discover. What a pity a drawing of the temple was not taken some hundred years ago. Posterity would have been grateful! But there were many more Roman temples in Britain of which no vestiges at all remain.

. . .

I have reached Guilford. Here is a stately almshouse built of brick with a quadrangle and a noble tower with a turret over the gate. There is a fair dining room at the upper end where there is a picture of the founder, George Abbot, Archbishop of Canterbury. Here is also a picture of Sir Nicholas Kempe, the knight who gave a hundred pounds in his lifetime at the laying of the first stone and at his death five hundred more to this hospital: a worthy benefactor.

. . .

In Our Lady's Chapel at Trinity Church in Guilford is a sumptuous monument of marble of Archbishop George Abbot. He was the son of a Sherman. When his mother was pregnant with him, she longed for pike, and dreamed that if she could eat pike her son would be a great man. The next morning, going down to the river to collect some water, she caught a pike in her pail and ate it.

. . .

Mayden-hair grows plentifully about Lothesley Manor (the seat of Sir William Moore) and about the heath nearby grows plentiful wild sage, St John's Wort, whorehound and a great store of Chamaepitys or ground-pine, which the apothecaries make much use of: they send for it from beyond the sea.

. . .

Here at Frensham is an extraordinary great pond, made famous by the London fishmongers for the best carp in England. It contains 114 acres and is accounted three miles about.

. . .

Waverley Abbey is situated low, but in very good air, and is as romantic a place as most I have seen. Within the walls are sixty acres. The walls are very strong, chiefly of ragstone, ten foot high. There are also remains of a fair church and cloister, and handsome chapel, which is now a stable, larger than that at Trinity College, Oxford. The windows are of the same fashion as the chapel windows at St Mary's Priory in Wiltshire.

. . .

Waverley was the mother church to the church at Farnham. The vicarage is a living of 80 li. per annum, in the gift of the Bishop of Winchester. My old tutor at Trinity College, Mr William Browne, became vicar of Farnham and lies buried here around the middle of the chancel, but without any memorial. I paid my respects to him today. He died of smallpox on 21 October 1669, after he had been vicar here for about eight years, appointed by Bishop Morley. He was born at Churchill in Dorset and his father was rector there. Like me he was educated at Blandford, then went on to Trinity College. He was an ingenious person, a good scholar and as admirable a disputant as any in the University at that time. It was my happiness to have been his pupil. He wrote often to me from Oxford after my father summoned me home during the civil wars.

. . .

Above the town of Farnham there is a stately castle, belonging to the Bishop of Winchester. At the beginning of the civil wars, in 1642, Sir John Denham of Egham was High Sheriff of this county. He secured the castle for the King for some time, but being so near to London, he could not hold it. It became a garrison for Parliament and was much damaged. After the wars, Bishop Morley repaired it, but without the advice of an architect, as may be seen from the way the windows are not placed exactly over one another. Not only does this weaken the building, it also offends the eye.

. . .

In Woking I spoke with a gravedigger today whose father gave him a rule whereby you may avoid digging a grave in ground where a corpse has already rotted. There is a certain plant – about the size of the middle of a tobacco pipe – which grows near the surface of the earth, but never appears above it. It is very tough and about a yard long, the rind of it is almost black and tender so that when you pluck it, it slips off, and underneath is red. It has a small button on the top, resembling the top of an asparagus. The gravedigger says he always finds two or three of these plants in a grave, and has promised to send me some. He is sure it is not a fern root, and finds that it springs from the putrefaction of the dead body. In this fine soil, graves quickly disappear: the wind and the scuffing of boys playing above them soon merge them back into the ground. So it is often not easy for the gravedigger to tell where graves have been before, but when he comes across the plant that feeds on putrefying flesh, he knows to dig no further. He tells me this holds true only for his own churchyard, and the one at Seend a mile or two away. Of others he would say nothing. The plant he described reminded me of μολη (moly), mentioned by Homer, except that Homer says it puts forth a little white flower just above the earth's surface.

. . .

The cheese of this county is very bad and poor. They rob their cheese by taking out the butter, which they sell to London. They are miserably ignorant as to making dairy produce, except butter. A gentle-woman of Cheshire moved into these parts (near Albury) and misliking the cheese here sent for a dairymaid out of her own county. But when the dairymaid came she could not, with all her Cheshire, make any good cheese here.

. . .

Croydon market is considerable for oats.

. . .

Bordering on Hampshire, Berkshire, Buckinghamshire and Middlesex lies the Hundred of Godley or Chertsey, which takes its name from the town Chertsey, lying on the banks of the River Thames.

. . .

I made diligent enquiry at Egham for Cooper's Hill, the setting of Sir John Denham's poem, which I remember printed at Oxford on brown paper during the war. But the inhabitants did not know any such place. At length an old man (Mr Ansted) sent his servant with me to the place.

. . .

I have reached Runnymede where the Great Charter – the Magna Carta – was first sealed in 1215.

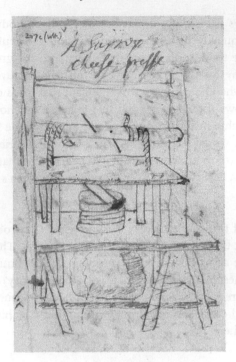

August

I have had the pleasantest pilgrimage that ever any man has had I think since the Reformation. Strangers in Surrey were very civil to me, much more so than the ones I met on my perambulations of Wiltshire.

I shall go next to Sussex if the weather holds and the ways are travellable, and afterwards to either Berkshire or Oxfordshire.

I am still searching for answers to Mr Wood's questions. He is still hard at work collecting information for his biographical register of the authors and bishops who have attended the University of Oxford since 1500.

. . .

Quaere: if Mr John Evelyn, who has written on planting and gardening, is an Oxford man? I know him from the Royal Society, but would like to know him better. During my perambulation of Surrey I visited his house at Wotton. It has a good prospect, which I made a sketch of.

. . .

I think and hope that Mr Wood will help find me some money to ease the cost of my perambulation: it would be a token in return for all the information I have been collecting to help him in his researches.

. . .

September

I am back at my lodgings in London and have seen Mr Hooke and Sir Christopher Wren and have talked to them of my description of Surrey. I have another week of work to do the other side of the Thames, which I kept for last. I have taken great pains over this task, but with much delight. If Mr Ogilby deals honourably with me, he will print all the extracts of the records in the Tower and in the Domesday Book, which I have obtained, and it will be a pretty piece. But I begin to fear that Mr Ogilby is a fickle and subtle man who cannot be trusted. I suspect he might discard the notes I have so diligently collected and not include them in his printed work.

. . .

20 September

On this day James, Duke of York, whose first wife died two years ago, married the Italian Princess Mary of Modena. She is fifteen years old and widely regarded as an agent of the Pope.

. . .

I met Mr Ogilby and Mr Hooke at Garraway's coffee house, which was, as usual, a hive of speculators and lotteries. Mr Hooke seemed weary.

Garraway's is Mr Hooke's favourite coffee house. It is in Exchange Alley, near the Royal Exchange. It was built above an old monastery crypt after the Great Conflagration. There are small rooms downstairs and a large coffee room upstairs, full of people reading or talking about the news.

. . .

October

My friend Christopher Wase – schoolmaster and scholar – has been commissioned by the Vice Chancellor and Regius Professor of Civil Law to report on the state of our free schools in England. He tells me it would greatly help to procure a table of the exhibitions for maintaining poor scholars at school or university. This is much needed as the corporations studiously suppress divulgence of their trusts, perhaps because they are afraid the funds will be seized if discovered. Mr Wase asks me to help him by seeing the Lord Mayor to this purpose. Here is a list of the questions about the free schools in each diocese that the enquiry will use to gather information:

1. Who was the founder?
2. When was it founded?
3. How endowed?
4. What schoolmaster and succession of masters? (Otherwise, such as are in memory to have been eminent, or authors of any extant work.)
5. What exhibitions and in which university?
6. Who are the governors, patrons and visitors?
7. What libraries are in the school, or in adjoining towns, with what manuscripts?

. . .

Three days into my journey to complete my survey of Surrey my horse either broke out of the pound at Esher, or else was stolen. I have been searching for him and heard nothing of him ever since. I walked yesterday from Esher to Richmond on foot. In some respects I would rather do this work pedestrian than equestrian anyway. But by the middle of next week I shall either buy another horse or have a friend lend me one.

I am ashamed to have discovered that no one from Magdalen Hall wrote to thank Mr Hobbes for his copy of his works. It cost him 25s. to have the book printed and bound, but he was not even sent word from the college that it had been received.

I hope that my Templa Druidum is to be printed at last.

. . .

I have news that my horse is at Kingston.

. . .

I went to collect my horse: his fees for pounds, etc. came to eight shillings. I have learnt that Mr Ogilby has changed his mind and will make no use of my work after all (he will include no more than four or five pages on any county in his book, and will get what scraps he can out of existing books or by hearsay). Nor will he reimburse the expenses I have incurred all this time on his account: for God, not a shilling. So I have perambulated Surrey to my very great content but am out of purse by about 4 or 5 li. at least. God deliver me of such men. Mr Hooke believes he will be able to bring Mr Ogilby round again by next spring. I do not much care, but I should have been glad to go on and survey Sussex.

PART IX

Penury

14 October

I have returned to London. Mr Hooke has lent me twenty shillings and I have promised to repay him.

. . .

28 October

I dined this evening with Mr Ashmole and Mr Dugdale. I talked to them about Mr Ogilby's treatment of me and they both assure me that unless he makes use of the notes I have collected for him, his book will be a mere bauble, a trifling thing. But I do not think Mr Ogilby will change his mind and do right by me.

Mr Ashmole once lived at Weston near Albury with his first wife. I asked him about the Roman temple on Blackheath. He says he remembers the ground pinning of the square, and also that of the circle surrounding it. I asked him too about the enormous snails I saw on the Albury downs. He says they were brought into England from Italy by the old Countess of Arundel, who dressed them and ate them.

. . .

November

I have sent Mr Hobbes's two lives in Latin (one in verse, one in prose) to Mr Wood. I pray that he takes care of them, for of the life in prose there is no other copy in England. I will collect it from Mr Wood when next I am in Oxford. Christmas will be a busy time, and I think it might be better to go to Oxford in May and walk to Botley to hear the winged choristers sing.

. . .

I have been to Richmond to see my old friend from Trinity College, William Radford, who is a schoolteacher there. While I was staying with him, he took to his bed. I stayed talking to him, remembering how he visited me when I had smallpox when I was a student and saved me from boredom. We spoke of old times and the frolic to London on foot that he made together with Mr Anthony Wood's elder brother Ned and Thomas Mariett.

. . .

To my great grief, my honoured friend William Radford has died.

. . .

I have sent Mr Wood information about Easton Pierse that is not shown on any map.

. . .

My friend Sir John Hoskyns has written to me announcing the birth of his son and asking me to send to Henry Coley for the horoscope. The baby was born on 14 November at 4.48 a.m.

. . .

I have drafted a list of questions that might be sent out to collect information on the geography, natural history, antiquity, etc. of different counties. There will be nineteen numbered questions under the heading: 'Queries in order to the Description of Britannia'. The questions could be sent through the counties to likely persons, invited to reply in writing, either upon certain knowledge, or else good authority, directing each of their remarks to the relevant numbered question and specifying the county and hundred wherein the remark falls.

. . .

20 November
Today I drank a bottle of wine with Mr Hooke and Mr Shortgrave. In payment of my debt to Mr Hooke, I sold him some of my books:

- Euclid – works in Greek and Latin (10s.)
- Plunia – *Purpur* (1s.)
- Censorinus – *De Mensura Anni* (8d.)
- Duret – *Histoire des Langues* and Scaliger – *Contra Caldanum* (6s. 4d)
- Baytins – *De Re Navali* (2s.)

So now I am acquitted of the 20s. Mr Hooke lent me.

. . .

21 November

I presented Mr Hooke with my book *Dell' historia naturale*, by Ferrante Imperato (published in Venice last year), which he intends to place in the Royal Society's library.

. . .

25 November

Mr Hooke has lent me another twenty shillings.

. . .

I visited the apothecary and collector John Conyers, who has premises in Shoe Lane. After the Great Conflagration he collected a world of antique curiosities during the excavations of the ruins of London. There are many Roman antiquities in his collection.

. . .

9 December

I was hoping to see Sir Christopher Wren in London yesterday, but he has had to go to Oxford. He has so much business in Whitehall at the moment that he has hardly any time to see me even when he is here in the city: he is one of my most necessary friends for securing some form of preferment. He is engaged in rebuilding London: St Paul's and fifty-two other city churches. I trust he will help me to some form of income, which I sorely need.

. . .

27 December

I was at Garraway's coffee house with Mr Hooke, Mr Hambden, Mr Hill and Mr Lodwick until late.

. . .

Anno 1674

I have moved into rooms within a stone's throw of Gresham College, from where I can easily help Mr Hooke with his experiments, and spend whole days with him.

My lodgings are with Mrs More in Hammond Alley in Bishopgate Street, the farthest house opposite old James Tavern. I have got to know some honest fellows and good workmen in the area: ivory-turners and cane-makers. Curious tortoiseshell knives and telescopes are made here.

. . .

5 February
I presented the Royal Society with some written observations concerning winds, their blowing down many hundreds of oaks at once and their blowing very differently in places little distant from one another.

. . .

23 February
The news is that England's alliance with France is over. Now we shall join the rest of Europe on the side of the Dutch and go to war with France.

I doubt how strongly the Church of England stands; and if it falls what shall I do? I am no enemy of Roman Catholics, unless they are Irish bigots. I say that a little superstition is a good ingredient in government. But what public spirit, what common honesty, is left? Among the clergy, humility and charity are very rare, except when you come across an honest bachelor parson. It is rumoured at the Vice Chancellor Mr Ralph Bathurst's table that Mr Wood has become a Roman Catholic.

I am so importuned that I could scarcely sleep last night. I am stormed anew by friends who would have me turn parson and keep an honest curate in a parsonage of 200 li. per annum. They drive me to my wits' end. Lord, how should I look in a cassock? But in some respects my friends are right: I love not business, and rising early in the morning is a death to me. As a parson I would not be troubled, could enjoy my friends in London and Oxford, and have a gentle competency.

. . .

Mr Hobbes tells me he has great esteem for Mr Hooke as man and philosopher. But he has considerably less for the Royal Society. Mr Hobbes knows that he stands in great esteem throughout the learned world, so has no need to seek endorsement from the Royal Society, which has not even protested against the evil words and disgraces put out against him by Dr Wallis, who has been engaged in a bitter controversy with Mr Hobbes ever since *De corpore* was published in 1655. He cannot see why the Royal Society would object to his vindicating himself when they do not bother to vindicate him themselves.

De corpore included a proof for squaring the circle, which Dr Wallis attacked. Mr Hobbes has since withdrawn it, but only to substitute new proofs. He believes the Royal Society to have unfairly taken Dr Wallis's side in their disputes, which are both philosophical and personal.

According to Mr Hobbes, Dr Wallis is no philosopher or geometrician of any standing, and is also a personal enemy. For this reason, Mr Hobbes will not agree to any of his work passing through Dr Wallis's hands. I have consulted their nativities and it is clear that their Mercuries are in opposition. Thus it is no surprise that they find themselves on such rancorous terms.

. . .

I have had to break the news to Mr Hobbes that the Dean of Christ Church, Dr Fell, has interfered with the account of his life in Mr Wood's book *Historia et antiquitates universitatis oxoniensis*. The Old Gent did not receive this news well. Mr Wood says that Dr Fell has inserted many base things into his book, about Mr Hobbes and others, to 'please his partial humor and undoe the author'.

Mr Wood's book is the result of ten years' work. In it he lists each of Oxford's colleges and halls, mentioning the writers that were educated there in order of their matriculation and listing the books they wrote. Dr Fell (who has plenipotentiary power over the University Press) is reading every page before it is printed and expunging and inserting whatsoever he pleases. It was Dr Fell who insisted the book appear in Latin.

. . .

1 *March*
I spent the day with Mr Hooke, helping to arrange his papers and things.

. . .

3 March

I was at Garraway's with Mr Hooke and Mr Wylde. Mr Wylde says the shriek that an oak gives before it falls can be heard a mile off, as if it were the genius of the oak lamenting its demise.

. . .

5 March

I was arrested on this day for a 200 li. debt by Sergeant Gardiner: a lusty, fair-haired fellow, proud, insolent, and everything like that (*et omnia id genus*).

. . .

9 March

On this day I was released. Providence provided better for me than I could have imagined or done for myself. A friend has undertaken to manage my concern in Brecon, one of the last remaining troubles from my father's estate, and I shall be able to pay my debts.

. . .

Mr Hooke has newly in print *An Attempt to prove the Motion of the Earth*. I hope it will hold. I am engaged in writing the Catalogue of the Repository of the Royal Society, which will hardly be finished by the beginning of May. I am doing it according to the incomparable method of Dr Wilkins's Philosophical Grammar. Mr Hooke began this before me, intending that the Royal Society's collection should be catalogued in accordance with the categories of Dr Wilkins's *Essay towards a Real Character, and Philosophical Language*.

. . .

April

Mr Hobbes has suggested that Mr Wood should write him a letter of complaint, of the kind he wrote to me, about the changes Dr Fell has made to *Historia et antiquitates*. Mr Hobbes will then be able to answer the letter and vindicate himself by correcting the errors that Dr Fell has introduced.

I saw Mr Hobbes on Good Friday (5 April) for his birthday. He is now aged eighty-six. We discussed the *Odyssey*. When Ulysses on his travels comes to a town where at one end it was day and at the other night, Mr Hobbes observes that Homer did not believe this, but took pleasure in contemplating how much the learned could make the ignorant believe.

I am reminded of the stories of King Arthur's court, Camelot, that are believed in Somersetshire. Stories verily believed by old women are often passed to their daughters, who can hardly be of any other opinion, since custom joined with ignorance is so powerful a thing.

. . .

I think I am likely to be spirited away to Jamaica by my lord John Vaughan, who is newly made governor there, and urging me to go with him. He promises to find me employment worthy of a gentleman. He intends to model Jamaica's government on our English Parliament, to stop piracy, to encourage sugar plantations and negotiate slave prices with the Royal African Company.

Other friends urge me to take a living in the church. But, fough! The cassock stinks: it would be ridiculous! Life in Jamaica with Lord Vaughan would be better – I would miss all my ingenious friends, but I could send letters to England every month or six weeks.

. . .

Mr Hobbes plans to vindicate himself against Dr Fell's charges at the end of his new translation of Homer's *Odyssey*, which is about to be printed.

I went to visit Mr Hooke, who had stayed in bed until 11 this morning after drinking a gallon of plain posset and vomiting last night. We went to Garraway's. He discussed an experiment where a magnet was found not to attract a stronger piece of iron after it had been touched there before.

. . .

The Earl of Thanet importunes me to accompany him to his estate in the Bermudas. He has written to me about old Richard Norwood who has recently died in the Bermudas, aged over ninety. Mr Norwood captained the ship in which my lord sent his gardener and vines to the Bermudas. His book, *The Seaman's Practice*, first printed in 1637, verifies a fundamental problem in navigation, namely the compass of the earth and sea and the quantity of a degree in our English measure. He has also written most usefully on plotting and surveying and the latitude of the principal places in England. The Royal Society used to send him questions.

. . .

May

I do not think it will be my fate to go to America this summer. I hope to see my mother and brother at or around Whitsuntide and to get to Oxford to see Mr Wood.

. . .

June

Mr Hooke and I observed the resistance of air to be duplicate to the velocity, or rather in musical proportion.

. . .

Mr Wood has suggested to Mr Hobbes that he write a letter of protest on a single folio broadside for inclusion in the second volume of his *Historia et Antiquitates Universitatis Oxoniensis*. Mr Hobbes needs to know how long and broad the paper must be and how many copies will be needed.

. . .

I have sent Mr Hobbes's letter of protest to Mr Wood. Mr Wood has shown it to Dr Fell, and Dr Fell has remarked that Mr Hobbes is an old man, has one foot in the grave, should mind his own business, and trouble the world no more with his papers. Little does Dr Fell know. Mr Hobbes recently saw the King in Pall Mall in St James's Park, and told him how ill served he has been by the nefarious Dean of Christ Church. The King seemed troubled and has given Mr Hobbes permission to vindicate himself as long as he limits his complaint to Dr Fell's ill treatment of him and does not criticise Oxford University more generally.

. . .

27 June
Mr Hooke lent me another ten shillings. He lent me twenty back in November, and another five since then.

. . .

2 July
Two dozen copies of Mr Hobbes's letter of protest have been sent to Oxford today, and other copies circulated in London.

. . .

6 July
I took leave of my cousin Sir John Aubrey's wife on her sickbed.
   I have given Mr Hooke more of my books for the Royal Society's library:

Pappus Alexandrinus, *Mathematicae Collectiones*, 1588
Apollonius Pergoeus, *Conicorum libri IV*, 1655, and *Conicorum libri V–VII*, 1661
Diophantes, *Arithmeticorum libri VI*, 1621
Copernicus, *De Revolutionibus Orbium Caelestium*, 1566
Bacon, *De Mirabilibus Artis et Naturae*, including Dr Dee's *Monas Hieroglyphica*, 1564
Gebri, *Alchimia*
Llull, *Testamentum*, 1663
Hartlib on engines and husbandry
Napier, *Mirifici Logarithmorum Canonis Descriptio*, 1614
Brerewood, *De ponderibus*, 1614
Alexander Anderson, Tracts LXXIV
Descartes, *De Lumine*
Pell in high Dutch: *An Introduction to Algebra*, by J. H. Rhan, translated out of high Dutch by T. Brancker, and altered by Dr John Pell, 1668
Pecquet, *Experimenta nova anatomica (Dissertatio de Circulatio Sanguinis)*, 1661
Galileo *Tractus de Proportionum Instrumento*, 1635

. . .

9 July
Mr Hooke lent me another five shillings.

. . .

11 July
Mr Hobbes's letter has been distributed today among all the coffee houses and stationers' shops in Oxford, crowded with visitors for the degree ceremony.

. . .

28 July
Mr Hobbes left London and went towards Derbyshire this morning.

Mr Wood has sent me a copy of his book, volume 1 of *Historia et antiquitates universitatis oxoniensis*, printed at Oxford earlier this month, in which he has included my name. Now, like a wild olive tree or polypedium, my name will live upon this never-dying structure.

. . .

1 August
A very rainy morning: I visited Mr Hooke.

. . .

3 August
Mr Hooke lent me another five shillings, which means I now owe him forty shillings.

. . .

Mr George Ent, my honoured friend and old acquaintance and fellow traveller to France, has moved to Oxford. I have given him a letter of introduction to Mr Wood, together with the manuscript Historia Roffensia, and my full set of the journal *Mercurius Pragmaticus*, all of which I intend to give to the Bodleian Library.

I have also sent to Mr Wood (via George Ent) the following:

− My precious drawings of Osney Abbey, which I had done when I was a student, so that one of them can be engraved for the volume of illustrations that will be published to accompany his book. I do not know, and I must find out, whether the plate that was made of one of the drawings of Osney Abbey for Mr Dugdale's *Monasticon* was melted in the Great Conflagration of 1666.

- A fine prospect of Godstowe nunnery and adjacent parts, taken from the bastion by St Giles' Church, which will be helpful when he prepares a description of Oxfordshire. I desire Mr Wood to return the originals after he has had the drawings engraved.
- The pamphlet description of the entertainments for the King and Queen at Bushell's Rock.

George Ent desires very much to have a copy of Mr Hobbes's life in prose, so I have asked Mr Wood to let him have one (Mr Ent has promised not to show it to anyone else).

I have a curious manuscript in the hand of Sir Thomas Pope, the founder of Trinity College, which I would give to the college library if I thought it would be chained there and safely kept, but I hesitate to do so, for fear it might be given away or lost.

I do not think I will get to Oxford again until the middle of October.

. . .

19 August
I went to Joe's coffee house in Mitre Court, Fleet Street, with Mr Hooke and Mr Wylde until late.

. . .

The Earl of Rochester has smashed the glass dials in the garden at Whitehall that were made by the Jesuit Father Franciscus Linus, who printed a discourse on dials in Latin. The Earl and his friends were returning from their evening revels: 'What!' said the Earl. 'Doest thou stand there to mark time?' Then he and his drunken friends set about destroying the dials. How it pains me to record this. I have heard Andrew Marvell say that the Earl of Rochester is the only man in England that has the true vein of satire, but nothing can excuse this wanton destruction.

. . .

I am reconsidering: perhaps it was not right to tell Mr Wood to show George Ent Mr Hobbes's life in prose. I could not see how to deny him, he was so importunate, but I think I was wrong and it is not fit.

. . .

I cannot persuade the booksellers to buy and insert Mr Hobbes's letter into the second volume of *Historia et antiquitates universitatis oxoniensis*. I fear they will include instead Dr Fell's abusively defiant reply to Mr Hobbes's complaints.

. . .

September

The more I think of it, the surer I am that my second thoughts are right: Mr Hobbes will be angry with me if George Ent obtains a copy of his life in prose. I have written again to Mr Wood and told him he should let George Ent read the life, but not to let him have a copy.

It is a shame that in his book Mr Wood has cut short some eminent lives: James Harrington's for example. He has left others out. I urged him to include Mr Hooke, but he has not done so, even though England has never produced a greater wit for mechanics.

. . .

I am very concerned. If George Ent gets a copy of Mr Hobbes's life it will fly about like lightning. Mr Hobbes, who is apt to be choleric about such matters, will be very angry and I will lose his friendship, which I have enjoyed since childhood.

The antiquary Dr Robert Plot of Magdalen Hall has been granted a letter of approval and recommendation from the Vice Chancellor, Ralph Bathurst, for his search after rarities (both natural and artificial) in His Majesty's kingdom. He will begin with Oxfordshire. I wish to help and can furnish him with many fine things I have collected myself. His plan for his book pleases me greatly. He concerns himself less with the chronicles and histories of the county than with the climate, geography, rivers and geology. He will follow Pliny's divisions in organising his natural history of the region and his researches are intended to extend knowledge of science as well as encourage the practical use of natural resources for trade. I hope the engraver will copy my drawing of Osney Abbey handsomely for inclusion in Dr Plot's book.

Meanwhile, Thomas Gore – the Cuckold of Alderton – has published his catalogue of all the authors who have written on heraldry and omitted my name! I let him peruse my manuscript, he has done his business, and now a fart for me.

The time seems long before I shall leave London and get to Oxford again. I fear I shall not get there in October, but if not, I shall, God willing, go at Christmas, by the coach or wagon.

. . .

26 September
Mr Hooke lent me another three shillings. Now I owe him forty-three shillings.

. . .

October
I have easily answered Mr Wood's question about the tower at Osney Abbey.

. . .

I have been to see my honoured friend Mr Francis Potter, whom I have not seen these past three years. His lippitude has now become blindness, which it grieved me to behold. He has let his beard grow unkempt, which used to be but little and trimmed. I asked him why he did not get some cousin of his to live with him and look after him at his great age of eighty. He said he had tried this but found it did not suit him, since his relatives begrudge what money he spends, thinking it is being taken away from them, whereas servants and strangers are kinder.

. . .

November
I am exceeding sorry that Mr Wood has left Mr Hooke – so eminent a person at home and abroad – out of his book. In one of my letters I know I gave him details of the tracts Mr Hooke has written.

I wish I had a copy of the astrological book *Leovicius de Directonibus*. I will ask Mr Wood to look out for it in the stationers at Oxford.

. . .

I am concerned about my lord the Earl of Thanet's health. He has consulted physicians and others, but their advice is that only Apollo can cure him completely! He says he would perform a pilgrimage to Apollo as far as the Bermudas, were he not in Diana's grove. He has read that Bacchus as well as Apollo and Aesculapius was adored as the God of health, and says he will partake of a few years of well-concocted wine in a southern clime. He needs an ingenious person to report for him on Bermuda. I do not think that person can be me.

. . .

December

I have been asked (together with Mr Collins) to help make a catalogue of all the gifts that the Royal Society has received and the names of the donors (one copy to be left with the keeper of the repository and the other with the treasurer); also a catalogue of all the instruments and other apparatus of the Society, paid for out of the public treasury; and a catalogue of all the books, discourses, letters and accounts brought to the Society, together with the names of the authors. These books and papers are to be kept somewhere convenient under lock and key (the President and the Secretaries will be keepers of the keys). Sir William Petty has suggested that all the discourses entered into the Society's register books should be divided into several sections and chapters.

Sir Jonas Moore was elected and admitted to the Society today.

. . .

10 December

I went to Garraway's coffee house with Mr Hooke and the Bishop of Sarum. Mr Hooke has bought my Greek *Chrysostom* from me for 4 li. 10s. I had planned to leave it to Jesus College in my will but am now forced to sell some of my books for want of money.

. . .

24 December

I went to Joe's coffee house with Mr Hooke and Mr Wylde. How much I like his lady, Mistress Jane Smyth! They cohabit – just as Mary, Countess of Pembroke, and Sir Martin Lister did. I feel I owe most of Mr Wylde's civility to Jane Smyth's goodness. She tells me she was born on Venus's day (Friday) on 15 April 1649, the year the late King was beheaded, and there was thunder and lightning and the house caught fire as she was born.

Mr Wylde has a fine collection of books and pictures including Jonas Moore's model of a citadel, which was made for Oliver Cromwell, and the manuscript of Sir Walter Raleigh's *A Tryall of oares and indications of metalls and mines.*

. . .

Anno 1675

January

I am in London trying to obtain some preferment at court. The days are now so short and cold.

. . .

I have asked Mr Wood to send to Weston for me for information for my Templa Druidum about the Rollright Stones: the diameter, how many yards or paces, and the height of the stones and the number.

I hear that in Oxford, George Ent and Mr Wood are quarrelling. Perhaps they can make peace over a glass of sack.

. . .

February

Sir John Hoskyns has been encouraging me to research and write the Natural History of England. He believes it will be important to examine different soils through the microscope and study them carefully. He tells me that Colonel Blunt and the munificent Sir Charles Howard will help, and that no man alive is so well suited to this work as me. He has already mentioned the project to my good friends Mr Ashmole, Mr Ettrick and Sir Christopher Wren.

. . .

Sir Christopher Wren says that all along the River Thames, many miles downwards from London Bridge, are great banks to keep out the river, which were chargeable to construct, and must be the work of the Romans, nobody else. He says London Bridge was built without diverting the river, by piles, which are not more than two feet under the riverbed, made of oak.

. . .

Mr Wood gave my brother a small amount of money for me, but my brother has not yet passed it on: he is very slow letting money go out of his hand.

If I can, I will go to see the Rollright Stones at Weston this Lent so I can study them more severely for myself.

In his book, William Camden described the tradition of the common people who believe that the stones were once men in the army of a would-be King of England: the largest of the stones the would-be King on horseback.

. . .

I have sent Mr Hobbes a printed copy of Sir William Petty's book, *Concerning the Use of Duplicate Proportion*, published at the end of last year. Its 'Appendix of Elasticity' sets out Petty's atomic theory, which Mr Hobbes tells me he believes is correct. I have passed on Mr Hooke's desire to publish through the Royal Society any of Mr Hobbes's treatises of philosophy or mathematics that are not already in print, but he writes to say there are none, and even if there were, he would not be content for them to pass through the hands of his enemy Dr Wallis.

. . .

All men cry out against Dr Fell's spoiling of Mr Wood's book. I have asked Mr Wood to mention my name, just briefly, in the preface to the next edition. He told me he intended to do this and I am sure Dr Fell scratched it out.

. . .

I was sorely mistaken! Mr Wood refuses to mention my name in the preface to his book: will only mention me as one of the authors of Trinity College if I have published something before the next edition of his book is printed. After all I have done to help Mr Wood in his researches this is hurtful indeed! He is right, though: I must publish my work. I have so much unfinished work upon the loom.

Mr Wood has asked me to find out what I can from Mr Ashmole and others about the claim that the skeletons of King Edward V and Richard Duke of Gloucester, murdered by King Richard III, were found lately in the Tower.

. . .

March
George Ent will give the librarian Mr Hyde five books to enter into the Bodleian Library under my name. His quarrel with Mr Wood gets worse and worse.

. . .

Now that the days lengthen and the weather is warmer, I will make progress with transcribing my manuscripts for the press.

George Ent has Dr Charleton's collection of all the Latin mistakes in Mr Wood's book: I believe there are 10,000. There is not a page without false Latin or solecisms, which are as bad. Last year Mr Wood and the Latin translator Dr Fell forced on him fell to fisticuffs.

. . .

25 March
On this day my nose bled at the left nostril at about 4 p.m. An ill omen, but nothing eventful followed.

. . .

8 April
Sir Robert Southwell read his discourse – or rather his collection of eight miscellanies – concerning water to the Royal Society today.

. . .

Mr Wylde is thinking of buying land in New York. But my lord the Earl of Thanet has been told that though the land is fertile in summer, the cold and deep snow of winter reduces the diet there to salt meat and fish. His advice to anyone buying land in America is: let it be in the Bermudas.

The Earl of Thanet complains that my lodging, like an enchanted castle, can never be found out, so he will continue to address his letters to me via Mr Hooke at Gresham College.

. . .

My friend George Ent has presented some books to the Bodleian Library on my behalf. The books I meant to give are a collection of the newssheet *Mercurius Pragmaticus* and a book on fencing. The librarian Mr Hyde would not enter so small a donation into the Benefactors' Book, so Mr Ent has added these others:

The Grounds of Obedience & Government, by Thomas White (London, '55)

Medela Medicinae, by Marchamont Needham (London, '65)

Bodie of the Common Law, by Edmund Wingate (London, '62)

Les Provinciales or the Mystery of Jesuitisme, by Blaise Pascal, done into English (London '57)

He says we must not fall out over this but discuss the matter further when we meet. He suggests that I should present any other books I wish to place in a library to Trinity College, but not my manuscripts, which the Vice Chancellor says should go to the Bodleian Library.

. . .

May

My lord the Earl of Thanet has offered me accommodation in his Garden House, which his mother has lent him, and which he intends to have fitted up as two or three chambers for his personal use when he comes to London. I will help look after his business in London, for an agreed salary.

. . .

I wait daily on courtiers for preferment and cannot leave London.

. . .

Mr Marvell, now fifty-four years old, has promised to write some notes on John Milton (who died last year on 8 November) for me to send to Mr Wood. I plan to go and visit Mr Milton's widow to collect details of his life that will otherwise be lost.

I have told Mr Wood to ask Mr Ashmole to show him the manuscript of Dr Gwyn, in which there are several letters from Dr John Dee concerning chemistry and magical secrets. I have left some notes on Dr Dee's life with Mr Ashmole, about three pages in folio concerning him.

I cannot deny that I owe kindness and respect to George Ent for his friendship and civility to me, but I am so heartily sorry that he is not a better friend to himself or his reputation. But every man to his humour! He puts me in mind of Plato's saying that perpetual drunkenness is the reward of virtue! His quarrel with Mr Wood will never mend now.

. . .

June
My mother has fallen sick of a burning fever at Langford, Somerset.

. . .

Mr Paschall has asked me to send him an account of the recent invention for improvement in beekeeping, which has been given a royal patent; it is said to prevent swarming and burning, and treble the profit of keeping bees.

He tells me his wife has had a letter from my mother complaining of ill health, on account of which she will stay a month longer at Langford, rather than going on to Bristol as she had intended.

. . .

I will visit my old friend Sir James Long at Draycot Cerne, near Easton Pierse, and stay with him until October. We will discuss Royal Society business. He is a good swordsman, horseman, and an admirable extempore orator, as well as a great historian, romancer and falconer. He is exceeding curious and has been searching for a long time into natural things.

Next time I am in Oxford, I wish to see the conjuring books in the Bodleian Library. I will ask Mr Wood whereabouts they are kept. Meanwhile, I have found out for him the exact spot of Sir Walter Raleigh's grave: he is buried in St Margaret's Church, next to Westminster Abbey.

. . .

I have reassured Mr Hobbes that he is not alone in being abused by Dr Wallis: Mr Hooke has been too, and so has Sir Christopher Wren. Dr Wallis is like a common spy, stealing from the discourse of ingenious people and printing what he takes. He is a most ill-natured man, an egregious liar and backbiter. He flatters and fawns on my lord Brouncker and his mistress, the actress Abigail Williams, who keeps up his reputation.

What can be said in Dr Wallis's favour is that although he steals flowers from others to adorn his own cap, some of the ideas he prints would be unrecorded otherwise. So while he does injury to the inventors, he does good to learning in publishing curious notions which would be lost to posterity if he did not set them down. Sir Christopher Wren especially is too busy to write himself.

Mr Hobbes is now translating the *Iliad*. His translation of the *Odyssey*, *The Travels of Ulysses* (1673), is much admired.

. . .

July
My mother has fallen sick with fever again.

. . .

August
Mr Hooke has written to me regarding my suggestion that he employ Mr Snell's young brother George. He says he would be glad to have him live with him and help him, but he must undertake to stay seven years and others must provide him with clothing, since Mr Hooke will supply him with meat, drink, lodging, washing and instruction.

. . .

September
I have written to Mr Hooke about George Snell.

. . .

In Minty Common, in Malmesbury Hundred, near the road that leads to Ashton Kayne, there is a boggy place called the Gogges, where springs rise up out of blue clay. Round about this place in hot weather there is a salt that looks like frost on the ground. I have seen it several times, and again today there was an incrustation of salt four feet around the edges of the bog. I made up about half a pint of a lixivium with ½lb of this nitrous earth, which I then evaporated. It yielded just under a quarter of an ounce of residue. This residue was evaporated to almost all crystallise in a cellar: the liquor turned deep red and the crystals flew like saltpetre on a hot iron, but some sediment, like burnt allum, remained.

. . .

In Stanton Parke, in my grandfather's time, there used to be martens. Now the species is lost in Wiltshire, but I think they are still in the New Forest, and in Cranborne Chase.

. . .

Michaelmas
Jane Smyth, Mr Wylde's good lady, is very unwell with pleurisy. I am very fond of her, and she of me. If I can, I will see her at Mr Wylde's house in the great square in Bloomsbury. On the first floor, over the hall, is Mr Wylde's study, where he keeps the deeds to his extensive estates, his rare books, pamphlets, manuscripts, jewels, watches, enamelled pictures, vessels of crystal, stone, glass, silver, gold, and other rare objects.

. . .

November
Mr Paschall has returned my book about bees. I sent it to him earlier this year, together with information about how to obtain the beekeeping licence.

. . .

Mr Meredith Lloyd, who was once my neighbour in Fleet Street, and a great collector of information about the Celtic languages, has sent me a list of Welsh words for my collection.

. . .

A good way of ending my days in peace and ingenious innocence would be to become principal of Gloucester Hall! I would make it an ingenious nest, and would decoy thither several ingenious persons of both universities and some from beyond the sea. Byrom Eaton has been the principal since 1662, but under him the establishment has fallen into neglect. It is a pity! The foundation can be traced back to 1283 and at the dissolution of the monasteries the hall was bought by Thomas Whyte, the founder of St John's College.

. . .

With the intention of helping Dr Plott, I have transcribed my Natural History of Wiltshire, my remarks of Surrey, and a sheet or two of other counties. I have asked my cousin Henry Vaughan to send me the Natural History of Brecknockshire and other adjacent counties to add to my collections. I began collecting memoirs and natural remarks in Wiltshire in 1656, almost twenty years ago. The Secretary of the Royal Society came to hear of it and has suggested I submit my remarks to the Society. I believe I am the first that ever made an essay of this kind for Wiltshire and (for aught I know) anywhere in the nation. Since seeing how excellently Dr Plot is doing with his Natural History of Oxfordshire, I have decided to give him all my papers and ask him to undertake Wiltshire too. I hope he will finish the task I have begun.

. . .

I have deposited with Mr Ashmole my notes on Dr Dee, two pages on Lord Bacon, and some remarks on other eminent men: Sir Christopher Wren, Mr Robert Hooke, Dr William Aubrey (my great-grandfather), John Pell, and Richard Boyle, the 1st Earl of Cork.

I remember that Lord Bacon's widow was still living after the beheading of the late King. After Lord Bacon's death she married her gentleman usher, Thomas Underhill, whom she made deaf and blind with too much of Venus. I must find out where and when she died.

. . .

1 December
On the first date of this month, I drank a sack with Mr Hooke and Mr Hoskyns at Mrs Story's.

. . .

Quaere: does the brain ferment in madness because of the extraordinary heat and motion of the spirits? Perhaps a hole bored in the skull would give some ease? Or a wet cap for the head to cool it? A good cure for headaches after drinking strong wine is putting one's head in a pail of cold water.

. . .

I think it is strange that magnifying glasses were so long unknown about in this world. Any good fellow at a tavern cannot escape noticing how much the threads of linen cloth are magnified by a glass (of sack or white wine) that has a stem and a hemispherical or conical bottom to it. At least, so it seems to me, when I stare into the bottom of my glass in a tavern and think about what I can see.

. . .

7 December
I went to Garraway's coffee house.

. . .

9 December
I was at Garraway's with Mr Hooke, Mr Hill, Mr Snell, and I smoked four pipes of tobacco.

. . .

10 December
Mr Hooke, Mr Hill, Mr Lodwick, Sir Jonas Moore, Mr Wylde and Mr Hoskyns and I are to set up a new club to meet at Joe's coffee house. The first meeting will be tomorrow night at 7 p.m.

. . .

11 December
At Joe's coffee house our new club – a small group of members of the Royal Society loyal to Mr Hooke – began. We discussed Mr Newton's new hypothesis and Mr Hooke explained his way of moving boiled alabaster dust and sand by magnetic filings.

. . .

15 December
I was with Mr Hooke until 11.30 p.m. this evening. He spoke to me of his new mechanical principle for flying.

. . .

16 December
Mr Newton read his *Discourse* to the Royal Society. Later I went to the Crown in Threadneedle Street with Mr Hooke, Mr Henshaw, Sir William Petty, Mr Barrington and Mr Hill.

. . .

18 December

I went to Garraway's with Mr Hooke, Mr Lodwick, Mr Hill and Mr Wylde: we talked of the Universal Character, Pre-Adamites and Creation; also about insects. Mr Hooke believes all vegetables are females. He told us about his principle for flying and we drank port. Mr Hooke claims that when he was a schoolboy at Westminster School he devised thirty different ways of flying. He imagines flying by some mechanical means: a chariot pulled by horses; or powered by vanes; or bending springs by gunpowder. I consider Mr Hooke the greatest mechanic alive in the world today.

. . .

19 December

I dined with Mr Hooke.

. . .

28 December

I was at Cardinal's until late this evening with Mr Hooke, Mr Wylde and Mrs Smyth.

. . .

30 December

I read a paper to the Royal Society. I presented my observations of Wiltshire, and have been asked to procure:

- Some of the iron ore of Sein that is said to be so rich that it can be melted in the smith's forge.
- Some of the blue clay from Easton Pierse that is free from sand and almost ultramarine in colour, since Mr Doight believes it might be good for making porcelain.

Mr Oldenburg has transcribed my observations of Surrey and Wiltshire, and papers on the springs and rocks of Herefordshire, Somerset and Gloucestershire. He will present them at the next meeting, which is on 13 January.

. . .

Anno 1676

1 January

On the first day of this month, I met Mr Hooke at Child's coffee house in St Paul's Churchyard after he had addressed the new Philosophical Club within the Royal Society. We stayed until 11 p.m. eating meat and drinking chocolate.

. . .

2 January

I was with Mr Hooke again today.

. . .

Mr Paschall says the bee colony licence is too expensive for the middle and mean classes of people who trade in bees. He has an idea as to how a cheaper method might be used by them instead, and thinks that it would pay the designer to publish it. The other method could be reserved for persons of estate.

. . .

Now I come (as Dr Ralph Kettell used to say) to the purpose: I have written ten sheets of my Natural History of Wiltshire and Surrey and some other counties for Dr Plot and have submitted them to the Royal Society: they were well received.

. . .

13 January

Mr Oldenburgh produced his transcriptions of my observations on Surrey at the Royal Society today, but the meeting was out of time, so they will not be considered until the next meeting.

. . .

14 January

I was at Garraway's with Mr Hooke and Mr Wylde until 11.30 p.m. Mr Wylde told Mr Hooke that the blood of a black cat can cure chilblains. This greatly irritated Mr Hooke and he muttered that Mr Wylde is not 'worth a whistle'.

. . .

17 January
I smoked at Garraway's with Mr Hooke until midnight.

. . .

20 January
On this day, my papers and some of Mr Newton's (on his theories of light and colour) were read at the Royal Society. Afterwards I went home with Mr Hooke.

. . .

22 January
There was much rain today. Mr Hooke and I went to visit Mr Henshaw. On the way we saw a Dutch carver at Pall Mall who makes gilded leather frames by wetting the gilded leather then lying it on fine heated brick dust and placing the mould hard on the leather until it is dry. The frames were very fine and cheap. We went on later to Sir Christopher Wren's.

. . .

27 January
Mr Paschall's letter to me was read before the Royal Society, containing natural observations of:

– The lead mines in the Mendip Hills
– The sulphur well in Spaw in Yorkshire
– A petrifying spring to rival the dropping well at Knaresborough in the north
– The motion of underground waters in the parishes of Zoylande, formerly recovered from the sea.

. . .

29 January
I visited Sir Christopher Wren again with Mr Hooke and Mr Hill. Mr Henshaw and Dr Holder were there too. We talked about petrifications of bodies, about plaisters, about framing glass, staining marble, filligreen sodering with bran, about printing stuffs and gilding stuffs, and about ghosts and spirits.

Dr Holder is beholden to no author and consults only with nature. He has a theory as to how to cure a deaf-mute, which has brought him into a terrible quarrel with Dr Wallis, who claims to have thought of the method before him. In his *Elements of Speech* (1669), Dr Holder derives the true and proper natural alphabet, discovered not through existing alphabets, but by investigating the organs of speech. He wishes that throughout the world there could be one sort of character for each letter to express it to the eye, exactly proportioned to the natural alphabet formed in the mouth.

. . .

As I was walking through Newgate Street today, I suddenly saw the bust of Dame Venetia (née Stanley) for sale as scrap metal on a stall at the Golden Cross, a brasier's shop. Even though the gilding had been burnt off in the Great Conflagration, I recognised it and pointed it out to my companion.
I must return and rescue it if I can. Before she married, Venetia Stanley was my friend Edmund Wylde's mistress, and afterwards she was mistress to the Earl of Dorset. Her picture, done by Van Dyck, hangs in the Queen's drawing room at Windsor Castle, over the chimney. She was a most beautiful, desirable creature who died suddenly in her bed aged thirty-three in 1633. When Sir Kenelm Digby married Venetia, against his mother's wishes, he said he could make a virtuous wife out of a whore. After her death, he retired to Gresham College to divert himself with chemistry and the professors' good conversation. He erected the sumptuous monument to his wife that the Great Conflagration destroyed.

. . .

February

My friendship with Mr Evelyn has grown since I sent him my notes on Surrey. He tells me Surrey is the county of his birth and his delight, but he was ashamed to discover how ignorant he is about it when he read my remarks. Nevertheless, he is sending me some material to add to my own. He tells me that the old house at Wotton was designed in the Italian manner on a mount fifty feet high. Under the mount was a grotto encrusted with shells and corals: their colours enhanced by the play of the water.

Mr Evelyn has drawn my attention to notable places in Surrey I have not yet visited, especially Bansted, which, he points out, is mentioned in Mr Burton's notes on Antonius's *Itinerary*. He says that to this day the rustics there dig up Roman coins, urns and bricks when they work the land.

. . .

Dr Plot says he has transcribed my notes on what a gravedigger told me concerning the roots that spring from dead bodies. He has similar purposes in his *History of Oxford* (that is about to go to press) as I do in my Chorographia Antiquaria. His book will include a new map, marking British and Roman camps and highways.

. . .

5 March
I went to Man's coffee house – over against Lincoln's Inn Gate in Chancery Lane – with Mr Hooke, Sir Robert Redding and Mr Chase. Afterwards at Sir Christopher Wren's, Mr Henshaw showed us Lapland boots and gloves, curious mosaic works in glass, and several brass antiquities. There was much discussion of ancient shipping and of music. We stayed until late.

. . .

My friend Jane Smyth, Mr Wylde's mistress, has chronic venereal disease: she is only twenty-seven years old. She was born the April after King Charles was beheaded. She came to London about half a year before the plague of 1665.

. . .

18 May
I told the Royal Society today that I have managed to arrange a loan of the astronomer Mr Samuel Foster's manuscripts, for their perusal, on the condition that they are returned afterwards. I arranged via my friend Mr Paschall to borrow them from Sir Francis Rolle via Mr Overton. Samuel Foster was Professor of Astronomy at Gresham College; he died in July 1652.

. . .

25 May

While I was with Mr Hooke and Mr Hoskyns today, Mr Hill gave us an account of Thomas Shadwell's new play *The Virtuoso*, which includes a character called Sir Nicolas Gimcrack said to be inspired by Mr Hooke. The play is a satire on the Royal Society. It draws on the Royal Society's *Philosophical Transactions*. Mr Hooke will see it for himself.

. . .

1 June

I observed the eclipse of the sun with Mr Hooke.

. . .

3 June

Mr Hooke saw *The Virtuoso* last night and is furious. He says people in the audience all but pointed at him as the inspiration for the buffoonish character Sir Nicolas Gimcrack. Sir Nicolas Gimcrack relates his ridiculous experiments and this is the source of much comedy in the play. When he is first on stage, Sir Nicolas Gimcrack seems to be swimming on land. He has bottled air, attempted to transfuse blood between dogs, and, like Mr Hooke, is fascinated by microscopy. Mr Shadwell insists that no individuals are ridiculed in his play – only the new science, which, he believes, aims at knowledge but never at useful discoveries. There can be no doubt that Mr Hooke has taken this as a personal attack. In Mr Shadwell's hands the Royal Society's experiments have become subjects for satire.

. . .

The Royal Society will make transcripts of my papers. I have been chosen for the committee that audits the Royal Society's accounts.

. . .

August

Mr Charles Snell has written to me of my nativity and accidents: 'Sickness at birth; ague and vomiting at about five or six years old; issue in my head; small-pox; amours with Madame Wiseman; selling away the manor etc.; hesitating in my speech . . .' All of which is accurate. He advises me that if my stammer hinders me, I could get a parsonage with a living of 400 or 500 li. per annum and give a curate 100 li. to officiate for me.

Mr Charles Snell has also sent me his judgement on Sir William Petty's horoscope.

. . .

My friend Thomas Mariett tells me there is extreme drought in Wiltshire: all the rivers, brooks and ponds are dry.

. . .

If I had wings (like a character in *The Virtuoso*), I would fly to see Mr Wood in Oxford! Instead, only my good wishes are continually sent. Mr Ralph Sheldon, the Roman Catholic, is another ever-honoured friend and lover of antiquities. If I should take a ramble into the country, I'd wait on him at Weston as soon as on any man in England. He has often invited me to stay.

. . .

If I were to visit my friend Mr Ralph Sheldon in Weston, I could go to Oxford first, but then how will I get to Weston? Maybe it would be possible for Mr Wood to help me get a horse, or perhaps there is a coach.

I will send Mr Wood a recipe of warm rye dough to apply to his ear to help his deafness; also a copy of Mr Evelyn's *Sylva*.

Today, Sir Henry St George, Clarencieux King of Arms, showed me manuscripts and good notes towards an account of my great-grandfather William Aubrey's life, written I suppose (given the hand-writing) by his son-in-law Daniel Dun, who married William Aubrey's third daughter, Joane. William Aubrey went to Oxford aged fourteen, became doctor by the time he was twenty-five, and about two or three years later, professor and Judge Advocate. I will ask Mr Wood if he would like to see a copy of his Life.

Quaere: what became of David King's collection of antiquities and antiquarian books, of which he had a great quantity at Yorke House?

My friends Sir William Petty and Sir John Hoskyns are still urging me to turn ecclesiastic to rescue my finances. Truly, if I had a good parsonage of 200 or 300 li. per annum, it would be a shrewd temptation. But this is no time to meddle in religion. People say the King of France grows stronger and stronger. What if the Roman religion were to come in again in England? I am no puritan, no enemy of the Pope, that old gentleman on the other side of the Alps. But as Mr Hobbes, that other old gent, says, I am better staying out of ecclesiastical matters in these unsettled times.

. . .

September
My lord the Earl of Thanet has invited me to return to Kent.

I am soon to go to Essex for a week with my good friend Mr Wylde, then afterwards perhaps to his estate in Worcestershire. Of all my friends who have helped me in my penury, he has done the most.

PART X

The Popish Plot

Anno 1676

Feeling against Roman Catholics is rising again in England. I am troubled by a letter I sent Mr Wood last year, or perhaps it was the year before, in which I expressed my friendship to the Church of Rome – I have asked him to burn the letter, or at least blot out the passage. I wrote the letter when I had been invited to take a benefice and was deciding what to do. God preserve us from another rebellion!

. . .

Mr Ogilby, the King's Cosmographer, has died and will be buried in the vault at St Bride's in Fleet Street. The church was damaged in the Great Conflagration and is being rebuilt according to Sir Christopher Wren's design.

. . .

Some time ago, I sent my friend Mr Paschall Mr Lodwick's essay on the Universal Character and communicated his responses to the author. Now Mr Lodwick has sent me further reflections on that subject and asked me to pass them on to Mr Paschall if I think he would be interested.

October
Mr Thomas Pigott of Wadham College doubts Mr Hooke's design for a pocket watch. He is interested too in the Philosophical Language and difficulties of the Universal Character.

. . .

20 October
I went to celebrate Sir Christopher Wren's birthday at Palgraves Head, near Temple Bar: he paid for everything. Sir John Hoskyns and Mr Hooke came too.

. . .

9 November
Today I was with Mr Hooke at Tooth's coffee house, then later at Garraway's.

. . .

15 November
I went home with Mr Hooke (Mr Crisp came too) and we drank two bottles of claret.

. . .

17 November
I went to Child's in St Paul's Churchyard and heard Mr Hooke and Mr Hill discourse about teaching children grammar by tables.

. . .

24 November
Mr Hooke and I went to dine with Lord Sarum.

. . .

7 December
I went to the Crown with Mr Wylde and Mr Hooke, where we drank brandy wine.

. . .

12 December
My friend the Reverend Andrew Paschall hopes that the outcome of Seth Ward the Bishop of Sarum's considerations on a Universal Language may be to reduce schism and babel to nothing.

. . .

Anno 1677

January

My lord the Earl of Thanet promises that he will acquaint his agent with the quality and quantity of shells I would like sent from the Bermudas.

. . .

March

My friend Mr Thomas Pigott has tracked down Dr Morison for me; he is putting out a general history of plants according to the order of nature. His proposals are in the Royal Society's Transactions and Mr Pigott will find out if Sir John Hoskyns wishes to subscribe. Further, he promises that as soon as he hears of anyone writing on medicinal waters, examined chemically, he will be sure to let me know.

. . .

My friend Mr James Boevey of the Inner Temple, who went to Florence in 1642 and enquired after Machiavelli's reputation, has also written many treatises on what he calls 'active philosophy': for example, 'The Government of Resolution' and 'The Art of Governing the Tongue'. He has sent me a list of his manuscripts and I am trying to persuade him to donate them to the library of the Royal Society.

Mr Boevey was a merchant before he was admitted to the Inner Temple. He is a great lover of natural philosophy and keeps a candle burning by him all night, with pen, ink and paper, so that he might not lose a thought. He is a person of great temperance, and deep thoughts, and a working head, which is never idle. He is only five foot tall, slenderly built, with extremely black hair, curled at the ends, an equally black beard, and the darkest of eyebrows hovering above dark but sprightly hazel eyes.

Mr Ashmole has made a list of the many books on magic in Mr Boevey's library.

. . .

12 March

Jane Smyth, who is somewhat better, and I met Mr Hooke this evening at Cardinal's Tavern in Lombard Street. We drank until past midnight and Mr Hooke vomited up wine.

Jane Smyth has the idea that men might metamorphose into trees and flowers planted in their graves. Her notion is that the soul of the deceased goes into the tree or plant and lives. It is lovely and ingenious.

. . .

25 March

Lady Day: my good friend Mr Wenceslaus Hollar has died. If he had lived until 13 July this year, he would have been seventy years old. He will be buried in St Margaret's churchyard, Westminster. He was a very friendly, good-natured man, but shiftless as to the world and died not rich.

. . .

James, Duke of York, has reluctantly consented to the marriage of his Protestant daughter Mary to William, the Prince of Orange, Stadholder of the Dutch Republic. Our present King, who still has no children born within wedlock, arranged the marriage. Many in England fear the prospect of a Roman Catholic monarch if James succeeds to the throne.

. . .

21 April

Mr Hooke saw the comet this morning (he learnt of it yesterday). He says it appeared in the sign of Taurus, between the base of the triangle and the unformed stars in the cloud of Aries. The head of it was in a right line with the heart of Cassiopeia and Alamak, or the south foot of Andromeda. As near as he could judge with his naked eye (he had no instrument or help to hand) it was 5/6 of the distance between the feet and the girdle of Andromeda.

. . .

24 April

I went to Mr Hooke's with Mr Wylde, Mr Merret, Mr Moxon and others to see the comet, but we missed it and drank two bottles of claret.

. . .

June

An abscess on my head broke.

July

Mr Charles Snell has written to explain my horoscope to me. He addresses me as 'Dear Gossip'! He says his brother will be glad to enter my lord the Earl of Thanet's employment as steward for his Barbados concerns, if he has not already engaged one.

. . .

I have sold some books to Mr Littlebury.

. . .

August

I am recovered now from my illness and will go soon into the country, where I hope to visit Mr Paschall in Somerset. We have much to discuss: the Universal Character, the cider press, etc. He tells me he has not yet been able to go to Salisbury to see the Bishop of Sarum, nor to visit my mother at Broad Chalke. I will go myself soon, I hope.

. . .

5 September

Mr Oldenburg, Secretary of the Royal Society, has died, aged about fifty-eight. He was made secretary when the Society was granted its royal charter in 1662 and was extremely active in that regard. He established the *Philosophical Transactions* in 1665. But it was through his default that some small tracts of Mr Hobbes's were not published in the *Philosophical Transactions*.

. . .

7 September

Mr Hooke came to dine with me and afterwards we went to see Sir John Hoskyns, then to visit Mr Alhurst, a perspective painter in Exeter Street, near the Red Cow.

. . .

11 September

My friend Mr Harrington died today at his house in Little Ambry. He will be buried in St Margaret's Church, Westminster, next to illustrious

Sir Walter Raleigh, under the south side of the altar, where the priest stands.

For this past year Mr Harrington's memory and speech were taken away by disease. It was a sad sight to see such a sample of mortality in one whom I had known to be a brisk and lively *cavaliero*. Henry Nevill continued to pay his visits to Mr Harrington during this illness as duly and respectfully as when his friend was in the prime of his understanding. Henry Nevill was a true friend and should never be forgotten for his constancy.

. . .

16 September
I coincided with Nell Young at Mr Hooke's.

. . .

4 October
Today I watched the demonstration of a new wind gun. It is made in the form of the head of a stick and from soldered brass, with two leather valves.

. . .

Mr Hooke has my picture done by my dear friend Mr Cooper, the prince of limners, before he died. Mr Cooper once gave Mr Hooke drawing lessons.

. . .

Mr Hooke has asked me to help find a new President of the Royal Society by discussing with Mr Ent, Dr Millington, etc. the manner of choosing one. Viscount Brouncker has been President since 1663, but has decided to resign, as it is clear he will not be re-elected at the Society's annual meeting on St Andrew's Day. The Society is declining and many members believe it needs a change in President.

. . .

I will undertake the correspondence for the election of the new President (although Sir John Hoskyns's cabal opposes this).

. . .

13 October
Today I was at the Rainbow and afterwards at Child's.

. . .

Since Mr Oldenburg's death, Mr Hooke has been elected Secretary of the Royal Society, together with Nehemiah Grew.

. . .

November
Viscount Brouncker sent me a note to give notice that next Friday, 30th of this month, the council and officers of the Royal Society are to be elected for the ensuing year, and my presence is expected for the election at Gresham College at nine o'clock in the morning precisely.

. . .

30 November
St Andrew's Day. Mr Henshaw was in the chair for the Royal Society vote. Mr Grew read out the votes and Mr Hooke marked them. Sir Peter Wych scrutinised for Mr Grew and I did it for Mr Hooke. The outcome was Sir Joseph Williamson President, Mr Hill Treasurer, Mr Grew and Mr Hooke Secretaries.

. . .

Anno 1678

March
Some of my letters reach me in London by being left with Mr William Crooke, the bookseller at the Green Dragon, outside Temple Bar. Mr Hobbes, who is in Hardwick, writes to me this way. He has not been able to write for some time and now has sent me a dictated letter. In it he says he is so weak that even dictating pains him. He is still bitter towards Dr Wallis. He says it is no surprise that Dr Wallis, or anyone else who studies mathematics only to gain preferment, should convert his study to juggling, conjuring and deciphering when his ignorance is discovered. According to Mr Hobbes, Dr Wallis is only esteemed in the universities because those who defended his geometry are too ashamed to recant.

I asked Mr Hobbes if he thought it possible to teach a man born deaf and dumb to speak. He answers me no: it is impossible. He says he is assured that a man born absolutely deaf must of necessity be made to hear before he can be made to speak.

. . .

In Oxford, Gloucester Hall, I am told, is in a terrible state. Not one student matriculated there these past four years, and only the incumbent Principal (Byrom Eaton) and his family and two or three other families living there keep some part of it from ruin. The paths are overgrown with grass and the hall and chapel have been nailed up with boards this year.

. . .

22 April
I dined with Sir John Hoskyns and Mr Hooke.

. . .

May
I have been misdirecting my letters to my friend George Ent: I have been sending them to The Crown, instead of The Rose! He has written to say he is hoping for my company when he comes to London in a week's time. He tells me that the University treasury is low, and so are Trinity College's coffers, on account of their building projects, but he believes Queens' or Emmanuel or some other Cambridge college might purchase Lady Dodington's medals.

My friend Andrew Paschall, so far as his rusticated life permits, is studying the natural way of making and learning a language, on different lines from the Bishop of Sarum. I am grateful to him for his kindness to my mother, whom he writes to and visits.

John Ray tells me he took up the study of plants only as a diversion, but since he is not qualified to serve God in his proper function – divinity is his profession, but he has not undertaken it for sixteen years – he has bestowed a good proportion of his time upon plants and has no thoughts of parting with any of his books on botany. In 1662, he forfeited his Fellowship at Trinity College, Cambridge, because he could not accept the terms of the Act of Uniformity, which prescribed the form of the public prayers and sacraments of the Church of England. Even so, he has remained a loyal member of the Church of England. At Trinity he had a small garden, planted with specimens that he had collected on his long walks in the Cambridgeshire countryside, or else had sent to him. His first botanising perambulation outside Cambridgeshire was to Northampton, Warwick and north Wales in 1658. Since then he has travelled north as far as Scotland and visited many places of antiquarian interest while searching for plants.

. . .

I have had such a good time in Oxford with my lady friend and ingenious company. Thomas Pigott would not be parted from us and even came to see us off on the coach at Abingdon.

. . .

The great lover of antiquities, Silas Taylor, has died. During his lifetime he accumulated many rare manuscripts, including those of the Church of Hereford and the Church of Worcester. Among them was King Edgar's original grant of the right to the sovereignty of the sea to the Kings of England. There is a printed copy in Mr Selden's *Mare Clausum*. I have seen the original many times and it is as legible as if it was writ yesterday. Mr Silas Taylor tried to sell it to the King for 120 li., but the King would not pay so much. Now that Silas Taylor has died a debtor, I fear his creditors will seize on his papers and belongings and this precious manuscript will end up being used to wrap herrings!

. . .

June
Yesterday on the Exchange it was reported that in the Roman Catholic countries there is a group of devotes that go up and down begging for money to make war on England: they have got about two million so far. They wear crosses and a crown of thorns on their heads.

. . .

I have heard that my old friend Francis Potter has died. He died between Easter and Whitsuntide on 22 April. He will be buried in the chancel at Kilmington where he was rector. His books have been sold for under 3 li. In Trinity College, Oxford, he will be remembered for the sundial he made on the north wall of Durham Quad and his copy of the portrait of the college's founder, Thomas Pope, which hangs in the hall.

. . .

Andrew Paschall has had an idea for promoting the Real Character. He suggests that sheets displaying tables of plants, with their names given in the Real Character, could be illustrated to hang in greenhouses like maps; the same for shrubs, trees, minerals and stones, insects, animals; also in pocket book size. This would be a clever way of getting the Real Character taken notice of.

. . .

4 July

Today I presented the herb called *terrara* to the Royal Society. It was brought over from Carolina by Sir Peter Colleton, and grown here in Mr Johnson's garden: it is the best antidote against all manner of poisons. Its virtues were a great secret among the Indians, until someone who married an Indian king's daughter discovered it. It is mentioned in the history of the Antilles, where it is called *herbe aux flesches*.

I also related an anecdote about a man whose feet rotted off from wearing shoes that had been taken off a malefactor's feet after he had rotted.

. . .

Thomas Pigott tells me that learned Dr Morison has talked to him of the Italian botanists Ambrosinus and Zeno, and shown him plates in Zeno's book.

. . .

Andrew Paschall has sent me an elaborate draft of his design for the table of plants. It sets out each separate part of the plant, botanical classifications, etc. The plant names are to be in several languages, in distinct columns. He asks me to assure Mr Lodwick that his proposals are intended to agree with the framework for the Real Character set out by the Bishop of Sarum. Mr Paschall has no ambition to be the author of a schism.

. . .

Mr Evelyn has been to see Mr Ashmole's library and collection of curiosities at South Lambeth. Mr Ashmole has many astrological manuscripts and is dedicated to the study of astrology.

. . .

September

I leave now for a few days in Oxford, where Mr Sheldon will send a horse for me, and I will travel on to his house at Weston, where Mr Wood has been staying and cataloguing his library.

I have promised to help Mr Wood by searching the register for the burial of John Milton. I have also encouraged him not to forget to mention Mr Wenceslaus Hollar, who so much obliged the world with his etchings and deserves to be remembered: he lies buried in St Margaret's Church, Westminster.

When I went to see Mr Milton's widow, she assured me that Mr Thomas Hobbes was not one of her late husband's acquaintances, that he did not like Mr Hobbes at all, but would acknowledge him to be a man of great parts and learned. Their interests and tenets were diametrically opposed.

. . .

Titus Oates, who was received into the Roman Catholic Church on Ash Wednesday last year, has accused the Jesuits of plotting to set fire to the City of London, murder the King and conquer England by Irish and French arms. The world runs madding.

Titus Oates now claims that he became a Roman Catholic only to spy on the Jesuits. Together with Israel Tonge, he wrote a manuscript outlining a Jesuit plot to assassinate the King. Today he was questioned by the King's Council and made allegations against over 500 Roman Catholic priests and nobles. Close members of the Duchess of York's circle are among those he has named. He has launched a public campaign against the 'Papists'.

. . .

12 October, Weston

Mr Sheldon's house has been searched today for arms by six men under the command of Sir Thomas Mordant, who is investigating the alleged Papist Plot, revealed by Titus Oates.

I will ask Mr Wood to lend me some money so that I can go straight back to London and stay out of the way of trouble.

. . .

15 October
Mr Wood agreed to lend me 3s. 6d: I will pay him back through his brother, whom I will meet at Staple Inn when he is next in London.

. . .

19 October
Mr Hooke and I watched the eclipse of the moon.

. . .

November
Mr Pigott tells me in his letter that every corner of Oxford is now full of rumours about the Papist Plot, so much so that other discourses seem silenced. Plots, policies and rumours in these troublesome and disordered times take away all thoughts of learning.

. . .

22 November
My old friend from Trinity, Thomas Mariett, now High Sheriff of Warwickshire, has gone to Weston with a warrant from the Privy Council and arrested Mr Sheldon, who has been taken to Warwick Gaol.

. . .

Titus Oates claims that the Queen is working with the King's Physician to poison His Majesty. The King will question Titus Oates himself.

. . .

The King has ordered the arrest of Titus Oates, whom he has caught out under questioning.

. . .

The Parliament has forced the release of Titus Oates. He is to be given an apartment in Whitehall and an annual allowance of 1,200 li.

. . .

Together with the future Earl of Pembroke, I have been chosen to inspect the proceedings of the Royal Society's Secretaries.

. . .

5 December
Today I left some books for Mr Wood at the Saracen's Head, including Mr Hobbes's *Leviathan*.

. . .

Anno 1679

January
I sent Mr William Howe the almanac of the Royal Society last year. He is sailing to Persia, from where he has promised me seeds and shells, and any rarities he finds on his travels. He says the Congo is not so pleasant a place as I believe it to be, but a trading seaport, which is barren and sandy. It is true that there are all sorts of fruit to be got there, but they are brought from elsewhere in the country. How I wish I were travelling with him.

. . .

27 January
Fire broke out in Middle Temple Lane last night and many of Mr Ashmole's collections have been burnt. His large paper book of faces, and another of marriage ceremonies and funerals, etc. are lost, along with all his subterranean antiquities and curiosities of nature. Some 9,000 brass, copper and silver coins and medals are missing or defaced. Mr Ashmole will spare no pains to rescue what he can from the ash.

. . .

I join Mr Wood in his lament for Mr Ashmole's collections: 'His losses are ours!' Before they burnt, those rarities were destined for Oxford.

. . .

The Commons have concluded that Papists started the fire in Middle Temple Lane, but others say it was a maidservant who lit a fire and went away.

. . .

February

Mr Crooke tells me there is competition for the printing of Mr Hobbes's life.

. . .

March

I have sent Mr Hobbes Sir George Ent's book on respiration. I sent it via Mr William Crooke's shop, and Mr Hobbes writes back to me the same way. My friend George Ent, son of Sir George, is seriously ill.

. . .

20 March

I was at Jonathan's coffee house, which is next door to Garraway's in Exchange Alley, with Sir John Hoskyns and Mr Hooke.

. . .

25 March

I was at Jonathan's coffee house again, but was expelled with Mr Wylde and Mr Sacwill.

. . .

At the Royal Society there has been further discussion of printing all Roger Bacon's works together, but before that can be done, it is necessary to find what writings of his are dispersed in private libraries. His *Computus Naturalium* is in the library of University College in Oxford, for example, but not in the Bodleian. I am to ask Mr Wood to send the Society a copy of the catalogue of Bacon's works that he included in his English edition of the Antiquaries of Oxford (which I have seen, even though it has yet to be printed).

. . .

2 April

I went to Child's coffee house this evening and saw Sir John Hoskyns, Mr Lodwick and Mr Hooke.

. . .

Often, as I lie in bed, I chide myself when I consider how much time Mr Wylde and I waste. I grow lethargic.

. . .

I dream often of my friend Ralph Sheldon's house in Weston.

. . .

Last night I decided that the scurrilous satirical pamphlet against Mr Pepys and his colleague Mr Hewer, *The Hue and Cry*, is one of the pleasantest things that I have ever read and nothing could more fit me. The pamphlet accuses them of coining money, selling jobs and licences and taking bribes. Mr Hooke and I laughed at it heartily.

. . .

Robert Pugh, the Roman Catholic controversialist, died in Newgate on 22 January, and is buried in Christ Church. I have found out that his (nearly finished) treatise on the several states and governments that there have been in this country since the Troubles is in the Earl of Castlemaine's hands; all his other works, including the almanac, were seized.

I am told that when his study was searched, his orders were there found and also a letter from the Queen Mother (whose confessor he had sometimes been) to the King to the effect that if he should fall into any danger of the law, upon sight of that letter he should have His Majesty's pardon.

. . .

11 April

My lord the Earl of Thanet has invited me to call on him tomorrow morning for a little business, followed by a dish of meat and a bottle of most excellent Portugal wine.

. . .

12 April

At Jonathan's coffee house, Mr Wylde and I discussed buildings with Mr Hooke.

. . .

My friend Mr Thomas Pigott claims the temptation of enjoying my company will attract him to London towards the end of May unless, still better, I visit him in Oxford. He writes to say he would be very glad to hear of the Bishop of Sarum's design for the Universal Character and Mr Hooke's and Mr Paschall's amendments, and what reception his letter to Mr Lodwick had had among them.

But alas, he informs me that my poor former-servant Robert Wiseman died some time ago. Mr Pigott helped carry him to the grave and is much afflicted by grief, as am I.

. . .

May Day

Today Mr Michael Dary, mathematician and a gunner of the Tower (by profession a tobacco-cutter), was buried in the churchyard near Bethlem. He was an old man, I guess over sixty-six, and an admirable algebrician. This past winter was so severe that he got gangrene in his fingers and they rotted from writing in the frosty weather.

. . .

15 May

On this day the foundation stone for a new building in Oxford to house Mr Ashmole's collection of rarities was laid next to Christopher Wren's Sheldonian Theatre. Mr Ashmole's collection includes that of the Tradescants of South Lambeth, which was assigned to him by Deed of Gift in 1659. He has agreed to donate all to the University, on the condition of the new building being completed. His intention in founding a public museum is to further knowledge of nature – necessary to human life, health and convenience – by promoting understanding of the history of nature. He hopes in this way to contribute to the development of medicine, manufacture and trade. Mr Evelyn has suggested to Mr Ashmole that Dr Plot would be a fit and proper appointment as the first keeper of the new museum when it is ready.

. . .

The Exclusion Bill has been introduced into the House of Commons, with the intention of excluding the Duke of York, a Roman Catholic, from succeeding to the throne. There is a faction that hopes to see the Duke of Monmouth – the King's bastard but Protestant son – succeed.

. . .

Sixteen days after the funeral of John Tradescant's widow Hestor, who was found drowned in her pond after losing her dispute with Mr Ashmole over her late husband's collection of rarities, Mr Ashmole has taken the lease on the Tradescant house and garden in South Lambeth. He had been leasing a neighbouring house since 1674. Some of the Tradescant collection had already been transferred to Mr Ashmole's house. Now that he is in full possession of the Tradescant inheritance, he hopes to move the collection to Oxford.

. . .

Mr Wylde Clerke, who is my friend Edmund Wylde's godson, has sent me a letter from Santa Cruz in Africa, dated November last year, reporting on the crops, berries, grapes, and horses of the country. He writes of the diet: camels' milk, ostrich meat; bread not commonly eaten; and the people's bare subsistence. He promises to explore for the herbs, etc. that I have enquired about.

. . .

Mr Thomas Pigott asks if I can help a learned friend of his, Mr Fairfax, a mathematician, who is reduced to great poverty. I fear I cannot.

. . .

20 June
On this day at Tyburn, the Jesuit William Barrow (known as Father Harcourt) and four others accused of the Popish Plot have been executed for conspiring to kill the King and subvert the Protestant religion.

There is a rumour that when Father Harcourt's entrails were tossed into the brazier by the hangman, a butcher's boy resolved to have a piece of his kidney, which was broiling in the fire, so burnt his fingers snatching it from the flames. I will see this piece of petrified kidney if I can. Mr Roydon, a brewer in Southwark, has it now.

I met Father Harcourt in 1650 and he told me that he was of the Stanton Harcourt family.

Since the discovery of the Popish Plot, the Penal Laws have been put into effect against Roman Catholics, who will be severely proceeded against if they do not receive the Sacrament according to the Church of England in their parish churches.

. . .

27 June

I met Mr Sheldon in London today (he was released from gaol in April, and treated very well there, so my friend Thomas Mariett tells me). My stammer was terrible. I still feel guilty for what I said about Mr Sheldon in a drunken letter I wrote to Thomas Mariett, which was full of gossip gleaned from the Parliament men and the courtiers who attend the Royal Society. As soon as I sent that letter to the posthouse, I regretted it, even though it was to my old acquaintance and intimate friend from boyhood. Mr Sheldon is so worthy and honest a gent: I would more easily incur anyone's displeasure than his.

The Queen has been accused of plotting to poison the King and convert the country to Roman Catholicism. I think there is shrewd evidence against her.

. . .

I have asked Mr Ent to try and recover for me the text of Mr Hobbes's Latin prose autobiography, which I lent to Anthony Wood and which he has refused to return.

. . .

Mr Hobbes tells me his treatise concerning law (The Dialogue of the Common Law) is imperfect at the end and he will not consent to it being printed, not by Mr Horne, nor by Mr Crooke. He tells me too that his book on the civil war (Behemoth: the history of the causes of the civil wars of England, and of the counsels and artifices by which they were carried on from the year 1640 to the year 1660) is in circulation, but he regrets this, as he could not get His Majesty to license it. The King has read and likes the book extremely, but is afraid of displeasing the bishops.

In his book, Mr Hobbes argues that our civil war was caused by Presbyterian clergy struggling to gain control over the people against the prerogative of the King. Speech was the main means by which the clergy sought to dominate the people. Mr Hobbes is suspicious of the power of eloquence, which he believes is a form of passion that distorts the meaning of words. Behemoth is written as a dialogue between 'A', an eyewitness of the civil war, and 'B', a younger student, concerning the years 1640 to 1660. It ends with a paean to General George Monck. Mr Hobbes offers a rational account of how the war and the regicide happened. He insists that there can be 'nothing more instructive towards loyalty and justice' than the memory, while it lasts, of that war.

. . .

23 July
I went to Bloomsbury coffee house with Mr Hooke.

. . .

September
My friend Robert Henley has invited me to go and take a little air at his country home, and when he comes back up to Parliament, he will carry me in his coach and set me down at the Middle Temple or near thereabout, from whence I shall know my way home.

. . .

October
My friend George Ent has died. He told me a few days before that he had seen a ghost (or *deceptio visus*, as he called it) that gave three knocks and called him away from this world. His father Sir George Ent is grief stricken.

. . .

14 November
I was at Jonathan's coffee house with Sir John Hoskyns and Mr Hooke.

. . .

I have suggested to Mr Edmund Halley – the prodigious young astronomer – that he study astrology. He tells me it seems an ill time for it, given that the arch conjuror Mr Gadbury is in danger of being hanged for it. But he will follow my recommendation and read around the subject. He went to the library and found the books I recommended, which were published in 1557.

I sent my letter to Mr Halley by way of my friend Thomas Pigott, so that these two would become acquainted.

. . .

24 November
My honoured lord the Earl of Thanet has died at the age of forty-nine. He was my refuge and patron.

. . .

I have heard that my old acquaintance John Birkenhead, who wrote the news in Oxford during the late wars, died on 4 December. He was chosen as a Member of Parliament for Wilton in the King's Long Parliament of 1661, but when he stood for election to Parliament this year, he was scorned and mocked and called 'pensioner'. As a result, he did not stand, but returned to London and insensibly declined, pining away in his lodgings in Whitehall.

. . .

My honoured friend Mr Hobbes died on 4 December at Hardwick. He was speechless for his last six days, and was buried on 6 December. I have sent for a full account of his funeral and will. Mr Wood will return Mr Hobbes's life in prose (which only goes up to 1651), so that I can continue it by six lines or so. They say that when a learned man dies, a great deal of learning dies with him. Mr Hobbes was a *flumen ingenii*, a stream of genius, never dry. The *recrementa* (or remains) of so learned a person are valuable. I must now fulfil my promise to my dear departed revered friend and write up the minutes of his Life, which I promised to do as long ago as 1667. 'Tis religion to perform the will of the dead. I am minded to begin it with a pleasant description of Malmesbury. I think first drafts or sketches ought to be rude as those of painters, for he that in his first essay will be curious of refining will certainly be unhappy in inventing. I do not know if I should print my memoirs of the Life of Hobbes in Latin, or English, or both. If in Latin, who will do the translation for me? And is my English style well enough?

. . .

Now that the sun has entered Capricorn, it will begin to mount a little higher and I shall become more vigorous and less lethargic again.

Mr Wood asks much of me. He has sent another list of questions:
- What is Francis Potter's epitaph; and which was the day and year of his burial?
- What were the titles of Dr William Petty's two published books, and where was he born?
- When did John Wagstaff die and where is he buried?
- When and where did Dr John Godolphin die, where is he buried, and who sold his books?
- Can I consult the register of St Pancras Church?

. . .

St John the Evangelist's Day

I am as good as promised Sir George Ent's assistance in continuing Mr Hobbes's life in Latin, even though he is still grieving for his son. I will get Mr Hobbes's life licensed by the Royal Society, or else print it in Holland or Scotland. Should I mention that it was at my request (about fifteen years ago) that Mr Hobbes wrote an account of his life and entrusted it to me as his countryman and acquaintance since I was eight years old? I will be zealously industrious to this purpose, and Mr Wood and I will be revenged on Dr Fell: *rumpatur quisquis rumpitur invidia* (may every man who bursts with malice burst himself).

Could one have thought that Dr Fell, that ghostlike ghostly father, so continual and assiduous in the prayers of the Church of England, that good exemplar of piety, a walking Common Prayer Book, could have made such a breach and outrage on morals and justice? Who would have thought Dr Fell to have such an itch for the tyranny of the press: scratching out an author's phrases, expunging and interponing? He has made the universities worse thought of than ever they were before. Who can pardon such a dry bone, a stalking consecrated engine of hypocrisy?

. . .

Anno 1680

January

Mr Henry Vaughan promises to search for me into distant and obscure nativities with all possible speed. If he finds anything in nature that may deserve the notice of the Royal Society he will present me with it. He finds the Ancients less unkind to astrology than most modern physicians.

. . .

At Burbage in Wiltshire the soil is an ash-coloured grey sand, and very natural for the production of good turnips. They are the best I have ever eaten, and are sent for from far and near. They are not tough and stringy, like other turnips, but cut like marmalade. Quaere: how old the trade in turnips is? Certainly all the turnips that were brought to Bristol eighty years ago came from Wales. But now none come from there, for it has been found that the red sand about Bristol breeds a better and bigger turnip. Burbage is also remarkable for excellent peas.

. . .

I have often wished for a map of England painted according to the colours of the earth and marks of the minerals.

. . .

My mother has written to tell me that she was seventy years old last Thursday (29 January).

. . .

Spectacles have been worn for about 200 years, and were sold, when first invented, for 3 or 5 li. a pair. The Germans call them Brill, from the beril-stone (or crystal) from which they were first made. I remember discussing the difference between spectacles and a vidette with Mr Hobbes.

PART XI

Brief Lives

Anno 1680

February

My friend the bookseller Mr William Crooke informs me that other authors are preparing lives of Mr Hobbes: he urges me to make haste with mine. I would not have believed that I could be so copious! I have written a draft, but still have more to add from letters and memoranda books. I would also like to write other lives: Sir William Petty's, Sir Christopher Wren's, Mr Robert Hooke's.

. . .

8 February

I was at Jonathan's coffee house with Mr Haak, Mr Hodby, Mr Tison and Mr Hooke.

. . .

I hope Mr Wood will help me by searching for the month and day of Mr Hobbes's matriculation. At Trinity College we wrote our names in the buttery book the day we were admitted to the University. It was probably the same at Magdalen Hall.

Mr Wood chides me for calling my Life of Mr Hobbes a supplement. Originally I intended it only to complement Mr Hobbes's own autobiography. But now Mr Wood advises me my work is worthy of the title: The Life of Thomas Hobbes.

I have been reading over some of my notes and it seems to me I could have written four times as much as I have on Malmesbury.

While I was smoking a pipe of tobacco in my chamber last Sunday night, it suddenly came to me that it would be a fine thing if I were to write my honoured friend Sir William Petty's life from his cradle; he can peruse it himself and then it shall be left for posterity hereafter. Now I have my hand in since writing the life of Mr Hobbes, I am minded to scribble a page or two on the lives of some eminent men. About five years ago I lodged with Mr Ashmole some sheets of minutes of the lives of Dr John Dee, Lord Bacon, Sir Christopher Wren, Robert Hooke, Dr William Aubrey, John Pell and Robert Boyle, etc. I have asked for these to be left with my friend Mr Wood so he can preserve them among his papers.

. . .

The science of astrology is not yet perfect. The way to make it perfect is to get an apparatus – or supellex – of true genitures. For this reason, I am taking much care collecting the nativities of the lives I am writing. Astrologers will be able to rely on these, for I have not compiled any of them on random or doubtful information. Instead, whenever possible, I have taken them down from the subject's own mouth.

. . .

This month the Penny Post has been set up. It was first invented by Mr Robert Murray, formerly clerk to the General Company for the Revenue of Ireland, and Mr Dockwra, who joined him in the enterprise. Previously, the post office collected and carried letters between postal towns, but there was no provision for delivering them, so many of them were lost, as I often found to my great chagrin. Now in London there will be a local delivery system charged at the rate of a penny per letter or packet weighing up to a pound. There will be several deliveries a day in London, and for the extra charge of another penny, letters can be delivered to addresses ten miles outside the city.

. . .

Today, at about 3 p.m., I was seized by a fainting fit. I fear that at the age of fifty-four, my death creeps up on me. I have written my last will and testament. I intend to leave my notes for the Lives I have begun to write to Mr Wood – they are like fragments from the shipwreck of the past.

Mr Wood warns me to be careful if I am to play any part in writing the life of Mr Hobbes: I should write fair things, or someone else will be on my back.

. . .

March

I have persuaded Sir William Petty to sit to have his picture painted by Mr Loggan the engraver. In 1659, Mr Samuel Cooper drew him in miniature and the result was one of the likest portraits that prince of limners ever drew.

. . .

12 March

Today is my birthday, which falls close to the Roman Quinquatria (19 March), the feast dedicated to Minerva.

. . .

My honoured friend Edward Davenant has died. I have heard Sir Christopher Wren say that he was the best mathematician in the world thirty or thirty-five years ago. But being a divine, he was unwilling to print his work, lest the world should know how he had spent the greatest part of his time.

I will write to his executor to ask if we may have the honour and favour of conserving his manuscripts in the library of the Royal Society, and of printing what is fit.

He was my singular good friend, to whom I have been more beholden than to anyone else besides. I once borrowed 500 li. from him for a year and a half and he would not let me pay him any interest on the loan.

. . .

25 March

Sir Jonas Moore was admitted as a Fellow of the Royal Society today.

. . .

Mr Dryden (Poet Laureate) has complimented Mr Blackbourne's style in compiling the life of Hobbes. These two are agreed on leaving out all the minuteness: they will have the truth, but not the whole truth. For example, they will make no mention of Mr Hobbes having been a page. I am letting the grass grow under my feet, and Mr Blackbourne will have all the glory if I do not hurry up. I say that the offices of panegyrist historians are one thing: but a Life is a short history in which minute details about a famous person should be gratefully recorded. I never yet knew a wit write a proper epitaph (unless he was an antiquary) which did not leave the reader ignorant about the subject's provenance, what countryman he was, etc.

I have made an index for my Book of Lives: it includes fifty-five persons (I have done ten of them already, including four pages on Sir Walter Raleigh). It will be a pretty thing when it is finished. I am so glad my researches for Mr Wood and my promise to write the life of Mr Hobbes have led me to collect these other lives. I do it playingly. This morning, I got up by 10 and wrote two lives. One of them was the life of Sir John Suckling, on whom I wrote a page and a half in folio. I will add to it the scoffing ballad that was made against him, his fine troop and his running away. Sir John replied with another ballad: 'I . . . thee foole, who ere thou be/ That maketh this fine sing song of me.' Perhaps Mr Wood will search Mr Sheldon's ballad collection for me.

If I could get up by 7 a.m., I could finish my Book of Lives in a month.

Here is a list of the Lives I have done so far:

Sir William Petty (the first)
Edward Davenant
Sir John Suckling
Mr Edmund Waller
Thomas Randolph
Mr Camden (half a page)
Mr William Oughtred (full)
Viscount Falkland

Quaere: who has Mr Camden's papers? I must remember to ask Mr Dugdale. I think he has Mr Camden's minutes of King James's life, and also his own life, written by himself, but very brief, just two sheets of paper in his own handwriting. Mr Dugdale got these manuscripts from the Bishop of Coventry, who filched them from Mr Camden as he lay dying. It is said that Mr Camden had bad eyes, lippitude I guess, or else was short-sighted, which is a great inconvenience to an antiquary.

Mr Dryden tells me he will write his life for me himself. I can then add it to my collection.

I could afford to put in the life of Dr Ralph Kettell, who was President of Trinity College when I first went there. Though no writer, he was a good man and a good governor of the college. I have among my books Dr Kettell's copy of Sir Thomas Overbury's translation of Ovid's *De remedio amoris*.

. . .

Philip Herbert, 7th Earl of Pembroke, my patron, has at Wilton fifty-two mastiffs and thirty greyhounds, some bears, a lion, and a matter of sixty fellows all more bestial than they.

. . .

1 April
Today I was at Jonathan's coffee house with Mr Hooke. He is a bachelor and I believe will never marry: a person of great suavity and goodness.

. . .

St George's Day
I have collected together my notes on Lives and I find I have written a book that is two quires of paper, which I will send to Mr Wood at the beginning of May.

. . .

I am sending Mr Wood a copy of Mr Hobbes's considerations on his own reputation and loyalty (first published anonymously in 1662). Originally, there were about 300 copies, and I had two or three. Now the book has been printed anew from one of my copies (the original having sold out).

. . .

May
I have been very ill with a cold lately. But even so, I have now written sixty-six of my Lives. Having begun my own Book of Lives, I feel I cannot be quiet until I have finished it. I have such an impulse on my spirit.

Recently, after coming round from a fainting fit, I wrote my will and humble request on the first page of my manuscript that my Book of Lives be transmitted to Mr Wood if I should die. They are fine things, my Lives, but few of them are fit to be printed in my lifetime, or Mr Wood's. If he dies, his papers will all fall into the possession of Dr Wallis (*ex officio*) as Keeper of the Archives, and there be stifled: for I am like Almansar in the play, who spares neither friend nor foe. I am religious John Tell-Troth.

I have decided to rename my Templa Druidum; now it will be called Monumenta Britannica.

. . .

3 June

Today at the Royal Society we discussed monstrous births. I read out Mr Paschall's letter about the two children born at Hilrewers in Somerset, joined into one body about the navel, but separated into two distinct bodies both above and below the belly. They eat, suck, cry, sleep and void their excrements separately and freely. They seem likely to live.

I also described a creature born to a rabbit but fathered by a cat, which Sir Christopher Wren has heard of too. Others spoke of cross-breeding between partridges and pheasants and poultry; and between ducks and sea fowl. It was generally observed that all the progeny of this cross-breeding are barren, and will not go on to propagate.

. . .

I have written my minutes of Lives tumultuarily, or as they occurred in my thoughts, or, occasionally, as I had information of them from others. My friend Mr Wood, antiquary of Oxford, could easily reduce them to order by numbering them according to time and place. They are Lives chiefly of contemporaries, but not only.

When I first began to write my Lives, I did not think I could have drawn out so long a thread. I have laid down the truth, as near as I can, and as religiously as a penitent to his confessor, nothing but the truth, the plain and naked truth, which is exposed so bare that the very pudenda are not covered, and there are many passages that will raise a blush in a young virgin's cheeks. I must ask Mr Wood to sew on some fig leaves, to make a castration, to be my *index expurgatorius*.

What uncertainty do we find in printed histories, which either tread too close on the heels of truth that they dare not speak plain, or else for want of intelligence (things being antiquated) become too obscure and dark. In my Book of Lives I do not repeat anything already published (to the best of my knowledge) and I imagine myself all along discoursing with Mr Wood. Thus he makes me renew my acquaintance with old or deceased friends: this is the pleasure of old men.

I have now lived over half a century of years in the world, and been much tumbled up and down in it, so I have a wide and general acquaintance. Also, I have the advantage of London's new coffee houses. Before they opened, men only knew how to be acquainted with their own relations or societies. They were afraid and stared at all who were not of their own communities.

I wish someone had written a Book of Lives like mine a hundred years ago. How many worthy men's names and notions are swallowed by oblivion because no such book exists for the last century! Perhaps this Book of Lives of mine is the most useful piece I have ever scribbled. Had Mr Wood not urged me to write it, many of these lives would have been swallowed up in oblivion too. General Lambert used to say: 'the best of men are but men at the best', and there are many examples in my rude and hasty collection of Lives, which is not fit to let fly abroad for another thirty years: the author and persons, like medlars, ought to be rotten first.

. . .

July
The Earl of Rochester, aged only thirty-three, has died of venereal disease at Woodstock Park. In his last illness, he was exceedingly penitent. He sent for his servants, even the piggard boy, to hear his palinode. His immature death puts me in mind of these verses of Propertius:

> Vere novo primoque in aetatis flore iuventae
> seu rosa virgineo pollice carpta, iaces.
> (In early spring and the first flower of youth,
> like a rose plucked by a maiden's hand, you lie dead.)

. . .

August

I have sent Mr Wood more answers to his questions, and in return asked him if, when he goes to Westminster, he will transcribe out of the ballad book the song on Lord Chancellor Egerton's son. I have also asked him to send me the name of the inventor of the engine for weaving silk stockings. Mr Wood has sent me some gloves, for which I am most grateful.

A friend tells me that in the time of the Rump Parliament they talked of the dissolution of the universities and concluded that they were unnecessary.

. . .

September

My Book of Lives will be in all about six-score individual lives, and I believe never before in England were lives delivered so faithfully and with such good authority. I will include in my Life of King James the hostile ballad that was sung at the time of his coronation in 1603:

> And at the erse of them marched the Scottish peers
> With lowzie shirts, and mangie wrists, went pricking-up
> their ears . . .

Perhaps Mr Wood can search Ralph Sheldon's ballad book for me to see if he can find it.

. . .

I have given my Book of Lives to Dr Pell, hoping he will make some additions and amendments. Before I gave it to him, I pleased myself reading over the Lives I have written so far and transcribing a few excerpts into this diary:

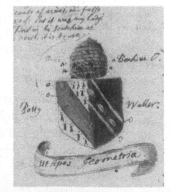

Sir William Petty, knight

His horoscope: Monday, Maii 26th, 1623: n h 42' 56" p.m., natus Gulielmus Petty, miles, sub latitudine 51 10' (tempus verum), at Rumsey in Hants.

This horoscope was done, and a judgement made upon it, by Charles

Snell, Esq., of Alderholt near Fording-bridge in Hampshire: Jupiter in Cancer makes him fat at heart. John Gadbury also says that vomits would be excellent good for him.

Sir William was the (eldest, or only) son of . . . Petty, of Rumsey in Hampshire, by . . . his wife. His father was born on the Ash Wednesday before Mr Hobbes, *scilicet* 1587. He died and was buried at Rumsey 1644, where Sir William intends to set up a monument for him. He was by profession a clothier, and also did dye his own clothes: he left little or no estate to Sir William.

Sir William was born at his father's house aforesaid, on Trinity Sunday. Rumsey is a little haven town, but hath most kinds of artificers in it. When he was a boy his greatest delight was to be looking on the artificers, e.g. smiths, the watchmaker, carpenters, joiners, etc. and at twelve years old he could have worked at any of these trades. He went to school, and learnt by 12 years a competent smattering of Latin, and was entered into the Greek. He has had few sicknesses. [Aged] about 8, in April very sick and so continued till towards Michaelmas,

About 12 (or 13), i.e. before 15, he has told me, happened to him the most remarkable accident of his life (which he did not tell me), and which was the foundation of all the rest of his greatness and acquiring riches.

He informed me that, about 15, in March, he went over into Normandy, to Caen, in a vessel that went hence, with a little stock, and began to merchandise, and had so good success that he maintained himself, and also educated himself; this I guessed was the most remarkable accident that he meant. He learnt the French tongue, and perfected himself in the Latin, and had Greek enough to serve his turn. Here (at Caen) he studied the arts. Memorandum: he was sometime at La Flèche in the college of Jesuits. At 18, he was (I have heard him say) a better mathematician then he is now: but when occasion is, he knows how to recur to more mathematical knowledge. At Paris he studied anatomy, and read Vesalius with Mr Thomas Hobbes (vide: Mr Hobbes's life), who loved his company. Mr Hobbes then wrote his *Optiques*; Sir William then had a fine hand in drawing and limning, and drew Mr Hobbes's optical schemes for him, which he was pleased to like. At Paris, one time, it happened that he was driven to a great strait for money, and I have heard him say that he lived a week on two pennyworth (or 3, I have forgot which, but I think the former) of walnuts.

Quaere: whether he was not sometime a prisoner there?

I remember about 1660 there was a great difference between him and Sir . . . , one of Oliver [Cromwell]'s knights, about . . . They printed one against the other: this knight was wont to preach at Dublin. The knight had been a soldier, and challenged Sir William to fight with him. Sir William is extremely short-sighted, and being the challengee it belonged to him to nominate a place and weapon. He nominated, for the place, a dark cellar, and the weapon to be a great carpenter's axe. This turned the knight's challenge into ridicule, and so it came to nought.

He is a person of an admirable inventive head, and practical parts. He hath told me that he hath read but little, that is to say, not since aged 25, and is of Mr Hobbes's mind, that had he read much, as some men have, he had not known so much as he does, nor should have made such discoveries and improvements.

His physique: his eyes are a kind of goose-grey, but very short-sighted, and, as to aspect, beautiful, and promise sweetness of nature, and they do not deceive, for he is a marvellous good-natured person. Eyebrows thick, dark, and straight (horizontal). His head is very large. He was in his youth very slender, but since these twenty years and more past he grew very plump, so that now (1680) he is *abdomine tardus*.

Robert Boyle

The honourable Robert Boyle Esq., the (fifth) son of Richard Boyle, the first Earl of Cork, was born at Lismor (anciently a great town with a university and 20 churches) in the county of Cork, the 25th day of January anno 1627.

He was nursed by an Irish nurse, after the Irish manner, where they put the child into a pendulous satchel (instead of a cradle), with a slit for the child's head to peep out.

He learnt his Latin, went to the University of Leyden, travelled in France, Italy, and Switzerland. I have oftentimes heard him say that after he had seen the antiquities and architecture of Rome, he esteemed none 'anywhere else'. He speaks Latin very well, and very readily, as most men I have met with. I have heard him say that when he was young, he read over Cooper's dictionary: wherein I think he did very well, and I believe he is much beholding to Cooper for his mastership of that language.

His father in his will, when he comes to the settlement and provision for his son Robert, thus – *Item to my son Robert, whom I beseech God to bless with a particular blessing, I bequeath, etc.* – the greatest part is in Ireland. His father also left him the manor of Stalbridge in Dorset, where is a great freestone house; it was forfeited by the Earl of Castlehaven.

He is very tall (about six foot high) and straight, very temperate, and virtuous, and frugal: a bachelor; keeps a coach; sojourns with his sister, the lady Ranulagh. His greatest delight is chemistry. He has at his sister's a noble laboratory, and several servants (apprentices to him) to look to it. He is charitable to ingenious men that are in want, and foreign chemists have had large proof of his bounty, for he will not spare for cost to get any rare secret. At his own costs and charges he got translated and printed the New Testament in Arabic, to send into the Mahometan countries. He has not only a high renown in England, but abroad; and when foreigners come to hither, 'tis one of their curiosities to make him a visit.

His works alone may make a library.

General Monck

George Monck was born at . . . in Devon (vide: Devon in Heralds' Office), a second son of . . . , an ancient family which had about Henry VIII's time 10,000 li. per annum (as he himself said). He was a strong, lusty, well-set young fellow and in his youth happened to slay a man, which was the occasion of his flying into the Low-countries, where he learned to be a soldier.

At the beginning of the late civil wars, he came over to the King's side, where he had command (quaere: in what part of England?). Anno . . . he was prisoner in the Tower, where his seamstress, Nan Clarges (a blacksmith's daughter), was kind to him in a double capacity. (The blacksmith's shop is still of that trade. It is the corner shop, first turning on the right hand as you come out of the Strand into Drury Lane.) It must be remembered that he was then in want and she assisted him. Here she was got with child. She was not at all hand-some, nor cleanly. Her mother was one of the five women barbers. Anno . . . (as I remember, 1635) there was a married woman in Drury-lane that had clapt (i.e. given the pox to) a woman's husband, a neighbour of hers. She complained of this to her neighbour gossips. So they concluded on this revenge, viz. to get her and whip her and shave all the hair off her pudenda; which severities were executed and put into a ballad. 'Twas the first ballad I ever cared for the reading of: the burden of it was thus:

> Did yee ever hear the like
> Or ever heard the same
> Of five women-barbers
> That lived in Drury-lane?
> (Vide: the Ballad-book)

Anno . . . her brother, Thomas Clarges, came a shipboard to George Monck and told him his sister was brought to bed. 'Of what?' said he. 'Of a son.' 'Why then,' said he, 'she is my wife.' He had only this child.

Anno . . . (I have forgot by what means) he got his liberty, and an employment under Oliver Cromwell (I think) at sea, against the Dutch, where he did good service; he had courage enough. But I remember the seamen would laugh, that instead of crying 'Tack about', he would say, 'Wheel to the right (or left)'.

Anno 16 . . . he had command in Scotland (vide: his life), where he was well beloved by his soldiers, and, I think, that country (for an enemy). Oliver [Cromwell], [Lord] Protector, had a great mind to have him home, and sent him a fine complimentary letter, that he desired him to come into England to advise with him. He sent His Highness word that if he pleased he would come to wait upon him at the head of 10,000 men. So that design was spoiled.

Anno 1660, February 10th (as I remember), being then sent for by the Parliament to disband Lambert's army, he came into London with his army about one o'clock p.m. He then sent to the Parliament this letter, which printed, I annex here. Shortly after he was sent for to the Parliament house, where, in the house, a chair was set for him, but he would not (in modesty) sit down in it. The Parliament (Rump) made him odious to the city, purposely, by pulling down and burning their gates (which I myself saw). The Rump invited him to a great dinner, in February, shortly after, from whence it was never intended that he should have returned (of this I am assured by one of that Parliament). The members stayed till 1, 2, 3, 4 o'clock, but at last His Excellency sent them word he could not come. I believe he suspected some treachery.

Annex: 'A Letter from his Excellencie the Lord General Monck and the officers under his command to the Parliament; in the name of themselves, and the soldiers under them', printed by John Macock, 1660.

The honours conferred on George Monck everyone knows.

His sense might be good enough, but he was slow, and heavy. He died Anno . . . and had a magnificent funeral suitable to his greatness.

Dr William Aubrey

William Aubrey, Doctor of Laws: – extracted from a manuscript of funerals, and other good notes, in the hands of Sir Henry St George – I guess it to be the handwriting of Sir Daniel Dun, knight, LL Dr, who married Joane, third daughter of Dr William Aubrey.

William Aubrey (the second son of Thomas Aubrey, the 4th son of Hopkin Aubrey, of Abercunvrig in the county of Brecon) in the 66th year of his age or thereabouts, and on the 25th of June, in the year of our Lord 1595, departed this life, and was buried in the cathedral-church of St Paul in London, on the north side of the chancel, over against the tomb of Sir John Mason, knight, at the base or foot of a great pillar standing upon the highest step of certain degrees or stairs rising into the quire eastward from the same pillar towards the tomb of the right honourable the lord William, Earl of Pembroke, and his funerals were performed the 23rd of July, 1595.

This gentleman in his tender years learned the first grounds of grammar in the College of Brecon, in Brecknock town, and from thence about his age of fourteen years he was sent by his parents to the University of Oxford, where, under the tuition and instruction of one Mr Morgan, a great learned man, in a few years he so much profited in humanity and other recommendable knowledge, especially in Rhetoric and Histories, as that he was found to be fit for the study of the Civil Law, and thereupon was also elected into the fellowship of All Souls College in Oxford (where the same Law hath always much flourished). In which college he earnestly studied and diligently applied himself to the lectures and exercise of the house, as that he there attained the degree of a Doctor of the Law Civil at his age of 35 years, and immediately after, he had bestowed on him the Queen's Public Lecture of Law in the University, the which he read with so great a commendation as that his fame for learning and knowledge was spread far abroad and he was also esteemed worthy to be called to action in the commonwealth. Wherefore, shortly after, he was made Judge Marshall of the Queen's armies at St Quentin in France. Which wars finished, he returned into England, and determining with himself, in more peaceable manner and according to his former education, to pass on the course of his life in the exercise of law, he became an advocate of the Arches, and so rested many years, but with such fame and credit as well for his rare skill and science in the law, as also for his sound judgement and good experience therein, as that, of men of best judgement, he was generally accounted peerless in that faculty.

Besides the great learning and wisdom that this gentleman was plentifully endowed withal, Nature had also framed him so courteous of disposition and affable of speech, so sweet of conversation and amiable behaviour, that there was never any in his place better beloved all his life, nor he himself more especially favoured of Her Majesty, Queen Elizabeth, and the greatest personages in the realm in any part of his life than he was when he drew nearest his death.

He was of stature not tall, nor yet over-low; not gross in body, and yet of good habit; somewhat inclining to fatness of visage in his youth; round, well favoured, well coloured and lovely; and albeit in his latter years sickness had much impaired his strength and the freshness of his hew, yet there remained there still to the last in his countenance such comely and decent gravity as that the change rather added unto them than ought diminished his former dignity. He left behind him when he died, by a virtuous gentlewoman Wilgiford his wife (the first daughter of Mr John Williams of Tainton in the county of Oxford, whom he married very young a maiden, and enjoyed to his death, that both having lived together in great love and kindness by the space of 40 years), three sons and six daughters.

Memorandum: – he was one of the delegates (together with Dr Dale, etc.) for the trial of Mary, Queen of Scots, and was a great stickler for the saving of her life, which kindness was remembered by

King James at his coming-in to England, who asked after him, and probably would have made him Lord Keeper, but he died, as appears, a little before that good opportunity happened. His Majesty sent for his sons and knighted the two eldest, and invited them to court, which they modestly and perhaps prudently declined. They preferred a country life.

You may find him mentioned in the History of Mary, Queen of Scots, 8vo, written, I think, by (John) Hayward; as also in Thuanus's Annales (insert his words here in honour to the Doctor's Manes).

He was a good statesman; and Queen Elizabeth loved him and was wont to call him 'her little Doctor'. Sir Joseph Williamson, Principal Secretary of Estate (first Under-Secretary), has told me that in the Letter-office are a great many letters of his to the Queen and council.

The learned John Dee was his great friend and kinsman, as I find by letters between them in the custody of Elias Ashmole, viz., John Dee wrote a book *The Soveraignty of the Sea*, dedicated to Queen Elizabeth, which was printed, in folio. Mr Ashmole has it, and also the original copy of John Dee's handwriting, and annexed to it is a letter of his cousin Dr William Aubrey, whose advice he desired in his writing on that subject.

Old Judge Sir (Edward) Atkins remembered Dr Aubrey when he was a boy; he lay at his father's house in Gloucestershire: he kept his coach, which was rare in those days. The Judge told me they then (vulgarly) called it a Quitch. I have his original picture. He had a delicate, quick, lively and piercing black eye, fresh complexion, and a severe eyebrow. The figure in his monument at St Paul's is not like him, it is too big.

Sir Lleuellin Jenkins, knight

Sir Lleuellin Jenkins, knight, was born at Llantrithid in the county of Glamorgan, Anno Domini . . . His father (whom I knew) was a good plain countryman, a copyholder of Sir John Aubrey, knight and baronet (eldest son of Sir Thomas), whose manor it is. He went to school at Cowbridge, not far off. David Jenkins, that was prisoner in the Tower (married a sister of Sir John Aubrey), was some remote kin to him; and, looking on him as a boy towardly, diligent, and good, he contributed something towards his education. Anno Domini 164(1), he was matriculated of Jesus College in Oxford, where he stayed till (I think) he took his degree of Bac. Artium. About that time Sir John Aubrey sent for him home to inform his eldest son Lewis Aubrey (since deceased, 1659) in grammar; and that he might take his learning the better, he was taught in the church-house where several boys came to school, and there were 6 or 7 gentlemen's sons boarded in the town. The young gentlemen were all near of an age, and ripe for the University together; and to Oxford they all went under Mr Jenkins's care about Anno 1649 or 50, but by reason of the disturbances of those times, Sir John would not have his son of any college. But they all studied at Mr (now Sir) Sampson White's house, a grocer, opposite to University College. Here he stayed with my cousin about 3 years or better, and then, in Anno 165 . . . (vide: Mr Hobbes's *De Corpore*, 'twas that year), he travelled with my cousin and two or 3 of the other gentlemen into France, where they stayed about 3 years and made themselves masters of that language.

He has a strong body for study, indefatigable, temperate and virtuous. God bless him.

Wenceslaus Hollar

Wenceslaus Hollar, Bohemus, was born at Prague. His father was a Knight of the Empire: which is by letters patent under the imperial seal (as our baronets). I have seen it: the seal is bigger then the broad seal of England: in the middle is the imperial coat; and round about it are the coats of the Princes Electors. His father was a Protestant, and either for keeping a conventicle, or being taken at one, forfeited his estate, and was ruined by the Roman Catholics.

He told me that when he was a schoolboy he took a delight in drawing of maps; which draughts he kept, and they were pretty. He was designed by his father to have been a lawyer, and was put to that profession, but then his father's troubles, together with the wars, forced him to leave his country. So it turned out that what he did for his delight and recreation only when a boy proved to be his livelihood when a man. I think he stayed sometime in Low Germany, then he came into England, where he was very kindly entertained by that great patron of painters and draughts-men (Thomas Howard) Lord High Marshall, Earl of Arundel and Surrey, where he spent his time in drawing and copying rarities, which he did etch (i.e. with *aqua fortis* in copper plates).

When the Lord Marshall went ambassador to the Emperor of Germany to Vienna, he travelled with much grandeur; and among others, Mr Hollar went with him (very well clad) to take views, landscapes, buildings, etc. remarkable in their journey, which we see now at the print shops. He hath done the most in that way that ever any one did, insomuch that I have heard Mr John Evelyn, RSS, say that at sixpence a print his labour would come to . . . li. (quaere: John Evelyn).

I remember he told me that when he first came into England (which was a serene time of peace) that the people both poor and rich did look cheerfully, but at his return, he found the countenances of the people all changed, melancholy, spiteful, as if bewitched.

I have said before that his father was ruined upon the account of the Protestant religion. Wenceslaus died a Roman Catholic, of which religion, I suppose, he might have been ever since he came to Arundel-house.

He was a very friendly good-natured man as could be, but shiftless as to the world, and died not rich.

Monsieur Renatus Descartes

Nobilis Gallus, Perroni dominus, summus mathematicus et philosophus; natus Hagae Turonum pridie Calendas Apriles, 1596; denatus Holmiae Calendis Februarii, 1650.

This inscription I find under his picture graved by C. V. Dalen.

How he spent his time in his youth, and by what method he became so knowing, he tells the world in his treatise entitled *Of Method*. The Society of Jesus glory in that their order had the educating of him. He lived several years at Egmont (near the Hague), from whence he dated several of his books.

He was too wise a man to encumber himself with a wife; but as he was a man, he had the desires and appetites of a man; he therefore kept a good conditioned handsome woman that he liked, and by whom he had some children (I think 2 or 3). 'Tis pity but coming from the brain of such a father, they should be well cultivated.

He was so eminently learned that all learned men made visits to him, and many of them would desire him to show them his . . . of instruments (in those days mathematical learning lay much in the knowledge of instruments, and, as Sir Henry Savile said, in doing of tricks), he would draw out a little drawer under his table, and show them a pair of compasses with one of the legs broken; and then, for his ruler, he used a sheet of paper folded double. This from Alexander Cooper (brother of Samuel), limner to Christina, Queen of Sweden, who was familiarly acquainted there with Descartes.

Mr Hobbes was wont to say that had Descartes kept himself wholly to geometry that he had been the best geometer in the world. He did very much admire him, but said that he could not pardon him for writing in defence of Transubstantiation, which he knew to be absolutely against his judgement.

Venetia Stanley

Venetia Stanley was daughter of Sir . . . Stanley. She was a most beautiful desirable creature; and being *matura viro* was left by her father to live with a tenant and servants at Enston Abbey in Oxfordshire: but as private as that place was, it seems her beauty could not lie hid. The young eagles had espied her, and she was sanguine and tractable and of much suavity (which to abuse was great pity).

In those days, Richard, Earl of Dorset (eldest son and heir to the Lord Treasurer), lived in the greatest splendour of any nobleman of England. Among other pleasures that he enjoyed, Venus was not the least. This pretty creature's fame quickly came to his lordship's ear, who made no delay to catch at such an opportunity.

I have now forgot who first brought her to town, but I have heard my uncle Danvers say (who was her contemporary) that she was so commonly courted, and by grandees, that 'twas written over her lodging one night *in literis uncialibus*:

> PRAY COME NOT NEAR, FOR DAME
> VENETIA STANLEY LODGETH HERE.

The Earl of Dorset, aforesaid, was her greatest gallant, he was extremely enamoured of her, and had one if not more children by her. He settled on her an annuity of 500 li. per annum.

Among other young sparks of that time, Sir Kenelme Digby grew acquainted with her, and fell so much in love with her that he married her, much against the good will of his mother; but he would say that 'a wise man, and lusty, could make an honest woman out of a brothell-house'.

Sir Edmund Wylde had her picture (and you may imagine was very familiar with her), which picture is now (vide) at Droitwych, in Worcestershire, at an inn in an entertaining-room, where now the town keep their meetings. Also at Mr Rose's, a jeweller in Henrietta Street in Convent garden, is an excellent piece of hers, drawn after she was newly dead.

She had a most lovely and sweet-turned face, delicate dark-brown hair. She had a perfect healthy constitution; strong; good skin; well proportioned; much inclining to a Bona Roba (near altogether). Her face, a short oval; dark-brown eyebrow, about which much sweetness, as also in the opening of her eyelids. The colour of her cheeks was just that of the damask rose, which is neither too hot nor too pale. She was of a just stature, not very tall.

Sir Kenelm had several pictures of her by Van Dyke, etc. He had her hands cast in plaster and her feet, and her face. See Ben Jonson's 2nd volumn, where he hath made her live in poetry, in his drawing of her both body and mind:

> Sitting, and ready to be drawne,
> What makes these tiffany, silkes, and lawne,
> Embroideries, feathers, fringes, lace,
> When every limbe takes like a face!

When these verses were made she had three children by Sir Kenelme, who are there mentioned, viz. Kenelm, George, and John.

She died in her bed suddenly. Some suspected that she was poisoned. When her head was opened there was found but little brain, which her husband imputed to her drinking of viper-wine; but spiteful women would say 'twas a viper-husband who was jealous of her that she would steal a leap.

I have heard some say, e.g. my cousin Elizabeth Falkner, that after her marriage she redeemed her honour by her strict living. Once a year the Earl of Dorset invited her and Sir Kenelm to dinner, where the Earl would behold her with much passion, and only kiss her hand.

Sir Kenelm erected to her memory a sumptuous and stately monument at . . . Friars (near Newgate-street) in the east end of the south aisle, where her body lies in a vault of brick-work, over which are three steps of black marble, on which was a stately alter of black marble with 4 inscriptions in copper gilt affixed to it: upon this alter her bust of copper gilt, all which (unless the vault, which was only opened a little by the fall) is utterly destroyed by the Great Conflagration.

How these curiosities would be quite forgot, did not such idle fellows as I am put them down!

PART XII

More Lives and Deaths

Anno 1680

September

About twenty years ago, I gave a quantity of petrified shells to the
Royal Society. They were something like cockles, but plain and with
a long neck rather than striated or invecked. I found them in south
Wiltshire. Mr Hooke says the species is now lost. The quarry at
Portland in Dorset is full of oyster shells, and a great deal of stuff
like sugar candy, that Mr Hooke says is petrified seawater.

I have often thought that there was a time when the whole globe
was covered with water, and that the world is like a pomegranate,
full of caverns. Anyone who has seen the caves at Wookey Hole or
the Peake in Derbyshire will have a strong and lively idea of what I
mean. Perhaps earthquakes caused the water to sink and then the
earth appeared. I am led to believe this by the great quantity of petrified fish shells that can be found on high hills.

. . .

26 September
I dined at Mr Hooke's. He has finished his Atlas.

. . .

27 September
Today I helped carry the pall for the satirist Samuel Butler's coffin. He died of consumption two days ago and we have buried him in the churchyard of Covent Garden, in the north part, next to the church at the east end. His feet touch the wall. His grave is two yards from the pilaster of the door and six foot deep. He printed a witty poem against religious fanatics, called *Hudibras*, in the early 1660s, which was extremely popular. He could have had preferments aplenty, but would not accept any good ones, so died in want.

. . .

Mr Hobbes's short Life by himself in Latin will be printed next week, and Mr Wood shall receive six copies.

. . .

October
I am at Gresham. Mr Pigott has written to tell me he intends to buy all the numbers of the Transactions of the Royal Society since no. 132 (1676), to complete the collection in their library at Wadham College. I reckon that since no. 132, there have been four by Mr Oldenburgh; six by Dr Grew; and two more by Mr Hooke; so twelve in total.

. . .

I have given the Royal Society a copy of the Life of Thomas Hobbes.

. . .

I am trying to find out whether the Ferraran library is at Ferrara, or Modena, and have written to Octavian Pulleyn, via contacts in Paris, to ask. All the princes of Italy are so careful to conserve their libraries and choice collections of manuscripts.

. . .

Mr Paschall has asked me if I can recommend any historical writers on the West Indies, particularly concerning what the Church of Rome has done in Peru and Mexico and the English Protestants in the northern tracts (Virginia and New England).

. . .

2 December

Today I have received an account of Ben Jonson's life from Mr Isaac Walton (who also wrote John Donne's life). Mr Walton is now eighty-seven years old. The account is in his own handwriting. I will send it on to Mr Wood for safe keeping.

. . .

Mr Wood has written to me to say that he is now back in Oxford and has leisure to read my Lives if I will send them to him. He encourages me to continue my collecting and researches and urges me to believe that these truly are my talents.

. . .

23 December

I went with Mr Hooke to Jonathan's coffee house, where Mr Henshaw refused the suggestion that he become president of the Royal Society.

Israel Tonge was buried today in the vault of the churchyard of St Mary Staining, where there was a church before the Great Conflagration, of which he was parson. He excelled at alchemy. He also set up an excellent school following the Jesuits' method of teaching at Durham in 1658 or 1659. Afterwards he taught in Islington at Sir Thomas Fisher's house. I went to see him there in the long gallery where he had put up several printed heads of Alexander the Great, Julius Caesar, Hannibal, Scipio, Aristotle, Archimedes, etc. with different declensions of verbs under them (the dative under one, the ablative under another, etc.). Then when the boys come to a verb that governs an ablative case, for example, it presently occurs to their memories: 'Oh, this verb is under Julius Caesar's head', etc. This way of local memory makes a fast impression or idea in their tender memories.

. . .

Anno 1681

January

Dr Pell has returned my book, but without any corrections or sugges-tions for improvements. Poor man! He is old and disconsolate, living in poverty. Soon I will send my remarks on 120 Lives to Mr Wood in Oxford. I ought to work some more on them first, but am distracted into reading French romances. I need to rub up my French, which has gone rusty with disuse.

. . .

Dr Blackbourne and I have published the 'Vitae Hobbianae auctarium' with Hobbes's accounts of his own Life. Mr Wood has been a great help to me in this. Dr Blackbourne is a young man of prodigious parts but ungovernable: he does not use me well in losing my papers. The mischief of it is that the great concern of the present politics drowns and takes away the venom of my sting as to the Right Reverend Fell. The felonies of the Reverend Fell seem insignificant amidst the present troubles. A pox take plots and plotters!

Quaere: what do the academics say at the coffee shops about Mr Hobbes's life?

. . .

18 January

On this day the King dissolved the Parliament. He refuses to compro-mise on the succession. The Whig, or Country, Party hopes to exclude the Roman Catholic James, Duke of York, but the King will not have it. A new Parliament will meet in Oxford in March. These turmoils remind me of my undergraduate days: God grant us peace!

. . .

Mr Dugdale has printed his *Short View of the Late Troubles*, which draws on the newsbooks that grew up during those years of civil war. He says in his preface that he has delivered in his own words what he knows, but for that which is beyond his own knowledge he has relied on other authors and the common Mercuries and other public licensed narratives of the events of the civil war.

. . .

The Earl of Berkshire has thanked me for my account of the waters of Leek and encouraged me to do some further experiments on their nature. He has left 10 li. for me at a draper's in St Paul's Churchyard and entreats me to accept it.

. . .

The King has dissolved Parliament again. He convened it at Oxford on 21 March and it lasted just eight days. Now he will rule without a Parliament and it is rumoured another Popish plot is afoot. My friend George Ent was wont to say, 'A pox take Parties!', and I say, 'A pox take plotters!'

. . .

I intend to send my Book of Lives to Mr Wood next week, but I cannot think how to do this safely, since if it gets lost there will be no retrieving it. I could take it myself and go and see my friend Sir James Long too, but Oxford is once again crammed to bursting point and I do not intend to end up sleeping by a fireside at my age.

How much work I would get done if I did not sit up with Mr Wylde until one or two in the morning, or if there was someone to get me up in the mornings with a good scourge! I think I could finish my Lives in a week, if I were to stop wasting time.˙ Sir James Long has invited me to stay again.

I intended to take down Sir Jonas Moore's memories, of the mathematician William Gascoigne especially, from whom he received most of his knowledge, but I delayed doing so, and now death has taken Sir Jonas away. I must set down what I can remember of what he used to say. Also, I remember that I did not take the measurements of Silbury Hill for my Monumenta Britannica because Sir Jonas had promised to give them to me. He had taken them accurately for the ordnance. I must find the measurements among his papers if I can.

Next week I will buckle to finish my Lives. I am sure I could do it in a week.

. . .

When I sent my small offering of books to the Bodleian Library in 1675, George Ent added to their number to make it up to a large enough donation for recording in the Benefactors' Book. He put in *The Mystery of Jesuitism*, or *Jesuit Morals*, I forget which. Now I have never meddled with controversy in my life, nor shall I ever! I am only for mathematics, philosophy and antiquities. It is for my gift of the Historia Roffensia manuscript that I should be remembered. But now I have fears I will be caught up in the religious strife on account of the book George Ent gave to the Bodleian Library on my behalf.

. . .

Mr Paschall has sent me an example of a desirable Utopia: a draft of a history entitled The American Adventure. The adventurers come from 'Eleutheropolis'. Strife has arisen between Christians and pagans. The Prince seeks to compose party differences but expels the strangers. The new adventurers are accepted and the Christianising of the populace is undertaken. Schism and dispute excluded, etc.

. . .

Mr Wood complains of his deafness and considers coming to London to consult a doctor; but he fears a cure might make him worse. He worries about how I can get my Lives to him securely.

. . .

June
Sir James Long tells me there is severe drought again in Wiltshire: there is no grass or hay to cut in the fields.

. . .

21 June
Yesterday evening Mr Wood sent his pretty niece – what amorous elegies I could write for her – to call on me, and I have let her take parts one and two of my book to him at last. I have a great many more things to insert, and ten more Lives I would like to add, but no time.

Mr Wylde has given me a recipe for curing Mr Wood's deafness. Mr Wood believes his deafness is caused by a cold moist head and a cold moist stomach, which give rise to noises in his head. I hope Mr Wylde's recipe will work!

. . .

Mr Wood has sent me 5s. He is pleased with my Lives even though they contain many things that are not fit to be published.

. . .

I went to a tavern with John Lacy, a player, who was Mr Ogilby's apprentice when he had his dancing school in Grays Inn Lane, and I took down notes to add to my Life of Mr Ogilby. Among other things, John Lacy told me that Mr Ogilby would never say where in Scotland he was born as he hoped (drollingly) that there would be as much contention over the place of his birth as there is over Homer's.

. . .

Sir William Petty writes from Ireland (where he feels he is living in a place full of exasperated enemies) to say he is not forward with the printing of his Political Arithmetic because he intends to compare his current draft with the one in Mr Southwell's hand, which he corrected in 1679.

On behalf of the Royal Society, Sir William has gone to some trouble over the elephant that was so unfortunately burnt. But the owner will not part with the skeleton, guts or trunk, which he hopes to show for profit (so they cannot be obtained for the Royal Society's repository). Sir William says he is surprised that English and Dutch surgeons living in India have not already made a perfect anatomy of the creature.

. . .

13 July

I told the Royal Society today that recently I saw a live marten in a shop in Cornhill. I think many of them are bred in England, and my friend Mr Wylde has received a number of skins from a tenant of his.

. . .

I hope, in a few weeks' time, to see my beloved Oxford again. How much I wish the history of Jesuitism which George Ent unluckily gave to the Bodleian on my behalf were erased out.

I am concerned that in my Lives there are things that will cut my throat if they are not cut out. There are, for example, severe touches in my account of the life of Sir Richard Boyle, Earl of Cork (father of Robert Boyle) – perhaps I should not have included what my friend Anthony Ettrick told me about his amours and bastards. My Life of Dr Wallis is another difficulty.

If I die in London, as seems most likely, I wonder where I should be buried? Perhaps in my parish church, St Martin's Outwych, near the door, like a poor penitent with a foot-square inscription. Or perhaps in the non-conformist churchyard by the artillery ground in Moorfields?

. . .

I fear the truths set out in my book will breed trouble – *veritas odium parit* (truth begets hatred). I have written too much truth, some of it of those who are still alive. In my book the truth is set down in its pure and natural state, not falsely coloured. This pleases me as an antiquary, but my Lives are not fit to be published. I have been writing them for my friend Mr Wood and have included many rude, undigested, unpolished and frivolous things.

. . .

I met with old Mr Beeston, 'the Chronicle of the Stage', today and we talked about the English poets he has known. He will give me notes on their lives. His father was master of the . . . playhouse. Knowing the uncertainty of life, and how few there are who transmit memories to posterity, I am ever more eager to pursue what I have begun.

. . .

I have written up the Lives of Mr Shakespeare and Mr Spenser:

Mr William Shakespeare

Mr William Shakespeare was born at Stratford-upon-Avon in the county of Warwick. His father was a butcher and I have been told heretofore by some of the neighbours that when he was a boy he exercised his father's trade, but when he killed a calf he would doe it in a high style, and make a speech. There was at that time another butcher's son in this town that was held not at all inferior to him for a natural wit, his acquaintance and coetanean, but died young.

This William, being inclined naturally to poetry and acting, came to London, I guess, about 18; and was an actor at one of the playhouses, and did act exceedingly well (now Ben Jonson was never a good actor, but an excellent instructor). He began early to make essays at dramatic poetry, which at that time was very low; and his plays took well.

He was a handsome, well shaped man: very good company, and of a very ready and pleasant smooth wit. The humour of . . . the constable, in Midsomernight's Dreame, he happened to take at Grendon in Bucks – I think it was Midsomer night that he happened to lye there – which is the road from London to Stratford, and there was living that constable about 1642, when I first came to Oxford: Mr Josias Howe is of that parish, and knew him. Ben Jonson and he did gather humours of men daily where ever they came. One time as he was at the tavern at Stratford-super-Avon, one Combes, an old rich usurer, was to be buried, he makes there this extempory epitaph:

> Ten in the hundred the Devill allowes,
> But Combes will have twelve, he sweares and vowes:
> If any one askes who lies in this tombe,
> 'Hoh!' quoth the Devill, "tis my John o Combe.'

He was wont to go to his native country once a year. I think I have been told that he left 2 or 300 li. per annum there and thereabout to a sister. Vide: his epitaph in Dugdale's Warwickshire.

I have heard Sir William Davenant and Mr Thomas Shadwell (who is counted the best comedian we have now) say that he had a most prodigious wit, and did admire his natural parts beyond all other dramatical writers. He was wont to say (Ben Jonson's *Underwoods*) that he 'never blotted out a line in his life'; said Ben Jonson, 'I wish he had blotted-out a thousand.'

His comedies will remain wit as long as the English tongue is understood, for that he handles *mores hominum*. Now our present writers reflect so much upon particular persons and coxcombeities, that twenty years hence they will not be understood.

Though, as Ben Jonson says of him, that he had but little Latin and less Greek, he understood Latin pretty well, for he had been in his younger years a schoolmaster, in the country – this from Mr . . . Beeston.

Mr Edmund Spenser

Mr Edmund Spenser was of Pembroke-hall in Cambridge; he missed the fellowship there, which Bishop Andrewes got. He was an acquaintance and frequenter of Sir Erasmus Dreyden. His mistress, Rosalind,

was a kinswoman of Sir Erasmus's lady's. The chamber there at Sir
Erasmus's is still called Mr Spenser's chamber. Lately, at the College
taking-down the wainscot of his chamber, they found an abundance
of cards, with stanzas of the *Faerie Queen* written on them. – This
from John Dryden, Esq., Poet Laureate.

Mr Beeston says he was a little man, wore short hair, a little band
and little cuffs.

Mr Samuel Woodford (the poet, who paraphrased the Psalms) lives
in Hampshire near Alton, and he told me that Mr Spenser lived sometime in these parts, in this delicate sweet air; where he enjoyed his
muse, and writ good part of his verses.

I have said before that Sir Philip Sidney and Sir Walter Raleigh were
his acquaintance. He had lived some time in Ireland, and wrote a
description of it, which is printed with Morison's History, or Description,
of Ireland.

Sir John Denham told me that Archbishop Usher, Lord Primate of
Armagh, was acquainted with him, by this token: when Sir William
Davenant's *Gondibert* came forth, Sir John asked the Lord Primate if
he had seen it. Said the Primate, 'Out upon him, with his vaunting
preface, he speaks against my old friend, Edmund Spenser.'

In the south crosse-aisle of Westminster abbey, next the door, is
this inscription:

Here lies (expecting the second coming of our Saviour Christ
Jesus) the body of Edmund Spenser, the Prince of Poets of his
time; whose divine spirit needs no other witness then the works
which he left behind him. He was borne in London, in the year
1510, and died in the year 1596.

. . .

8 August
My mother has written to tell me that she has been ill for three weeks
and now her eyes are a little sore.

. . .

At my mother's request, Mr Paschall has supplied his wife's recipe for
lapis calamine for sore eyes, and has explained how to apply the cure.

The ointment is made from finely powdering the *lapis calamine* and mixing it with butter.

. . .

15 August
On this day my brother Tom died at Sarum. I will write to my friend the astrologer Charles Snell, for an account of my poor brother's demise.

. . .

Charles Snell tells me he had not heard my brother was ill until he was dead. He had no learned physician with him, only drunken Jack Chapman, the sometime apothecary at Bath.

. . .

September
I have brought more of my Lives to Oxford for Mr Wood. I have been here a week, refreshing my soul among ingenious acquaintances. I feel I owe adoration to Oxford's very buildings and groves, and am ready almost to offer sacrifice, when I find myself growing young again here. I am reminded of Ovid's account of Medea rejuvenating old Aeson that gave my friend Francis Potter the idea of blood transfusion.

. . .

October
It is ringing all over St Albans that Sir Harbottle Grimston, Master of the Rolls, removed the coffin of renowned Lord Bacon to make room for his own in the vault of St Michael's Church.

. . .

December
I am an ignorant fellow of but little learning. It has been suggested to me that I might succeed Dr Lamphire as Principal of Hart Hall. But surely they will choose some more learned man, like Dr Plot.

Mr Ashmole and I have been making a collection of the nativities of learned men from the manuscripts of old English astrologers who lived over a hundred years ago. These manuscripts used to belong to Mr William Lilly – who died at his house in Hersham on 9 June this

year – but now they are in the possession of Mr Ashmole. We work
on the manuscripts together: Mr Ashmole turning over the pages and
reading them aloud while I transcribe. By April I hope we will have
got through forty volumes. After Christmas I will visit him at his
house in Lambeth every Sunday to this purpose. Each volume takes
us about an hour. Also, after Christmas, when the opiating quality of
the mince pies has been exhaled, I will continue with Mr Beeston
recording the details he remembers of the lives of the poets.

Mr Ashmole also has Mr Lilly's account of his own life. He was
born on May Day and if he had lived until next May he would have
been full fourscore. In the last almanac that Mr Lilly wrote by his
own hand in 1677, before he went blind, he predicted the great comet
that appeared last year. I must remember to bind up the almanac with
some other pamplets, for it is very considerable and should not be
lost.

But what encouragement does one have to do such things, for
which one receives no thanks, but only scorn and contempt: *O curva
in terras anima* (Oh, crooked souls that bow to earth).

. . .

St John the Evangelist's Day
Today I was smoking a pipe of tobacco at my friend Mr Wylde's house
when it suddenly came to me that Mr Wood might succeed Dr
Lamphire at Hart Hall and secure himself an income. He is a man
who makes no bustle in the world, but who is there to compare with
him in merit?

. . .

I am too late! Old Mr Beeston has died before I could get from him
more details of the lives of the English poets! Alas! Alas! Those details
have gone with him into oblivion and nothing can retrieve them now.
He died at his house in Bishopgate Street. Mr Shipey in Somerset
House has his papers.

. . .

I went to visit Mr Fabian Philips and took down his life from his
mouth. His house is over against the middle of Lincoln's Inn garden
in Chancery Lane. He reproached me with never finishing any of my

work. He was a barrister at Middle Temple, but grows blind and lonely and miserable now. I must see him again to cheer him. He told me that sixty-nine years ago, there were only two attorneys in the whole of Worcestershire. But now there is one in every market town, about a hundred, he believes.

Two days before Charles I was beheaded Mr Fabian Philips wrote a 'Protestation Against the Intended Murder of the King' and printed it and caused it to be put upon the posts. When all the courts in Westminster Hall were voted down, he wrote a book to justify them and the Speaker and Keepers of the Liberty sent him thanks. Mr Fabian Philips assures me that King Charles's plain coffin cost just six shillings.

. . .

The Earl of Clarendon tells me that when his father was writing his history of our times – from the reign of Charles I to the Restoration of Charles II – the pen fell out of his hand. He picked it up to continue writing and it fell again. This is how he realised that he had palsy. It is said the history is very well done, but his son will not print it. Nor will he print his father's Life, written by himself, because he says it is too soon (his father died in 1674).

. . .

I have consulted Sir James Long, of Draycot Cerne in Wiltshire, on the cutting of a canal to join the rivers Thames and Avon. He has referred me to Bills in Parliament for this and another such project, but expresses himself strongly against it (considering the plan unfeasible, spoiling of land, and proposed only by adventurers who do not intend to act on their proposals, etc.). He mentions alternative routes for the cutting, and the objection to each. Cutting through Cricklade is a possibility, and Sir James Long has consulted his cousin, who will help. He warns of stony ground and scarcity of water, but is glad to be of service, even so, and will await my response. Meanwhile, he interests himself in witch trials.

. . .

I have taken care of Sir James Long's hawk, and he has reimbursed me.

. . .

The second reading of the Bill for marrying the rivers Thames and Avon by a three-mile cut near Malmesbury has revived in my mind the notion I have entertained for many years of making a boat to be rowed with sheels, or paddles, by a crank instead of oars. Such a boat would suit better the narrowness of the cut and be easier to propel against the strong stream. I think Mr Potter's concave cylinders could be fitted to the bottom of the boats.

. . .

London has become so big and populous that the New River of Middleton can only serve the pipes to private houses twice a week.

. . .

Anno 1682

Easter Eve

Now that the warmer weather comes on I grow exceedingly active and begin to consider that we are all mortal men, and that we must not lose TIME.

If Mr Wood confirms he is alive and in Oxford, I will send him my collections – I would not have them go astray.

When Lord Norris of Rycote comes to Oxfordshire, I will certainly wait on him, for he has been kind in presenting me with a map of Rome by Pyrrho Ligurio, which should be engraved by Mr White, Mr Loggan's scholar. I hope Mr Wood will subscribe to this good work.

. . .

I have had my Designatio de Easton Piers bound up between hard boards to preserve it.

. . .

I have now sent to Mr Wood the third volume of my Lives. I have also sent him Mr Hobbes's recently published Tracts.

. . .

When I was staying with Sir Robert Henley in Hants., in solitude and secluded among the beech trees, I wrote a trifle that I am minded to show to Mr Wood. It is a description in verse and prose of the land-scape that was within range of view.

. . .

August
Mr William Penn, the Quaker, has set off towards Deale to sail for Pennsylvania, which was named after him last year (4 March 1681) when the King granted him and his heirs a province in America, in payment of the 10,000 li. that was owed to his father (20,000 li. considering the interest). His patent is from the beginning of the 40th degree to 43 degrees in latitude, and 5 degrees longitude from Chisapeake Bay. God send him a prosperous and safe voyage. He is my countryman, since his ancestors lived in Minty in the Hundred of Malmesbury.

. . .

September
My time is taken up with mundane affairs and I am out of humour.

. . .

Today I was sent a trunk of my books, papers, manuscripts and precious objects from Wiltshire that I have not seen for the last eleven years. I wish I could have all my books together in one place.

. . .

From Africa, Mr Wylde Clerke has written to tell me that the plant I enquired about is unknown to the Moors. As to poisons, they know only mercury. He says he might be able to find out more about the plant if he could have more details of it. He promises to observe the methods of preserving plants and berries. As to magic, he finds that alleged manifestations are spurious and no prescription can be found in books. Alleged control of death is also shown to be false. He says they practise cruel tortures on rebels.

. . .

Sir Henry Blount, who is over eighty years of age, his mind still strong, has been taken very ill in London: his feet extremely swollen. He has gone to Tittinghanger. His motto is: *Loquendum est cum vulgo, sentiendum cum sapientibus* (Speak with the vulgar, think with the wise). He is fond of saying that he does not care to have his servants go to church lest they socialise with other servants and become corrupted into visiting the alehouse and debauchery. Instead he encourages them to go and see the executions at Tyburn, which, he claims, have more influence over them than all the oratory in the sermons.

. . .

October
Thomas Merry, who was Sir Jonas Moore's disciple and an excellent logist, has died. He redid all of Euclid in a shorter and clearer manner than ever before, but he left his work unstitched so that when I called to enquire for it after his death, the pages had departed like *Sybillina folia*, and several were lost. I collected up what I could and took the loose sheets to the Royal Society. There they were committed to the care of Mr Paget, but he deemed them imperfect and unfit to be printed. What will become of them now, God knows!

. . .

Anno 1683

January
My mother tells me she is seventy-three years of age.

. . .

21 February
Today at the Royal Society we discussed medicated springs. Sir John Hoskyns and I confirmed that in Surrey and Kent, as far as Shooter's Hill, the earth is full of the pale yellow mineral known as pyrites.

. . .

The curious clock that Mr Nicholas Mercator made and presented to His Majesty is for sale from Mr Fromantle's for 200 li. It is a foot in diameter and it shows the difference between the sun's motion and apparent motion. The clock was neglected at court, even though the King commended it. It was sold to a watchmaker for 5 li., then on to Mr Fromantle.

. . .

Whitsun

My loyal, dear, useful, faithful friend George Johnson has died. He was
a strong and lusty man, but caught a malignant fever from the Earl of
Abingdon's brother, which carried him off. He left London last Monday,
got home on Tuesday, was ill that night, better the next day, but then
fell ill again with intermitting fever and died. He was born at Bowdon
Park within four miles of where I was born. We studied at Blandford
School and the Middle Temple together. If he had become Master of
the Rolls, as he was expected to do, he would have made me one of
his secretaries with 500 li. a year. I shall never see such an opportunity
again. If I had 500 li. a year I would use it to the greater glory of God
and to help my ingenious friends, Mr Wood above all.

. . .

I fear that I should not have put my Book of Lives, concerning so many
great persons still living, into even Mr Wood's hands. I ought to casti-
gate and castrate some of the things in it that are too true and biting,
and cast them aside somewhere at the end of the book to be referred
to in an occult and secret way (e.g. 125 to be 521 or done retrograde).

I think it will be a long time before I get to Oxford again.

The chalybeate spring I discovered at Seend, near Devizes, in 1666,
will now, I hope, become a fashionable resort. When I presented
samples of the water to the Royal Society, they were much admired.
I did not have enough authority personally to bring the waters into
vogue, but I will insert notice of them into next year's almanac and
the gazette.

. . .

24 May

On this day Mr Ashmole's museum in Oxford was opened to the
public. It is a large stately new building next to the Bodleian Library,
which will house the collection of rarities, curiosities and antiquities
that he has given to the University. The collection was sent from South
Lambeth to Oxford by barge: enough to fill twelve carts. Dr Robert
Plot has been appointed the first Keeper of the Museum.

. . .

June

William Penn, the Quaker, writes to me from Pennsylvania, and sends his greetings to Sir William Petty, Mr Hooke, Mr Wood and Mr Lodwick. He says he prides himself on the good opinion of the gentlemen of the Royal Society and professes himself a votary of the prosperity of our enquiries since 'It is one step to Heaven to return to nature.' He praises our experimental age where everything is tried by the measure of experience, as against the ill tradition of foolish credulity, and he solicits the continuation of our friendship to his undertaking.

In his letter, Mr Penn describes the fertility of the country in trees, forests and crops. The soil is good and there are many springs. There are delightful fruits, as good as any in Europe, plentiful fish in the rivers and an abundance of vines, which he intends to cultivate with the help of Frenchmen from Languedoc and Poitou. The river is full of sturgeon that can be seen leaping from it by day and heard at night. The fish can be roasted or pickled. Several people from other colonies – Virginia, Maryland, New England, Road Island, New York – are moving to Pennsylvania.

Mr Penn is making it his business to establish a virtuous economy and so he sits in council twice a week and has held two assemblies, which, he says, received him with all kindness.

. . .

August

My friend Jane Smyth is in extreme danger of dying due to suppression of urine. Her ureter is stopped.

. . .

September

Earlier this month I was robbed. My friend Thomas Pigott hopes the mishap has not spoilt my Knightsbridge rounds by moonlight and that he may be merry with me again in the middle of the night at the World's End.

. . .

I have called on Mr Bushnell, an ingenious stonecutter, who lives opposite St James's Park on the road that runs to Knightsbridge. He gave me an account of the curious marble that was used to build Charing Cross, which was pulled down around 1647. Afterwards, there was a fashion for using the marble for salt cellars and knife-handles. It was a sort of hair-coloured grey and full of little (as it were) kernels. Recently the quarry from which the marble came was rediscovered in Sussex; it was overgrown with trees and bushes, but came to light when the roots of an old oak tree were grubbed up.

. . .

Sir Jonas Moore's books are for sale – it is such a pity that so good a collection is at risk of being scattered. I will catalogue them, and price them as far as possible, for Dr Wallis, in the hope that he can find a buyer.

Sir Jonas Moore intended to leave his books to the Royal Society, but when he died in August 1679, he had not made a will, to the Royal Society's great loss. At the Restoration, he was made Master Surveyor of His Majesty's ordinance and armouries. I often heard him say how Mr Wylde, who studied mathematics with him, interested him in surveying in the first place. When he surveyed the fens, he observed that the line that the sea made on the beach is not straight. He made banks to follow the line and got much credit as a result for keeping the sea out of Norfolk.

. . .

December
Alas, Oxford's Vice Chancellor has not agreed to purchase Sir Jonas Moore's books for the Bodleian Library. Dr Wallis tells me they will take the chance of picking up at the auction sale such important mathematical works as they lack. Perhaps one of the Cambridge colleges will purchase the collection so it can stay together.

. . .

Sir Isaac Newton tells me the cost of building prevents Trinity College, Cambridge, from buying books at present. He has been to the Vice Chancellor, who asks the price and desires to see the catalogue of Sir Jonas Moore's books, but it is not clear whether the University will be able to purchase them either, being at present very low. Mr Newton intends to bring the matter before the Heads of Colleges at the next opportunity.

PART XIII

PART XIII

Manuscripts

Anno 1684

January

The Great Freeze is upon us.

. . .

I am still grieving deeply for my friend George Johnson, and since his death last Whitsun another friend – the mathematician John Collins, Fellow of the Royal Society – has also died. Their deaths have discomposed me and left me lethargic. But I begin to consider my own mortality, and am resolved to send Mr Wood all my poor scribbles by Easter term. I hope he will have the goodness to pardon and pity my melancholy and long silence.

. . .

I am ordering and revising my manuscripts. Since 1669 I have been reflecting on education. I have hundreds of notes on the design of a school for gentlemen and have taken one of my epigraphs for my Idea of Education from Seneca's *Epistulae Morales*.

Mr Paschall urges me to go on with my design. He says he believes this is the great thing the world needs and it would be worth the while of a good angel to come down from heaven to promote such work.

My mind turns back to the school days I shared with George Johnson in Blandford. Plato says that the education of children is the foundation of government. It follows then that the education of the nobility must be the pillars and ornament of government: they bear the weight of it, like Atlas. But while there is ample provision in both our universities for the education of divines and clerks, no care has been taken for the right breeding of gentlemen of quality, which could not be of greater importance in a nation, since they are the root and source of a good administration of justice. It may seem paradoxical, but no nobleman's son in England is so well bred as the King's Mathematical Boys at Christchurch Hospital in London, which our King Charles, founded in 1673 for producing navigators. Arithmetic and geometry are the keys that open to us mathematical and philosophical knowledge, and all other knowledge as a consequence. Arithmetic and geometry teach us to reason right and carefully and not to conclude hastily or make a false step.

Without doubt it was a great advantage to the learned Mr William Oughtred's natural parts that his father taught him common arithmetic perfectly while he was a schoolboy. The like advantage may be supposed of the learned Edward Davenant, whose father taught him arithmetic when a schoolboy. The like may be said of Sir Christopher Wren, Mr Edmund Halley and Mr Thomas Axe. In some men it makes no matter if they learn in later life, e.g. Mr Hobbes was forty years old, or more, when he began to study Euclid's *Elements*. But more commonly, learning arithmetic after a good number of years is difficult: 'tis as if a man of thirty or forty should learn to play on the lute when the joints of his fingers are knit: there may be something analogous to this in the brain and understanding.

A banker in Lombard Street assured me that most tradesmen are ruined for want of skill in arithmetic. For the merchants sell to them by wholesale and the retailers (through ignorance) over shoot themselves and do not make their money again.

. . .

14 April

William Brouncker, President of the Royal Society for about fifteen years, was buried today in the vault he had built in St Katharine's, near the Tower of London (the vault is eight foot long, four foot broad, and about four foot high). He died on 4th of this month. He was governor of St Katharine's and shortly before his death he gave the church a fine organ. He told me he lived in Oxford when it was a garrison for our late King, but was not of the University. Instead he addicted himself to the study of mathematics, at which he was a great artist.

. . .

Sir William Petty's thirty-two questions for the trial of mineral water have been printed in the Royal Society's *Philosophical Transactions*. I will include them all in my Natural History of Wiltshire, where I take notice of the springs in that county:

1. How much heavier is it than brandy?
2. How much common water will extinguish its taste?
3. What quantity of salt upon its evaporation?
4. How much sugar, allum, vitriol, nitre will dissolve in a pint of it?
5. Whether any animalculae will breed in it, and in how long time?
6. Whether fish, viz. trout, eels, etc. will live in it, and how long?
7. Whether it will hinder or promote the curdling of milk, and fermentation of liquors, etc.?
8. Whether soap will mingle with it?
9. Whether it will extract the dissolvable parts of herbs, roots, seeds, etc. more or less than other waters, i.e. whether it be a more powerful menstruum?
10. How galles will change its colour?
11. How it will change the colour of syrup of violets?
12. How it differs from other waters in receiving colours, cochineal, saffron, violets, etc.?
13. How it boils dry peas?
14. How it colours fresh beef, or other flesh in boiling?
15. How it washes hands, beards, linen, etc.?
16. How it extracts malt in brewing?
17. How it quenches thirst, with meat or otherwise?
18. Whether it purges; in what quantity, time, and with what symptoms?
19. Whether it promotes urine, sweat, or sleep?
20. In what time it passes, and how afterwards?
21. Whether it sharpens or flattens the appetite to meat?
22. Whether it vomits, causes coughs, etc.?
23. Whether it swell the belly, legs; and how, in what time and quantity, etc.?
24. How it affects sucking children, and (if tried) the foetus in the womb?
25. Whether it damps or excites venereal disease?
26. How blood let while the waters are drunk looks, and how it changes?

27. In what degrees it changes, in different degrees of evaporation, and brewed?
28. Whether it breaks away by eructation and downwards?
29. Whether it kills the asparagus in the urine?
30. What quantity may be taken at a time impure?
31. Whether a sprig of mint or willow grows equally as out of other waters?
32. In what time they putrefy and stink?

. . .

August
I am beset by the fear that my two volumes of notes on the antiquities of Wiltshire, which I sent to Mr Wood via his friend Mr Allan, have been lost, since I hear that Mr Allan has now died of smallpox! Last week my Natural History of Wiltshire reached Mr Paschall, but when it arrived the box was all broken to splinters and it had been months in transit. Thus we see how manuscripts are apt to be lost!

. . .

12 August
This evening I was eyewitness to one of my ever-honoured friend Mr Edmund Wylde's experiments. Just before we sat down to dinner this evening, he sowed in an earthen porringer of prepared earth seeds of parsley, purslane, balm, etc. The porringer was then set on a chafing dish of coals and by the time we had finished dinner (about an hour and a half later) the seeds had sprung up visibly: nineteen or twenty young plants. More appeared afterwards, their leaves as big as pinheads. We drew out some of them with pliers and found the roots were about half an inch long. The dish was put out in the garden overnight. It is raining very hard now. Quaere: if the plants will survive?

. . .

Mr Paschall has written me a long and generous letter about my Idea of Education, which he has read through carefully. He thinks that it might be wise to make no mention of particular schools and universities, particularly not of their defects. He urges me to give some thought to educational proposals for the first nine or thirteen years, whereas at present my scheme only covers education after these years. He is particularly concerned that I should add a scheme for moral, legal and religious education.

. . .

The great stone at Avebury has fallen and broken into two or three pieces (it was but two foot deep in the earth!). The attorney Walter Sloper of Winterbourne Monkton (the next village north of Avebury) has let me know this. I must go to Avebury and see it if I can.

. . .

23 October

I dined tonight with Mr Wood, who came up to London last Friday (17 October). He paid for our meal.

. . .

I have asked my friend Mr Paschall to be sure to send some berries of the Holy Thorn of Glastonbury to my mother this Christmas. (The old tree was cut down in the late wars, but by grafting and inoculation it was preserved for the country.) Mr Paschall tells me that recently labourers at Glastonbury found a manuscript indicating treasure nearby, and a search was carried out. A man who obtained stone from a renter of the abbey found gold in it. The gold came from chimney stones, where it was perhaps hidden at the time of the Dissolution.

. . .

November

Dr Plot has printed a small treatise on the origin of springs, *De Origine Fontium*, which he has dedicated to Mr Ashmole. He has finished his natural history of Staffordshire and I hope he will turn now to Wiltshire. I asked him to undertake this work in 1675, and offered him all my papers and assistance to this end. But Dr Plot says he is too busy at the museum and will not meddle any more in work of this kind unless for his native county of Kent. He urges me to finish and publish the work on Wiltshire I began almost thirty years ago. I fear that if I do not do this myself, my papers will perish or be sold in an auction, or somebody else will put their name to my work.

. . .

17 December

I related to the Royal Society Colonel John Windham's observation about the height of the barometer in Salisbury Cathedral. That steeple is 404 foot high; the weather door is 4,280 inches and at that height the mercury subsides 42/100 of an inch.

. . .

Anno 1685

January

Mr Wood tells me he has lately heard that most, if not all, of the library at Wilton House is to be sold. I remember the books I read in that library, especially Sir Philip Sidney's translation of the Psalms. No one knows that library better than my friend Christopher Wase, who was a tutor at Wilton. I must ask him for more information about it.

. . .

2 February

On this day the King suffered a sudden apoplectic fit.

. . .

6 February

On this day the King died at Whitehall Palace. His brother James, the Roman Catholic Duke of York, has succeeded him.

. . .

14 February

The dead King's body was buried today in Westminster Abbey, without any manner of pomp. James II of England is our new King.

. . .

St George's Day

Today I saw the coronation of King James II. I watched the procession. After the King was crowned, according to ancient custom, the peers went to the throne to kiss him. The crown was nearly kissed off his head. An earl set it right, but as the King left the abbey for Westminster Hall, the crown tottered extremely.

Just as the King came into Westminster Hall, the canopy of golden cloth carried over his head by the wardens of the Cinq Ports was torn by a puff of wind (it was a windy day). I saw the cloth hang down very lamentably. Perhaps this is an ill omen. Storm clouds of religious strife are gathering.

. . .

St Mark's Day

Tonight stately fireworks were prepared on the banks of the Thames to celebrate the coronation of the King. But they all took fire together and the flames were so dreadful that several of the spectators leaped into the river, preferring to be drowned than burnt.

. . .

King James has ordered the trial of Titus Oates on charges of perjury.

. . .

May

Titus Oates has come before Judge Jeffreys and been found guilty of false testimony, on account of which many innocent Roman Catholics were arrested and some executed. He has been sentenced to be stripped of his clerical habit, to be pilloried in Palace Yard, to be led round Westminster Hall with an inscription declaring his infamy over his head, to be pilloried again in front of the Royal Exchange, to be whipped from Aldgate to Newgate, and, after an interval of two days, to be whipped from Newgate to Tyburn. If, against all probability, he survives this punishment, he is to be kept a prisoner for life, brought forth from his dungeon five times a year and exposed on the pillory in different parts of London.

. . .

My honoured friend Sir James Long has promised to send me cloth for a new suit and four cheeses from Draycot. Wiltshire is good for cloth and cheese.

. . .

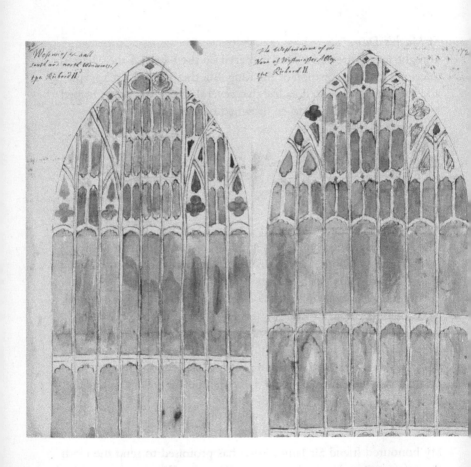

B is true: A should have been made like it.

men at ye points of A. and B, are Angels, holding ye Armes Royal

Queere if at
Prague in Behem
& at Padoa Italy.

The Roof of Westminster-hall

by King Richard 2.d

The Breadth of this Hall is 78 foot: wch is the greatest
breadth of any Roome in Europe without Pillars.

June

I have nearly finished my revisions to my Natural History of Wiltshire. It is now fifteen years since I left Wiltshire, but I spent so long travelling between north and south Wiltshire on the road from Easton Pierse to Broad Chalke that I have a strong enough image of it in my mind to make some additions to my old notes even at this distance. My discourse on Wiltshire is like the portrait of Dr Kettell of Trinity College that Mr Edward Bathurst (one of Ralph Bathurst's brothers) painted some years after his death. It was not done from life, but it did well resemble him. If I had had the leisure I would have willingly searched the whole county for natural remarks.

I hope hereafter my work will be an incitement to some ingenious and public-spirited young Wiltshire man to polish and complete what I have delivered rough-hewn, for I have not leisure to heighten my style. I will dedicate my Natural History of Wiltshire to my patron Lord Pembroke. He is hard in his bargaining but as just a paymaster as lives.

. . .

I need to move my mother from Bridgwater, where she has been living of late, back to Broad Chalke, and will need to spend time helping her settle. Mr Paschall and his wife will be sad at parting from her. They have been good neighbours and friends to her in Bridgwater.

. . .

There is a hill in Wiltshire under which three streams rise: one runs to Sarum, then on to Christ Church and into the French sea; another runs to Marlborough and on to Reading, where it runs into the Thames; and a third runs to Calne and on until it disgorges into the Avon which runs to Bristol.

It seems to me that the city of Bristol very well deserves the pains of some antiquary (Gloucester too). I think the best-built churches of any city in England are in Bristol, excepting the London churches that have been built since the Great Conflagration. Bristol had a great many religious houses in the old days; the Priory of Augustine is a very good building, especially the gatehouse. I think Bristol is the second city in England both for greatness and trade, and yet is not so much as mentioned in *Antonini Itinerario*.

. . .

12 *June*

Yesterday I came to Chedzoy, near Bridgwater, to meet Mr Paschall's friend who is rector here. They have a scheme afoot to operate some lead mines in the Mendips – I thought perhaps this scheme might mend my fortunes. But alas! More menacing plots and plotters thwart me. I arrived here on the very night the Duke of Monmouth, the late King's bastard son, landed at Lyme Regis to begin his rebellion. Monmouth's soldiers entered the house and came into my chamber as I lay in bed. They took away horses and arms.

. . .

July

After his landing at Lyme Regis, the Duke of Monmouth collected a following of 3,000 men and was proclaimed King at Taunton. From there he went to Bristol, but the city shut its gates on him, so he retired to Bridgwater. Government forces were encamped nearby at Sedgemoor. There was fierce battle on the evening of 5 July, after which Monmouth fled. He was captured on Shag Heath and is now being held at the house of my old friend Anthony Ettrick (Recorder and Magistrate of Poole and Wimborne), from whence he will be sent to trial. Deo Gratias that storm cloud is over-blown!

. . .

August

I hope to find out from Sir William Dugdale when glass painting was first used in England.

I have heard William Dugdale say that although Mr Camden has the better reputation, the antiquary Mr Robert Glover was the best Herald of the College of Arms. He took a great deal of pains in searching out the antiquities of several counties, participating in heraldic visitations in the north of England especially.

. . .

September

I have quarrelled furiously with my tiger brother William over money.

. . .

I cannot read or write for grief! I cannot go to Salisbury to search out answers to Mr Wood's questions. My brother and I are at such a difference that it completely distracts my mind.

. . .

December
John Pell has died. I could not persuade him to make a will, so his books and manuscripts have fallen into the hands of his son-in-law.

. . .

I have visited Dr Pell's last home and rescued some letters in his own handwriting from the pies! I cannot bear to think how many letters of ingenious men have been lost at the hands of cooks who value them not.

. . .

Anno 1686

January
I am back now in the city from Broad Chalke, thank goodness, since my domestic troubles there are so great that I could not read or write this past six weeks, and could find no time to visit Salisbury to answer Mr Wood's questions, which I would otherwise have willingly done! My tiger brother William and I have such great differences that I believe we will never be close again. I do not know if I shall ever shake off this grief.

. . .

February
Captain Poyntz has made me a grant of a thousand acres of land on the island of Tobago, for services I have done him with regard to the Earl of Pembroke and the Earl of Abingdon. He advises me to send over people to settle and to get subscribers to sign up for a share of this land, since he says 200 acres will be enough for me personally.

. . .

I have started composing a list of ideas for rescuing my fortunes.

– Obtain a patent to open the passage to make it wider for ships to come to Bristol, whereas now they come no nearer than Hungerode. Also to blow up the little island, or collection of rocks, in the key (called the Lidds?) at Bristol which occupies the room of two or three barks. Also to make obtuse the sharp angular rock at St Vincent's which is a great nuisance to the merchants.
– Put somebody on to merging the Thames and Avon, and get a share in it.
– Obtain a patent to dig for the coal that I have discovered in Slyfiend Common in Surrey, near Guilford.
– Discover and find out the lands concealed and embezzled by the Fishmongers' Company, which was to maintain so many scholars in Oxford and for the ease of poor Roman Catholics in Lent. Mr Fabian Philips tells me I may find out the donation in Stow's *Survey of London*. Edmund Wylde says that the old Parliament intended to have an inspection into charitable uses.
– My discovery of the nitrous springs at Minty in Wiltshire called the Gogges (1665), where there is good fuller's earth. I will engage Sir Edward Hungerford to help me get the ground from our friend George Pitt, Esq.
– It would be a prudent way of laying out money to build a handsome commercial house of entertainment for the water-drinkers at Seend and to make a fine bowling green etc.
– William Penn, Lord Proprietor of Pennsylvania, has given me a grant of 600 acres and advises me to plant it with French Protestants.

. . .

My friend Mr Edward Lhwyd, who is Dr Plot's assistant at the Ashmolean and Register to the Chymical Course at the Laboratory, thanks me for my continual favours to the museum, but tells me that most people at Oxford do not yet know what it is. They simply call the whole building the Laboratory and distinguish no further. In fact, the museum consists of three principal rooms open to the public, each about fifty-six feet long and twenty-five broad. The uppermost room is called the Musaeum Ashmoleanum, and this is where rarities are shown to visitors; the middle room is the School of Natural History, where Dr Plot, who is Professor of Chemistry as well as Keeper of the Museum, lectures three times a week; the third room, in the basement, is the laboratory, for demonstrations and experiments.

. . .

Mr Loggan will draw a picture of me in black and white that can be engraved for my Natural History of Wiltshire when it is printed. I also desire him to draw Wilton House so that a picture of it can be included in my book.

. . .

24 March

Today I told the Royal Society of a series of six drawings of sea battles done by Mr Hollar: the Society hopes to obtain them.

. . .

31 March

I described to the Royal Society how Sir Jonas Moore arranged for several curious observations of the tides at London Bridge to be made by means of a rod buoyed up at the bottom by a cork, so rising and falling with the water. I think the record of these observations is in the keeping of Mr Flamstead or Captain Hanway, and I will do my best to procure them for the Society.

I also mentioned that the greatest tide found on the coast of England is at Chepstow Bridge. I hope Sir John Hoskyns might pursue further investigations into that tide. Captain Collins is currently engaged in a survey of the sea coast of England, so he too could communicate his observations to the Society of the tides in various ports and headlands.

. . .

My friend Mr Paschall writes to tell me that our country is a pleasant land! Under his influence, Chedzoy, though close to the centre of the uprising last year, provided very few recruits for the Duke of Monmouth's army. And yet Mr Paschall is still saddened to see the common people's folly: many of them will not believe that the King is living, or that the late Duke of Monmouth is dead.

. . .

My good mother is unwell and distressed by the quarrel between me and my brother William. She is close now to the end of her life and wishes she could leave us friends.

. . .

21 April

On this day my dear and ever honoured mother died; my head is a fountain of tears. My brother William has decided my mother will be buried at Kington St Michael with my father.

. . .

May

Aside from necessary business, I have not written a word since my great grief. I have not touched my Natural History of Wiltshire since the evening of 21 April when I heard the news of my mother's death. Earlier that day I just finished the last chapter, rough-hewn.

I am troubled by the death of my mother and the financial troubles that have resulted. Chalke must now be sold.

May I live to publish my papers. I must make haste for I am now sixty years old.

. . .

Mr Paschall tells of a holy day at Bridgwater (on Tuesday, 6 July) in remembrance of last year's deliverance from the Duke of Monmouth (bells, guns, bonfires). The people there are hoping that the King, who pardoned the rebels, will welcome this voluntary act of loyalty and gratitude.

. . .

My friend Thomas Mariett tells me that his deceased first wife appeared to him: he is certain that if he could tell me all the circumstances, I would believe him.

. . .

18 August

I have been reflecting on the fate of manuscripts after the death of their author, and since I intend to take a journey into the west of the country soon, I have made a new will today. If I should depart this life before I return to London, I bequeath the unfinished manuscript of my Natural History of Wiltshire to my friend Mr Hooke of Gresham College. I humbly desire him to have my sketches of the noble buildings and prospects of Wiltshire engraved by my worthy friend Mr David Loggan. I signed this will today in the presence of four witnesses, one of them Mr Francis Lodwick.

. . .

Mr Paschall has described to me a case of gonorrhea in a man of sixty who has led a temperated sedentary life. He asks me to ask my friends for advice. I will send him a recipe with egg white and sugar that will help.

. . .

I have given Sir William Petty the extracts I copied out of the register books of half a dozen parishes in south Wiltshire.

. . .

8 December

Today I showed the Royal Society a nautilus cast in the substance of the pyrites or vitriol stone: a brass colour, found in a chalk-pit.

In the Royal Society's *Philosophical Transactions* for this month and last (no. 185) there is an account of the discovery of an ancient sepulchre by the River Eure at Cocherel, Rouvray, near Pacy-sur-Eure, in Normandy. Since it slightly resembles the Sanctuary at Avebury, I have inserted this account into my manuscript. I am still working on it. I will have to change the dedication since King Charles died last year. It was he who originally set me on the task of writing about Avebury, after I showed it to him in 1663. I must finish and publish if I can.

. . .

Anno 1687

February

I have begun to collect records of folk customs. I find there are many connections between the customs of classical Rome and modern England.

The Britons imbibed their Gentilisme from the Romans; and as the British language has crept into corners (like Wales and Cornwall) so the remains of Gentilisme are still kept there. I do not doubt that those customs were anciently over all Britain and Gaul; but the Inundation of the Goths drove them out, together with the language.

Quaere: How comes it to pass that while the British language is so utterly lost in England, so many Roman customs yet remain? But indeed they are most northwards, and towards Wales, while the south retains but few of them.

The Gentiles would not perfectly relinquish all their idols; so they were persuaded to turn the image of Jupiter with his thunderbolt into *Christus crucifixus*, and Venus and Cupid into the Madonna and her Babe, which Mr Thomas Hobbes said was prudently done, in his *Leviathan*.

I am reminded of my friend Thomas Browne's critique of miracles wrought by relics in his *Religio medici*, which first opened my understanding when I was a young man.

. . .

I am embattled in a lawsuit with my brother William, who plagues me with letters and running up and down to lawyers. I have had no time of late to think my own thoughts, to help Mr Wood, or to work on my Natural History of Wiltshire. I need to fulfil my promise to Mr Dugdale to make my Templa Druidum fit for publication. Perhaps I can get to Oxford for three or four days in April, to paste some notes and memoranda into my collection of Lives. Meanwhile, I must move out of my lodgings near Gresham College, where I have lived these past ten years.

. . .

I have acquainted Sir Thomas Langton, one of the aldermen of Bristol, with my design to remove the Lidds, and he has imparted it to the common council of the city, who kindly received it, but troubles and debts come upon me and I do not think I will be able to emerge from them to fulfil my plan for reviving my fortunes.

. . .

March
Sir James Long invites me to consult him about natural history. He offers

good horses from Reading to get me in three hours to Hungerford and
thence to Bath.

Meanwhile he writes to me about ferns of the district, the many
deer in Auburn Chase and the plants they feed on, the kinds of fish
(lampreys plentiful in flood time) and birds of the district: water fowl
and sea birds especially.

. . .

April

My friend Mr Paschall tells me the Quakers do all they can in town
and county to make a great show. He believes the active ruling men
among them were principals in the rebellion, and owe their lives to
a scarce-hoped-for mercy from the King. He fears that the Republicans
who were at the bottom of the rebellion may be exerting a mischievous influence for the overthrow of the monarchy and that their joy
over the indulgence is due to their hopes of overthrowing the Church
of England with the help of the Roman Catholics.

Robert Barclay's book, *System of the Quakers' Doctrine in Latin*, first
appeared in English in 1678, dedicated to King Charles, now to King
James. Barclay is an old, learned man, mightily valued by the Quakers.
His book is common.

. . .

6 July

Today at the Royal Society we discussed the plant called Star of the
Earth, which grows plentifully about the mills near Newmarket and
Thetford. I explained that it can also be found at Broad Chalke.

. . .

Mr Dugdale has criticised me for putting hearsays into writing. For
example: when I was a schoolboy in Blandford there was a tradition
among the country people of Dorset that Cardinal Morton – Bishop of
Ely, then Archbishop of Canterbury during the reign of Henry VII – was
the son of a shoemaker of Bere Regis. Mr Dugdale believes such things
should not be part of a written life. But if I do not collect these minute
details, they will be lost for ever. I do not say they are necessarily true,
only that they have been believed true and have become part of local
traditions.

I am setting out now on an excursion to Yorkshire.

. . .

On a rocky mountain above Netherdale there is a kind of moss that also grows in Scotland. I have pressed a piece of it, together with its roots, between two sheets of paper.

. . .

September

In Yorkshire I have seen the pyramid stones called the Devil's Arrows today, near Borough-Bridge, on the west side of the Fosse Way. They are a kind of ragstone and not much weather beaten. I did not have the right idea about this antiquity until I saw it for myself. The stones stand almost in a straight line except the one near the Three Greyhounds, which is about two and a half yards out of line with the rest. I could not see any sign of a circular trench around the monument, like that at Avebury or Stonehenge.

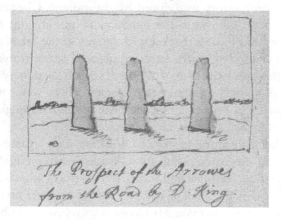

The Prospect of the Arrowes from the Road by D. King.

The crosses at Borough-Bridge and nearby villages are the highest I have ever seen. I think the early Christians must have re-used the stone from these Devil's Arrows to save themselves the trouble of drawing new stones out of the quarries to make their crosses. This would have reduced the number of the Devil's Arrows still in place.

In this county, the women still kneel on the bare ground to hail the new moon every month. The moon has a greater influence on women than on men.

From Stamford to the bishopric I saw not one elm on the roads, whereas from London to Stamford there are elms in almost every hedge.

. . .

Sir Charles Snell has sent me my poor brother Thomas's ill-starred horoscope, which he had refrained from sending until now lest dread of the event might have killed him. But since poor Thomas died in 1681, no harm can come of it now.

. . .

October

This month I have dipped my fingers in ink. I am transcribing all the British place names I can find in Sir Henry Spelman's *Villare Anglicanum* (printed in 1656) and interpreting them with the help of Dr Davies's Dictionary and some of my Welsh friends. Spelman's book was made from Speed's maps, but in the maps many names are false written, so Spelman has transcribed them wrongly in his book, and in addition there are some errors introduced by the printer. I began reading Spelman's book with only the intention of picking out the small remnant of British words that escaped the fury of the Saxon conquest. But then I decided to list the hard and obsolete Saxon words too and interpret them with the help of Whelock's Saxon Dictionary. We need to make allowances for these etymologies. There were, no doubt, several dialects in Britain, as we see there are now in England: they did not speak alike all over this great isle.

Following my Natural History of Wiltshire, I am tempted to write memoirs of the same kind for Gloucestershire, Herefordshire, Monmouthshire, Flintshire and Surrey. I am fearful of what will happen to my work if I die. What shall I say or do with these pretty collections? I had thought to make Mr Hooke my executor to publish them after my death, but he has so much of his own work to do that he will not be able to finish mine. I think Mr Wood would take more care than anyone else, but many of the remarks I have collected will be lost if I do not stitch them together myself.

. . .

16 December

On this day Sir William Petty died of a gangrenous foot caused by gout at his house in Piccadilly Street opposite St James's Church. As soon as I can, I must visit his house and take note of the manuscripts he has in his closet. His last two printed tracts were comparisons of London and Paris. I expect to find much unprinted or unfinished work.

. . .

I have been chosen to serve again on the committee that audits the Royal Society's accounts.

. . .

I am grateful to Mr Wood for remembering my great-grandfather, Dr William Aubrey, in his book. I am grateful too to his brother, who entertains me so well when I am in Oxford.

. . .

Anno 1688

10 June

On this day King James's son was born. He will surely be raised a Roman Catholic and succeed to the English throne ahead of his Protestant half-sister Mary, wife of William, Prince of Orange. Anti-Catholic sentiment has reached a climax and many talk of inviting Mary and William to England. It is not clear what this might achieve. Perhaps their presence would help overturn some of the King's policies, or perhaps there could be some kind of regency.

. . .

12 June

I dined this evening at the Mermaid Tavern with Mr Wood and Dr Plot. He told Mr Wood that when his book is published, he would give him 5 li. for a copy. I have asked Mr Wood to give all the papers of mine that he has to the museum for safe keeping.

. . .

I have decided to donate to the museum in Oxford a miniature of myself by Samuel Cooper, and one of Archbishop Bancroft by Nicolas Hilliard, the famous illuminer in Queen Elizabeth's time, together with a collection of thirty-seven coins (seven silver, the rest brass) and other things of antiquity dug up from the earth. The picture of me is done in water colour and set in a square ebony frame; that of Archbishop Bancroft is set in a round box of ivory, not much bigger than a crown piece. I have sent all these things to Mr Wood in Oxford and asked him to deliver them for me. I promised him he could peruse all that I am giving first, before passing the box and its contents to the museum.

. . .

May, June, and July this year have been very sickly and feverish.

. . .

October
Dr Plot complains that Mr Wood has not yet delivered my box to the museum. He has let the museum have the two miniatures and the coins I sent, but kept back the rest together with the manuscripts of mine that are in his keeping.

. . .

New troubles arise upon me like hydras' heads.

I am concerned about my papers and collections, which are still with Mr Wood. He will not surrender them to Dr Plot for the museum as I have asked. Dr Plot has told Mr Ashmole what has happened and he is outrageously angry, as Mr Wood is suspected of being a Papist, and in these tumultuous times his papers will surely be searched. My manuscripts must not fly around like butterflies.

My brother William, whom I have injured, is very violent. In our shared troubles over money, I have not always behaved well and have put my interests above his when I needed to. In my father's will he was left a portion but it was always hard for me to pay it and lately impossible. He is keen to meet me, but I must avoid him. He writes to me often, sending his letters to me via Mr Hooke. This strife between us gravely disturbs me.

My heart is almost broke and I have much ado to keep my poor spirits up. I pray God will comfort me.

I am separated from my books. They are all at Mr Hooke's or my old landlord Mr Kent's, so even if I had any leisure to enjoy them, I could not.

To divert myself since the removal of my books, I have been perusing Ovid's works. I have picked up a sheet or so of references for my Remaines of Gentilisme (my collection of folklore which I have been working on since February last year); some of them are from his *Epistles* and *Amores*, where one would not expect to find anything. See what a strange distracted way of studying the Fates have given me.

To rescue my finances, I need to sell my last remaining interest in Broad Chalke farm and keep an annuity of 250 li. for myself if I can. My brother William must not hear of it.

I desire of God Almighty nothing but for the public good.

My time is running out.

PART XIV

Transcriptions

Anno 1688

5 November
On this day William, Prince of Orange, landed at Torbay with an army.
He has been formally invited to England by a small group. They are:

The Earl of Danby
The Earl of Shrewsbury
The Earl of Devonshire
The Viscount Lumley
The Bishop of London
The Earl of Orford
The Earl of Romney

. . .

Here in London the rabble has demolished Popish chapels and the
houses of several Popish lords, including Wild House, the residence
of the Spanish ambassador. They pillaged and burnt his library. I am
afraid the unrest will spread to Oxford and Mr Wood's papers, many
of my own among them, will be searched and destroyed, as the whole
University believes him to be a Papist.

. . .

18 December
On this day William, Prince of Orange, reached London.

. . .

I went to see Mr Ashmole last Tuesday; he is very ill. He told me Mr Wood is still refusing to send my box of papers to the museum for safe keeping, but if he does not do so without further delay he will no longer look on him as a friend and will not give another farthing to the University. Mr Wood is suspected of being a Roman Catholic and my papers will not be safe with him if (or when) his own are searched and burnt. Mr Ashmole says much more care is taken now at the museum and books are safer there than they are even in the Bodleian Library. He suggests that the papers I desire kept secret should be sealed up in a locked box in the museum and not opened until after my death. I think his advice very solid and sedate: there are some things in my Lives that make me open to scandal, and I have written a letter or two which I wish were turned to ashes!

My shirt, cap and cravat are with my laundress Mrs Seacole in Oxford: I hope she keeps them safe. I was meant to pick them up from her within a fortnight, but the times prevent me going back to Oxford at the moment. I wish I could go next month, or in February, but I fear I will need to be in hiding then from my brother and other creditors.

. . .

I have been collecting my thoughts on education and compiling a manuscript of recommendations for an ideal school for gentlemen. I foresee that my design is likely to be opposed by the clergies of both parties. But I hope it will find some champions and supporters, especially among the Fellows of the Royal Society.

I would have my school be in a fair house with a little park, high-walled, of about a mile about.

The only time of learning is from age nine to sixteen; afterwards, Cupid begins to tyrannise, jealousies, marriage and worldly cares intertwine with studies. It is a mistake to keep boys at their books at an age more proper for matrimony, when their minds chiefly run on propagating their race. Nature will be nature at 18+. At this age their information is like writing on greasy parchment: it will not stick or leave an imprint. Trying to educate boys over eighteen is like painting anew on an old picture: the colours will not be imbibed.

My school would need:

- A grammarian (one for every class)
- A mathematics teacher (elected by the President of the Royal Society and the teacher of the King's Mathematical Boys at Christchurch Hospital School)
- A rhetorician (who may be a Scot)
- A logician (who should also read to the boys the rudiments of the civil law and ethics)
- Ten or twelve Swiss, Dutch or Scottish boys of about fifteen years old that speak Latin well, to play with and instruct the young gentlemen
- An excellent pen-man or writing master
- A dancing master (French)
- A cook (French or Swiss)
- A butler (Swiss)
- A governess (unmarried and with no daughters)
- A porter (not an old fellow or a scabby old servant in a tattered gown like a scarecrow, but a lofty young Swiss with a decent livery and long sword)
- A chaplain (who might also be library-keeper and/or logic reader)

I would like to see the boys carrying Euclid's *Elements* in their coat pockets as religiously as a monk carries his breverie. I believe Euclid's is the best book ever written. But I would have the boys go no further than Euclid's ninth or tenth book, not only for lightness of carriage, but also to avoid them being too perplexed.

I think the best way of improving boys' memories is to have one of them read aloud to the class a page at a time of Appianus (which Mr Thomas Cooper in his dictionary commends as a most excellent work on the Roman civil war) and after a time of recollection the boys should give an account of what they have heard. The boys will vie with one another to see who will remember most.

It is certain that too much reading of the poets spoils a good prose style, wherefore I would have the boys meddle as little with the poets as is possible. Ovid's *Metamorphoses* and Homer they should be very perfect in, for the delight and delicacy of the fancy and the lively descriptions which they should imitate in English blank verse like Mr Milton's *Paradise Lost*. Yet I would not have them ignorant of how to make a Latin or Greek verse.

Mr Hobbes told me that he thought boys should read Catullus before Martial, since the former are passions and the latter jests in verse. He also recommended Caesar's *Commentaries* because he thought them the best Latin style and most courtlike.

I would have nothing of terror in my school. There would be no turning up of bare buttocks for pedants to exercise their cruel lust. Instead there would be mild punishments: to stand in the middle of the school; to be prisoners in their chambers; to be kept at their books when their fellows are at play; not to drink wine or eat tarts and fruit. In the statutes of my school I would include this command: 'The scholars are not to be beaten about the head.'

I would let the children sleep out their full sleep, otherwise rheumes and catarrhs, dullness, etc. follow. Some of my friends impute their unhealthiness to their too early rising at Westminster School.

I believe the disposition of a boy is the same when he is a man, only he covers it with a cloak of cunning and dissembling, so school fellows know one another's blind-sides or foibles, and some come to be their servants who were their play-fellows at school.

I envisage my ideal institution to be both school and university; the boys who attend it will not need to go on to any other house of scholarship, except to some particular college of law or physic where they mean to be practitioners.

I would furnish my school with microscopes, telescopes and a camera obscura for taking pictures of one's self or of the landscape. It will set the boys agog.

I would have those inclined to drawing practise it for their recreation. I would have these lovers of drawing make perspectives of walls, of Cyprus trees and of pillars, in level, uphill and downhill, which is easy to do and extremely pleasant to the eye. This will train them to draw figures in perspective, which few painters understand. It will prepare and fit them for starting in landscapes, and indeed for the drawing of everything that is drawn from life. Then let them practise drawing horses as big as life on sheets of paper pasted together. This will make them understand horses better than other men. Let them draw a greyhound standing: it is reducible to a square and oblong.

In the chapel of my ideal school, at the east end, I would have a picture of Gratitude taken from *The Golden Age: Aurea*, by the Flemish artist Gérard de Lairesse: namely, a modest and beautiful virgin pouring frankincense into an aurum with live coals. Underneath is written *Gratitude* and these words of Cicero's: *Religio est Justitia Nostra Adversus Deum.*

I would have the boys read the prayers of Sir Francis Bacon. The first called by his lordship The Student's Prayer; the second The Writer's Prayer.

The Student's Prayer

To God the Father, God the Word, God the Spirit, we pour forth most humble and hearty supplications; that he, remembering the calamities of Mankind and the pilgrimage of this our Life, in which we wear out days few and evil, would please to open to us new Refreshments out of the Fountains of His Goodness, for the alleviating of our miseries . . .

The Writer's Prayer

Thou, O Father, who gavest the Visible Light as the First-born of thy Creatures, and didst put into Man the Intellectual Light, as the top and consummation of thy Workmanship; be pleased to protect and govern this Work, which coming from thy Goodness, returneth to thy Glory . . .

We are taught our religion by our nurses and pedants, but when we become men every one makes a religion to himself.

In my school I would have the solstices and equinoxes observed as holidays, but I would have the boys mix with their jollity arithmetical observations of the sun. Also, being Christians, we should remember with Holy Church 16 December, the day on which the first antiphon to Wisdom is sung in the last days of Advent.

Gloucester Hall in Oxford would be a good place for one of these schools, but the other colleges would envy it.

I think seven of these ideal schools in England would be enough, with up to sixty scholars in each. I envisage one near London at Kensington, at Merton in Wiltshire, at Cranborne in Dorset, at Oxford, in north Wales, in Glamorgan and in Lancashire. While the expense of the education would be great, perhaps greater than that of the Inns of Court, there would be great advantages to possessing such fine learning.

It gives me much pleasure to consider and foresee how many young gentlemen's minds would be cultivated and improved and their understandings opened by good information of the sciences. But now I think I see a black squadron marching from Oxford, set up by Dean Fell under the crozier staff he carries as Bishop of Oxford, to discomfort this pretty little flock I have imagined. And so this pleasing dream of mine is at an end.

. . .

I do not know what to do with my manuscript on the Idea of Education. If I die and leave it here, it will be lost, or seized upon by my old landlord Mr Kent's sons. If I send it to the Ashmolean Museum, the Oxford tutors will burn it because it is very much against their interests; if I send it to Mr Wood, when he dies, his nephew will use the pages to stop up his guns. I had thought to send it to the Earl of Abingdon, but he has other fish to fry now. Perhaps the Earl of Pembroke would do best? If I had the money for an amanuensis, I would leave a copy in the hands of each of these earls.

. . .

22 December
On this day King James fled to France, two days after the Queen. London has been consumed by rioting against the Roman Catholics.

. . .

Anno 1689

13 February
On this day the Convention, which was summoned to resolve the constitutional crisis created by the flight of King James, presented its Declaration of Rights to William and Mary, who are now proclaimed King and Queen of England, following the abdication, or at least vacant throne, of King James.

. . .

The residentiary canon, Isaac Vossius, has died at his lodgings in Windsor Castle and left what is said to be the best private library in the world. It is rumoured that King William will buy it and send it to Holland. Vossius was once city librarian of Amsterdam and librarian to Queen Christina of Sweden. He was a Fellow of the Royal Society. I hope either Oxford or Cambridge University will buy his library and keep it in England.

. . .

My friend Mr John Ray the naturalist writes to me from his home in Black Notley. He tells me that Mr Evelyn countenances my observation that elms grow no further north than Stamford. My observation supports Mr Evelyn's view that elms were originally strangers, not native trees of England; I think the Romans brought them here. Mr Ray has sent me two plant samples pasted on to a paper, and he says that the plant I found on the downs, which resembled wild thyme, was Dwarf Holy Rose.

Mr Ray approves my design for a work interpreting the names of places in England; he says it is sure to be acceptable. He thinks that ancient records and monuments will be useful and says there exists a good Saxon dictionary. The Welsh, as I have told him, is very imperfect.

I will soon make a journey into Wales, and Mr Ray has asked me to send him notice of anything extraordinary relating to natural history or experiment that I encounter on my travels.

. . .

Around 1650, in Verneditch Walk, which is a part of Cranborne Chase, there were a thousand or twelve hundred fallow deer; but now there are not above five hundred left.

A glover at Tisbury says he will give sixpence more for a buckskin of Cranborne Chase than a buckskin of Groveley.

At Groveley there are badgers. The grease of the badger is an admirable recipe for sciatica and old aches, but the hedgehog's grease is even better. Some women in Bedfordshire perform wonderful cures with it.

. . .

March

I grow old and my candle burns low. From now on I must transcribe my manuscripts an hour a day at least. My notes are so confused and so interlined that if I do not do it in my lifetime, they will signify nothing. I hope that by Michaelmas I will have gone through the most difficult and perplexing parts. I will write only on one side of the paper, so that the notes can be cut and transposed or pasted into a new order later on.

My brother William is insistent that we should meet to discuss our financial difficulties. He says he is sorry for anything he said amiss in passion to hurt me. I will not meet him yet. I fear he will bring me to debtors' prison. This business grieves and vexes me.

. . .

My friend Edward Lhwyd has provided me with a Welsh glossary to help with my collection of words.

. . .

11 *April*

Today was the Coronation of William III and Mary II, who are co-regnant over England, Scotland and Ireland. May they bring us peace!

. . .

My brother William desires to meet me to discuss the sale of Broad Chalke farm. I will not see him. He is suspected of being a Roman Catholic and has lost his job as a groom-keeper.

. . .

My candle burns low, heartbreaking cares shorten my days and I fear my Lives are not fit to be published. I sent them to Mr Wood in their natural state – *puris naturalibus* – more pleasing to an antiquary than to have them fricasseed. Dr Plot must not see my Surrey papers. I fear he will wrong me by putting my work under his own name – a thing too common in this world.

. . .

I have asked Mr Wood to help find a college lease for Jane Smyth, just as he did for Edward Shirbourne. I feel more obliged to her than to anybody. If only I could get Mr Wood to help her in this way. I have also asked him to find out the price of a rare medicine that she needs for the stone from Mr Kit White, the chemist in Holywell.

. . .

Since Seth Ward, Bishop of Sarum, died, I have searched all the papers that were at his house in Knightsbridge. I have asked his nephew and heir to look over the papers in his study at Sarum too, but when the Bishop of Sarum dies, the custom is that the Dean and Chapter lock up his study and put a seal on it. When Seth Ward's study is reopened I hope his nephew will send me an account of his papers so I can pass it on to Mr Wood. I have rescued some of Seth Ward's scattered papers from being used by the cook to put under pies. One that I have rescued concerns his study of Common Law. It will be useful to include it in my Idea of Education.

. . .

Yesterday I went to see Mr John Rushworth, author of the *Historical Collections*, which gather together records of the debates and passages in the House of Commons during the years of our civil war. He was licenser of the press between 11 April 1644 and 9 March 1647. Mr Rushworth claims to have invented a new method of writing history: i.e. writing and declaring only matter of fact in chronological order, without observation or reflection. He boldly set down what was said at the trial of Charles I, and after the execution of the King became personal secretary to Oliver Cromwell.

My visit to him yesterday was mortifying. He has quite lost his memory with drinking brandy to keep his spirits up. He lodges with the widow Mrs Bayley in the Rules-court Alley, Southwark; she takes good care of him and wipes his nose like a child. He has forgotten his own children and entered a second childhood of his own. He does not recognise any of his four daughters. He tells me he is superannuated.

. . .

14 July

I dined with Mr Ashmole. We discussed Sir Richard Napier, the nephew of the astrologer. There is a story that before he died he lay at an inn where he saw a premonition of himself dead on the bed.

I have been setting aside legal business and my time is wholly taken up with transcribing my manuscripts. I hope I can be finished in six weeks. Then I shall go and see Mr Wood in Oxford and make myself happy in good company.

August

Thank God I have almost finished the tedious task of transcribing my manuscripts. Life is so uncertain. This morning I was in such anguish at the thought I might die before sending these transcriptions to Mr Wood, in which case they will all be lost. There is no trust, or hardly any, in anybody. It is so common for people to publish another person's labour under their own name, but I know Mr Wood is too much of a gentleman to wrong me in this way.

. . .

I have collected together my samples of handwriting that reach from the Conquest to this present time. By a collection of several hands or fashions of characters one may know prima facie the king's reign in which a manuscript was writ. It may also be useful for the detection of forgeries. It is now over twenty years since I had this wish, to get some graver to set forth the hands of several reigns or centuries, but only now am I preparing my work to be printed. I was led on to it by my Chronologia Architectonica.

Just as the Roman architecture degenerated into Gothic in like manner did the Roman character. I have heard that in the Vatican library at Rome are conserved still some copies of books written in the time of the Roman government. I shall not adventure to retrieve any so high as that here in England. The highest in antiquity that I know of in our nation is the charter granted by King Athelstan to the corporation of Malmesbury of which I hope to exhibit a copy in my book.

. . .

September

Anyone would think that there is an evil genius haunting me. I moved into pleasant lodgings at the end of last January here in London, and a week later a schoolmaster moved into the room above me. He came in around midnight or one o'clock in the morning and woke me, and rose very early hammering around for about a quarter of an hour every morning before he left for his work. The following week a man, wife and child breeding teeth moved in too. The child cried day and night and the mother's shrill tongue and singing to the cradle were intolerable. Even so, I kept on with my transcribing. But just as I had about a week's more work to do to finish, read over and correct, the child in the next room fell sick of the smallpox, and then the mother got it too. My friend Mistress Smyth is afraid of catching smallpox, since she has never had it, so I had to leave my lodgings and lie at inns to avoid being in contact with the disease and passing it to her. I brought my manuscript with me but am without my Pliny, Homer, etc. for quotations.

Last week I had the good luck to move to an empty house, where I am writing this, but just today I have heard there will be a new tenant moving in. I could have gone to stay with Mr Kent, but he has two children also sick with smallpox.

It is said that the party who is first infected in a family with smallpox has the disease most mildly. Those that are infected by that person have it more malignly by degrees, and so the more who are infected, the more pestilent the disease becomes, until at last it is a plague.

I hope I can go to Oxford next month. I have written to Mr Wood to ask him to consider where I should lie. Perhaps I could board at Mr Kit White's, the chemist in Holywell, or some other private place. Wherever it is, I wish the windows would be south- or east-facing. I need to retrieve my laundry: I hope Mrs Seacole hasn't lost it. There should be a shirt, cap and cravat waiting for me in Oxford. I would much prefer not to stuff up my breeches by wearing two shirts and sweltering on the coach.

. . .

15 September

I spent the day with Mr Hooke and he told me of his controversy with Mr Newton, whom he has known ever since the latter was elected to the Royal Society in January 1672. Together we wrote a letter to Mr Wood about Mr Hooke's 'An Attempt to prove the motion of the Earth', which he first read to the Royal Society in 1670, long before Mr Newton published his *Principia* in 1687.

It is clear to me that it was Mr Hooke, not Mr Newton, who made the greatest discovery in nature that ever was since the world's creation. In 1679, Mr Hooke proposed an inverse square law to explain planetary motions. Mr Hooke is certain that he first discovered the properties of gravity and showed them to the Royal Society years before Mr Newton printed and published them as his own inventions.

I hope Mr Wood can read what Mr Hooke wrote today and do him credit for his genius. I must get from Mr Hooke a catalogue of what he has written and as many of his inventions as I can. He believes there are around a thousand of them. It is so hard to get people to do right by themselves.

. . .

I am kept busy and am likely to be involved in a Chancery suit regarding the sale of Broad Chalke and my brother's rights. I have entrusted what remains of my estate at Broad Chalke to my brother (about 250 li. per annum) and instructed him to pay a debt of 20 li. I owe to Captain Stumpe of Malmesbury. This debt is on a bond I borrowed in 1660. There is a further debt of 80 li. also.

. . .

Michaelmas

I have decided to sell my last interest in Broad Chalke to Mr Kent, my landlord. My brother William must not hear of this since he believes I have entrusted my interest in the farm to him. I find that the only way I can put off my grief is to concentrate on putting my papers in order before I die. There are still some good old books of mine left in Broad Chalke farm, which I am hoping to be able to send to Oxford (the Venerable Bede's works in two volumes, etc.).

. . .

October

Mr Kent and all his family have gone to Broad Chalke to take possession of it. My books are still there and I must find a way to retrieve them. My brother will not be spoken to and has absented himself. Perhaps I can go to Broad Chalke with Mr Kent at Christmas and settle matters then.

. . .

November

Mr Paschall has a manuscript on Stonehenge by an antiquary to show me that argues that it is British; and he tells me that a Roman pavement has been discovered at Bawdrip: it is a shame I did not see it when I was at Chedzoy.

. . .

Mr Hooke affirms that the whole of the City of London has been raised since the time of the Romans by nearly twenty feet. Since the Great Conflagration in 1666 it has been raised another two feet more or less. When the city was first built, the ground was only a little above the high-water mark, as at Southwark.

. . .

Mr Ralph Bathurst has been long replying to my last letter because I omitted to tell him how to reach me in London. He declines my suggestion that he write an epitaph for Sir William Petty. At the age of seventy he thinks that it would be more proper to write his own epitaph. He tells me that he has seen many good wits miscarry before reaching his present age, and he has much less reason to hope for better success.

. . .

December
Mr Paschall tells me of a manuscript by Philantiquarius (Peter of Langtoft), dating from the early fourteenth century, concerning the treasures of Claudius and other Roman emperors found in Somerset and tracing the advance of the invader. He also sends an account of Stonehenge as an old British triumphal temple erected to the idol Anaraih to which captives and spoils were sacrificed; and an explanation of the layout of the circles and stones.

. . .

This month the child in the next chamber to mine is much quieter so I am making progress transcribing a fair copy of my Monumenta Britannica and writing the Preface.

. . .

Mr Wood claims that everyone seems to complain these past few months that money is dead and there is no trading (because of the taxes and wars, especially the lingering war in Ireland between the abdicated King James and King William). In Oxford the University is very thin of scholars: only eighty or so matriculated last Michaelmas, and half have gone home for Christmas.

It is said that when King James entered Ireland from France earlier this year, one of the gentlemen who went before him bearing the mace stumbled without any rub in his way. The mace fell out of his hands and the little cross upon its crown fell off and stuck fast between two stones in the street. This is well known all over Ireland and it much troubled the King and his attendants. It was an ill omen.

. . .

Anno 1690

March

I have made a collection of all my learned and philosophical letters from 1643 to the current year. It took me three days. I will send them to Mr Wood and hope they will be safe: not put under pies as the Bishop of Sarum's were!

. . .

I have begun to draw up an apparatus for the lives of our English mathematicians. Dr Richard Blackbourne has suggested that I do this. I have made a list of all the mathematicians I intend to include. Thomas Hobbes, Thomas Allen, John Collins, William Lilly, etc. I have written about before now, so I have simply marked them as 'done'. I will not meddle with the Lives of our own writers in mathematics before the reign of Henry VIII, but will prefix those excellent verses of Mr John Selden's printed in Arthur Hopton's *Concordance of Years* in 1616.

. . .

The other day I was at Thomas Mariett's house and heard Dr Henry Birket tell a story about Dr Ralph Kettell at Trinity College in 1638 or 1640. Dr Birket heard Dr Kettell preaching, as he was wont to do on Trinity Sunday. He told them they should keep their bodies chaste and holy, 'But,' he said, 'you fellows of the college here eat good commons and drink good double beer and breed seed, and that will get out!' It is rumoured that next year Trinity's chapel will be demolished and rebuilt. How the good old Doctor would have ranted and beat up his kettledrum if he had lived to see such luxury in the college as there is now. *Tempora mutantur!*

. . .

April

I am afraid I will die with so much work still on the loom. I have been ill for two of the past three months with my gallstone and gout. But not seriously ill, except for two days from the stone.

Between Mr Kent and my brother all my best things – my papers and my books – are embezzled.

I will go to Oxford to see Mr Wood, but I shall stay only a little while: I have little money to spare: and a great deal of business to do.

. . .

Mr Fabian Philips has died. I will visit his family to see if I can gather up his literary remains and find a safe place for them. His daughter is his executrice. I hope she will set up a tablet with her father's name and date of death in the church where he has been buried in his wife's grave.

. . .

May

How I wish my papers were in Mr Wood's hands, for death seems to threaten. I shall send a wagon to him with a box full of manuscripts and printed books, which the noble Earl of Pembroke gave me not long ago, and pray they arrive safely. God bless us in this in-and-out world.

. . .

I have been speaking to Captain Edmund Hamden about his poet cousin Edmund Waller, who was born in the parish of Agmundesham in Buckinghamshire at a place called Winchmore Hill. The house was sold by Edmund Waller's father, but not long before his death in 1687, Edmund had a very great desire to buy it back again: part of the house had been rebuilt, but the room in which he was born is still standing. He told his cousin: 'A stag, when he is hunted, and near spent, always returns home.' This makes me think of my family home at Easton Pierse, where I was born, and where I shall not be able to go to die.

. . .

From Bath, the physician Thomas Guidott has written to me with news of Mr and Mrs Ashmole, who are taking the baths with enjoyment and effect: 'He is stronger in his limbs and she much better in her bowels.' He hopes to increase the number of baths that they take. Elizabeth Ashmole is Mr Ashmole's third wife and the daughter of our mutual friend and antiquary Mr William Dugdale.

Thomas Guidott tells me too that he has recently been given some Roman coins. He says the only important find among them is a fine silver Triumvir piece depicting a trireme, which is inscribed:

ANT IIIVIRRP ANTONIUS TRIUMVIR REPUBLICA

. . .

July

The Royal Society have done me the honour of taking charge of a transcription of my manuscript on the Natural History of Wiltshire, which I have entrusted to Mr Hooke's hands.

How I long to see Oxford once more and to put my writings in order before I die. But I fear I will be arrested and must hide for a while yet. I am so grateful to Mr Kent, even if he has embezzled my books, for letting me stay with him, and even if his giddy wench of a maid interferes with my letters and piles them in a box, so looking for anything is like looking for a needle in a bottle of hay. She even lost one letter out of her breast!

My brother's rough humour has put my business so out of order that I have had to deal with some odd people. *Heu, heu, quid faciant homines, cuive habeant fidem?* (Alas, alas! What are men to do or in whom should they put their trust? Catullus 30, 6.)

If the bailiffs catch me, my brother having been so unkind, I will go and end my days with that good woman Mrs Bayley: the widow who looked after the historian Mr John Rushworth of Lincoln's Inn before he died, in the debtors' prison in Rules-court Alley in Southwark.

. . .

Mr Wood sends me so many queries. I trouble myself to find the answers for him, despite the troubles that press upon me. I desire to give Mr Wood my watch, which was a gift from the Earl of Pembroke, to remember me by. I will be my own executor and send it to him as soon as the watchmaker has finished mending it.

. . .

I am fearful of sending valuable things to Oxford by the wagon for I hear there is exceeding robbing.

. . .

Anno 1691

January

In the box I will send Mr Wood I will include two excellent volumes of the Venerable Bede's works, to be deposited in the museum until further notice, but they should not remain there, nor in the Bodleian Library. Perhaps there will be a library at New Inn Hall, in which case I will give them to it, or else to Jesus College Library.

I am so continually troubled in mind I cannot write. I intend to finish the second part of my Natural History of Wiltshire, but must go down to Wiltshire before the end of this month, and that will disorder my plans.

I asked my brother to pay Captain Stumpe of Malmesbury a debt of 20 li. upon bond, which I borrowed in 1660. But my brother never did it. I threw myself on the mercy of my friend Mr Kent, who will appease my creditors, but I shall be in danger of imprisonment. If my brother learns that I have an annuity from Mr Kent for Broad Chalke, he will seize upon it.

My brother's ill humour has landed me in bankruptcy!

. . .

I wish Mr Wood would do right by Mr Hooke. When I sent him my box, I included Mr Hooke's account of the discovery Mr Newton runs away with all the credit for. But I do not think he has taken notice of it in his biographical book, which will be called *Athenae Oxonienses*, since only Athens could rival Oxford in its array of distinguished writers.

. . .

February

I have decided to place my Natural History of Wiltshire, my Antiquities of Wiltshire and my other manuscripts in the museum.

. . .

I hoped to go to Oxford last Friday, but when I went to the coach I found five women, two of them old and very sick, and no room for my dog: a pretty little bitch that I have lately grown extremely fond of. So I will hope to go on Monday. On Monday night, God willing, I shall be in Oxford, and will stay for just a week. I hope I can lodge somewhere near to Mr Wood.

. . .

Mr Lhwyd, who was Dr Plot's assistant at the Ashmolean, has taken over as Keeper of the Museum.

. . .

From New Inn Hall, Oxford, Thomas Bayley writes to thank me for the gift of St Jerome's bible and Bede's works: they are the first benefactions to be presented to their library. I shall be inscribed in the book of benefactors. My coat of arms is already pasted in the binding of the St Jerome bible and Thomas Bayley has asked me to send some more to put upon the other books I have given them.

. . .

Next week I think I will finish Part 2 of my Natural History of Wiltshire. In the chapter on architecture, I would like to insert Dr Wren's animadversions on Salisbury Cathedral. I remember that he was invited by Seth Ward, Bishop of Sarum, to survey the cathedral. He spent at least a week on it and produced a curious discourse, no more than about two sheets. I am told it has been lent to someone, but no one seems to know whom. I will attempt to trace it.

. . .

I think there is about ten times as much gardening around London now as there was in Anno 1660. In the time of King Charles II gardening was much improved and has become more common. Over the last twenty years we have many more foreign plants and since 1683 many exotic plants have been brought into England, no less than seven thousand. I have heard this from Mr Watts, the gardener of the apothecary's garden at Chelsea, and other botanists. As for Longleat Garden, it was lately made; I have not seen it, but they say it is noble.

. . .

April

Mr Hooke has been very ill, and we were afraid we would lose him. I assured him that Mr Wood would do right by him and give him the credit for the idea Mr Newton takes the credit for. This comforted his spirits.

I have written to Mr Lhwyd to tell him that among the other things I have given to Mr Wood for the Ashmolean Museum, there is my unfinished Villare Anglicanum, or collection of English place names. I can think of no one more suited to finishing the task than Mr Lhwyd, and I only hope he will do right by me and make mention of me if he does so.

. . .

Mr Wood has complained that the watch I gave him does not work well, but it kept time indifferently when I had it. The days of the month were always faulty but that isn't worth a chip. I have told him that if he has it mended he should do so in London rather than Oxford. I believe it cost at least 10 li. when the Earl of Pembroke bought it for me.

. . .

I have heard that my old friend Tom Mariett died about ten days ago. His third wife broke his heart.

. . .

I hope to get to Oxford – our English Athens – in July.

. . .

May

I have been to the Tower to see the Earl of Clarendon, who received my visit very kindly. He has been imprisoned since the beginning of the year for corresponding with King James in exile. I was surprised to learn how few people go to visit such a great person in prison. I explained to the Earl how to write to Mr Wood, but he says he cannot write his father's life, as Mr Wood would like, until he is at liberty to return to his papers.

. . .

Mr Hanson of Magdalen College, Oxford, tells me that he has observed that almost all the well waters about the north part of Wiltshire are very brackish. At Highworth the apothecary, Mr Allmon, told him he had often seen milk coagulated with the water, and yet the common people brew with it, which gives their beer an ungrateful taste. At Cricklade their water is so very salty that the whole town is obliged to have recourse to a nearby river for their necessary uses. At Wotton Bassett they have a medicinal spring, some small distance from the town, which a neighbouring divine says Dr Willis gave this judgement on: it is the same as that at Astrop. They have also a petrifying spring. At Devizes, almost a quarter of a mile from the town, there is another petrifying spring, which a local physician, Dr Merriweather, showed me. At Bagshot, near Hungerford, is a chalybeate spring: some gentlemen drank of it with good success.

. . .

June
Mr Wood has published the first volume of his *Athenae et Fasti Oxonienses: An exact History of all the Writers and Bishops who have had their Education in the most Antient and Famous University of Oxford from the fifteenth year of King Henry the Seventh, 1500 to 1690, to which are added the Fasti or Annales of the said University.*

The costs of publication have almost ruined him!

. . .

Since there has been such a long friendship between me and Mr Wood, I shall present one of his books to a public library (e.g. New Inn Hall, or wherever he thinks fit) as a memorial of the friendship between us. When he comes to London, I hope he will bring with him Sir Christopher Wren's observations of Salisbury church.

The Earl of Abingdon kindly invites me to stay with him at his house in Lavington. I shall do so in about a month after my visit to

Oxford. His wife died suddenly in May and I must comfort him in his sadness if I can.

. . .

July

Today I sent to Oxford a great bundle of books via the Saracen's Head carrier. I intended to add into the box four volumes of my manuscripts in folio, plus a thick folio of letters written to me, but the Royal Society got to hear of this yesterday, and insisted on delaying the manuscripts and letters so transcriptions can be made before they are sent to Oxford. They will not charge me for the transcriptions: I did not expect so great an honour. I would willingly print my Templa Druidum in my lifetime, since it is finished and only wants an Aristarchus to polish the style.

. . .

I have been chosen again to serve on the committee that audits the Royal Society's accounts.

. . .

St Thomas's Day

The Royal Society's transcription of my Natural History of Wiltshire has cost 7 li. (including the paper). It is a folio as thick as the Common Book of Prayer. I did not think it would prove so bulky.

. . .

August

Mr William Fanshawe asks me where he may get Samuel von Pufendorf's book of natural religion, and at what price. He applauds my Treatise on Education and encourages me to perfect it, send it abroad, and so cause posterity to celebrate my name with more respect than any of the great men who first civilised and cultivated rude and untaught mankind.

. . .

Mr John Ray has agreed to read over my memoirs of the Natural History of Wiltshire, and asks me to send them to him by the Braintree carrier, who innes at the Pewter Pot in Leaden Hall Street and goes out of town on a Friday morning every week. He says he has never had anything miscarry this way, either coming or going. He believes there is great variety of plants in Wiltshire and if it were well searched perhaps some new discoveries might be made. Also, he identifies the two kinds of tree (hornbeam is one) about which I enquired.

I have sent Mr Ray a list of the titles of my works in manuscript, and by this he can see that I have not been idle. He hopes that in time I will gratify the learned and ingenious by publication. He imagines there would be many as desirous of reading them as he is himself.

. . .

September

I have now been seven times to try and see Mr Heyrick, the stationer, on Mr Wood's behalf. When at last I found him, he seemed to me to be the most morose and unmoral man I ever met with. He cares not for Mr Wood and said he would not take pains to answer his queries.

. . .

Mr John Ray has read my History of Wiltshire in manuscript and offered some gentle criticisms.

. . .

October

I went to Bayworth – about three miles south of Oxford – with Mr Wood and Mr Dyar.

. . .

Mr John Ray is delighted with my History of Wiltshire, where he says I mingle *utile dulci*. He believes all kinds of readers would appreciate it and urges me not to be deterred from publishing it by fear of giving offence.

He says there is only one thing in the manuscript that might justly give offence and that is my hypothesis of the Terraqueous Globe, which is in fact Mr Hooke's theory. I think it the best thing in the whole work, even though it interferes with Chapter One of the Book of Genesis. Mr Ray says he cannot accept it. Mr Hooke first brought his theory before the Royal Society in 1663 or 1664.

There are lots of lacunae in my manuscript that must be filled in before it can be published, and Mr Ray criticises some of my new coined

words, which he says do not sound well. Mr Boyle has also been criticised for using new coined words. Here are some examples: to apricate,
to reficate, 'continently' put as opposite to incontinently, etc.

. . .

The Ashmolean Museum has been robbed. Three years ago, I gave
several things to it, including my picture in miniature by Mr Samuel
Cooper (which would be worth 20 guineas at auction) and Nicolas
Hilliard's miniature of Archbishop Bancroft, the famous illuminer of
Queen Elizabeth's time. I do not know if the thieves have taken them
or not.

. . .

My friend Mr Lhwyd, who became Keeper of the Museum this year
upon Dr Plot's retirement, has confirmed that the two miniatures I
donated were among the stolen items.

. . .

My brother has been unkind to me and (God forgive me) I have
undone him and myself. The truth is, I was never made to manage
an estate: I was predestined to be cozened and cheated.

. . .

November
I am plagued by worries because I have not yet received back my
manuscript from Mr John Ray. He tells me that this has never happened
before. He was confident of its safe arrival for he had laid strict charge
on his man to see it carefully lodged in the wagon. But it has not
arrived.

. . .

I have prepared my notes on Surrey for printing. My papers are chaotic,
like *sybillina folia*! I wish I had transcribed them into a fair copy soon
after my perambulation of the county in 1673. I cannot take the pains
to digest them in better order now (which would require the drudgery
of another transcribing); instead I have set them down tumultuarily,
as if tumbled out of a sack, as they come to hand, mixing antiquities
with natural history. In this state I shall expose them to the view of

the candid reader, wishing him as much pleasure in the perusal of them as I had in the collecting of them.

. . .

December

I think someone should run over a good English–Latin dictionary and make a collection of the primitives for English, French and endenizened Latin words, together with the few British and Danish words that are yet retained in our language, and then number them, and reduce them to their least forms to see what proportion they are in relation to one another. I guess the greatest proportion would be Latin, or that there would be as many Latin as true English words.

The Earl of Pembroke has given me a fine picture in wax that I will send to Mr Lhwyd for the museum even though Mr Ashmole and I are both concerned about the way the pictures in the museum are being looked after. They need to hang so they are reclining from the walls, otherwise the salt and saltpetre in the walls will rot the canvases. Sadly, this has already happened to the picture of the Queen in the room by the museum's laboratory.

. . .

Anno 1692

February

My friend Edmund Gibson, who is editing the new edition of Mr Camden's *Britannia*, bemoans the corruption of the nation's genius, which gives no encouragement to books of learning and antiquity, not even my Monumenta Britannica, which is ignored by the booksellers, despite its august title!

I have asked him whether to print my new book (which I hope will have more success) in Oxford or London, and he feels obliged to recommend London because Oxford's press has few men, only a small stock of letters, and many obstructions. He says the Oxford press is so slow that it would take four or five years to print my Monumenta Britannica.

. . .

The Earl of Clarendon is prosecuting Mr Wood for libelling his father. In his Life of Judge Jenkins, Mr Wood included information about the old Earl of Clarendon, which I passed to him, never thinking he would print it. I obtained it from Judge Jenkins himself.

. . .

Mr Wood always warned me not to lend my manuscripts. How right he was. After I had lent my Natural History of Wiltshire to Mr John Ray, he wrote me a very kind letter advising me not to include in it the digression on Mr Hooke's theory of the Terraqueous Globe. Now he has published a book of his own, *The Wisdom of God manifest in the Works of Creation*, in which Mr Hooke's theory is published without mention of either Mr Hooke or my book, where Mr Ray learnt of it. Mr Hooke is much troubled by this.

. . .

March
Mr Hooke is very anxious to have a copy of what Mr Wood proposes to print about him and will willingly pay for a transcript.

. . .

My brother William came to town yesterday and has gone on to Sussex today, after serving me and Mr Kent with a subpoena. So I have got a new law suit that I never expect to wear out: God help the oppressed. About two years ago, when I entrusted my brother with the remnants of my estate at Broad Chalke (about 250 li. per annum), I asked him to pay a debt to Captain Stumpe of Malmesbury for 20 li., on a bond borrowed in 1660, but he never did it. Nor did he take up a further debt of 80 li. on my behalf. In the circumstances, I had to throw myself on Mr Kent's favour to appease my creditors. In return for an annuity I gave Mr Kent my Broad Chalke estate without telling my brother. Now he is pursuing me for it through the courts.

I hope to get to Oxford by the end of April.

. . .

At the request of Sir Charles Howard and Mr John Evelyn I am endeavouring to complete my History of Surrey in manuscript. I need to write about the River Thames and have asked Mr Lhwyd's opinion as to the derivation of the word Tam or Tame. The Romans, in their conquests, gave Latin endings to the names of places or rivers, so the name was perhaps Thamys originally, to which they added the termination 'is', making it Thamesis (or perhaps Thamysis). As to what Tham or Tam signifies, I cannot find either of these words in the Welsh dictionary. Perhaps the word is lost among the Welsh, but it could possibly be retrieved from a manuscript Welsh dictionary, now in the possession of Sir William Williams, in which there are 1,500 more words than there are in Mr Meredith Lloyd's printed dictionary. I will write to him to ask his opinion about this.

. . .

April

Currently I am collecting my post from The Tobacco Roll & Sugar Loaf, at the upper end of Maidenhead Lane, parish of St Giles in the Fields, Bloomsbury.

I have started preparing an account of Southwark, which is a troublesome task. I hope Mr Wood can help me by telling me something of Bermondsey Abbey. I have taken enough pains to help him in the past.

When I undertook my perambulation of Surrey, I left out Southwark because it had already been surveyed by Mr Stow. But now I am set to transcribe and print my minutes, all these years later, I do not think I can leave the principal town of the county untouched.

. . .

Mr Lhwyd says he cannot answer my question about the etymology of Thamesis. He says the hypothesis of the Terraqueous Globe could be very useful to him, since he intends to write a treatise on formed stones.

He says he is very glad to hear that I am taking care to leave my papers in order. He will take it as an honour to pay for my letters, and asks for a catalogue of the tracts I have written.

. . .

The account of Southwark, which is now upon my hands, is a hard task.

. . .

Dr Hooke is concerned about what Mr Wood has written about him: he says that if Mr Wood makes any mention of him, he must see a copy before the book goes to press.

. . .

May

I have left the manuscript of my Idea of Education with my honoured friend Mr Evelyn and told him that if I should happen to die before I call to collect it, he should send it to Mr Hooke at Gresham College to be put into my chest marked 'Idea', which is full of books for this design.

Lately I have added some notes to my manuscript, concerning especially the books the boys in my ideal school should read or keep with them.

I would have them carry in their coat pockets Mr John Ray's *Synopsis of English Plants*, or Mr Andrew Paschall's *Botanic Tables* from Mr Ray's book done in the Real Character in three sheets. It is proper for a gentleman to know soils. As they follow their botanics, let them make notes on the earth and minerals. Let them travel several times over all England and Wales making observations. To see the sea and harbours and rocks or cliffs will be a strange sight to them.

Sir Roger L'Etrange's *Aesop's Fables* would be a delightful book for the young to read: it would open their understanding and teach them to write in a clear gentle style.

As for history, it is a large field and too long a work for my Idea of Education, and too sour to be relished sweetly by the young. But if the boys have leisure and inclination, so that they are not without guidance, I think they should be given Mr Degore Whear's *Praelectiones*. Mr William Prynne's advice to me for the seeking of our English history was to read the authors that wrote of their own time.

I imagine the boys in my ideal school to be like pretty bees always excerpting information of some kind or other. This habit will be a considerable advantage to them later in life. One may take a hint from an old woman or a simple person. I would have them treat nobody with contempt, but aim always at truth.

. . .

18 May

My honoured friend Mr Ashmole died on this day at his house in Lambeth. He will be buried in St Mary's Church, South Lambeth.

. . .

My pretty little bitch is with puppy and I will not leave her behind when I go to Oxford next. Maybe I could take her with me?

. . .

I am staying with my friend Mr Baskervill of Bagworth. I have been here nearly a week and have been exploring in Bagley Wood. Noticing the presence of ironstone, I sent for powder of galles and tried several springs, which turned violet, or else black as ink. I will carry some samples to Oxford.

. . .

Here in Oxford I cannot get anyone to take any notice of my water samples from Bagley Wood. No one will drink them.

. . .

As a mourner, I have visited St Mary's Church, South Lambeth, to perform my last office at the grave of my worthy friend Mr Ashmole, whose body lies in the south aisle, at the east end on the north side under a black marble inscription, which I have transcribed for my survey of Surrey.

His greatest memorial is his museum in Oxford. Over the entrance to the door, fronting Broad Street, is the inscription:

Musaeum Ashmoleanum, Schola Naturalis Historiae,
Officina Chymica

. . .

July
The second volume of Mr Wood's book has been published.

. . .

28 July
Mr Wood's book came before the Royal Society today, but no one had read it yet; there will be plenty of censors by the next meeting. As the University will not allow the Appendix to be printed, I think Mr Wood should have it printed in Holland.

I have sent two of my own volumes to Mr Wood for his perusal and castigation.

My survey of Surrey is now in Dr Gale's hands, and from him it will go to Mr John Evelyn.

I go tomorrow to stay with Mr Ray in Essex for a week. Our quarrel is mended and the manuscripts of mine he sent back arrived safely, thank goodness. Then, about the middle of August, I will visit Broad Chalke and Wilton, and from thence to Oxford around the beginning of September.

. . .

August

I have seen Mr Wood's books at Dr Gale's and found that he has not inserted some of the epitaphs I sent him. The Royal Society is adjourned until 18 October, so we will not know what it makes of these volumes until then.

Mr Gadbury is incensed because Mr Wood refers disparagingly to his achievements in astrology as fortune-telling, and has printed an old scandal about his provenance (namely that his father, a farmer of Wheatley, Oxfordshire, made a stolen marriage with a daughter of Sir John Curson of Waterperry). Scholars have generally supposed that Mr Gadbury was bred an academician, since he was born in Oxford, but actually his father was a tailor who married a lady who came to him for a fitting. Mr Wood believes this confirms even more glory on Mr Gadbury's intellectual achievements, but Mr Gadbury is furious.

It is a great relief to hear that my two volumes have reached Mr Wood safely.

In September I go to Broad Chalke, then to Wiltshire, then to Oxford, where I hope to lodge by Turle Gate. I intend to see Sir Christopher Wren on Monday.

I have had a very civil letter from Dr Garden, Professor of Theology at Aberdeen, and an admirable account of my Templa Druidum; he has explained several monuments in Scotland I did not understand before, and thanks to him I now understand an antiquity in Wiltshire that was altogether dark to me.

. . .

Mr John Ray's daughters are much pleased with the glass microscope I sent them as a present.

. . .

October

Mr John Ray has read my inch-thick commonplace book of scientific observations Adversaria Physica a second time and believes it very worthy of the public; he urges me to prepare it for the press for issue in my lifetime, both for my own honour and the instruction of others. He has ordered me a copy of his physico-theological discourses (2nd edition), printed this year. These are miscellaneous writings concerning the dissolution and changes of the natural world, including a discussion of fossils. Mr Ray insists that fossils were once alive.

. . .

Quaere: how the pebbles on the beach came to be of the ovallish figure; there was a time when they were soft.

. . .

Mr Wood now regrets having written rather unkindly of Mr Gadbury.

. . .

I have asked Mr Wood to send me my verses on Robin-red-breast as I would be sorry to lose them and I see one is sure of nothing that is not in one's own custody, and when one is dead all is lost that is not deposited in some public repository.

. . .

November

In Oxford, I am enjoying Mr Lhwyd's civilities, and the company of all my other ingenious friends in this city.

. . .

Mr Wood has received a summons to appear in the Vice Chancellor's court. He is accused of libel in his Athenae against the Earl of Clarendon's father, Lord Chancellor under King Charles II.

. . .

18 November

Today Mr Lhwyd got me to make a list of my works (which I will leave in the museum):

1. Antiquities of Wiltshire, after the method of Sir William Dugdale Description of Warwickshire, 2 parts in folio
2. Monumenta Britannica, 3 parts fol.
3. Memoirs of Natural Remarks in Wilts. 2 parts fol.
4. Perambulation of Half the County of Surrey fol.
5. Miscellanies fol.
6. Lives 3 parts
7. Mr Thomas Hobbes's Life in English
8. An Apparatus of the Lives of English Mathematicians (a copy at Gresham College)
9. Idea of Education of Young Gentlemen from 9 to 18 fol. (the correct copy is with Anthony Henley, Esq. at the Grange in Hantshire)
10. Remaines of Gentilisme 3 parts (copy with Mr Kennet)
11. Villare Anglicanum to be interpreted fol.
12. A Collection of Divine Dreams from persons of my acquaintance worthy of belief
13. Hypothesis Ethics & Scala Religionis
14. A Collection of Genitures . . .
15. Easton Pierse delineated
16. Villa or a Description of the Prospects from Easton Pierse
17. Faber Fortunae, a private essay
18. A Collection of approved Recipes
19. A Collection of Letters written to me by about 100 ingenious Persons
20. Adversaria Physica
21. An Introduction to Architecture
22. Some Strictures of Hermetick Philosophy collected by J. Aubrey

. . .

December

Since coming back to London, I have distributed the copies of his preface that Mr Wood sent me for his friends, except that I was one copy short, so Mr Evelyn does not have it. Mr Gadbury remains incensed by Mr Wood's book. I wish Mr Wood would return my papers to me and give Mr Hobbes's *Leviathan* to New Inn Hall. I cannot move back into my old lodgings because someone else has taken them, so I am not yet settled in London, but am once again imposing on my friends.

Dr Gale of St Paul's School will receive mail for me until I have a settled address once more.

. . .

Mr Meredith Lloyd has written to me with further reflections on the origins of the name of the River Thames. But Dr Thomas Gale affirms that the Saxons called the Thames Eams, which signifies water. This is confirmed by the *Chronicon Saxonicum*, published this year by Mr Edmund Gibson, Fellow of Queen's College, Oxford.

. . .

I was ill all last week, but managed to go to my lord Abingdon on Sunday. He met me with a sad face and told me that terrible trouble is coming my way. I was mightily surprised. The Earl of Clarendon has told Lord Abingdon that Mr Wood told him that the libel, and other information he included in his book, came from ME! I cannot believe that Mr Wood would deal so unkindly with me, when I have been such a faithful friend to him. I have served him since 1665! The libel that has so offended the Earl of Clarendon was printed anyway, and not unknown. It is the claim that the old Earl, Lord Chancellor at the Restoration, sold offices for money. Surely Mr Wood could have said he found out this information by buying it, rather than pin the blame on me? Or else he could have said he heard it from George Ent, or someone else who is already dead? I must find out from Mr Wood what it is exactly that he has said against me, so I can try and defend myself from the wrath of the Earl of Clarendon, who is resolved to ruin me. Nothing grieves me more than the thought that I shall not now see any of my books in print. I fear I will never see Mr Wood or Oxford again. I will write to Mr Wood and ask him to respect the wishes of a dying man by sending my papers to Dr Gale, who is a Fellow of the Royal Society, headmaster of St Paul's School and my faithful friend. My heart is ready to break at Mr Wood's betrayal and unkindness.

. . .

Mr Wood has written to me this morning to assure me that – in the name of God – he did not betray me to the Earl of Clarendon. He urges me to tell Lord Abingdon and thanks me for distributing his preface. But still he does not return my papers.

. . .

Anno 1693

February

I have written to Mr Thomas Hanson of Magdalen College to try and further Mr Hooke's claims against Mr Newton's. He feels obliged to communicate the contents of my letter to Mr Newton and receive his vindications.

. . .

I do not think a bookseller will print my Monumenta Britannica. I have shown my manuscript to several, and though they like it and think it will sell well, they will not take a risk on a book that costs above 5s., paper being so dear. My three, or rather four, volumes (for I will add my Miscellanies) will not be less than 15s. Mr Smyth, the bookseller of St Paul's Churchyard, and others have advised me to get subscriptions to print it at Oxford. So next Monday I will advertise for subscriptions in the press; I will have a prospectus printed and will send 200 copies to Oxford and ask Mr Lhwyd to help distribute them.

As soon as I have time, I will get my collection of correspondence bound and dedicate it to the Ashmolean Museum. My letters from many ingenious persons contain many rarities and I hope posterity will make use of them. It would be a great pity if they were lost.

. . .

My prospectus for Monumenta Britannica is ready for distribution. The four proposed volumes will be:

Volume I

1. Templa Druidum
2. A Review
3. Religion and Manners of the Druids

Volume II

1. Camps
2. Castles
3. Military Architecture of the Old Times
4. Roman Towns

5. Pits
6. Horns

Volume III

1. Barrows
2. Urns
3. Sepulchres
4. Ditches
5. High-ways
6. Roman Pavements
7. Coins
8. Embanking and Draining

Volume IV Miscellanea

1. Architectonical
2. Of Scutcheons
3. Hand-writings
4. Habits
5. Of Weights
6. Prices of Corn
7. Of Diversities of Standards, and the Value of Money
8. Nouvelles
9. The Proportion of the Languages, Ingredients of our Present English

I expect the whole work to be about 160 sheets printed in folio with an abundance of illustrations. Every subscriber will pay eighteen shillings (nine at the time of subscribing and nine upon receipt of the books). The price for non-subscribers will be a pound and four shillings. Very few copies will be printed so there will be no danger of unsold copies. The books will be printed by next Candlemas and delivered to the following booksellers' shops:

Mr Clavel at the Peacock in St Paul's Churchyard
Mr Smith at the Feathers in St Paul's Churchyard
Mr Bennet at the Half-Moon in St Paul's Churchyard
Mr Nott in Pall Mall
Mr Hensman in Westminster Hall
Mr Hindmarsh at the Black Bull in Cornhill

Mr Sam Crouch over against the Royal Exchange
Mr Horne at the entrance to the Royal Exchange
Mr Wilkinson at the Black Boy in Fleet Street
Mr Henry Clements, bookseller in Oxford
Mr Henry Dickenson, bookseller in Cambridge

In Templa Druidum, the first part of my Monumenta Britannica, I proceed gradually from the less imperfect remains of antiquity to the more imperfect and ruinated. The stones give evidence for themselves.

. . .

March
Mr Lhwyd longs to have my Monumenta Britannica in the press; he has all my pamphlets safe in the museum. He says that if I would like to dedicate my collection of letters to the museum, he will have them bound for me at once, which will save me the expense of doing it myself.

PART XV

Crepusculum

Anno 1693

20 March

I was attacked and wounded by thieves. They set upon me around 11 p.m., robbed me and left me with fifteen wounds to my head. I have been ill since and had to stay a whole week in my chamber trying to recover. I am weary from taking medicine.

. . .

April

A severe bout of gout has nearly carried me away. It struck just after I recovered from the wounds inflicted by the thieves. I had intended to visit my cousin Elizabeth Freeman (the daughter of Sir John Aubrey who married Ralph Freeman of Aspeden Hall) and my friend Dr William Holder in Hertfordshire, but ill health prevents me.

Mr Dryden will try to help me get my Monumenta Britannica published by his bookseller, who normally only prints plays and romances. I am exceedingly obliged to him, but I think I will have to print it by collecting subscriptions instead. I have begun gathering them already and been lucky so far. And I have sent a copy of my prospectus for publishing my book to Mr Wood. I hope he can find me some more subscribers.

I intend to be in Cambridge towards the end of next week, where I shall be glad to serve Mr Wood. People are shy of speaking to me about his book; the Peers (I can tell) are offended by his liberties. Mr Evelyn is very cross because he asked Mr Wood to send him what he intended to write about him in his book before it was published, but Mr Wood did not do so. Now Mr Evelyn complains that Mr Wood

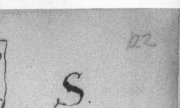

M S

JOHANNES AllBREY

de EASTON-PIERS in Agro Wilton.

Arm͞: Regalis Societatis Socẏ^ius

infra situs est.

Obijt

Anno { D͞ni.
{ Ætat.

or

I woold desire this Inscription, should be a stone of white
marble, about the bignesse of a Royal sheet of paper, scilicet,
about two foot square.   a stone-cutter
    Mr Reynolds of Lambeth [Fox-hall] who married Mrs Elias
Ashmoles Widow) will help me to a marble, as square as an Imperiall
sheet of paper for eight shillings.

has called him a virtuoso: he hates the title so much he says he would
rather have been called a coxcomb.

Frances Sheldon and her niece were at dinner and they were angry
with Mr Wood for disparaging their gentility. I told them that it was
only drollery, not disrespect.

. . .

May
I have now been indoors for three weeks with this bad attack of the
gout.

. . .

I have designed my own epitaph:

JOHANNES AUBREY

de EASTON PIERS in Agro Wilton

Arm: Regalis Societatis Socius

Infra situs est

Obÿt

Anno . . .

. . .

I desire this inscription to be a stone of white marble about the bigness
of a royal sheet of paper, i.e. two foot square. Mr Reynolds of Lambeth
(Foxhall), a stone-cutter who married Mr Elias Ashmole's widow, will
sell me a marble as square as an imperial sheet of paper for eight
shillings.

. . .

Mr Thomas Tanner urges me, before I pass away, to lose no time
in communicating the best part of my laborious collections to the
world, and offers me every help. He will be delighted to receive my
Natural History of Wiltshire and see to its printing with Mr Lhwyd's
assistance. He is much interested in my Remaines of Gentilisme,
and asks me to send him too my Wiltshire Antiquities, which will
be of great use to the collections which he intends to set about
himself.

. . .

June

At the Saracen's Head I delivered to Mr More, the carrier, a locked box of manuscripts addressed to Mr Tanner, and an envelope for him containing the key. This must be a secret from Mr Wood whom it might exasperate: he could do me great mischief if he decided to betray me. There are secrets in my book of Lives that I would not have exposed to common view before I am dead.

. . .

July

Mr John Ray says he has read at once and with great satisfaction my Perambulation of Surrey in manuscript, and judges it well worth printing, as he does all my other manuscripts, which he has read. He thinks that the only reason for the booksellers' shyness is that I am not yet known to the learned world by any published work. He says let them only have a taste of my writings. Dr Gale has told Mr Ray that he thinks well of my Monumenta Britannica.

. . .

Dr William Holder has asked to be inserted as a subscriber to my book. He invites me to go and stay with him, suggesting I take the Buntingford coach which leaves from the Dolphin, Bishopsgate, three days a week (every Tuesday, Thursday and Saturday). If I give him notice of my arrival, he will send his chariot to meet me and take me on four miles to his home.

. . .

I will go to Lavington, then Cambridge. So far I have only 112 subscriptions for my Monumenta Britannica, which is not enough, so I must ask if the University will subsidise the printing of it; I hope my friend Mr Thomas Tanner at Oxford will help me by talking about this with Dr Charlett and Dr Bathurst. Perhaps between them they can persuade the University to help.

My brother went to Kington St Michael yesterday, which has a great collection of heraldry.

. . .

20 July

I set out, at last, for Hertfordshire this morning. I will visit my cousin Elizabeth Freeman first, then go on to Therfield to stay with Mr William Holder. We will set off for Cambridge together.

. . .

August

Dr Ralph Bathurst tells me he is pleased I have resumed thoughts of publishing my Monumenta Britannica, improved by Dr Gale's annotations, with many cuts or illustrations. He claims that Mr Charlett will be very ready to advise and assist in the work of printing it. He has asked to be put down as a subscriber to my book. But I need to find more subscribers or my manuscript will never be printed.

. . .

30 August

I am in Cambridge, where the news has reached me that my dear friend Mr Wood was fined 40 li. and expelled from the University of Oxford last month on 29 July. I read of it in the Gazette as I sat in the coffee house. The Heads of Houses in Oxford were offended by Mr Wood's book. So at about ten o'clock, on the morning of 31 July, the Parator made a fire of two faggots in the Sheldonian Theatre yard and burnt Mr Wood's offending pages.

Dr Holder has introduced me to some of the Heads of Houses in Cambridge, very few of whom have read Mr Wood's book; I told them I thought it would be good if someone wrote a similar book about Cambridge, but they slighted the proposal as useless learning. There are excellent philologists in Cambridge, but the worst antiquaries I ever conversed with.

I hope my brother William, despite our quarrels and differences, and Mr Thomas Tanner will live to finish my Wiltshire Antiquities for me. I have been dragged into the legal proceedings between William and my old landlord Mr Kent. Even though my brother has not been kind to me, I must do right by him in court, even to my own detriment.

I will visit Rycot and thence to Sir John Aubrey's house at Borstall, near Brill in Buckinghamshire, then to Oxford. Dr Bathurst has kindly offered me assistance in printing my book but says that Dr Charlett and the Principal of Jesus can be of more help.

. . .

I called on Mr Coley, who is still very cross with Mr Wood for calling astrologers conjurors.

. . .

I have sent a boxful of antiquities to Mr Lhwyd for the Ashmolean Museum (they are deposits, for now, not donations, because there are some things among them reflecting on Dr Wallis that are not fit to be seen by everybody yet). I hope Mr Wylde will give Mr Lhwyd the Armenian dictionary for the museum too.

. . .

September

Mr Thomas Tanner has spent the last three months in Wiltshire, on the business of promoting our common design of illustrating a new translation and edition of Mr Camden's *Britannia*. He admits that one who had spent all his life in Wiltshire – as I have – might have done more than he could, but he has left room for insertions. He has made several finds: the track of the Fosse Way; nearly a hundred villages not mentioned in the former map; several places mentioned in the Saxon histories; and around twenty stations and encampments of the Romans, Danes and Saxons.

. . .

October

Mr Lhwyd – who has been in Wales collecting information to add to the new translation and edition of Mr Camden's *Britannia* – has asked me to send him my memoirs of Caerphilly Castle, which I visited in 1656.

He promises he will do me right and not rob me of honour and thanks due to me from the curious and ingenious. He asks too if he may open my box of papers in Oxford for his own private use.

I am fearful that all the credit for my unprinted work will be stolen from me.

. . .

I have asked Mr Thomas Tanner to peruse my manuscript, but not to let Mr Lhwyd excerpt from it, lest he put an extract into the new *Britannia* and spoil the sale of my book. I will send all my manuscripts to Oxford; I hope my brother and Mr Tanner will finish my Antiquities of Wiltshire. And if I die, I hope Mr Gibson will print my other antiquities manuscripts, and that Mr Lhwyd will print my Natural History of Wiltshire.

. . .

Mr Thomas Tanner has read my Templa Druidum (the first part of my Monumenta Britannica) with great satisfaction, together with Dr Garden's letter about it, which he believes will be an ornament to the book.

. . .

I am back from a short visit to Oxford, during which I scarcely spoke to Mr Wood, and now I am staying with James, Earl of Abingdon, at Lavington, where I have leisure enough. The fine garden here is a monument to the ingenuity of Sir John Danvers. It came into the Earl of Abingdon's possession through his first wife, who was Sir John's granddaughter. Through the length of the garden there runs a fine clear trout stream, walled with brick on each side. The garden is full of irregularities both natural and artificial. It is almost impossible to describe this garden, it is so full of variety and unevenness; it would even be difficult for a good artist to make a draft of it.

I am reading over Dr Locke's book *On Education* printed this year. But my leisure to read and think will soon disappear when I return to London, where I shall sink under trouble. Mr Kent and my brother are up to their ears in Chancery and I shall be dragged further into it.

. . .

November

Mr Lhwyd is trying to reassure me that he only meant to ask for my thoughts on Caerphilly Castle and anything else I might communicate about Wales. He says he had no intention of stealing from my Monumenta Britannica manuscript. He thought just one or two pages of my three volumes might be made use of (under my own name). He was asking to see only a transcript of those few pages, not the whole manuscript. He says he would welcome Mr Wylde's Armenian dictionary for the museum. It was Mr Wylde who first encouraged Mr Lhwyd to the study of British antiquities, which he now relishes and will never forsake.

. . .

December

Mr Thomas Tanner now advises me to abridge the first part of my
Monumenta Britannica for printing to about forty sheets, partly to
make a cheaper book. He points out that the cheaper a book is, the
more buyers it will have. He suspects that the reason why I have not
sent him the other parts of my Monumenta or my Natural History
of Wiltshire is that I have changed my mind about doing so on hearing
that he is now engaged in preparing a new edition of Mr Camden's
Britannia. He insists emphatically that I need not fear he will play the
plagiarist with my manuscripts or treat me ungently as Mr Wood has
done: he bids me trust his good will. He assures me that his reason
for asking to see my Wiltshire Antiquities was chiefly that he might
make many pertinent additions to my book. He asks me to trust my
papers in his hands as soon as possible.

. . .

St John's Day

I came back to London with Lord Abingdon ten days ago. I intend to
go to Oxford this coming March for a month, and I hope Mr Wood will
have returned to me before then the ten pages he cut from my collection
of Lives. If, and only if, he has done so, I shall let him peruse the rest
of the Lives when I go to Oxford. I am deeply hurt by Mr Wood's rough
dealing with me. I have returned his letters, as he asked me to, but he
will not give back my pages, even though I have asked him often.

. . .

Anno 1694

January

At a party yesterday, I ate a couple of good fowl, as good as any I
have ever eaten, and drank some very good wine. My friends and I
were ingeniously merry!

. . .

5 January

I had an apoplectic fit today around 4 p.m.

. . .

Mr Lhwyd says the University's instrument maker is willing to make a quadrant for me – I desire a copy of the one my old friend Mr Potter gave me many years ago. The instrument maker says he will do it for 10s. even though he cannot see what use the quadrant will be. Mr Lhwyd asks if he can copy one of the Roman inscriptions that Mr Tanner showed him in my Antiquities of Wiltshire.

. . .

I hope to see Mr Wood in Oxford early in April. I hope he has delivered Mr Hobbes's *Leviathan* to Dr Bayley (which I promised to their library). I must take care that Mr Wood deposits the draft of Osney Abbey and the verses on Mr Bushell's works in the Ashmolean Museum.

. . .

February
I have told Mr Thomas Tanner that while I welcome his encouragement to print my book about Druid temples, further consideration is needed. Soon the wagonner will be delivering my Natural History of Wiltshire to Oxford and I would be content for some excerpts to be printed in the *Britannia*, but not the cream, leaving only the skimmed milk to be published as my own.

Among other papers I have put in the box some for Mr Tanner's private use. I have several letters to add to my volume, but they are not fit for the young critics of Oxford to peruse and scoff at.

I am busy compiling my collection of Hermetick Philosophy from manuscript notes I have been keeping for years in a box named 'Dreams'. There are millions of dreams that too little notice is taken of, but those who have the truest dreams have the IXth House well dignified in their star charts, which I do not.

For the past fifty years, Natural Philosophy has been exceedingly advanced, but Hermetick Philosophy has lain long untouched. I think this strange. Hermetick Philosophy holds that the three parts of wisdom are alchemy, astrology and theurgy (or supernatural intervention in human affairs). It is a subject worthy of consideration.

I do not think I will ever have the leisure to put my papers in order. They will all need to be copied anew. I hope Mr Lhwyd will oblige me in this.

. . .

On behalf of my friend the Earl of Pembroke, I hope to buy a picture from one Mrs Hall: she is asking 14 li. for it. I will not give more than 12 li. and have asked Mr Lhwyd to offer her this sum. The painting is *The Executioner with John the Baptist's Head*, by William Dobson. The Earl of Pembroke asks that his identity not be disclosed (for fear Mrs Hall will raise the price). If I can arrange this purchase for him, the painting will be safe at Wilton House.

The Earl of Pembroke has read over my Idea of Education and approves of it, but he is not active in helping me print it. I am concerned that if I die before my manuscript is printed, it will be coffined up together with the books I have collected that relate to it. Nobody will have the generosity to set my design afoot after my death.

I doubt I will live to see my school established at Cranborne, or anywhere else. If the nobles have a mind to have their children in the clergy's pockets, much good may it do them.

. . .

March

The Earl of Pembroke has agreed to pay the sum Mrs Hall is asking for the picture. He desires it be sent to him without delay (but is not interested in the frame it is currently in). If Mrs Hall will appoint someone to receive the money, I will meet them in Dirty Lane in Bloomsbury and conduct them to his lordship, so this business can be settled. I hope this can be done soon because I intend to leave London for Hertford, where Dr Holder invites me. But I must finish the Earl of Pembroke's business first.

I never go out of my lodgings until noon these days.

. . .

2 March

Mr Thomas Tanner called on me.

. . .

I am receiving my letters via my friend Dr Gale, Master of St Paul's. I have received one from Mr Lhwyd asking if I have given the books I sent to the Ashmolean Museum, or only temporarily deposited them there for custody. He says Mr Thomas Tanner gave him the key to my box and that Mr Tanner now has my Monumenta Britannica, and will send for my History of Wiltshire.

. . .

Mr Thomas Tanner has asked me to do him the favour of visiting his brother, who lives at an address in Clement Lane, near Lombard Street. He urges me to visit Oxford too, where I am promised good company.

. . .

The Earl of Pembroke is very impatient for his picture. I have asked Mr Lhwyd to send it on as soon as possible. I have decided to make a gift to the museum of the books I sent with Mr Kent. Mr Tanner has obtained a history of Wiltshire in which there is a pedigree of the Aubrey family. I would like a copy for my cousin Sir John Aubrey.

. . .

I have been ill with a fever.

. . .

I need to send Mr Lhwyd the information he needs.

. . .

Several Roman coins have been found lately at Caerphilly Castle. Sir John Aubrey tells me he welcomes my help in making Caerphilly better known in the new edition of Camden.

. . .

I have written to Mr Lhwyd asking if he has my manuscript of Remaines of Gentilisme. I fear it is too light for the University. I have asked him to insert my manuscript of the Antiquities of Wiltshire in the museum catalogue, but not my letters.

Major Beach of Bradford says he would be glad to have Mr Lhwyd visit him. There is a woman living near him who is celebrated for botany and who supplies all the Bath doctors with samples.

Lord Pembroke has received his picture and is very pleased with it. He has put it in a noble gilt frame and sent it this week to Wilton.

Sir John Aubrey will get Mr Webb to draw and paint a copy of the
Aubrey pedigree.

. . .

April

Mr Lhwyd has written to thank me for my observations on the
Remaines of Gentilisme, which he hopes may encourage study of that
subject at Oxford. There are only a few at present in the University
who pursue the study of antiquities. But Mr Lhwyd's view is that even
if some young man or other might undervalue my work, that should
not prevent it being presented to the library. He says that Mr Gibson,
noting my family's pedigree in Wiltshire, may be able to trace it into
Brecknock. He thinks that my letters are a valuable treasure, but
recognises that it would be improper to prevail on me to donate them
to the museum.

. . .

At last, Mr Thomas Tanner has consigned to the carrier, called Matthew's
Wagon, my Monumenta Britannica, my dreams manuscript, and a sheet
of Dr Pell's notes about the taking of Rome. His delay this past three
weeks made me angry. Now he has apologised for keeping them so
long and explained that he has marked the passages that he has borrowed,
that he has borrowed very sparingly, and has taken care not to plagiarise.
He is very pleased that I have donated my Antiquities of Wiltshire to
the museum, but agreed to leave the manuscripts in his hands until he
has completed them with the illustrations he is engaged on.

. . .

It seems more and more unlikely that my Monumenta Britannica will
be printed. I despair of the manuscript ever becoming a book in four
volumes. I begin to wonder if I should print another of my manuscripts, one that is less lengthy perhaps? My collection of Hermetick
Philosophy? Before I die, I hope to dedicate at least one printed book
to my patron, Lord Abingdon.

. . .

I have got to know Sir Henry Chancey, Serjeant at Law, who is writing
the Antiquities of Hertfordshire, with more diligent extraction of the

records than anyone else has done. He requires the names of the last abbots of St Albans and I said I would ask Mr Wood.

Sir John Aubrey has invited me to Borstall for the last week of April.

. . .

May

By Mores' Wagon I have sent my English copy of Pliny's *Natural History* and my Reden and Holyoks Dictionary to Oxford for the museum. My Pliny is in three volumes and has annotations by me throughout. I have carefully distinguished the cures Pliny lists that depend on magic from those that depend on herbal remedies. The dictionary is not worth much, but I am sending it to show how I found out the proportion of the several different languages of which present English consists.

I hope to be in Oxford with my friends in a fortnight.

. . .

I remember that on Shotover Hill in Oxfordshire, not long before the civil wars, and within living memory, there was an effigy of a giant cut in the earth, like the white horse by Ashbury Park.

. . .

I hope Mr Lhwyd received the books I sent by Mores' Wagon ten days ago: I made sure to pay the carriage. I think I will get to Oxford by about the middle of June. Mr Gibson tells me that the University will not print my manuscripts: they let them lie amongst the rubbish.

. . .

Mr Lhwyd says the books I have given to the museum have arrived and he has entered my English Pliny in the catalogue. He will make a list of all my pamphlets and donations, but he can say nothing about the printing of my manuscript of Monumenta Britannica till the Press has perused it. At the present time, Dr Lister and I are the library's only benefactors of note for books and other curiosities, aside from Mr Ashmole.

. . .

St John the Baptist Day

Today is Midsummer's Day. I was walking in the pasture behind Montagu House, Bloomsbury, around ten o'clock, when I saw twenty-two or three young women, most of them well dressed, busy on their knees, as though weeding. I could not understand what they were doing, until a young man explained that they were looking for a coal under the root of a plantain, to put under their heads tonight, so they will dream of their future husbands. It is said that the coal can only be found on this day at that hour.

There are other magical secrets women have handed down for this purpose. On St Agnes Night, 21 January, take a row of pins and pull out every one, one after another, saying an Our Father and sticking the pins in your sleeve, and then you will dream of him or her you shall marry. This makes me think of Ben Jonson's verse:

> And on sweet Agnes Night
> Please you with the promis'd sight,
> Some of Husbands, some of Lovers,
> Which an empty Dream discovers.

I never married.

. . .

July
I am at Borstall. I find it more troublesome to write to my friends from here than from London, because Sir John Aubrey's servants are full of business and have no time to carry my letters to the post.

. . .

August
Mr Wood makes such demands of me! His most recent list of queries includes:

– Where does Mr Bagford live?
– Can I find out from Mr Hooke the Christian name of . . . Oliver, the glass painter?
– Can I send him Mr John Gadbury's almanac for the year 1693?
– Can I ask Mr Thomas Jekyll for an account of himself and find out from him the date and place of burial of Sir William Waller?
– Whom did Dr Walter Charleton succeed: John Davies of Kidwelly or Sir Edward Sherburne?
– Can I ask Mr Birkhead about Sir Henry Janson?

– Where did Mr Robert Boyle live and die?
– What is Mr Ashmole's obit?

. . .

I have had an unsuccessful visit to Oxford.

. . .

September

I have been ill since returning from Oxford of a surfeit of peaches. I wondered if I should send to the chemist Mr Kit White for a good lusty purge, but I have not eaten a piece of flesh for six days and abstinence has pretty well settled me again. Mr Wood's unkindness and choleric humour added to my illness.

He treats me badly. I do not know how to deal with him and must seek the advice of Mr Lhwyd and Mr Tanner. His unkindness almost breaks my heart. I have asked him to return my prospects of Osney Abbey, which I paid to have drawn by Mr Hesketh when I was a student at Trinity College, and the pamphlet for the entertainment of the King and Queen at Bushell's Rock. I know that if Mr Wood should die, his nephews and nieces will not value them, and they will be lost. Worse, he has cut out the index and around forty pages from one of my volumes of Lives – was ever any lady so unkind? I thought he was a dear friend, in whose hands I could have trusted my life. His unkindness breaks my heart.

Lord Abingdon has told me that the Earl of Clarendon never maligned me or blamed me for the libel in Mr Wood's book. He only told me he had in banter and to frighten me (which he certainly did succeed in doing!).

Sir John Aubrey and his lady, who treat me with all kindness and respect, urge me to accompany them to Glamorganshire in a fortnight's time. I have not been very fit for riding of late.

. . .

Mr Wood is furious with me. He says I have treated him badly by not letting him know sooner that Lord Abingdon was only bantering when he said the Earl of Clarendon suspected me to be the source of the libel printed in his book. He says I left it a long time to pass this

comforting news on to him and then only mentioned it by accident.
He berates me further for running away with 'my books in my
codpiece' and abandoning him when the Earl of Clarendon commenced
his libel suit. Nevertheless he proposes a meeting. He says he will
come to Beckley next Monday afternoon, which is two or three miles
away from Borstall, and he asks me to meet him around 2 p.m. at an
alehouse called the Earl's Arms. He has more work for me to do.

. . .

October

I am with my lord Abingdon in Lavington again. I wish I could go to
Oxford for ten days, or even two weeks, but my lord desires me to
travel through Wiltshire with him en route to London, where I will be
until round about the time the sitting of Parliament begins in November.

I miss my friend Mr Wood and will answer more of his queries
when I get back from London. I regret now that I wrote a page about
his ungrateful dealings with me to be bound up with my Lives after
he cut ten pages from them and removed the index. I have asked my
friend Mr Lhwyd to remove that page of my complaints against Mr
Wood from the stitched volume.

. . .

When I last wrote to Mr Lhwyd, I forgot to ask him to insist that Mr
Wood give back my original drafts of Osney Abbey and the sheets he
has cut out of my Book of Lives.

. . .

Anno 1695

March

I have been ill with a great cold since 25 January, St Paul's Day, and have
only been up and about for a week. While I was ill, I received an angry
letter from Mr Wood that very much discomposed me and made my
illness worse. I have always been ready to serve him, but have received
no thanks or credit. I wish him well, even so, and will answer his queries.

It has been a most unnatural start to the year: no signs of spring
yet, while the cold weather continues.

. . .

St Mark's Day

Coming through Bagley Wood, on my journey to Oxford from Abingdon today, I discovered what I think are two chalybeate springs in the highway. At the gate of Wotton Common, near Cumnor in Berkshire, is a spring which I have great reason to believe is such another. And also, at the foot of Shotover-hill, near the upping-stock, I am confident by the clay, is such another spring. Deo Gratias.

. . .

26 April

I was in Fleet Street at the Fleur-de-luce today with Mr Wood, Mr Martin, Mr Kennett and Mr Tanner.

. . .

10 May

Today I tested the Bagley Wood springs. When I mix the waters with powder of galles they give as black a tincture as ever I saw. Afterwards, one may write as legibly with the waters as with black lead. Bagley Wood belongs to St John's College, so I have presented a phial of the water to the President, Dr Levins. He tells me there are a number of water-drinking Fellows of the college who go every summer to Astrope in Hertfordshire. Tomorrow morning a group of us will set out to try the Bagley Wood water together to see how it compares.

. . .

The water-drinking Fellows of the college found the Bagley Wood water much more diuretic than the Astrop water. Word will soon spread through Oxford. Tomorrow I plan to show the Principal of Gloucester Hall the little spring called Woodroffs Well near Wotton Gate that I discovered in 1692.

. . .

June

Mr Wood has been pardoned and allowed to return to the University.

. . .

July

My friend William Holder has suggested a cure for the trouble in my eye. He recommends medicine sold by the apothecary who lives at the Pestle & Mortar in St Martin's Lane.

. . .

I cannot now read because of a mist that has come over my eyes ever since I left Oxford. I had to cut my visit short owing to business in London. I think my visit to the barber's on the Saturday morning before I left caused the mist. I was hot and sweaty so I went to the barber's to have my head shaved. He had no hot water, so since I was in a hurry, I let him do it in cold water. On the following Monday I was in the coach by five o'clock in the morning and it was very cold. My fellow passengers were women and out of respect for them I sat on the coldest side of the coach. I was vexed at being torn away from Oxford on business and ever since then there has been this mist in my eyes.

I can hardly read a letter and write by guess. Lady Russell's French doctor believes the mist will wear off, but meanwhile I am advised to drink only Stretham waters. I will go to Oxford again on my way to Wales with Sir John Aubrey, but God knows when I will get back to my beloved city after that.

. . .

August

I write now by guess and cannot properly see the page. My eyes are not mending. Dr Goodall is hoping Mr Wood will undertake to write the Antiquities of Cambridge University. About half the Heads of Houses have expressed an interest in this.

. . .

I am in London, but my mind wanders in Bagley Wood, which is so lovely and pleasant in the summertime. It is a most romantic place, with such a great variety of plants: no garden is more delightful. I think there should be a fair there every summer, for finery, etc. It would draw together all the young people of both sexes for twenty miles around.

. . .

Mr Wood has written to me with advice on how to cure my eyes. I can hardly read his letter. He suggests I make an incision in one of my shoulders, or between my shoulder and neck-bone on the left side, through which the issue in my head will drain in three months; or else take pills; or lay plasters of mastic to my temples and leave off sleeping on a bed after dinner. He tells me too that the chalybeate spring I found earlier this year in Bagley Wood on my way to Oxford has been dismissed because it is not running water.

Mr Wood asks me to bring Norden's *Surveyors' Dialogues* to Oxford with me when I go. He desires to see Dr Holder's collection of old musical printed books, as he intends to publish the lives of English musicians and writers on musical theory and practice, just as there are accounts of English dramatic poets.

. . .

I have sent by Mr Rush, the bargeman, two trunks, one of sealskin and the other black leather, and two great boxes addressed to Mr Lhwyd at the Ashmolean Museum. I will go to Oxford myself in a week or so to divide the contents between the museum and the library of Gloucester Hall, then send the boxes on to Borstall, where I will be staying with my relative Sir John Aubrey.

My eyes are mending very slowly. My candle burns low. My dear friend Mr Edmund Wylde grows very weak and I fear cannot long continue.

. . .

September
My eyes mend but slowly. I will go to Llantrithyd with my cousin Sir John Aubrey on Monday. If I live long enough, I hope I will be able to go to Oxford to see Mr Wood again.

. . .

October, Llantrithyd
My cousin spoils me with all the varieties of sustenance that the sea and land afford. But, oh! How much I would rather eat a simple commons in a college with good ingenious company. I should love to converse with my friend Mr Llwyd, for example. My cousin and I pass the tankard and bottle between us all afternoon and drink his good health.

. . .

November

I have written to Mr Hooke to thank him for all his favours and kind-
nesses to me. How much I miss him and our Wednesday meetings at
Gresham College!

My eyes are failing, but I am still working on my collection of
Hermetick Philosophy, which I hope to see in print before I die.

I have given the Royal Society three more books: *Chronicon Saxonicum*
(by my friend Edmund Gibson); *Margarita Philosophica*; and *Wardi
Astronomica Geometrica*. The books will be delivered to the Society's
library keeper accordingly.

. . .

December

I shall never see my old friend, correspondent, collaborator and fellow
antiquary Mr Wood again. He died on 28 November. I am extremely
sorrowful. Even though his spleen used to cause him to chagrin and
chide me, we could not be asunder. He would always come to see
me at my lodgings with his dark lantern, which should now be a relic.
Mr Tanner has his papers and will be faithful to him and finish what
he left undone. Mr Wood has bequeathed his papers to the University
to be placed next to Mr Dugdale's.

. . .

It is so cold! I do not think it has been this cold since the Great Freeze
of 1684!

. . .

My dear friend Mr Wylde has died. When I was most in need, he took
me in his arms and it was with him that I most commonly took my
diet and sweet otiums. Nor was I, by any means, the only friend in
need whom he helped. He will be laid to rest in Glazeley church.

. . .

Anno 1696

January

I will stay with Lady Long in Wiltshire for a month. I wish to know if Mr White Kennett proposes to do anything with my Remaines of Gentilisme, and if not I hope Mr Lhwyd will get it out of his hands. I have also told him to get Mr Rowland to give back my Idea of Education so it can be placed in the museum again.

. . .

February, Llantrithyd

When Mr Lhwyd comes to visit me here at my cousin's house in Wales, I hope he will bring with him a small piece of the alum stone he found in Whitby, for comparison with some local stone here.

I am told another chalybeate spring has been discovered near Oxford. Quaere: if it is at Wytham? I found one there but Lord Norris would not let me publicise it, as he thought it would bring him too many visitors.

. . .

At long last a book of mine has been published. Today I have held a printed copy of my *Miscellanies* in my hand. The publisher is Edward Castle, in Whitehall next to Scotland Yard Gate. I have dedicated my book to the Earl of Abingdon, in whose gardens at Lavington last summer I found time to review some of my papers and put them in order to make this book. I had hoped to dedicate my Description of Wiltshire to his lordship, but it is still only half finished and I am too far spent in age for that undertaking now. Instead I make my honoured friend, who has taken me into his favour and protection for many years, this smaller offering of my *Miscellanies*.

The matter of this book of mine is beyond human reach, we being miserably in the dark as to the workings of the invisible world, which knows what we do, or incline to do, and works upon our passions. I have collected some remarks of visions and prophecies, etc. within my own remembrance or that of persons worthy of belief in the age before me.

My book begins with a copy of Mr John Gibbon's *Day Fatality*, which was printed on two sheets in folio in 1678. But I have omitted Mr Gibbon's concluding remarks on the 14 October, the birthday of King James II, who was Duke of York when *Day Fatality* first appeared. Mr Gibbon offered eulogies to James that should not be reprinted now he is disgraced. In this way I hope that what is useful in Mr Gibbon's book for the advancement of Hermetick Philosophy can be separated from the politics of the time at which he wrote it. There have been such changes in politics and power in my lifetime.

After Mr Gibbon's remarks, I present my own on fatalities of families and place, portents, omens, dreams, apparitions, voices, impulses, knockings, blows invisible, prophecies, marvels, magic, etc. There are twenty-one short chapters in my book, the last dedicated to second-sighted persons.

In my chapter on magic I have included some spells:

To Cure the Thrush

There is a certain piece in the beef, called the mouse-piece, which given to the child or party so affected to eat does certainly cure the thrush. An experienced midwife told me this.

Another to Cure Thrush

Take a living frog and hold it in a cloth, so it does not go down the child's mouth. Put the head of the frog into the child's mouth until it is dead, then take another frog and do the same.

To Cure the Tooth-ache

Take a new nail and make the gum bleed with it, then drive it into an oak. This cured William Neal, Sir William Neal's son, a very stout gentleman, when he was almost mad with pain and minded to pistol himself.

To Cure the Tooth-ache

(Out of Mr Ashmole's manuscript, written in his own hand)

Mars, hur, abursa, aburse.
Jesu Christ for Mary's sake
Take away this Tooth-ach.

Write the words three times; and as you say the words, let the afflicted party burn one paper, then another, and then the last. Mr Ashmole told me he saw this experimented with and the party was cured.

For the Jaundice
The jaundice is cured by putting the urine after the first sleep
to the ashes of the ash tree, bark of barberries.

. . .

I am at Llantrithyd. I hoped that Mr Lhwyd would be able to visit me
here, but he cannot at the present time. I hope I will see him here in
the autumn. In the meantime, I have sent him the dividing compasses
invented and made by Mr Potter for the museum.

When I next go to Oxford I will take one of Sir John Aubrey's
guineas for Mr Thomas Tanner as a small token of the great respect
I bear him.

. . .

13 July
Tonight I sail from Cardiff, on my way to Borstall, from whence Sir
John and I will take the coach to London.

I am hoping that when I get to London, via Rycot, I will be able
to borrow the original of Van Dyck's painting of the Earl of Danby
in St George's robes, which is in possession of Lady Derham, of
Derham Abbey, Norfolk. To do this, I will need assistance from my
well-connected kinsman John, and help from the Earl of Abingdon.

I hope to be at Oxford or Borstall by the end of August at the latest
and to meet my brother then. I feel surprised by age.

. . .

November
The printer and Mr Churchill are shamefully long in producing my
Monumenta Britannica. I fear I will never see it in print.

. . .

December
In the country recently, I found my old copy of Mr Christopher Love's
unlicensed pamphlet, Scripture Rules, from 1647 – the other copies were
burnt in the Great Conflagration – and I have had it reprinted. I am
sending some of the reprints to Mr Lhwyd to distribute among his
friends.

How clearly I still remember the summer day in 1651 on which I saw Christopher Love beheaded on Tower Hill for plotting against the Commonwealth. The sky went black.

. . .

Anno 1697

January

I have presented the Royal Society with a copy of my *Miscellanies*: the only book of mine that has been printed so far. I have made corrections and additions throughout by hand. There are many things I would like to have included that are not in the printed text.

. . .

I have written to ask Mr Lhwyd to give my Remaines of Gentilisme to Dr Charleton to revise. And I have asked him to have my manuscript on the Idea of Education ready for transcription when I visit Oxford.

. . .

June

I will visit Oxford on my way to visit my long-honoured friend Lady Long.

Men think that because everybody remembers a memorable event soon after it is done, it will never be forgotten; and so it ends up not being registered and cast into oblivion.

I have always done my best to rescue and preserve antiquities, which would otherwise have been utterly lost and forgotten, even though it has been my strange fate never to enjoy one entire month, or six weeks, of leisure for contemplation.

I have rescued what I could of the past from the teeth of time.

Matters of antiquity are like the light after sunset – clear at first – but by and by *crepusculum* – the twilight – comes – then total darkness.

Aubrey is buried in an unmarked grave.
The Register of St Mary Magdalen, Oxford reads:

'1697. John Aubrey, a stranger, was buryed Jun. 7th'

He would have preferred burial in a barrow near
Broad Chalke farm because:

'Our bones, in consecrated ground, never lie quiet.'

MISCELLANIES,

VIZ.

I. Day-Fatality.	XIV. Transportation in the Air.
II. Local-Fatality.	
III. Oftenta.	XV. Vifions in a Beril, or Glafs.
IV. Omens.	
V. Dreams.	XVI. Converfe with Angels and Spirits.
VI. Apparitions.	
VII. Voices.	XVII. Corps-Candles in *Wales*.
VIII. Impulfes.	
IX. Knockings.	XVIII. Oracles.
X. Blows Invifible.	XIX. Exftafie.
XI. Prophefies.	XX. Glances of ⎰ Love. ⎱ Envy.
XII. Marvels.	XXI. Second - Sighted-Perfons.
XIII. Magick.	

Collected by *J. Aubrey*, Efq;

LONDON:
Printed for *Edward Caftle*, next *Scotland*-Yard-Gate by *Whitehall*. 1696.

Aubrey's Afterlife

After his death in 1697, almost three centuries passed before Aubrey was fully recognised as a pioneer biographer, antiquarian, archaeologist and historian of nature, science, mathematics, language, folklore and architecture. The only book he published in his lifetime, *Miscellanies: A Collection of Hermetick Philosophy* (1696), was considered a 'mad book' of spells and hocus-pocus in the rational eighteenth century. After waiting so long and fighting so hard to publish a book of his own, Aubrey almost lost his purchase on posterity in a single ill-judged dash into print at the end of his life. His posthumous reputation was partially rescued by the next generation of antiquaries. Early in the eighteenth century, the scholar and editor Thomas Hearne rightly credited Aubrey with arranging for the remains of Osney Abbey to be recorded, 'before the Destruction made by the late horrid Rebellion (against King Charles the First)'. Hearne noted that details of Osney's tower and various other parts had been delineated 'by the Care and Charge of the late Mr John Aubrey, who began the study of antiquities very early when he was Gentleman-Commoner of Trinity College in Oxford, and had no inconsiderable Skill in them as may appear from his History of the Antiquities of Wiltshire, his Native County, now remaining in the Museum Ashmoleanum'. Hearne argued that though imperfect and unfinished, it was apparent from Aubrey's manuscripts that he wrote well on antiquities, 'to the study of which he was led by a Natural Inclination'. Unfairly, Hearne blamed Elias Ashmole for distracting Aubrey in his later years into 'the Whimseys and Conceits of Astrologers, Sooth-Sayers and such like ignorant and superstitious Writers, which have no Foundation in Nature, Philosophy, or Reason'. Aubrey's passion for astrology needed no encouragement. But nothing could detract from the fact that he was 'a very ingenious man and the world is indebted to him for so carefully preserving the remains of the old Abbey of Osney and for assisting Mr Wood and others in their searches after Antiquities'.

The first of Aubrey's manuscripts to be published in the eighteenth century was his study of Surrey. Richard Rawlinson, a young antiquary, Oxford bibliophile and friend of Hearne's, came across Aubrey's manuscript in the Ashmolean. Accompanied by his brother and the bookseller Edmund Curll, Rawlinson followed in Aubrey's footsteps through Surrey to finish his work. Aubrey's manuscript, with Rawlinson's additions and omissions, was published by Curll in five volumes costing twenty-five shillings as *Natural History and Antiquities of the County of Surrey* (1718–19). Rawlinson complained in his introduction that Aubrey's original manuscript was 'huddled together in a very confused and immethodical Order', and set about reducing or regularising Aubrey's notes. As is often the wont with confident standardisers, he introduced some mistakes, including the claim that Aubrey got married after he returned from his travels in France. Nevertheless, once published, Aubrey's natural history of Surrey became a valued work of reference, albeit one studded with gaps and holes where names and facts could not be ascertained.

Aubrey's pioneering work on the megaliths at Avebury and Stonehenge was recognised by the eighteenth-century antiquary William Stukeley, who surveyed both sites and became the first secretary of the London Society of Antiquaries in 1718. Stukeley followed Aubrey in attributing the stone monuments to the Druids. But whereas Aubrey imagined the Druids were members of a savage culture, Stukeley thought they were bearers of Mosaic wisdom and the highest of all high priests of nature. He read Aubrey's friend Thomas Gale's notes on the unpublished Monumenta Britannica manuscript and consulted the original in the Ashmolean. Keen to assert his own scholarly prowess, Stukeley is sometimes criticised for not crediting Aubrey with the ideas he borrowed from him. Aubrey would not have been surprised. Throughout his biographical work, he always did his best to defend other people's intellectual property; towards the end of his life, he knew he had not done enough to secure his own. Aubrey's prospectus for publishing his Monumenta was fanciful in the extreme and the small number of subscribers he secured for the project could not have seen the chaotic state of the manuscript. But even without publication, Aubrey's work influenced the next generation and played a formative part in the development of archaeology in England. He has a claim to be recognised as the first English archaeologist.

During Aubrey's lifetime, Anthony Wood extracted information from the Brief Lives manuscripts for inclusion in *Athenae Oxonienses* (vol. 1, 1691 and vol. 2, 1692). Scandalously, he did not include a single acknowledgement to Aubrey. It was not until 1797, a hundred years after Aubrey's death, that further printed extracts were included in a miscellany, *The Minutes of Lives, The Oxford Cabinet, Consisting of Engravings from Original Pictures, in the Ashmolean Museum, and other Public and Private Collections, with biographical anecdotes by John Aubrey FRS, and other Celebrated Writers*. But soon after this volume appeared, the publisher, James Caulfield, and his transcriber were denied further access to the Aubrey archive by Edmond Malone, the Shakespearean scholar, who had been preparing his own edition of the Brief Lives and claimed an exclusive right to the manuscript. Malone's edition never appeared. In 1813, substantial extracts from Aubrey's Brief Lives were published in *Letters Written by Eminent Persons in the Seventeenth and Eighteenth Centuries, to which are added Hearne's Journey to Reading, and to Whaddon Hall the Seat of Browne Willis, Esq. and Lives of Eminent Men, by John Aubrey, Esq. The whole now first published from the originals in the Bodleian Library and Ashmolean Museum, with biographical and literary illustrations*. This was the edition through which Victorian biographers came to appreciate Aubrey. The editors, the Revd Dr Philip Bliss and the Revd John Walker, censored Aubrey's seventeenth-century candour out of consideration for the prim sensibilities of nineteenth-century readers.

In 1898, two centuries after Aubrey's death, a near-complete transcript of the Brief Lives manuscripts was edited by the Revd Andrew Clark: scholar, diarist and rector of Great Leighs, Essex. There were still excisions to spare the blushes of readers. For example, in his life of General Monck, Aubrey describes how the mother of Monck's mistress was one of the 'five women barbers' of Drury Lane who punished another woman for passing venereal disease to one of their husbands. The five women resolved 'to gett her and whippe her and to shave all the hair off her pudenda'. Clark transcribes this as 'to gett her and whippe her and . . .' so it is impossible to understand from his edition why the five women were described as barbers. Clark was not shy of making high-handed value judgements entirely out of sympathy with Aubrey's inclusive biographical approach. 'It is plain, from a glance over the MSS, that many of the lives are of little interest; in some cases, because they contain more marks of omission than statements of fact; in other cases, because they give mainly excerpts from prefaces of books; and so on. A much more interesting, as well as handier, book would be produced, if the editor were to reject all lives in which Aubrey has nothing of intrinsic value to show,' Clark pronounced. But for all its shortcomings, his edition, which included over 500 lives and gathered together material Aubrey had left scattered, was the best and most definitive for the next 100 years.

During the nineteenth century, Aubrey won renown for his work on Wiltshire. In his lifetime he divided his Wiltshire collections into two projects: the antiquities and the natural history of the county. Before he died, he entrusted his countryman and fellow antiquary Thomas Tanner with completing both. At the time, Tanner was assisting Bishop Gibson with the new 1695 edition of Camden's *Britannia*, into which a lot of Aubrey's Wiltshire remarks were incorporated. Almost 150 years later, further selections from the Natural History of Wiltshire collections were published by John Britton, who was born, as Aubrey was, in Kington St Michael. Britton was Aubrey's first biographer. His book, *Memoir of John Aubrey, FRS, embracing his autobiographical sketches, a brief review of his personal and literary merits, and an account of his works; with extracts from his correspondence, anecdotes of some of his contemporaries, and the times in which he lived*, was published by the Wiltshire Topographical Society in 1845. Also in the mid nineteenth century, the Revd Canon John Edward Jackson, rector of Leigh Delamere, where Aubrey once went to school, published an edition of the Wiltshire antiquities manuscript. When Aubrey donated it to the Ashmolean Museum, it was in two parts: Hypomnemata Antiquaria A, and B. Aubrey's brother William borrowed part B in 1703 and never returned it. Again, Aubrey would not have been surprised: this kind of common carelessness and the resultant loss to scholarship was what he spent his life fighting. Canon Jackson thought that whilst many of Aubrey's remaining Wiltshire remarks 'do not at first sight appear to be very important', excuses could be made for retaining and publishing them, given 'that he was the first, and for a long time the only collector for Wiltshire; and that almost any notices of days long past are better than no notices at all'. In 1862, Canon Jackson's largely inclusive approach resulted in *Wiltshire: the Topographical Collections of John Aubrey, FRS*, an expensive, thick quarto book of nearly 500 pages with more than 40 plates.

In the twentieth century, Aubrey's reputation developed dramatically. Anthony Powell began work on his biography of Aubrey in the 1930s and had completed an outline when war broke out in 1939. After six years in the army and subsequent demobilisation 'in circumstances not always ideal for sifting historical material', Powell published *John Aubrey and His Friends* in 1948. There was a deep resonance between Powell's sensibility and Aubrey's own: both saw England at war; both mapped the manners of their very English milieus. Powell understood that Aubrey would stand the test of time: 'Aubrey, without the least conceit, possessed an exceptional sense of his own existence as part of history; and it is perhaps appropriate that he should have been subjected to history's mechanical process in a marked degree. For a long time he was not much thought of, partly on account of his deprecatory attitude towards himself. Humility is a rare quality. Those who possess it sometimes encounter neglect in life and run some risk of oblivion after death; but in the end history grinds exceeding small.' In 1949, Powell published a new popular edition of over 200 of the Brief Lives, and the scholar Oliver Lawson Dick's edition appeared the same year, together with a brief biography of Aubrey.

Aubrey's popularity was further boosted by Patrick Garland's one-man stage play *Brief Lives*, which premiered in London at the Hampstead Theatre in 1967, had two runs on Broadway and was adapted for television. Closely based on Aubrey's own writing and starring Roy Dotrice, the play broke box office records on both sides of the Atlantic. For forty years, Dotrice played Aubrey as a lovable, eccentric, gossipy old man, and as a result entered the *Guinness Book of Records* for the greatest number of solo performances (1,782). Dotrice's representation of Aubrey on stage was a partial portrait: Aubrey's youthful enthusiasm, pioneering intellectual curiosity, originality and generosity to other scholars played no part in it. But the success of the play indirectly inspired a revisitation of the manuscripts. In 1972, the publisher and editor John Buchanan-Brown compiled a new edition of the *Miscellanies* together with extracts from Aubrey's

Remaines of Gentilisme and Judaisme manuscript and other fragments. Buchanan-Brown argued that to understand who Aubrey was, 'one must forget the figure created so persuasively and with such little historical basis upon the stage and television'. He emphasised that far from being backward-looking, Aubrey belonged to the intellectual avant-garde of his age. Also in 1972, J. E. Stephens published the first (and to this day the only) edition of Aubrey's Idea of Education manuscript, taking a simplistic and somewhat irritated approach to his working methods: 'Much of the manuscript is ill-arranged and repetitive, and despite the fact that the author returned to it at intervals to amend and to annotate parts of the text, it remains incomplete. There are several hundred insertions in the margins vertically and on the reverse side of the manuscript sheets. Many of the additions are no more than personal memoranda to the writer reminding him to seek out this or that paper or to ask advice on some point at issue: others record his second thoughts and the opinions of the virtuosi in whose company he mixed.'

In 1975, the distinguished historian of science Michael Hunter published the first study of Aubrey's ideas, *John Aubrey and the Realm of Learning*. This is still the best book on Aubrey's intellectual milieu. Hunter intended his book to supplement Powell's focus on Aubrey's social life. Powell referred often to Aubrey as someone primarily interested in the past, whereas Hunter argued that the present and the future were at least as imaginatively important to him. Hunter explained the nature of Aubrey's intellectual preoccupations and compared and contrasted them with those of his contemporaries, arguing that there was still no straightforward distinction between mechanist moderns and mystical ancients in Aubrey's time: in fact, 'he was typical in deriving scientific and magical theories and explanations from all sorts of old and new sources'.

In 1980, John Fowles, a novelist fascinated by the collector's quest, noted that generations of scholars had sunk their lives into trying to order Aubrey's Monumenta Britannica manuscript, before he rushed in himself 'where angels fear to tread' and together with the historian Rodney Legg published for the first time a quasi-facsimile edition of *Monumenta Britannica*, nearly 200 years after Aubrey's death. In his brief foreword Fowles wrote: 'I think not even with Pepys are we closer to an existential awareness of what it was like to be alive then:

the anxieties, the delusions, the hopes, the joys, the melancholies and poetries.'

In the twenty-first century, Aubrey's afterlife, slowly but surely accumulating since he died, is flourishing. In 2010, the literary and intellectual historian William Poole organised an exhibition at the Bodleian Library, 'John Aubrey and the Advancement of Learning', to coincide with the Royal Society of London's 350th anniversary. Poole's accompanying book offers an introduction to Aubrey's intellectual world: 'Aubrey was a very clubbable man in a very clubbable century.' As part of Oxford University's Cultures of Knowledge project, 'Networking the Republic of Letters 1550–1750', Poole is coordinating the publication and digitalisation of Aubrey's correspondence. This will make the collection of over 800 letters Aubrey exchanged with the pre-eminent philosophers, scientists and scholars of his day accessible in print and online: a gift to posterity beyond his wildest dreams. In 2015, Clark's long-standing edition of *Brief Lives* has been superseded by Kate Bennett's magisterial new scholarly edition for the Clarendon Press. In Bennett, Aubrey has found at last an editor after his own heart. More fastidious in the pursuit of truth than Aubrey was himself, Bennett's *Brief Lives* is the first to be faithful to Aubrey's own vision of the form and meaning of his biographical collections. Her edition includes censored and deleted material, title pages, antiquarian notes and indices, together with a critical introduction and comprehensive commentary. It is the result of two decades of painstaking work in archives: Aubrey would have been delighted.

Aubrey hoped that his name would live on after his death and that posterity would benefit from the paper and material collections it was his life's work to assemble. Most of these collections were successfully preserved in the Ashmolean Museum. In 1860, Aubrey's paper collections were moved to the Bodleian Library. Aside from *Brief Lives* very recently, none of them has been adequately edited, and many are in urgent need of conservation. With two exceptions (Faithorne's portrait of Aubrey and Hollar's engraving of the drawing of Osney Abbey Aubrey commissioned), all the illustrations in my book are Aubrey's own, reproduced from his manuscripts, by kind permission of the Bodleian Library. Hollar's engraving of Osney Abbey is rare: it was mysteriously omitted from a large number of the first editions of the second volume of Dugdale's *Monasticon Anglicanum*, and afterwards the plate was lost or melted in the Fire of London. The engraving is reproduced in my book with thanks to Olivia Horsfall Turner, Curator of Designs at the Victoria and Albert Museum, who is preparing an edition of Aubrey's Chronologia Architectonica. From childhood and throughout his life, Aubrey loved to draw and paint. The final image included in *John Aubrey: My Own Life* is his only known self-portrait: a sketch of himself and Sir James Long of Draycot out hawking. Typically, it is clear which figure is Sir James, at the centre of the picture, with a telescope and the sword Oliver Cromwell permitted him to wear. But which figure is Aubrey? My bet is that he drew himself the least defined of all the figures: the one lightly shaded beside Sir James, through whom the outlines of some trees are visible; the one who has dismounted from his horse and is looking intently at a building in the valley beyond.

Acknowledgements

I am grateful to the Master and Fellows of Gonville & Caius College, Cambridge; the Principal and Fellows of Brasenose College, Oxford; Drue Heinz and the electors to the Hawthornden Castle Fellowships for enabling me to write uninterruptedly in spring 2012; the staff in the Bodleian Library's Special Collections; the staff in the British Library Manuscripts Reading Room; the staff in the Royal Society Library and the Ashmolean Museum.

My editor Jenny Uglow believed in and understood my book from the beginning; her companionship on this biographical journey has been a blessing and a privilege. Juliet Brooke, Senior Editor at Chatto & Windus, guided my book through publication with grace and imagination.

For generous scholarly and literary help I am also deeply indebted to the following friends and colleagues: Mary Beard, Kate Bennett, John Casey, John Dunn, Antonia Fraser, Heather Glen, Mark Goldie, Jonny Grove, Olivia Horsfall Turner, Claerwen James, John Kerrigan, Anne Malcolm, William Poole, Hamish Robinson, Ali Smith, Peter Stothard, Peter Straus, Richard Tuck. I am grateful to Jane Selley for her careful copy-editing, to Joanne Hill for her thorough proof-reading and to Helen Smith for the index.

Soon after I began writing about Aubrey, my father, John Scurr, moved to Hankerton, near Malmesbury, giving me many opportunities to explore north Wiltshire. I first came to know south Wiltshire through my friend Canon Timothy Russ, who died before my book was finished; may he rest in peace.

Aubrey was a wonderful friend. He has led me to deepen old friendships and discover new ones. My last expression of gratitude is to him.

Endnotes

Abbreviations

For full details, see Bibliography.
Bennett: John Aubrey, *John Aubrey: Brief Lives*
Clark: John Aubrey, *'Brief Lives', chiefly of Contemporaries*
Monumenta: John Aubrey, *Monumenta Britannica*
Natural History: John Aubrey, *The Natural History of Wiltshire*
Surrey: John Aubrey, *The Natural History and Antiquities of the County of Surrey*
Wiltshire Collections: John Aubrey, *Wiltshire: The Topographical Collections*
Education: John Aubrey, *Aubrey on Education*
Three Prose Works: John Aubrey, *Miscellanies, Remaines of Gentilisme and Judaisme, Observations*

England's Collector

2 *He offered as a 'probability'*: MS Aubrey 14, fol. 25.

2 *In the aftermath of*: Powell (1949), p.xxii.

2 *The historical and scientific interests*: K. J. Williams (2012); Poole (2010).

2 *Looking back*: Powell (1948), p.274; MS Aubrey 3.

3 *Antiquities, according to Bacon*: Robertson (ed.) (2013), p.82.

4 *One of the drawings*: William Dugdale collaborated with Roger Dodsworth. *The Monasticon Anglicanum* was first published in Latin, vol. 1 (1655), vol. 2 (1661) and vol. 3. (1673). Hollar's engraving was published in vol. 2 (1661) facing p.136.

4 *Aubrey records that*: Keynes (1968); Bennett, vol. 1, p.432; Clark, vol. 1, p.37.

4 *After the Restoration*: Compare the work of William Somner in Canterbury and see, *A treatise of the Roman ports and forts in Kent*.

5   *Before Printing: Three Prose Works*, p.290.

5   *From here the book trade:* Raymond (2003), p.83.

5   *He became a Fellow:* Hunter (1975), p.64; Hunter (1981), p.21; Hunter (1989), p.8–9.

7   *He promised to give his own important collection:* Ovenell (1986), pp.14–15.

7   *At the end of his life:* MS Aubrey 6, MS Aubrey 7, MS Aubrey 8. Bennett; Clark.

8   *About himself Aubrey concluded:* Bennett, vol. 1, p.429; Bobrick (2006), p.231.

8   *He cursed the classical tradition:* MS Wood 39, fol. 340r.

8   *A Life, he insisted:* MS Wood 39, fol. 340r.

9   *His idea was to get at the truth:* MS Aubrey 6, fol. 12; Bennett, vol. 1, p.38.

9   *An example is the Life:* Bennett, vol. 1, p.406.

9   *In Elizabeth and Essex, Lytton Strachey writes:* Powell (1949), pp.xxi–xxii.

10   *Among the manuscripts and letters:* MS Aubrey 7, fol. 3; Bennett, vol. 1, p.429.

11   *When he could no longer afford:* Or occasionally with antiquarian services, see Thanet's archive.

11   *In describing himself:* MS Wood 39, fol. 196; MS Aubrey 9, fol. 8.

11   *In the pencil portrait of Aubrey:* Portrait of John Aubrey by William Faithorne, in the Ashmolean Museum, Accession Number WA1904.3, graphite and wash on vellum, with red chalk and graphite.

12   *I was inspired: The Diary of Samuel Pepys:* Latham and Matthews (1971–1983); de Beer (1955); Robinson and Adams (1935).

12   *Pepys kept his diary for a decade:* Even though he wrote in shorthand, Pepys took care over the final copy of his diary, which was elegantly bound and shelved for posterity.

Part I: Wiltshire

18   *My grandfather tells me:* Wiltshire Collections, pp.240–1.

18   *I like to ask:* MS Top. Gen. C.25, fol. 207.

19   *I lie on the bank:* MS Aubrey 10, fol. 117.

19   *The north part:* Three Prose Works, p.312; Wiltshire Collections,
      p.236.

19   *The stones at Easton:* MS Aubrey 1, fol. 84.

19   *I am so bored:* MS Aubrey 10, fol. 7b.

19   *When I was learning:* Natural History, p.43.

19   *I love to read:* MS Top. Gen. C.25, fol. 203v. In his *Idea of Education*,
      Aubrey complained about the use of hornbooks that taught
      children to read using gothic characters instead of Latin:
      Education, p.51.

20   *I started school:* Clark, vol. 1, p.33; MS Ballard 14, fol. 133.

20   *There is another:* Natural History, p.17.

20   *I have moved:* MS Aubrey 2, fol. 18b.

21   *My fine box top:* MS Aubrey 10, fol. 8b.

21   *In Latin lessons:* Education, p.53.

21   *My most distinguished ancestor:* Bennett, vol. 1, pp.114–19; Clark,
      vol. 1, pp.210–15. Dr John Dee (1527–1609), mathematician, astrol-
      oger and antiquary.

21   *My nurse, Kath:* Bennett, vol. 2, p.439.

22   *Kath knows the history:* Three Prose Works, pp.287, 290.

22   *I am newly recovered:* Bennett, vol. 1, p.439.

22   *It is venison season:* Aubrey is mistaken. In fact Hobbes's father
      was vicar of the small neighbouring parish of Brokenborough,
      one of the poorest livings in the area. See Malcolm, p.2. Hobbes
      went to school in Westport when Robert Latimer was teaching
      there. Clark, vol. 1, pp.331–2.

23   *Mr Hobbes went to Oxford:* Malcolm, pp.4–12. Hobbes returned to
      England in October 1636.

23   *Here are some:* Clark, vol. 2, p.325.

23   *I rode over:* Natural History, p.44; Monumenta, p.103.

23   *Sir Philip Sidney:* Monumenta, p.98. Note that in his manuscript
      transcription of Sidney's poem Aubrey writes 'stones' instead of
      'stone'. Duncan-Jones (1973), p.102.

24   *My honoured teacher:* 'Here lieth Mr Robert Latymer, sometime
      rector and pastor of this church, who deceased this life the second
      day of November, anno domini 1634'.

24   *I love the music:* Bennett, vol. 1, p.36; Clark, vol. 2, p.319.

24   *Above alderman and woollen draper:* Bennett, vol. 1, p.259; Clark,
      vol. 2, pp.249–50; Duncan-Jones (1991), p.299.

25   *My grandmother, Rachel Danvers:* Bennett, vol. 1, pp.712–13; Clark, vol. 2, pp.298–9.

26   *Since Alderman Whitson's death:* Monumenta, pp.47, 65.

26   *When we are not:* Dr William Aubrey and William, Earl of Pembroke, were distantly related (by descent from the Welsh princes Melin and Philip ap Elydr) and fought together at the Battle of St Quentin (1557). See Powell (1948), p.22.

27   *I have seen a book:* MS Aubrey 2, fols 36, 167.

27   *Here is the 1st Earl of Pembroke:* Bennett, vol. 1, pp.247–50; Clark, vol. 1, pp.314–17.

27   *Here is Mary, Countess of Pembroke:* Bennett, vol. 1, p. 251–3; Clark, vol. 1, pp.310–3.

28   *Here is Sir Philip Sidney:* Bennett, vol. 1, pp.256–60; Clark, vol. 2, pp.247–50.

29   *The situation of Wilton House:* MS Aubrey 2, fol. 31.

29   *There is a picture:* MS Aubrey 2, fol. 32.

29   *Peacock has run:* Natural History, p.117.

30   *This autumn, Broad Chalke:* MS Aubrey 1, fol. 171.

30   *Mr Peyton is now:* Bennett, vol. 1, p.527; Clark, vol. 2, p.307. Francis Bacon, Viscount St Albans (1561–1626), Lord Chancellor, politician and philosopher.

31   *Lord Bacon has argued:* Bacon (2013), p.82.

31   *I have found:* Education, p.20.

31   *A terrible day:* Education, p.18.

32   *Sir Walter Raleigh:* Bennett, vol. 1. p.232, pp.241–2; Clark, vol. 2, p.191.

33   *I have heard my grandfather:* Bennett, vol. 1, p.35.

33   *Sometimes, on holy days:* MS Aubrey 4, fol. 21a(r).

33   *Sauntering through Blandford:* Aubrey is referring to the Thirty Years War.

34   *7 November:* Malcolm, pp.15–16.

Part II: Oxford

39   *Mr Hobbes encouraged me:* Clark, vol. 2, p.322. Magdalen Hall was originally next to Magdalen College. The Hall, unlike the College, had no chapel: see Malcolm, p.4. It was re-founded as Hertford College in the nineteenth century.

39   *All this time: Education*, p.86.

40   *Because I am busy:* On Aubrey's knowledge of rattlesnakes see Bennett, pp.321–2.

40   *'Turds! Tarrarags!':* Brief Lives, Kettell; MS Ballard 14, fol. 127.

41   *In Dr Ralph Kettell's dining room:* Gloucester Hall is now Worcester College.

42   *May Day: Three Prose Works*, p.137.

42   *Today I heard:* Clark, vol. 2, p.294.

42   *This morning, I saw:* Manning.

42   *At St John's College: Three Prose Works*, p.350.

43   *There has been a brush:* Bennett, vol. 1, pp.448–9; Clark, vol. 1, p.188.

44   *Now the place is full:* MS Aubrey 15; MS Top. Gen. C.25, fol. 89.

44   *Today Dr Kettell:* Bennett, vol. 1, p.175; Clark, vol. 1, p.250.

45   *Dr Kettell upbraided:* MS Top. Gen. C.25, fol. 204.

45   *Today I visited Abingdon:* Bennett, vol. 1, p.352; Clark, vol. 1, p.185.

46   *How now Bellona thunders:* Bennett, vol. 1, p.432.

46   *I have regretfully obeyed: Natural History*, p.15.

46   *The eldest son: Natural History*, p.81.

47   *Francis Potter, a reclusive:* Revd Francis Potter BD FRS (1594–1678) was a commoner of Trinity College, Oxford, and in 1637 succeeded his father, Prebendary Richard Potter (Fellow 1579–85), as rector of Kilmington in Somerset. His brother, Revd Hannibal Potter DD (1592–1664), was elected into the Trinity Fellowship in 1613.

48   *I have met:* Bennett (2009), p.330; Bennett, vol. 1, p.134; Clark, vol. 1, p.200; MS Aubrey 6, fol. 44.

50   *I am made much of:* Powell (1948), p.54.

50   *Tonight I watched: Three Prose Works*, pp.27–8.

50   *Many of the courtiers:* Bennett, vol. 1, pp.181–2;

51   *I have seen Dr William Harvey:* Bennett, vol. 1, p.200; Clark, vol. 1, p.300.

51   *I have heard another:* Bennett, vol. 1, p.198; Clark, vol. 1, p.298.

52   *In George Bathurst's rooms:* Harvey (1628), p.34; Frank (1981). Harvey's *Exercitationes de Generatione Animalium, quibus accedunt quaedam de Partû, de Membranis ac Tumoribus Uteri, et de Conceptione* was printed in 1651.

52   *I hope I can find:* Bennett, vol. 1, p.432;

53   *Camp fever is raging*: MS Ballard 14, fol. 96; 'unpolished' by smallpox
      is a phrase Aubrey uses about Sir John Denham: Bennett, vol. 1,
      p.505. Grim the Collier is a figure in seventeenth-century folklore
      appearing in songs and stories.

54   *Smallpox is periodical: Three Prose Works*, p.24.

54   *I am not there*: Wiltshire collections, p.263.

54   *Sir William Waller's soldiers*: Wiltshire Collections, p.258.

Part III: War

59   *My father's caution*: Clark, vol. 1, p.38.

59   *Dr Ralph Kettell has died*: MS Ballard 14, fol. 131.

60   *I went to visit Mr Bushell*: Clark, vol. 1, pp.133–4.

61   *In this time of civil war*: Bennett, vol. 1, pp.314–5.

61   *My friend and tutor*: MS Aubrey 12, fols 47, 48.

62   *According to William Browne*: Clark, vol. 1, p.173.

62   *William Browne says*: MS Aubrey 12, fols 49, 50.

63   *I rode over: Natural History*, p.99.

64   *The Parliament's soldiers*: Hartmann.

64   *On this day*: Wood, *Athenae Oxonienses* I, p.515.

64   *Mr William Browne writes*: MS Aubrey 12, fols 43, 44.

65   *When I was a boy*: Wiltshire Collections, p.136.

65   *There is a church*: Bennett, vol. 1, pp.587–8; Clark, vol. 1, p.244.

65   *My friend William Browne*: MS Aubrey 12, fols 35–6.

67   *Old Mr Broughton*: Bennett, vol. 1, p.335; Clark, vol. 1, p.128.

67   *There are otters*: MS Aubrey 1, fol. 132r.

67   *The Middle Temple gardens*: MS Aubrey 4, fol. 23r.

68   *Sir Thomas Fairfax*: Bennett, vol. 1, p.651; Clark, vol. 1, p.251; MS
      Aubrey 8, fol. 60.

68   *While the King*: Bennett, vol. 1, p.267; Clark, vol. 1, p.104.

69   *My honoured neighbour*: MS Aubrey 15 (MS Top. Gen. C.25, fol. 57v).

69   *To my great joy*: Bennett, vol. 1, p.433.

69   *The Parliamentarian Visitation*: Hopkins, p.119.

70   *Ralph Bathurst says*: Clark, vol. 2, p.11.

70   *My Trinity friends*: Bennett, vol. 1, p.399.

70   *I went to visit William Stumpe: Natural History*, p.79.

71   *Despite all the disruptions*: MS Wood 49, fol. 42. Matthew Hale
      (1609–76), judge and writer; his integrity was founded on puritan

manners and religion. Henry Rolle (1589–1656), politician and judge. Both men served on the King's Bench. Hale edited the treatise on common law which Rolle composed for students.

71 *How it comes to pass:* Natural History, p.17; Three Prose Works, p.25.

72 *Mr Lydall has not yet received:* MS Aubrey 12, fols 296–7; Frank (1973); Frank (1981), p.165.

73 *Mr Lydall has done:* MS Aubrey 12, fols 298–9.

73 *Hannibal Potter:* Hopkins, p.119.

74 *The south front:* Natural History, p.82.

74 *At Morecomb-bottome:* Natural History, p.33.

74 *The walls of the church:* Natural History, p.43.

74 *The River Thames:* Natural History, p.30.

74 *Clay abounds in Wiltshire:* Natural History, p.35.

74 *I believe the name:* Wiltshire Collections, p.251.

75 *We set off with the hounds:* Natural History, p.44.

75 *On this day, at last:* Bennett, vol. 1, pp.184–95; Clark, vol. 2, pp.161–70.

77 *These are the peaks:* Natural History, p.38.

77 *Mr Potter tells me stories:* Bennett, vol. 1, pp.336–9; Clark, vol. 1, p.108.

78 *Mr Emanuel Decretz:* Bennett, vol. 1, p.558; Clark, vol. 1, p.10.

Part IV: Learning

81 *In our present times:* Frank (1973).

81 *Since the Parliamentary Visitation:* The King's Cabinet Opened, or certain packets of secret letters and papers written with the King's own hand and taken in his cabinet in Nasby-field, June 14, 1645 by victorious Sir Thomas Fairfax, wherein many mysteries of state, ending to the justification of that cause, for which Sir Thomas Fairfax joined battell that memorable day are clearly laid open, published by special order of the Parliament by Robert Bostock, London, 1645.

81 *At Hullavington:* Three Prose Works, p.358.

82 *Old good-wife:* Natural History, p.69.

82 *I attended the baptism:* Clark, vol. 2, p.229.

82 *It is rumoured:* MS Aubrey 12, fol. 306.

82 *Mr Lydall and I:* MS Aubrey 12, fol. 302.

83 *Mr Lydall has written:* MS Aubrey 12, fols 304–5.

83 *I have been hunting:* Clark, vol. 2, p.317; MS Aubrey 1, fols 135–6.

84 *My friend Mr Christopher Wase:* Wase (1654).

84 *I have been to Verulam:* Bennett, vol. 1, pp.205–27; Clark, vol. 1, pp.66–84.

86 *Gorhambery House is large:* Virgil (1999–2000), *Eclogues* 4, vol. 1, p.50.

87 *My friend John Lydall:* MS Aubrey 12, fols 306–7.

87 *There has been a remarkable occurrence:* Bennett, vol. 1, p.43; Clark, vol. 2, p.141.

88 *I have acquired:* Williams, 'Training the Virtuoso'.

88 *Mr Lydall is leaving:* MS Aubrey 12, fols 310–11.

88 *I have acquired:* Bacon (1648).

88 *My friend Mr Francis Potter:* Royal Society, London, Classified Paper XII (I) 17; Bennett, introduction.

89 *Sir John Danvers's house:* MS Aubrey 2, fol. 56.

89 *Lord Bacon came often:* Bennett, vol. 1, p.206; Clark, vol. 1, p.70; MS Aubrey 6, fol. 67v.

89 *Mr Potter is greatly obliged:* Wilkins.

89 *Mr Potter considers:* MS Aubrey 13, fols 141–3.

90 *I am like Virgil's Dido:* Bennett, vol. 1, p.440; Virgil (1818), p.202.

90 *Here are some:* MS Aubrey 12, fols 308–9; Kircher.

91 *On this day:* Three Prose Works, p.29; MS Wood 39, fol. 247; Powell (1948), pp.70–1.

91 *The bookseller Mr Crooke:* Malcolm, pp.200–29.

92 *My friend Dr William Petty:* Bennett, vol. 1, p.43; Clark, vol. 2, p.140; MS Aubrey 9, fol. 51. On Hobbes's treatise on optics, see Malcolm, p.13.

92 *At last I have met:* Bennett, vol. 1, p.198; Clark, vol. 1, p.302.

92 *Mr Harrington was:* Bennett, vol. 1, p.244.

93 *I have been to see Mr Hobbes:* Clark, vol. 1, pp.351–2.

93 *It was Mr Mudiford:* MS Top. Gen. C.25, fol. 207; Ellis.

94 *Dr William Petty:* Bennett, vol. 1, p.45; Clark, vol. 2, p.142.

94 *Sir Charles Cavendish:* Bennett, vol. 1, p.90; Clark, vol. 1, p.153.

94 *The London physician:* MS Aubrey 12, fols 29–30.

94 *On this day my father:* Three Prose Works, p.73.

95 *My friend Mr Potter:* MS Aubrey 13, fol. 144.

95 *At Wilton House:* Bennett, vol. 1, p.348; Clark, vol. 1, p.218.

95 *Today I went:* 26 April 1649.

96 *Then we talked:* Bennett, vol. 1, pp.52–3; Clark, vol. 1, p.121.

96 *Mr Boyle speaks Latin:* Bennett, vol. 1, p.291; Clark, vol. 1, p.183.

96   *I returned to Eynsham:* Bennett, 'John Aubrey and the Circulation';
     MS Aubrey 6, fol. 100; MS Ashmole 1722.

97   *Despite these troubles:* MS Aubrey 12, fols 315–16.

97   *Mr Lydall has sent:* MS Aubrey 12, fols 319, 320.

97   *Mr Hartlib has a manuscript:* MS Aubrey 12, fols 155a–156b.

98   *Mr Potter was to come:* MS Aubrey 13, fol. 145.

98   *I am trying to find:* MS Aubrey 12, fols. 312, 313.

98   *Dr Harvey has prescribed:* MS Aubrey 12, fol. 107.

98   *My friend Anthony Ettrick:* Natural History, p.121; Gaskill (2007).

99   *Mr Potter's brother:* MS Aubrey 13, fols 146, 162.

99   *Following my questions:* MS Aubrey 12, fols. 314, 315.

99   *Mr Potter has written:* MS Aubrey 13, fol. 147; Robert Boyles's
     Memoirs for the Natural History of Human Blood (1684): Hunter and
     Knight; Frank (1981), p.170.

100 *At Kington St Michael:* Natural History, p.15.

100 *As you ride:* Three Prose Works, p.314; MS Aubrey 1, fol. 17.

100 *Captain Stokes:* Natural History, p.12.

100 *More Roman money:* Wiltshire Collections, p.5.

101 *I think I will send:* Bennett, vol. 1, p.400–2; Clark, vol. 2, p.219–225.

101 *In Weekfield:* Wiltshire Collections, p.5.

101 *Mr Samuel Hartlib:* Lodwick, p.22.

102 *The draft of my will:* MS Aubrey 21, fol. 75.

102 *Mr Potter has still not:* MS Aubrey 13, fol. 149.

103 *Mr Hobbes's friend:* MS Top. Gen. C.24, fol. 219.

103 *Mr Selden meant:* Bennett, vol. 1, pp.400–6; Clark, vol. 2, pp.219–25.

103 *Mr Hobbes's* De Corpore: Malcolm, p.148.

104 *Mr Hales is a pretty little man:* Bennett, vol. 1, p.399; Clark, vol. 1,
     p.280.

105 *Slough, near Eton:* MS Aubrey 5, fol. 60v.

105 *I find it strange:* Monumenta, p.90.

105 *The downs surrounding Avebury:* Aubrey is an early user of the word
     'romantic', and he also uses the word 'romancy' (see Surrey, vol.
     1, p.8).

105 *Ever since I came upon:* Monumenta, p.20.

106 *I have asked Dr Harvey:* Natural History, p.43.

106 *Dr Harvey's brother:* Bennett, vol. 1, p.198; Clark, vol. 1, p.298.

106 *Dr Harvey tells me:* Bennett, vol. 1, p.201; Clark, vol. 1, pp.300–1.

106 *I have seen Dr Harvey:* Bennett, vol. 1, p.203; Clark, vol. 1, p.302.

107 *I had a fall:* MS Aubrey 4, fol. 180.

107 *I have evaporated water:* Natural History, p.20.

107 *Hancock's well:* Natural History, p.20.

107 *I have received:* Clark, vol. 1, p.305; MS Aubrey 21, fol. 112.

107 *My friend Lord Nicholas Tufton:* Became 3rd Earl of Thanet in May 1664; imprisoned in Tower December 1655–September 1656 and September 1657–June 1658; married Elizabeth, daughter of Richard Boyle (Earl of Burlington) in April 1665.

107 *I visited Sherborne House:* Natural History, p.38.

108 *Mr Lydall tells me:* MS Aubrey 12, fols 317, 318.

108 *I have been visiting:* Bennett, 'John Aubrey and the Circulation'.

109 *Here at Draycot:* Wiltshire Collections, p.233; Natural History, p.21.

109 *Mr Potter has suggested:* MS Aubrey 13, fols 152, 153.

110 *My friends:* Bennett, vol. 1, pp.586–7; Clark, vol. 2, p.32.

110 *I have started collecting:* MS Aubrey 1, fol. 6.

110 *Henry Lyte:* MS Aubrey 2, fol. 51.

110 *I have drawn:* Bennett, vol. 1, p.212; Clark, vol. 1, p.78.

111 *A second coffee:* Bennett, vol. 1, p.338; Clark, vol. 1, p.110.

111 *My tedious lawsuit:* Powell (1948), p.80.

112 *Mr Rumsey is much troubled:* Bennett, vol. 1, p.689; Clark, vol. 2, p.207; Rumsey; Ellis, pp.132–3.

112 *As I rode:* MS Aubrey 15 (MS Top. Gen. C.25, fol. 65).

112 *I visited Caerphilly Castle:* Aubrey's erroneous identification of Caerphilly Castle as Roman is discussed by K. J. Williams (2012), in his thesis, John Aubrey's Antiquarian Scholarship, see chapter entitled 'Monumenta Britannica: II. Mapping Roman Britain'.

112 *I went to Monmouth church:* Surrey, vol. 1, pp.15–16.

113 *Veneris morbus:* Bennett, vol. 1, p.440.

113 *In his will:* Bennett, vol. 1, p.195; Clark, vol. 1, p.295.

113 *My honoured friend:* Clark (1891–1900), vol. 1, p.229.

113 *He left the college:* Notes and Records of the Royal Society of London, vol. 27, no. 2 (Feb. 1973), pp.193–217, 208; Mydorgius.

114 *Dining at Hampton Court:* Natural History, p.190; Powell (1948), p.91.

114 *John Wilkins has been made:* Bennett, vol. 1, p.294; Clark, vol. 2, p.301; Bennett (2009), p.336.

114 *On this day Oliver Cromwell:* Three Prose Works, p.27.

115 *The experimental philosophical club:* Bennett, vol. 1, p.506; Clark, vol. 2, p.322; MS Aubrey 8, fol. 6.

115 *On this day:* MS Aubrey 1, fol. 1b; Clark, vol. 1, p.252.

115 *Wiltshire is too great:* Wiltshire Collections, p.3.

116 *Sir George Penruddock: Natural History,* p.102. Sir George Penruddock of Broad Chalke was born at Westminster: MS Aubrey 23, fol. 61.

116 *Today, riding at a gallop:* MS Ballard 14, fol. 158b.

116 *I have gone:* MS Aubrey 9, fols 32–3; Clark, vol. 1, pp.326–7.

117 *Mr Hobbes's horoscope:* Clark, vol. 1, p.328; MS Aubrey 9, fol. 33.

118 *Mr Stafford Tyndale:* MS Aubrey 13, fol. 230.

118 *I have sold the old manor:* MS Aubrey 13, fols 245r, 255r.

118 *I am sharing lodgings:* Bennett, vol. 1, p.56; Clark, vol. 2, p.75.

119 *I am an auditor:* Bennett, vol. 1, pp.318–19; Clark, vol. 1, pp.289–90.

119 *My Trinity College friend:* Bennett, vol. 1, p.532; Clark, vol. 2, p.148.

Part V: Restoration

123 *On this day:* Aubrey includes in his life of Monck *A Letter from his Excellence the Lord General Monck, and the Officers under his Command, to the Parliament, In the name of themselves and the souldiers under them,* printed by John Macock, London, 1660. The letter is dated 11 February 1659.

123 *Someone anonymous:* Bennett, vol. 1, pp.59–60; Clark, vol. 2, p.78.

124 *The news has spread:* Bennett, vol. 1, p.57; Clark, vol. 2, p.76.

125 *Mr Harrington's Rota Club:* Bennett, vol. 1, p.320; Clark, vol. 2, p.74.

125 *Samuel Pordage:* Bennett, vol. 1, p.459; Clark, vol. 2, p.160.

125 *Earlier this month:* MS Aubrey 1, fol. 85v.

126 *The aurora:* Uglow, p.35.

126 *As the morning:* Clark, vol. 2, p.153.

126 *On this day:* Uglow, p.40.

127 *Last month, I wrote:* Foskett, p.36.

127 *At Rye: Three Prose Works,* p.331.

128 *Mr Hobbes tells me:* Clark, vol. 1, p.340; MS Aubrey 9, fol. 41.

128 *The King and Mr Hobbes:* MS Aubrey 9, fol. 41.

128 *I have heard:* Wiltshire Collection, p.255.

128 *My turquoise ring has changed:* MS Aubrey 1, fol. 85v.

129 *I am one of the signatories: Notes and Records of the Royal Society of London,* vol. 28, no. 2 (1 April 1974), p.167.

129 *My most honoured:* Bennett, vol. 1, p.633; Clark, vol. 2, p.82.

129 *My servant saw:* McMains.

129 *The astrologer:* Joyce escaped with his family to the Netherlands, where he was last heard of in August 1670.

130 *I have been to visit: Natural History*, p.97.

130 *The cloudy spot:* MS Aubrey 1, fol. 85v.

130 *Since the return:* Hannibal Potter was reinstated as President of Trinity College on 3 August 1660.

130 *Sir John Hoskyns:* MS Aubrey 12, fol. 189.

131 *I discussed the lace: Three Prose Works*, p.28.

131 *Mr Hollar is very short-sighted:* Bennett, vol. 1, p.77; Clark, vol. 1, pp.407–8.

131 *Sir John Hoskyns writes:* MS Aubrey 12, fols 224, 190.

132 *My cousin James Whitney:* Bennett (2009), p.334.

132 *The natives seem:* Hobbes (1994), vol. 2, p.520.

132 *In Dublin we met: Three Prose Works*, p.349.

133 *Mr Tyndale writes:* MS Aubrey 13, fols 231–2.

133 *I am delighted:* Clark, vol. 1, p.394.

133 *My friend Mr Wenceslaus Hollar:* Hunter (2010), p.97.

135 *Mr Samuel Cooper:* John Evelyn's diary, January 1662.

135 *Sir John Hoskyns writes:* MS Aubrey 12, fol. 193.

135 *Mr Hobbes has silenced:* Clark, vol. 1, p.335; MS Aubrey 9, fol. 38. Note this summary of *Leviathan* is from *Mr Hobbes Considered in his Loyalty, Religion, Reputation and Manners. By way of Letter to Dr Wallis* (1662), which Aubrey is quoting.

136 *Mr Hobbes says: Education*, p.128; Malcolm, pp.21–2.

136 *Mr Tyndale complains:* MS Aubrey 13, fol. 235.

136 *Parliament has passed:* Malcolm, p.348.

136 *Mr Hooke is of but middling stature:* Clark, vol. 1, p.411.

137 *Sir William Petty presented:* Bennett, vol. 1, p.51; Clark, vol. 2, p.146.

137 *Dr Walter Charleton:* Birch, vol. 1, p.166.

137 *On this day:* Birch, vol. 1, p.172.

137 *To my great joy:* Birch, vol. 1, p.179; Aubrey, *Three Prose Works*, p.359.

137 *The minister of Avebury: Natural History*, p.44.

138 *I presented the Society:* Gunther (1925), vol. 6, p.116; Birch, vol. 1, p.206.

138 *Mr Hooke's report:* Gunther (1925), vol. 6, p.116; Birch, vol. 1, p.207.

138 *I mentioned before:* Birch, vol. 1, p.212.

138 *Mr Potter has been invited:* MS Aubrey 13, fols 154–5.

139 *I also described:* Birch, vol. 1, p.234.

139 *Quaere: if a bladder*: Clark, vol. 2, p.327.

139 *The new charter*: Birch, vol. 1, p.236.

139 *When I was about*: Natural History, p.23.

139 *At Crudwell*: Natural History, p.23.

140 *Sir Kenelm Digby*: Birch, vol. 1, p.300.

140 *I have found*: Hobbes (1994), vol. 2, p.555.

140 *I have also found*: MS Aubrey 12, fols 162–3.

140 *The rivulet that runs*: Natural History, p.28. Crawfish are crayfish.

141 *In his book*: Monumenta, pp.25, 129.

141 *I think Mr Charleton*: Monumenta, p.85.

141 *Today I met*: Monumenta, p.21.

142 *Afterwards, as we were leaving*: MS Top. Gen. C.24, fols 23–5.

142 *His Majesty also*: Monumenta, p.34.

142 *While I think it*: Monumenta, p.92.

142 *The monument is still*: Monumenta, p.86.

144 *Mr Francis Potter*: Birch, vol. 1, p.329.

144 *St Andrew's Day*: Bennett, vol. 1, p.48.

145 *I am lovesick*: MS Aubrey 12, fol. 194.

145 *I have been elected*: Lennard.

145 *I have described*: Birch, vol. 1, p.422.

Part VI: Stone, Water, Fire

149 *I have reached Paris*: Hobbes (1994), vol. 2, p.620.

150 *The shopkeepers here*: Powell (1948), p.8.

150 *About a mile*: MS Aubrey 15 (MS Top. Gen. C.25, fol. 56).

150 *Not far from the road*: MS Aubrey 15 (MS Top. Gen. C.25, fol. 56).

150 *I have paid*: MS Aubrey 21, fol. 56.

150 *I hear that Mr Hooke's*: Bennett, vol. 1, p.98; Clark, vol. 1, p.411.

151 *I have seen Mr Hobbes*: Aubrey claims to have inspired Hobbes's treatise *De Legibus*, which was bound up with his book on rhetoric, so 'one cannot find it but by chance': MS Aubrey 7, fol. 5r.

151 *Mr Hobbes always has*: MS Aubrey 9, fol. 54; Hobbes (1994), vol. 1, p.xxx.

151 *My friend Mr George Ent*: MS Aubrey 12, fols 102–3.

154 *I have written*: The preface to Templa Druidum.

154 *The similarity between*: Monumenta, p.42.

154 *I have made a close study*: MS Aubrey 11, fols 1b, 3.

154 *Mr Charlton claims:* MS Aubrey 11, fols 13b, 14.

155 *Southward from Avebury:* MS Aubrey 15 (MS Top. Gen. C.25, fol. 63).

155 *How well I remember:* Bennett, vol. 1, p.315; Clark, vol. 1, p.134.

155 *I missed seeing:* MS Aubrey 13, fol. 236.

156 *The bush in Mr Hinton's garden: Three Prose Works,* p.330.

156 *The widow of:* Bennett, vol. 1, p.455; Clark, vol. 1, p.127. Aubrey comments: 'but it was his Father-in-lawes invention'.

156 *Looking on a serene sky:* Boyle (2001), vol. 3, p.111.

157 *Mr Samuel Pepys:* Birch, vol. 2, p.13.

157 *Sir John Hoskyns:* MS Aubrey 12, fol. 196.

157 *The poet Sir John Denham:* Bennett, vol. 1, p.349; Clark, vol. 1, p.219.

157 *I have been to see:* Bennett, vol. 1, p.171; Clark, vol. 2, p.304.

157 *Mr Wenceslaus Hollar:* MS Aubrey 12, fol. 174.

158 *In Mr Camden's* Britannia: Bennett, vol. 1, p.359; Clark, vol. 1, p.145.

158 *I discovered the waters:* MS Aubrey 1, fol. 34.

158 *I sent my servant: Natural History,* pp.21–2.

159 *In about a month:* Boyle (2001), vol. 3, pp.111–12; Pell.

160 *I have shown:* Boyle (1772), vol. 1, section VIII, p.451; vol. 3, p.148.

161 *Mr Hobbes is disturbed:* Hobbes (1994), vol. 1, p.xxv.

161 *The Parliamentary Committee:* Hobbes (1994), vol. 1, p.xxv.

161 *Following the Great Conflagration:* Bennett, vol. 1, p.98; Clark, vol. 1, p.411.

162 *I saw Bishop Braybrook's body: Three Prose Works,* p.349.

162 *I spoke to some:* MS Top. Gen. C.25, fol. 37.

162 *A little before:* MS Top. Gen. C.25, fols 37r–38r; Bennett (2014).

163 *Lord Henry Howard:* Birch, vol. 2, pp.121–2.

163 *I have been chosen:* Birch, vol. 2, p.123; *Notes and Records of the Royal Society of London,* vol. 28, no. 2 (1 April 1974), p.167; MS Aubrey 8, fol. 60v; MS Top. Gen. C.25, fol. 38r.

163 *Blood has been moved:* Birch, vol. 2, p.123.

164 *The band of my turquoise ring:* Boyle (1772), vol. 3, p.151.

164 *At the meeting today:* Birch, vol. 2, pp.127, 142.

164 *At the Royal Society's:* Birch, vol. 2, pp.129–30.

164 *My lord Brouncker:* Britton, p.96.

165 *Lady Denham died:* Bennett, vol. 1, p.350; Clark, vol. 1, p.219; MS Aubrey 12, fols 96–7.

165 *My friend Edward Davenant:* Bennett (2009), p.330.

165 *Since the Great Conflagration: Natural History,* p.38.

165 *Many Roman remains:* Monumenta, pp.498–9.

166 *I have promised:* MS Aubrey 9, fol. 31v; Wiltshire Collections, pp.251, 255.

167 *We talked of Mr Hobbes:* Clark (1891–1900), vol. 5, p.10.

167 *This summer, Mr Wood:* Bennett (1998); Clark (1891–1900), vol. 1, p.286. Wood began to look at the registers, etc. in Christ Church Treasury in October 1659.

168 *I have received:* MS Ballard 14, fol. 80r.

168 *At a meeting:* Birch, vol. 2, p.224.

168 *Today, before the Royal Society:* Gunther (1923–45), vol. 6, p.321; Birch, vol. 2, p.226.

169 *I am at last:* MS Ballard 14, fol. 80.

170 *I went today:* Bennett, vol. 1, p.145; Clark, vol. 1, pp.208–9.

170 *Thomas May translated:* Bennett, vol. 1, pp.573–4; Clark, vol. 2, pp.55–7; Raymond (1996), p.285.

170 *I have seen Mr Hobbes:* Hobbes (1994), vol. 1, p.xxv. On the dating of Hobbes's tract on heresy, see Willman.

170 *The Council:* Birch, vol. 2, p.265; Lewis (2001).

170 *Today I brought before:* Birch, vol. 2, p.272.

171 *I have decided:* MS Top. Gen. C.24, fol. 251.

171 *Exploring the sky:* Register Book Copy 3, 128; Classified Paper VIII (I) 24.

171 *The Royal Society:* Birch, vol. 2, p.283; Lodwick, pp.19–20.

171 *When I was a boy:* MS Wood 39, fol. 118.

173 *I have been told:* MS Wood 39, fol. 318.

173 *My servant Robert:* MS Ballard 14, fol. 81.

173 *I have been to see:* MS Aubrey 4, fol. 211r.

174 *As soon as my lawsuit:* MS Ballard 14, fol. 82.

174 *The great poet:* Clark, vol. 1, pp.190–1.

175 *St Paul's Day:* MS Ballard 14, fol. 86.

175 *If Mr Wood needs:* MS Ballard 14, fol. 84.

175 *I brought my drawing:* Register Book Copy 3, 128.

175 *Sir John Denham:* Bennett, vol. 1, p.350; Clark, vol. 1, p.219.

176 *Today, I brought before:* Birch, vol. 2, p.361.

176 *In Mr Samuel Cooper's studio:* Bennett, vol. 1, p.295; Clark, vol. 1, p.151; Mortimer, p.68.

176 *Lord Cary adhered:* Bennett, vol. 1, p.298; Clark, vol. 1, pp.152, 173.

176 *I have sent:* MS Aubrey 12, fols 94–5.

177 *Mr Wood has quarrelled:* Clark (1891–1900), vol. 2, pp.163–4.

177 *The work of making:* Natural History, p.27.

177 *Seth Ward tells me:* Natural History, p.37. Wilkins became Bishop of Chester in November 1668.

177 *This searching:* MS Aubrey 3, fol. 11.

177 *At Bemarton:* Natural History, p.95.

178 *Mr Wood has been summoned:* Ballard MS 14, fol. 84.

178 *A new idea:* MS Aubrey 10, fol. 2.

178 *I am in Broad Chalke:* MS Ballard 14, fol. 88.

178 *I have heard:* MS Aubrey 4, fol. 142v. Mr William Browne died on 21 October 1669.

178 *I have presented:* Hobbes (1994), vol. 2, p.521.

179 *I was to see:* MS Aubrey 12, fols 153–4.

179 *I have a short poem:* MS Aubrey 21, fol. 3; Bennett, vol. 1, p.323; Clark, vol. 1, p.293.

179 *Mr Harrington suffers:* Bennett, vol. 1, p.321; Clark, vol. 1, p.292.

179 *My former servant:* MS Aubrey 13, fols 256–7.

180 *Easter Tuesday:* MS Tanner 456a, fol. 9.

180 *Many of the old ways:* Wiltshire Collections, p.236.

180 *I remember how my grandfather:* Wiltshire Collections, p.236.

182 *I have collected together:* MS Aubrey 17, fols 1–2; Ovid, *Metamorphoses*, lib. 9.

183 *I saw Mr Wood today:* Clark (1891–1900), vol. 2, p.192.

183 *I am at Broad Chalke:* MS Aubrey 12, fols 116–17.

183 *My former servant:* MS Aubrey 13, fol. 258.

183 *This year, not far:* Three Prose Works, p.50.

184 *Mr Lodwick, my friend:* MS Aubrey 12, fol. 264; Lodwick, pp.33–4.

184 *Between south Wales:* MS Wood 39, fol. 128.

184 *When I was a boy:* MS Ballard 14, fol. 133; Clark, vol. 1, pp.146–7.

184 *Also in Yatton Keynell:* Monumenta, p.126.

185 *Mr Samuel Butler:* Bennett, vol. 1, p.396; Clark, vol. 1, pp.145–6.

185 *The Roman architecture flourished:* MS Aubrey 15 (MS Top. Gen. C.25, fol. 168).

185 *The Roman architecture came again:* MS Aubrey 16, fol. 8.

185 *Today I presented:* Notes and Records of the Royal Society of London, vol. 28, no. 2 (1 April 1974), p.168.

185 *Today I gave:* Notes and Records of the Royal Society of London, vol. 28, no. 2 (1 April 1974), p.168.

185   *I have also presented:* Birch, vol. 2, p.462.
186   *I am pleased to hear:* MS Wood 39, fol. 163; Clark, vol. 2, p.10.
186   *Glass is becoming:* Clark, vol. 2, p.329.
186   *I have been helping:* MS Wood 39, fol. 165.
186   *I have introduced:* MS Wood 39, fol. 165.
187   *My friend Walter Charleton:* MS Aubrey 12, fol. 66.
187   *Surely my stars:* MS Wood 39, fol. 166.
187   *I have now completed:* Wiltshire Collections, p.119.

Part VII: Work

191   *I am concerned:* MS Ballard 14, fol. 92.
192   *In London I have received:* MS Aubrey 12, fols 82, 83.
192   *Henry Coley was born:* Bennett, vol. 1, p.753; Clark, vol. 1, p.181.
192   *John Florio was born:* MS Wood 39, fols 131, 133; Clark, vol. 1, p.254.
193   *If you dissolve sugar:* Three Prose Works, p.356.
193   *It is a relief:* Clark, vol. 1, p.42.
193   *I am interested:* MS Wood 39, fol. 131: 14 June 1671.
193   *Mr Gadbury assures me:* Bennett, vol. 1, p.580; Clark, vol. 2, p.324.
193   *I think it might be said:* MS Wood 39, fol. 131.
194   *Mr Wood writes:* MS Wood 39, fols 135, 183.
194   *I am rumoured:* MS Wood 39, fol. 141.
194   *Mr Thomas Gore:* MS Aubrey 12, fols 140–1.
194   *Sir John Hoskyns:* MS Aubrey 12, fol. 197.
194   *I have asked:* MS Wood 39, fols 141–5.
195   *I have drawn inspiration:* MS Aubrey 21, fol. 24.
195   *I shall set my play:* Clark, vol. 2, p.268; vol. 1, p.277; MS Aubrey 21, fol. 24v.
196   *Before I leave England:* MS Wood 39, fol. 141.
196   *Sir James and I:* Bennett, vol. 1, pp.561–2; Clark, vol. 2, p.37.
197   *After the mosaic:* MS Aubrey 15 (MS Top. Gen. C.25, fol. 104).
198   *I have noticed:* MS Aubrey 15 (MS Top. Gen. C.25, fol. 155),
198   *I have sought advice:* Clark, vol. 2, p.149.
198   *Two trunks full:* MS Ballard 14, fol. 89.
198   *I wish to go:* MS Wood 39, fol. 149.
198   *I have been sending:* MS Wood 39, fol. 155; Bennett, vol. 1, p.261; Clark, vol. 2, p.90; Dr Muffet's book was *Healths improvement, or,*

Rules comprizing and discovering the nature, method, and manner of preparing all sorts of food used in this nation, ed. Christopher Bennet (1655); Bennett, vol. 1, p.491; Clark, vol. 1, p.275.

200 *Mr Edward Bradsaw:* Clark, vol. 2, p.85.

200 *My lord the Earl:* MS Aubrey 13, fol. 209.

200 *Mr Isaac Newton:* Birch, vol. 3, p.1.

201 *To help Mr Wood:* MS Wood 39, fol. 195.

201 *Sir John Hoskyns:* MS Aubrey 12, fols 209–10.

201 *I am going to Somerset:* MS Aubrey 26, fol. 10v.

201 *The headmaster of Brentwood:* MS Aubrey 13, fols 49–51.

202 *I know of men:* MS Aubrey 10, fol. 7.

202 *For his collection:* Boyle (2001), vol. 4, p.319.

202 *Mr Wood is a candid historian:* MS Aubrey 12, fol. 8.

203 *My honoured friend:* Bennett, vol. 1, p.7; Clark, vol. 1, pp.182–3.

203 *Mr Cooper gave me:* Clark, vol. 1, p.368; Foskett, p.63. An unfinished portrait of Hobbes is among others listed as being in the artist's studio after his death.

203 *Mr Paschall tells me:* MS Aubrey 13, fol. 2; Salmon.

203 *Sir John Hoskyns:* MS Aubrey 12, fol. 202.

203 *I have discovered:* MS Wood 39, fol. 181.

204 *In his youth:* Bennett, vol. 1, pp.609–19; Clark, vol. 2, pp.102–4; Ogilby.

204 *Mr Ogilby's list:* MS Aubrey 4, fol. 244; Bennett (2014).

204 *Mr Hooke is ill:* MS Aubrey 12, fol. 203.

205 *I have found out:* MS Wood 39, fol. 185.

205 *Mr Thomas Browne:* MS Aubrey 12, fols 52–4.

205 *About a hundred:* MS Wood 39, fol. 188.

205 *I am staying:* Boyle (2001), vol. 4, pp.319–20.

205 *Sir John Hoskyns insists:* MS Aubrey 12, fol. 205.

205 *My lord the Earl:* MS Aubrey 13, fol. 210.

206 *My thoughts keep returning:* MS Wood 39, fol. 192, October 1672; MS Top. Gen. C.25, fols 23–33.

206 *I have in my possession:* MS Wood 39, fol. 190; *Surrey*, vol. 1, p.v (introduction).

206 *Mr Hobbes has given:* Birch, vol. 3, p.58.

206 *I have a great desire:* MS Wood 39, fol. 147.

207 *Sir John Hoskyns has written:* MS Aubrey 12, vol. 206.

207 *I hope to retrieve:* MS Wood 39, fol. 181.

207 *According to Goody Faldo:* MS Wood 39, fol. 192, 18 January; Bennett (2009), p.338.

208 *My friend and fellow antiquary:* Bennett, vol. 1, pp.114–19; Clark, vol. 1, pp.210–15; MS Aubrey 8, fol. 6v.

208 *My friend Henry Coley:* MS Aubrey 23, fol. 113.

208 *I am back:* Hooke (1935), p.18.

208 *It has been decided:* MS Wood 39, fol. 253. Dr Poole has argued that Aubrey's identification of his manuscript as Historia Roffensia is mistaken. The manuscript is a copy of 'Flores Historiarum' now MSe Musae 149.

208 *I think my former servant:* MS Wood 39, fol. 261.

209 *I dined yesterday:* MS Wood 39, fol. 195.

209 *Christopher Wren's sister:* Bennett, vol. 1, p.280; Clark, vol. 1, p.405.

209 *I have succeeded:* MS Wood 39, fol. 196; MS Aubrey 9, fol. 8.

210 *Mr Ashmole has shown:* MS Wood 39, fol. 255.

210 *I would like to return:* MS Wood 39, fols 261, 258.

210 *My books:* MS Wood 39, fol. 199, 7 April 1673.

211 *I dined recently:* Bennett, vol. 1, p.573; Clark, vol. 1, pp.170–1.

Part VIII: Surrey

215 *Sir Lleuellin Jenkins:* Bennett, vol. 1, pp.75–6; Clark, vol. 2, p.8.

215 *My spirit is dejected:* MS Wood 39, fol. 206.

215 *At last, Mr Ogilby:* Surrey, vol. 1, introduction; Clark (1891–1900), vol. 2, p.265; MS Aubrey 4, fol. 243r; see also Ogilby (1673). Also Aubrey's note that the Royal Society considered these queries at several meetings (MS Aubrey 4, fol. 244).

216 *Alas, I must wait:* MS Wood 39, fol. 214.

216 *Dr Fell:* Clark (1891–1900), vol. 2, p.200.

216 *I have sent:* Clark (1891–1900), vol. 2, p.265.

216 *Two days ago:* Clark (1891–1900), vol. 2, p.265.

217 *Robert Moray's death:* Bennett, vol. 1, p.633; Clark, vol. 2, p.82; Monumenta, p.128; Birch, vol. 3, p.113.

217 *I have decided:* Surrey, vol. 1, introduction. The earliest notes regarding Aubrey's perambulation of Surrey are from July 1673 (MS Aubrey 4, fols 235r–242v). He later reworked them, as did his editor, Rawlinson.

217 *The celebrated River Thames:* MS Aubrey 4, fols 5a(r), 13.

217 *London Bridge:* MS Aubrey 4, fol. 10r.

218 *It is generally agreed:* MS Aubrey 4, fol. 14r.

218 *The Tradescant collection: Surrey*, vol. 1, pp.12–13.

218 *In the ditches:* MS Aubrey 4, fols 25, 32.

219 *East of Kingston:* MS Aubrey 4, fol. 37r.

219 *All Saints' Church:* Horsfall Turner, p.182; *Surrey*, vol. 1, pp.18–19; MS Aubrey 4, fol. 38.

219 *At Cobham: Three Prose Works*, p.318; MS Aubrey 4, fol. 44r.

219 *At Norbury:* MS Aubrey 4, fol. 48.

219 *At Deepdene:* MS Aubrey 4, fols 49–50, 53–4.

220 *There is a vineyard: Three Prose Works*, p.318.

220 *I have copied:* MS Aubrey 4, fols 51–2.

220 *As I rode:* MS Aubrey 4, fol. 59r.

221 *On Letherhed Down:* MS Aubrey 4, fol. 89r.

221 *In Albury Park:* MS Aubrey 4, fol. 99r.

222 *Ben remembers:* MS Aubrey 4, fol. 105r.

222 *I went to see the remains: Surrey*, vol. 4, pp.79–80; MS Aubrey 4, fols 102r–103.

222 *I have reached Guilford:* MS Aubrey 4, fol. 108r; for illustrations see fol. 183v.

223 *Mayden-hair grows:* MS Aubrey 4, fol. 117v.

223 *Here at Frensham:* MS Aubrey 4, fol. 140ar.

223 *Waverley Abbey is situated: Surrey*, vol. 3, p.360; MS Aubrey 4, fol. 141r.

224 *Waverley was the mother church:* MS Aubrey 4, fol. 142v.

224 *Above the town:* MS Aubrey 4, fol. 148r.

224 *In Woking I spoke: Three Prose Works*, p.319; MS Aubrey 4, fol. 163r.

225 *The cheese of this county:* MS Aubrey 4, fol. 170r.

225 *Croydon market:* MS Aubrey 4, fol. 180r.

225 *Bordering on Hampshire:* MS Aubrey 4, fol. 182r.

225 *I made diligent enquiry:* MS Aubrey 4, fol. 189a(r). Aubrey notes that according to his friend Christopher Wase, Sir John Denham called the place Cooper's Hill after his man Cooper, who took a great delight in going there because of the prospect.

225 *I have reached Runnymede:* MS Aubrey 4, fol. 189a(r).

226 *I am still searching:* MS Wood 39, fol. 221.

226 *Quaere: if Mr John Evelyn:* MS Wood 39, fol. 221; MS Aubrey 4, fol. 95r.

227 *I think and hope:* MS Aubrey 13, fol. 246.

227 *I am back:* MS Wood 39, fol. 223; Wattie, p.214.

227 *I met Mr Ogilby:* Hooke (1935), p.62.

228 *My friend Christopher Wase:* MS Aubrey 13, fols 247–9; Wase (1678).

228 *I am ashamed:* MS Wood 39, fol. 231.

Part IX: Penury

233 *I have returned:* Hooke (1935), p.65.

233 *I dined this evening:* MS Ballard 14, fol. 96.

233 *Mr Ashmole once lived:* Surrey, vol. 4, pp.70, 79; MS Aubrey 4, fol. 99.

233 *I have sent:* MS Tanner 456a, fol. 15.

234 *I have been to Richmond:* Clark, vol. 2, p.177.

234 *I have sent Mr Wood:* MS Wood 39, fol. 243.

234 *My friend Sir John Hoskyns:* Clark, vol. 1, p.425; MS Aubrey 23, fol. 63.

234 *I have drafted:* MS Ashmole 1829, fol. 5.

234 *Today I drank:* Hooke (1935), p.70.

235 *I presented Mr Hooke:* Notes and Records of the Royal Society of London, vol. 28, no. 2 (1 April 1974), p.169.

235 *Mr Hooke has lent me:* Hooke (1935), p.71.

235 *I visited the apothecary:* See MS Top. Gen. C.24, fol. 244v; MacGregor, p.86.

235 *I was hoping:* MS Wood 39, fol. 241.

235 *I was at Garraway's:* Hooke (1935), p.77.

236 *My lodgings:* Bennett, vol. 1, p.438; Clark, vol. 1, p.44; MS Wood 39, fol. 261.

236 *I presented:* Birch, vol. 3, p.122.

236 *I am so importuned:* MS Wood 39, fol. 255.

237 *Mr Hobbes tells me:* MS Aubrey 12, fols 166–7.

237 *I have had to break:* Clark (1891–1900), vol. 2, p.290.

237 *Mr Wood's book:* Clark, vol. 1, p.343; MS Aubrey 9, fol. 43.

237 *I spent the day:* Hooke (1935), p.89.

238 *I was at Garraway's:* Hooke (1935), p.90.

238 *On this day:* MS Wood 39, fol. 261; Wattie; Hooke (1935).

238 *Mr Hooke has newly:* MS Wood 39, fol. 261; Lodwick, p.30.

238 *I saw Mr Hobbes:* MS Ballard 14, fol. 98.

239 *I am reminded:* Surrey, vol. 3, p.367; MS Aubrey 4, fol. 140a(r).

239 *Other friends urge me:* MS Ballard 14, fol. 98.

239 *Mr Hobbes plans:* MS Ballard 14, fol. 99.

239 *I went to visit:* Hooke (1935), p.99.

239 *The Earl of Thanet:* MS Ballard 14, fol. 99; Bennett, vol. 1, p.745; Clark, vol. 1, p.97.

240 *I do think:* MS Wood 39, fol. 268.

240 *Mr Hooke and I:* Hooke (1935).

240 *I have sent:* Clark (1891–1900), vol. 2, p.293.

241 *Mr Hooke lent me:* Hooke (1935), p.109.

241 *Two dozen copies:* MS Ballard 14, fol. 103.

241 *I took leave:* Hooke (1935), p.111; *Notes and Records of the Royal Society of London,* vol. 28, no. 2 (1 April 1974).

242 *Mr Hooke lent me:* Hooke (1935), p.112.

242 *Mr Hobbes's letter:* Clark, vol. 1, p.345.

242 *Mr Wood has sent me:* MS Ballard 14, fol. 105.

242 *A very rainy morning:* Hooke (1935), p.115.

242 *Mr Hooke lent me:* Hooke (1935), p.116.

242 *George Ent desires:* MS Ballard 14, fol. 108.

243 *I have a curious manuscript:* Clark, vol. 2, p.158.

243 *I do not think:* MS Ballard 14, fol. 107.

243 *I went to Joe's:* Hooke (1935), p.118.

243 *The Earl of Rochester:* Bennett, vol. 1, pp.151, 171; Clark, vol. 2, pp.34, 54.

243 *I am reconsidering:* MS Ballard 14, fol. 110.

244 *I cannot persuade:* Hobbes (1994), vol. 2, pp.918–19.

244 *It is a shame:* MS Ballard 14, fol. 111.

244 *The antiquary:* Ovenell, p.31.

244 *Meanwhile, Thomas Gore:* MS Wood 39, fol. 282.

245 *Mr Hooke lent me:* Hooke (1935), p.123.

245 *I have easily answered:* MS Wood 39, fol. 282; MS Ballard 14, fol. 111.

245 *I have been to see:* Bennett, vol. 1, p.191; Clark, vol. 2, p.170.

245 *I wish I had:* MS Ballard 14, fol. 113.

245 *I am concerned about:* MS Aubrey 13, fols 211–12.

246 *Sir Jonas Moore:* Birch, vol. 3, pp.158–9.

246 *I went to Garraway's:* Hooke (1935), p.135; *Notes and Records of the Royal Society of London,* vol. 28, no. 2 (1 April 1974), p.181.

246 *I went to Joe's:* Hooke (1935), p.138; Clark, vol. 2, pp.230, 229.

247 *Mr Wylde has:* Turner; see Powell, Add MS 82701.

247   *I am in London:* MS Wood 39, fol. 288.

247   *I have asked Mr Wood:* MS Wood 39, fol. 265.

247   *Sir John Hoskyns:* MS Aubrey 12, fol. 215.

247   *Sir Christopher Wren says:* MS Aubrey 15 (MS Top. Gen. C.25, fols 133, 132).

248   *If I can:* MS Aubrey 13, fol. 265r.

248   *In his book: Monumenta,* p.72.

248   *I have sent:* Hobbes (1994), vol. 2, pp.751–3.

248   *All men cry out:* MS Wood 39, fol. 291.

248   *I was sorely mistaken:* MS Aubrey 13, fol. 265v.

249   *George Ent will give:* MS Aubrey 12, fols 105–6.

249   *Now that the days:* MS Ballard 14, fol. 115.

249   *On this day:* Clark, vol. 1, p.45.

249   *Mr Wylde is thinking:* MS Aubrey 13, fol. 213.

249   *My friend George Ent:* MS Aubrey 12, fol. 109.

250   *My lord the Earl:* MS Aubrey 13, fol. 217.

250   *I have told:* Clark, vol. 1, p.211; MS Aubrey 6, fol. 37.

250   *I cannot deny:* MS Wood 39, fol. 296.

251   *Mr Paschall has asked:* MS Aubrey 13, fol. 4.

251   *Next time:* MS Wood 39, fol. 299.

251   *I have reassured:* Hobbes (1994), vol. 2, pp.753–6.

252   *What can be said:* Bennett, vol. 1, p.301; Clark, vol. 2, p.282.

252   *Mr Hooke has written:* Gunther (1923–45), vol. 7, pp.434–5.

252   *I have written:* Hooke (1935), p.184.

252   *In Minty Common: Three Prose Works,* p.324.

253   *In Stanton Parke: Three Prose Works,* p.325.

253   *Jane Smyth:* Clark, vol. 2, p.229; Bennett (2014), pp.317–32.

253   *Mr Paschall:* MS Aubrey 13, fol. 5.

253   *Mr Meredith Lloyd:* MS Aubrey 5, fol. 4.

253   *A good way:* MS Tanner 456a, fol. 19r.

254   *I have deposited:* MS Ballard 14, fol. 127.

254   *I remember:* Bennett, vol. 1, p.210; Clark, vol. 1, p.71; MS Aubrey 6, fol. 68.

254   *On the first date:* Hooke (1935), p.197.

254   *Quaere: does the brain: Three Prose Works,* p.340.

254   *I think it is strange:* MS Hearne's Diaries 159, fol. 204; Bennett, introduction.

255   *I went to Garraway's:* Hooke (1935), p.198.

255 *I was at Garraway's:* Hooke (1935), p.199.

255 *Mr Hooke, Mr Hill:* Hooke (1935), p.199.

255 *At Joe's coffee house:* Hooke (1935), p.200; Hunter (1981), p.45.

255 *I was with Mr Hooke:* Hooke (1935), p.201.

255 *Mr Newton read:* Hooke (1935), p.201.

256 *I went to Garraway's:* Hooke (1935), p.202; M. Hunter and S. Schaffer (eds), p.174; Bennett, vol. 1, p.99; Clark, vol. 1, p.411.

256 *I dined:* Hooke (1935), p.202.

256 *I was at Cardinal's:* Hooke (1935), p.204.

256 *Mr Oldenburg:* Classified Paper VII (I) 28; Birch, vol. 3, p.271.

257 *On the first day:* Hooke (1935), p.207.

257 *I was with Mr Hooke:* Hooke (1935), p.208.

257 *Mr Paschall says:* MS Aubrey 13, fol. 6.

257 *Now I come:* MS Ballard 14, fol. 116.

257 *I was at Garraway's:* Hooke (1935), p.211.

258 *I smoked at Garraway's:* Hooke (1935), p.212.

258 *On this day:* Hooke (1935), p.213.

258 *There was much rain:* Hooke (1935), p.213.

258 *Mr Paschall's letter:* Birch, vol. 3, p.280.

258 *I visited Sir Christopher Wren:* Hooke (1935), pp.214–15.

259 *Dr Holder is beholden:* Lodwick, p.32.

259 *As I was walking:* Bennett, vol. 1, p.333; Clark, vol. 1, pp.224–33.

259 *My friendship:* MS Aubrey 4, fol. 28; *Surrey*, vol. 1, Evelyn's letter.

260 *Dr Plot says:* MS Aubrey 13, fols 137–8, 222–3.

260 *I went to Man's:* Hooke (1935), p.218.

260 *My friend Jane Smyth:* Clark, vol. 2, p.229.

260 *I told the Royal Society:* Birch, vol. 3, p.316.

261 *While I was with:* Hooke (1935), p.235.

261 *I observed the eclipse:* Hooke (1935), p.235.

261 *The Royal Society: Notes and Records of the Royal Society of London*, vol. 28, no. 2 (1 April 1974), p.167.

261 *Mr Charles Snell has written:* Clark, vol. 1, p.50; MS Aubrey 23, fols 116, 117.

262 *Mr Charles Snell has also:* Bennett (2009), p.343.

262 *My friend Thomas Mariett:* MS Aubrey 1, fol. 30b.

262 *If I had wings:* MS Ballard 14, fol. 118.

262 *Today, Sir Henry:* Bennett, vol. 1, p.60; Clark, vol. 1, p.53; MS Ballard 14, fol. 119; MS Aubrey 6, fol. 19v.

262 My friends: MS Ballard 14, fol. 119.

263 My lord the Earl: MS Wood 39, fol. 301.

263 I am soon to go: MS Ballard 14, fol. 119.

Part X: The Popish Plot

267 Feeling against: MS Wood 39, fol. 301.

267 Mr Ogilby: MS Wood 39, fol. 316. Ogilby died on 4 September 1676: Bradley and Pevsner.

267 Some time ago: MS Aubrey 12, fol. 264.

267 Mr Thomas Pigott: MS Aubrey 13, fol. 105.

268 I went to celebrate: Hooke (1935), p.254.

268 Today I was with: Hooke (1935), p.255.

268 I went home: Hooke (1935), p.257.

268 I went to Child's: Hooke (1935), p.257.

268 Mr Hooke and I: Hooke (1935), p.259.

268 I went to the Crown: Hooke (1935), p.261.

268 My friend the Reverend: MS Aubrey 13, fol. 14. Note example of Universal Language in MS Aubrey 13, fol. 15.

269 My lord the Earl: MS Aubrey 13, fol. 226.

269 My friend Mr Thomas Pigott: MS Aubrey 13, fol. 112.

269 My friend Mr James Boevey: Bennett, vol. 1, pp.467–70; Clark, vol. 1, p.115.

269 Jane Smyth, who is somewhat: Hooke (1935), p.278.

270 Jane Smyth has the idea: Turner.

270 Lady Day: Bennett, vol. 1, p.78; Clark, vol. 1, p.408.

270 Mr Hooke saw: Hooke (1677), p.1.

270 I went to Mr Hooke's: Hooke (1935), p.287.

271 Mr Charles Snell: MS Aubrey 13, fol. 189.

271 I have sold: Clark, vol. 1, p.45.

271 I am recovered now: MS Aubrey 13, fols 21, 22, 24.

271 Mr Oldenburg: Clark, vol. 1, p.362.

271 Mr Hooke came to dine: Hooke (1935), p.311.

271 My friend Mr Harrington: Clark, vol. 1, p.294.

272 I coincided: Hooke (1935), p.313.

272 Today I watched: Hooke (1935), p.317.

272 Mr Hooke has my picture: Hooke (1935), p.318.

272 I will undertake: Hooke (1935), p.319.

273   *Today I was at the Rainbow:* Hooke (1935), p.320.

273   *St Andrew's Day:* Hooke (1935), p.331.

273   *Some of my letters:* MS Aubrey 9, fol. 9.

274   *In Oxford:* Clark (1891–1900), vol. 2, p.398.

274   *I dined:* Hooke (1935), p.354.

274   *I have been misdirecting:* MS Aubrey 12, fols 111–12.

274   *My friend Andrew Paschall:* MS Aubrey 13, fol. 29.

274   *John Ray tells me:* MS Aubrey 13, fols 170, 171.

275   *I have had:* MS Aubrey 13, fol. 115.

275   *The great lover:* Bennett, vol. 1, p.510; Clark, vol. 2, p.255.

275   *Yesterday on the Exchange:* MS Wood 39, fol. 324.

275   *I have heard:* MS Wood 39, fol. 307.

276   *Andrew Paschall has had an idea:* MS Aubrey 13, fol. 31.

276   *Today I presented:* Birch, vol. 3, p.423.

276   *Thomas Pigott tells me:* MS Aubrey 13, fol. 116.

276   *Andrew Paschall has sent me:* MS Aubrey 13, fols 32–3.

277   *Mr Evelyn has been:* MacGregor, p.45; Evelyn's diary, 23 July 1678.

277   *I have promised:* MS Wood 39, fol. 311.

277   *When I went to see:* Bennett, vol. 1, pp.663–4; Clark, vol. 2, p.72.

277   *Mr Sheldon's house:* Clark (1891–1900), vol. 2, p.420.

278   *Mr Wood agreed:* Clark (1891–1900), vol. 2, p.420.

278   *Mr Pigott tells me:* MS Aubrey 13, vol. 119, 3 November 1678.

279   *Together with the future:* Notes and Records of the Royal Society of London, vol. 28, no. 2 (1 April 1974), p.167.

279   *Today I left:* MS Wood 39, fol. 312.

279   *I sent Mr William Howe:* MS Aubrey 12, fols 232–3.

279   *I join Mr Wood:* Clark (1891–1900), vol. 2, p.435.

280   *Mr Crooke tells me:* MS Aubrey 12, fol. 88.

280   *I have sent Mr Hobbes:* Hobbes (1994), vol. 2, p.770.

280   *I was at Jonathan's coffee house:* Hooke (1935), p.404.

280   *I was at Jonathan's coffee house again:* Hooke (1935), p.404.

280   *At the Royal Society:* Birch, vol. 3, p.472.

280   *I went to Child's:* Hooke (1935), p.405.

281   *Often, as I lie:* MS Wood 39, fol. 319.

281   *I am told:* MS Wood 39, fol. 321.

281   *My lord the Earl:* MS Aubrey 13, fol. 227.

281   *At Jonathan's:* Hooke (1935), p.406.

282   *My friend Mr Thomas Pigott:* MS Aubrey 13, fol. 120.

282 *Today Mr Michael Dary:* Bennett, vol. 1, p.4; Clark, vol. 1, p.198; MS Aubrey 6, fol. 1v. On the winter of 1678–9 see Clark (1891–1900), vol. 2, pp.426, 432, 439.

282 *On this day:* See Ashmole's own account, quoted in Gunther (1925) and (1933), p.148.

283 *Sixteen days after:* MacGregor, pp.43–5.

283 *Mr Wylde Clerke:* MS Aubrey 12, fols 80, 81.

283 *Mr Thomas Pigott asks:* MS Aubrey 13, fol. 121.

283 *There is a rumour:* Bennett, vol. 1, p.32; MS Aubrey 6, fol. 10. See histories of the Civil War published at the time of the Popish Plot, when events were interpreted through the experiences of 1637–42. Raymond (1996), p.280; Bennett, vol. 1, p.672; Clark, vol. 1, p.284.

283 *Since the discovery: Miscellanies,* p.31.

284 *I met Mr Sheldon:* MS Wood 39, fol. 328.

284 *Mr Hobbes tells me:* Hobbes (1994), vol. 2, pp.772–3, 820; Clark, vol. 1, p.342; MS Aubrey 9, fol. 42v.

284 *In his book:* Raymond (1996), pp.290–1.

285 *I went to Bloomsbury:* Hooke (1935), p.418.

285 *Mr friend Robert Henley:* MS Aubrey 12, fols 160–1.

285 *My friend George Ent: Three Prose Works,* p.71.

285 *I was at Jonathan's:* Hooke (1935), p.430.

286 *I sent my letter:* MS Aubrey 12, fols 147–8.

286 *I have heard:* Bennett, vol. 1, p.268; Clark, vol. 1, p.105.

286 *My honoured friend:* Clark, vol. 1, pp.17, 20, 21; MS Aubrey 9, fol. 29.

286 *Now that the sun:* MS Wood 39, fol. 331.

287 *Mr Wood asks much:* Clark (1891–1900), vol. 2, p.475.

287 *Could one have thought:* MS Wood 39, fol. 327.

287 *Mr Henry Vaughan:* MS Aubrey 13, fols 238–9.

288 *At Burbage: Natural History,* p.36.

288 *I have often wished: Three Prose Works,* p.313.

288 *Spectacles have been worn:* Bennett, vol. 1, p.33; Clark, vol. 2, pp.319–20; MS Ballard 14, fol. 126.

Part XI: Brief Lives

291 *I was at Jonathan's:* Hooke (1935), p.438.

291 *I hope Mr Wood:* MS Ballard 14, fol. 127.

291   *Mr Wood chides me:* Clark, vol. 1, p.17.

291   *While I was smoking:* MS Ballard 14, fol. 127.

292   *The science of astrology:* Bennett, vol. 1, p.39; Clark, vol. 1, p.9.

292   *This month:* Bennett, vol. 1, p.581; Clark, vol. 2, p.91.

292   *Today, at about 3 p.m.:* MS Aubrey 6, fol. 2.

292   *Mr Wood warns me:* Clark (1891–1900), vol. 2, p.480.

293   *I have persuaded:* Bennett, vol. 1, p.48; Clark, vol. 2, p.145.

293   *He was my singular:* Bennett, vol. 1, p.136; Clark, vol. 1, p.201.

293   *Sir Jonas Moore:* Birch, vol. 4, p.29.

294   *I have made an index:* MS Ballard 14, fol. 131.

294   *If I could get up:* MS Ballard 14, fol. 131.

294   *Quaere:* MS Ballard 14, fol. 133; Bennett, vol. 1, p.395; Clark, vol. 1, pp.144–5.

295   *Mr Dryden tells me:* Bennett (2009), p.344.

295   *I could afford:* Bennett, vol. 1, p.676; Clark, vol. 2, p.119.

295   *Today I was:* Hooke (1935), p.442; Clark, vol. 1, p.411.

295   *I am sending:* Clark (1891–1900), vol. 2, p.472.

295   *I have been very ill:* MS Wood 39, fol. 340.

296   *I have decided:* MS Wood 39, fol. 340.

296   *I also described:* Birch, vol. 4, p.41.

297   *I wish someone:* Bennett, vol. 1, p.37; MS Aubrey 6, fol. 12.

297   *The Earl of Rochester:* Bennett, vol. 1, p.171; Clark, vol. 2, p.304.

298   *A friend tells me:* MS Wood 39, fol. 343.

298   *My Book of Lives:* MS Wood 39, fol. 347.

298   *I have given:* MS Wood 39, fol. 351.

298   *Sir William Petty, Knight:* MS Aubrey 6, fol. 12; Bennett, vol. 1, pp.41–52; Lawson Dick, pp.237–241.

300   *Robert Boyle:* MS Aubrey 6, fol. 16; Bennett, vol. 1, pp.52–3, Lawson Dick, pp.36–7.

301   *General Monck:* Bennett, vol. 1, pp.53–60; Clark, vol. 2, pp.72–8.

303   *William Aubrey, Doctor of Laws:* Bennett, vol. 1, pp.60–74; Clark, vol. 1, pp.53–66.

305   *Sir Lleuellin Jenkins, knight:* Bennett, vol. 1, pp.74–6; Clark, vol. 2, pp.7–9; Lawson Dick, pp.174–6.

306   *Wenceslaus Hollar:* Bennett, vol. 1, pp.76–8; Clark, vol. 1, pp.407–8, Lawson Dick, pp.163–3.

307   *Monsieur Renatus Descartes:* Bennett, vol. 1, pp.104–5; Clark, vol. 1, pp.221–2; Lawson Dick, pp.94–5.

308 *Venetia Stanley:* Bennett, vol. 1, pp.330–4; Clark, vol. 1, pp.229–33; Lawson Dick, pp.100–1.

Part XII: More Lives and Deaths

313 *About twenty years ago:* Three Prose Works, p.316.

313 *I have often thought:* Three Prose Works, p.317; MS Aubrey 1, fol. 89.

314 *I dined:* Hooke (1935), p.455.

314 *Today I helped carry:* Bennett, vol. 1, p.388; Clark, vol. 1, pp.136–7.

314 *Mr Hobbes's short autobiography:* Clark, vol. 1, p.17; MS Wood 39, fol. 347.

314 *I am at Gresham:* MS Aubrey 13, fols 127, 128.

314 *I have given:* Notes and Records of the Royal Society of London, vol. 28, no. 2 (1 April 1974), p.168.

314 *I am trying:* MS Aubrey 13, fol. 165.

315 *Mr Paschall has asked:* MS Aubrey 13, fols 43, 44.

315 *Today I have received:* Bennett, vol. 1, p.357; Clark, vol. 2, p.14; MS Aubrey 6, fol. 107.

315 *Mr Wood has written:* MS Wood 45, fol. 181.

315 *I went with Mr Hooke:* Hooke (1935), p.460.

315 *Israel Tonge was buried:* Bennett, vol. 1, p.153; Clark, vol. 2, p.262; Education, p.89.

316 *Dr Blackbourne and I:* MS Wood 39, fol. 351.

316 *Mr Dugdale has printed:* Raymond (1996), p.282.

317 *The Earl of Berkshire:* MS Aubrey 12, fols 57–8.

317 *The King has dissolved:* MS Ballard 14, fol. 130b.

317 *I intend to send:* MS Ballard 14, fol. 129.

317 *I intended to take:* MS Top. Gen. C.25, fol. 11.

317 *When I sent:* MS Wood 39, fol. 358.

318 *Mr Paschall has sent:* MS Aubrey 13, fols 45, 46.

318 *Mr Wood complains:* MS Wood 45, fol. 184.

318 *Sir James Long:* MS Aubrey 1, fol. 30b.

318 *Mr Wylde has given:* MS Wood 39, fol. 354.

318 *Mr Wood has sent me:* Clark (1891–1900), vol. 2, p.545.

319 *I went to a tavern:* Bennett, vol. 1, p.618.

319 *On behalf:* MS Aubrey 13, fols 101–2.

319 *I told the Royal Society:* Birch, vol. 4, p.94.

319 *I hope:* MS Wood 39, fol. 360.

319 *I am concerned:* Bennett, vol. 1, p.299; Clark, vol. 1, p.119.

320 *I fear the truths:* MS Wood 39, fol. 397.

320 *I met with:* MS Wood 39, fol. 357.

320 *Mr William Shakespeare was born:* MS Aubrey 8, fol. 81. Bennett, vol. 1, pp.365–6; Clark, vol. 2, pp.225–7; Lawson Dick, pp.275–6.

321 *Mr Edmund Spenser:* Bennett, vol. 1, pp.260–1; Clark, vol. 2, pp.232–3; Lawson Dick, pp.282–3.

322 *At my mother's request:* MS Aubrey 13, fol. 48.

323 *On this day:* MS Wood 39, fol. 357.

323 *I have brought:* MS Tanner 456a, fol. 27.

323 *Mr Ashmole and I:* MS Ballard 14, fol. 134.

324 *Mr Ashmole also has:* Bennett, vol. 1, p.32; Clark, vol. 2, p.33.

324 *Today I was smoking:* MS Ballard 14, fol. 135.

324 *I am too late:* Bennett, vol. 1, p.447; Clark, vol. 1, p.97.

324 *I went to visit:* Natural History, p.141; Bennett, introduction.

325 *Two days before:* Bennett, vol. 1, p.343; Clark, vol. 2, p.150.

325 *The Earl of Clarendon:* MS Wood 39, fol. 365. The Earl of Clarendon's History was eventually printed in 1704 and the profits used to establish the Clarendon Press. Bennett, vol. 1, p.8; Clark, vol. 1, p.426.

325 *I have consulted:* MS Aubrey 12, fols 279–80.

326 *The second reading:* MS Aubrey 12, fol. 5.

326 *London has become:* Bennett, vol. 1, p.654; Clark, vol. 2, p.60. See also Aubrey's life of Mr Inglebert, where he claims Inglebert 'was the first inventor, or projector, of bringing the water from Ware to London (called Middletons water) he was a poore-man, but Sir Hugh Middleton, Alderman of London moneyed the business, undertook it, and got the profit, and also the credit of that most useful invention': Bennett, vol. 1, p.606.

326 *When Lord Norris:* MS Aubrey 12, fol. 8; Lord Norris of Rycote, later Earl of Abingdon.

326 *I have had:* MS Aubrey 17, fol. 18.

326 *I have now sent:* Clark (1891–1900), vol. 3, p.14.

326 *When I was staying:* MS Wood 39, fol. 369.

327 *Mr William Penn:* Bennett, vol. 1, p.594; Clark, vol. 2, p.133; MS Aubrey 2, fol. 27.

327 *From Africa:* MS Aubrey 12, fol. 78.

327 *Sir Henry Blount:* Bennett, vol. 1, p.339; Clark, vol. 1, p.111.

328 *Thomas Merry:* Bennett, vol. 1, p.749; Clark, vol. 2, p.60.

328 *Today at the Royal Society:* Birch, vol. 4, p.186.

328 *The curious clock:* Bennett, vol. 1, p.647; Clark, vol. 2, pp.58–9.

329 *My loyal, dear, useful:* MS Ballard 14, fol. 137.

329 *The chalybeate spring:* MS Ballard 14, fol. 136.

329 *On this day:* Ovenell, pp.21–2; Wood, 20 March 1683 (cited in MacGregor, p.49).

330 *Mr Penn is making:* MS Aubrey 13, fols 98–9.

330 *My friend Jane Smyth:* Clark, vol. 2, p.229.

330 *Earlier this month:* MS Aubrey 13, fol. 132.

330 *I have called on:* MS Aubrey 4, fol. 299.

331 *Sir Jonas Moore's books:* MS Aubrey 13, fol. 243. Aubrey had known Sir Jonas Moore since 1664: see Willmoth, p.164.

331 *Sir Jonas Moore intended:* Bennett, vol. 1, p.305; Clark, vol. 2, p.78.

331 *Alas:* MS Aubrey 13, fol. 244.

331 *Sir Isaac Newton:* MS Aubrey 12, fols 347–8.

Part XIII: Manuscripts

335 *I am still grieving:* MS Ballard 14, fol. 137.

335 *I am ordering:* MS Aubrey 10, fol. 6b.

335 *Mr Paschall urges me:* MS Aubrey 13, fol. 66b. For Aubrey's manuscript, see MS Aubrey 10.

336 *Without doubt:* MS Aubrey 10, fols 9, 8a.

336 *A banker:* MS Aubrey 10, fol. 35a.

336 *William Brouncker:* Bennett, vol. 1, p.478; Clark, vol. 1, pp.128–9.

337 *Sir William Petty's:* Philosophical Transactions, vol. 14 (1684), pp.802–3; Natural History, p.26.

338 *I am beset:* MS Wood 39, fol. 375.

338 *Mr Paschall has written:* Surrey, vol. 1, pp.xviii–xix, introduction.

339 *The great stone:* Monumenta, p.56.

339 *I have asked my friend:* MS Aubrey 13, fols 71–2.

340 *I related:* Birch, vol. 4, p.348.

340 *Mr Wood tells me:* MS Wood 45, fol. 192; Bennett, vol. 1, p.252.

341 *Just as the King:* Three Prose Works, p.29.

341 *Tonight stately fireworks:* Three Prose Works, p.29.

341 *Titus Oates has come:* Macaulay, Chapter IV.

344 *I have nearly finished:* MS Aubrey 1, fol. 7.

344　*I need to move:* MS Aubrey 13, fol. 87.

344　*There is a hill:* Three Prose Works, p.317.

344　*It seems to me:* Bennett, vol. 1, p.713; Clark, vol. 1, p.147; MS Aubrey 8, fol. 105; MS Aubrey 15 (MS Top. Gen. C.25, fol. 133).

345　*Yesterday I came:* MS Wood 39, fol. 374.

345　*I hope to find out:* MS Wood 39, fol. 375.

345　*I have heard:* Bennett, vol. 1, p.698; Clark, vol. 1, p.267.

346　*I cannot read:* MS Wood 39, fol. 377.

346　*John Pell:* Bennett, vol. 1, p.163; Clark, vol. 2, p.127.

346　*I have visited:* MS Aubrey 13, fol. 89.

346　*I am back now:* MS Wood 39, fol. 377.

346　*Captain Poyntz:* Clark, vol. 1, p.45; MS Aubrey 26, fol. 6.

347　*I have started composing:* MS Aubrey 26, fols 2–6; MS Aubrey 15 (MS Top. Gen. C.25, fol. 137).

347　*My friend Mr Edward Lhwyd:* MS Aubrey 12, fol. 240; Ovenell, p.23.

348　*Mr Loggan will draw:* MS Aubrey 1, fol. 3; MS Aubrey 2, fols 2, 31.

348　*Today I told:* Birch, vol. 4, p.468.

348　*I also mentioned:* Birch, vol. 4, p.469.

348　*My friend Mr Paschall:* MS Aubrey 13, fol. 77.

349　*My good mother:* MS Aubrey 13, fol. 77.

349　*I am troubled:* MS Ballard 14, fol. 139.

349　*May I live:* MS Ballard 14, fol. 139.

349　*Mr Paschall tells:* MS Aubrey 13, fol. 78a, b.

349　*My friend Thomas Mariett:* MS Aubrey 12, fols 330–1.

350　*Mr Paschall has described:* MS Aubrey 13, fols 79, 80.

350　*Today I showed:* Birch, vol. 4, p.511.

351　*I am embattled:* MS Ballard 14, fol. 141.

351　*I have acquainted:* MS Aubrey 15 (MS Top. Gen. C.25, fol. 134v).

352　*Meanwhile he writes:* MS Aubrey 12, fols 283–4.

352　*My friend Mr Paschall:* MS Aubrey 13, fol. 81.

352　*Robert Barclay's book:* Clark, vol. 1, p.86; MS Aubrey 8, fol. 53v. The book first appeared in Latin in 1678, *Theologiae verae Christianae apologia.*

352　*Today at the Royal Society:* Birch, vol. 4, p.546.

352　*Mr Dugdale has criticised:* Clark, vol. 2, p.89; MS Wood 39, fol. 397.

353　*On a rocky mountain:* MS Aubrey 1, fol. 14b.

353　*In Yorkshire:* Monumenta, p.110.

353　*In this county:* Clark, vol. 2, p.324.

354 *Sir Charles Snell:* MS Aubrey 13, fol. 190.

354 *Following my Natural History:* MS Wood 39, fol. 392; MS Aubrey 5, fol. 17.

354 *On this day:* Bennett, vol. 1, p.51; Clark, vol. 2, p.148.

355 *I have been chosen:* Notes and Records of the Royal Society of London, vol. 28, no. 2 (1 April 1974), p.167.

355 *I dined this evening:* Clark (1891–1900), vol. 3, p.269.

355 *I have decided:* MS Aubrey 13, fol. 140; Ovenell, pp.67–8.

356 *May, June:* MS Aubrey 1, fol. 171.

356 *I am concerned:* Ovenell, p.58.

357 *I desire of God:* MS Tanner 456a, fol. 34.

Part XIV: Transcriptions

362 *I went to see:* MS Aubrey 12, fol. 2.

362 *My school would need:* MS Aubrey 10, fol. 10.

363 *I would like to see:* Bennett (2009), p.335; *Education*, p.115.

363 *I think the best:* MS Aubrey 10, fol. 23.

363 *It is certain:* MS Aubrey 10, fol. 24.

364 *Mr Hobbes told me:* Education, p.61.

364 *I would have nothing:* MS Aubrey 10, fol. 137.

364 *I believe the disposition:* MS Aubrey 10, fol. 10.

364 *I envisage:* MS Aubrey 10, fol. 10.

364 *I would furnish:* Robert Boyle and Robert Hooke invented a portable camera obscura in 1665–6.

364 *I would have those:* Education, p.112.

365 *I would have the boys:* MS Aubrey 10, fols 127–9.

365 *We are taught:* Aubrey attributes this remark to the Italian doctor, scientist and natural philosopher Fortunius Licetus (1577–1657), a friend of Galileo.

365 *In my school:* Education, p.70.

365 *Gloucester Hall:* MS Aubrey 10, fol. 133b.

367 *I will soon make:* MS Aubrey 13, fol. 172.

367 *At Groveley:* MS Aubrey 1, fol. 132r.

367 *I grow old:* MS Wood 39, fol. 386.

368 *My friend Edward Lhwyd:* MS Aubrey 5, fol. 6.

368 *My candle burns low:* MS Wood 39, fol. 397; MS Wood 40, fol. 372.

368 *I have asked Mr Wood:* Clark, vol. 2, p.230.

369 *Since Seth Ward:* Clark, vol. 2, p.289; MS Aubrey 10, fols 64–5.

369 *Yesterday I went:* Raymond (1996), p.270.

369 *My visit to him:* Clark, vol. 2, pp.207–9; MS Wood 39, fol. 386v.

369 *I dined with Mr Ashmole:* Clark, vol. 2, p.92; MS Wood 39, fol. 390.

369 *I have been setting:* MS Wood 39, fol. 389.

370 *Thank God:* MS Wood 40, fol. 372.

370 *I have collected:* MS Aubrey 15 (MS Top. Gen. C.25, fol. 185).

370 *Just as the Roman:* MS Aubrey 15 (MS Top. Gen. C.25, fol. 186).

371 *It is said:* Three Prose Works, p.354.

371 *I hope I can go:* MS Wood 39, fol. 395.

372 *I hope Mr Wood:* Bennett, vol. 1, p.104; Clark, vol. 1, p.415.

372 *Mr Paschall has:* MS Aubrey 13, fol. 83.

373 *Mr Hooke affirms:* Monumenta, p.505.

373 *Mr Ralph Bathurst:* MS Aubrey 12, fols 21, 22.

373 *Mr Paschall tells me:* MS Aubrey 13, fol. 84.

373 *This month:* MS Aubrey 12, fol. 11.

373 *Mr Wood claims:* Clark (1891–1900), vol. 3, p.319.

374 *It is said:* Three Prose Works, p.31.

374 *I have made a collection:* MS Wood 39, fol. 402.

374 *I have begun:* Clark, vol. 1, p.16; MS Aubrey 8, fol. 70.

374 *The other day:* Kemp; MS Wood 39, fol. 400.

375 *I will go to Oxford:* MS Wood 39, fol. 402.

375 *How I wish:* MS Ballard 14, fol. 142.

375 *I have been speaking:* Bennett, vol. 1, p.379; Clark, vol. 2, p.278.

376 *Thomas Guidott:* MS Aubrey 12, fol. 144.

377 *My brother's ill humour:* MS Wood 39, fol. 411.

377 *I wish Mr Wood:* MS Wood 39, fol. 412.

378 *I have decided to place:* MS Wood 39, fol. 414.

378 *I hoped to go:* MS Wood 39, fol. 414.

378 *From New Inn Hall:* MS Aubrey 12, fols 31–2.

378 *Next week I think:* MS Wood 39, fol. 417; Clark, vol. 2, p.312; MS Aubrey 21, fol. 69; MS Aubrey 7, fol. 8v.

378 *I think there is:* Natural History, p.93.

379 *Mr Hooke has been:* MS Wood 39, fol. 424.

379 *I have written:* MS Aubrey 5, fol. 2.

379 *I have heard:* MS Wood 39, fol. 426.

379 *I hope to get:* MS Ashmole 1814, fol. 95.

379 *I have been to the Tower:* MS Wood 39, fol. 427.

380 *Mr Hanson of Magdalen: Natural History*, pp.25–6.

380 *Since there has been:* MS Ballard 14, fol. 143.

381 *Today I sent to Oxford:* MS Wood 39, fol. 405.

381 *I have been chosen: Notes and Records of the Royal Society of London*, vol. 28, no. 2 (1 April 1974), p.167.

381 *The Royal Society's transcription:* MS Wood 39, fol. 429.

381 *Mr William Fanshawe:* MS Aubrey 12, fol. 115.

381 *Mr John Ray has agreed:* MS Aubrey 13, fol. 173.

382 *I have now been:* MS Wood 39, fol. 433.

382 *Mr John Ray has read:* MS Ballard 62, p.123.

382 *I went to Bayworth:* Clark (1891–1900), vol. 3, p.372.

382 *He says there is only:* MS Aubrey 13, fol. 174.

383 *The Ashmolean Museum:* Foskett, p.54. Dr Plot acknowledged receipt of the portraits on 18 October 1688.

383 *My brother has been unkind:* MS Wood 39, fol. 435.

383 *I am plagued:* MS Aubrey 13, fol. 175.

383 *I have prepared: Surrey*, vol. 1, To the Reader, 1691; MS Aubrey 4, fol. 31.

384 *I think someone:* MS Aubrey 5, fol. 8b.

384 *The Earl of Pembroke:* MS Ashmole 1814, fol. 98.

384 *I have asked him:* MS Aubrey 12, fols 138c, d.

384 *The Earl of Clarendon:* Hearne (1906), p.102.

385 *Mr Hooke is very anxious:* MS Ballard 14, fol. 145.

385 *My brother William:* MS Ballard 14, fol. 146.

385 *At the request:* MS Ashmole 1814, fol. 99.

386 *I have started preparing:* MS Ballard 14, fol. 147.

386 *He says he is very glad:* MS Aubrey 12, fols 243–4.

386 *The account of Southwark:* MS Wood 51, fol. 3.

386 *Dr Hooke is concerned:* MS Ballard 14, fol. 149.

387 *I have left:* MS Aubrey 10, fol. 1.

387 *Sir Roger L'Etrange's:* MS Aubrey 10, fol. 66b.

387 *As for history:* MS Aubrey 10, fol. 97.

387 *I imagine the boys: Education*, p.69.

388 *My pretty little bitch:* MS Tanner 456a, fol. 40.

388 *I am staying:* MS Wood 51, fol. 11.

389 *I go tomorrow:* MS Ballard 14, fol. 153.

389 *I have seen Mr Wood's books:* MS Wood 51, fol. 4.

389 *I have had a very:* MS Wood 51, fol. 4; Clark, vol. 1, p.258.

389 *Mr John Ray's daughters:* MS Aubrey 13, fol. 176.

390 *Mr John Ray has read:* MS Aubrey 13, fol. 177.

390 *Mr Wood now regrets:* MS Ballard 14, fol. 154.

390 *I have asked Mr Wood:* MS Wood 39, fol. 437.

390 *In Oxford:* MS Ashmole 1814, fol. 101.

390 *Today Mr Lhwyd:* MS Aubrey 5, fol. 123v.

391 *I was ill:* MS Tanner 456a, fol. 41.

391 *Mr Wood has written:* MS Wood 45, fol. 208.

392 *I have written:* MS Aubrey 12, fols 149, 150.

392 *As soon as I have time:* MS Ashmole 1814, fol. 102.

392 *Mr Lhwyd longs:* MS Aubrey 12, fols 241–2.

Part XV: Crepusculum

399 *Mr Dryden will try:* Clark (1891–1900), vol. 3, p.420.

401 *Frances Sheldon:* MS Wood 51, fol. 5.

401 *I have now been:* MS Ashmole 1814, fol. 91.

401 *I have designed:* MS Aubrey 5, fol. 122.

401 *Mr Thomas Tanner urges:* MS Tanner 25, fol. 40.

402 *At the Saracen's Head:* MS Tanner 25, fol. 49.

402 *Mr John Ray says:* MS Aubrey 13, fol. 178.

402 *Dr William Holder:* MS Aubrey 12, fol. 168.

402 *My brother went:* MS Tanner 25, fol. 66.

403 *Dr Ralph Bathurst:* MS Aubrey 12, fols 23, 24.

403 *I am in Cambridge:* MS Tanner 25, fol. 82; Clark (1891–1900), vol. 3, p.429.

403 *I will visit Rycot:* MS Tanner 25, fol. 82.

404 *I called on Mr Coley:* MS Wood 51, fol. 6.

404 *I have sent a boxful:* MS Ashmole 1814, fol. 92.

404 *Mr Thomas Tanner:* MS Tanner 25, fol. 83.

404 *Mr Lhwyd:* MS Aubrey 12, fol. 248; MS Aubrey Top. Gen. C.25, fol. 153v.

404 *I have asked Mr Thomas Tanner:* MS Tanner 25, fol. 94.

405 *Mr Thomas Tanner has read:* MS Aubrey 13, fol. 201.

405 *I am back: Natural History,* p.93.

405 *I am reading over:* MS Aubrey 10, fol. 4; MS Wood 51, fols 6, 21.

405 *Mr Lhwyd is trying:* MS Aubrey 12, fols 249–50.

406 *Mr Thomas Tanner now advises:* MS Aubrey 13, fol. 204.

406 *I came back to London:* MS Wood 39, fol. 442; MS Ashmole 1814, fol. 114.

406 *At a party yesterday:* Add MS 1388, fol. 149.

406 *I had an apoplectic fit:* Clark, vol. 1, p.45.

407 *Mr Lhwyd says:* MS Aubrey 12, fol. 251.

407 *I hope to see:* MS Wood 51, fol. 8.

407 *I am busy:* Three Prose Works, p.42.

407 *I do not think:* MS Tanner 25, fol. 118.

408 *On behalf of my friend:* MS Ashmole 1814, fol. 94; MS Aubrey 12, fols 260–1; Bennett, 'John Aubrey, William and Judith Dobson'.

408 *The Earl of Pembroke has read:* MS Aubrey 10, fol. 2.

408 *I doubt I will live:* Education, p.16.

408 *I never go out:* MS Ashmole 1814, fol. 107.

408 *Mr Thomas Tanner called:* MS Wood 39, fol. 450.

408 *I am receiving:* MS Aubrey 12, fols 252–3.

409 *Mr Thomas Tanner has asked:* MS Aubrey 13, fol. 196.

409 *The Earl of Pembroke:* MS Ashmole 1814, fol. 106.

409 *Several Roman coins:* MS Ashmole 1814, fol. 119; MS Aubrey 12, fols 6–7.

409 *Lord Pembroke has received:* MS Ashmole 1814, fol. 109.

410 *Mr Lhwyd has written:* MS Aubrey 12, fols 254–6.

410 *At last, Mr Thomas Tanner:* MS Aubrey 13, fols 202–3.

411 *Sir John Aubrey:* MS Wood 39, fol. 440.

411 *I hope to be:* MS Ashmole 1814, fol. 112.

411 *I remember that:* MS Top. Gen. C.25, fol. 242v.

411 *I hope Mr Lhwyd:* MS Ashmole 1814, fol. 113.

411 *Mr Lhwyd says:* MS Aubrey 12, fols 256–7.

411 *Today is Midsummer's Day:* Three Prose Works, p.83.

412 *I am at Borstall:* MS Wood 39, fol. 447.

412 *Mr Wood makes such demands:* Clark (1891–1900), vol. 3, p.440.

413 *Sir John Aubrey and his lady:* MS Ashmole 1814, fol. 116; MS Ballard 14, fol. 155.

413 *Mr Wood is furious:* MS Tanner 456a, fol. 48.

414 *I miss my friend:* MS Ashmole 1814, fol. 117.

414 *When I last wrote:* MS Tanner 25, fol. 240.

414 *I have been ill:* MS Wood 39, fol. 450.

414 *It has been a most unnatural:* Clark (1891–1900), vol. 3, p.483.

415 *Coming through Bagley Wood:* Natural History, p.26.

415　*I was in Fleet Street:* Clark (1891–1900), vol. 3, p.483.

415　*Today I tested: Natural History*, p.26.

416　*My friend William Holder:* MS Aubrey 12, fol. 173.

416　*I cannot now read:* MS Wood 39, fol. 452.

416　*I can hardly read:* MS Ashmole 1829, fol. 25; MS Wood 51, fol. 9.

416　*I am in London:* MS Wood F 51, fol. 9–10.

417　*Mr Wood has written:* MS Aubrey 13, fol. 269.

417　*Mr Wood asks me:* MS Aubrey 13, fol. 269.

417　*My eyes are mending:* MS Ashmole 1829, fol. 28; MS Wood 39, fol. 440.

417　*My eyes mend:* MS Wood 51, fol. 11.

417　*My cousin spoils me:* MS Ashmole 1829, fol. 31.

418　*I have written:* MS Sloane 1039, fol. 108.

418　*I have given: Notes and Records of the Royal Society of London*, vol. 28, no. 2 (1 April 1974), p.179.

418　*I shall never see:* MS Tanner 24, fol. 108.

418　*It is so cold:* Evelyn's diary, 24 January 1684.

418　*I will stay:* MS Ashmole 1814, fol. 118.

419　*I am told another:* MS Ashmole 1829, fol. 56.

419　*At long last: Miscellanies.*

420　*In my chapter on magic: Miscellanies*, p.87.

421　*I am at Llantrithyd:* MS Ashmole 1829, fol. 13.

421　*When I next go:* MS Tanner 24, fol. 108.

421　*I am hoping:* MS Tanner 24, fol. 196.

421　*The printer:* MS Ashmole 1829, fol. 78.

422　*How clearly:* MS Ashmole 1829, fol. 86.

422　*I have presented: Notes and Records of the Royal Society of London*, vol. 28, no. 2 (1 April 1974), p.169.

422　*I have always done my best:* MS Aubrey 7, fol. 4v.

422　*Matters of antiquity:* MS Aubrey 9, fol. 29r.

422　*Aubrey is buried:* Hearne (1906), vol. 7, p.153; *Surrey*, vol. 1, p.ix, introduction.

Aubrey's Afterlife

425　*The only book: Miscellanies* was republished in 1721 and 1784; I am grateful to Dr William Poole for drawing my attention to the fact that on the contents page of the Ashmolean's copy an early reader has written 'superstitiosi'.

425 *Hearne noted that details:* The Itinerary of John Leland the Antiquary, published by Thomas Hearne (James Fletcher, 1770), p.124.

426 *Rawlinson complained:* Surrey, vol. 1, p.ii.

426 *He read Aubrey's friend:* Haycock, pp.126–32.

427 *The five women resolved:* Bennett, vol. 1, p.54.

427 *it is impossible to understand:* Clark, vol. 2, p.73.

428 *A much more interesting:* Clark, vol. 1, p.5.

429 *Those who possess it:* Aubrey, *Brief Lives and other selected writings*, p.xxii.

429 *In 1972, the publisher and editor:* A less satisfactory edition of the *Remaines of Gentilisme and Judaisme* first appeared in 1881.

430 *Many of the additions:* Education.

430 *Hunter explained:* Hunter (1975), p.21.

430 *In his brief foreward:* The edition looks like a facsimile but is not. There are many omissions and the plates have been reordered.

431 *As part of Oxford University's Cultures of Knowledge project:* see emlo.bodleian.ox.ac.uk

Bibliography

Manuscript sources

The Bodleian Library

MS Ashmole 1722 Aubrey's annotations to Robert Plot's *The Natural History of Oxfordshire*

MS Ashmole 1814 Letters from Aubrey to Edward Lhwyd

MS Ashmole 1829 Letters from Aubrey to Edward Lhwyd

MS Ashmole 1830 Letters from Aubrey to Edward Lhwyd

MS Aubrey 1 *The Natural History of Wiltshire*

MS Aubrey 2 *The Natural History of Wiltshire*

MS Aubrey 3 *An Essay Towards a Description of the North Division of Wiltshire*

MS Aubrey 4 *A Perambulation of Surrey*

MS Aubrey 5 *An Interpretation of Villare Anglicanum*

MS Aubrey 6 *The Minutes of Lives* (Part 1)

MS Aubrey 7 *The Minutes of Lives* (Part 2)

MS Aubrey 8 *The Minutes of Lives* (Part 3) including an *Apparatus for the Lives of our English Mathematical Writers*

MS Aubrey 9 *The Life of Mr Thomas Hobbes*

MS Aubrey 10 *An Idea of Education of Young Gentlemen*

MS Aubrey 11 *An extract or Summary of the Lemmata of Stone-heng restored to the Danes*, by Walter Charleton

MS Aubrey 12 Letters to John Aubrey (1644–95), A–N

MS Aubrey 13 Letters to John Aubrey (1644–95), O–W

MS Aubrey 14 *Monumenta Britannica* (Parts 1 and 2); also MS Top. Gen. C.24

MS Aubrey 15 *Monumenta Britannica* (Parts 3 and 4); also MS Top. Gen.
  C.25
MS Aubrey 16 Copy of part of *Chronologia Architectonica*
MS Aubrey 17 Designatio de Easton-Piers in Comitatu Wilts
MS Aubrey 19 Medical Recipes in English
MS Aubrey 20 Two Essays written in 1659–60 by H. Milborne 'For the
  better orderinge the poore'
MS Aubrey 21 *The Countrey Revell, or the Revell at Aldford*, and miscel-
  laneous papers
MS Aubrey 23 A Collection of Genitures Well Attested
MS Aubrey 24 An Astrological Treatise, *Zercobeni, seu Claviculæ Salmonis
  Libri IV*, with additional recipes and incantations
MS Aubrey 25 *Musica*, Nicolaus Mercator
MS Aubrey 26 *Faber Fortunae*
MS Aubrey 28 A letter from Mr Thomas Hobbes

MS Ballard 14 Letters from Aubrey to Anthony Wood
MS Ballard 62 Scribal copy

MS Hearne's Diaries 158–9 Thomas Hearne's transcript of Robert
  Plot's notes on Aubrey's Adversaria Physica

MS Rawlinson D.26 The Journal of Anthony Wood
MS Rawlinson D.727 Fair copies of three of Aubrey's Lives
MS Rawlinson J.F.6 The Accidents of John Aubrey

MS Tanner 22 Letters to Thomas Tanner, 1698
MS Tanner 23 Letters to Thomas Tanner, 1697
MS Tanner 24 Letters from Aubrey to Thomas Tanner, 1696
MS Tanner 25 Letters from Aubrey to Thomas Tanner, 1695
MS Tanner 102 The Journal of Anthony Wood
MS Tanner 456 Letters between Aubrey and Anthony Wood

MS Wood 39 Letters from Aubrey to Anthony Wood
MS Wood 40 Letters from Aubrey to Anthony Wood
MS Wood 46 Letters from Aubrey to Anthony Wood
MS Wood 49 Letters from Aubrey to Anthony Wood
MS Wood 51 Letters from Aubrey to Anthony Wood

The British Library
MS Lansdowne 231 Remaines of Gentilisme and Judaisme
MS Sloane 1039
Add MS 82700–4 Anthony Powell Manuscripts. *John Aubrey and His Friends*; 1937–89. First published in 1948. 5 vols.
Add MS 1388

The Royal Society
Classified Paper VII (I) 28
Classified Paper VII (I) 30
Classified Paper VIII (I) 24
Classified Paper XII (I) 17
MS 92, copy of Natural History of Wiltshire, commissioned in 1691
Register Book Copy 3

Journals

Notes and Records of the Royal Society of London, www.rsnr.royalsociety publishing.org
Philosophical Transactions of the Royal Society, first issue 6 March, 1665, www.rstl.royalsocietypublishing.org
Oxford Dictionary of National Biography, www.oxfordnb.com (2004–)

Printed sources

Aubrey, J., *Miscellanies: A Collection of Hermetick Philosophy* (London, Edward Castle, 1696)
_____, *John Aubrey: Brief Lives with an Apparatus for the Lives of our English Mathematical Writers*, ed. Bennett, K. (Oxford: Oxford University Press, 2015)
_____, *Aubrey's Brief Lives, edited from the Original Manuscripts and with a Life of John Aubrey*, ed. Lawson Dick, O. (London: Secker & Warburg, 1949)
_____, *Brief Lives and other selected writings*, ed. Powell, A. (London: Cresset Press, 1949)
_____, *'Brief Lives', chiefly of Contemporaries, set down by John Aubrey, between the Years 1669 & 1696, edited from the author's mss.*, ed. Clark, A., 2 vols (Oxford: Clarendon Press, 1898)

_____, *Letters Written by Eminent Persons in the Seventeenth and Eighteenth Centuries, to which are added Hearne's Journey to Reading, and to Whaddon Hall the Seat of Browne Willis, Esq. and Lives of Eminent Men, by John Aubrey, Esq. The whole now first published from the originals in the Bodleian Library and Ashmolean Museum, with biographical and literary illustrations*, ed. Bliss, P., and Walker, J. (London: Longman, Hurst, 1813)

_____, *The Minutes of Lives, The Oxford Cabinet, Consisting of Engravings from Original Pictures, in the Ashmolean Museum, and other Public and Private Collections, with biographical anecdotes by John Aubrey FRS, and other Celebrated Writers* (London: printed for James Caulfield, 1797)

_____, *Monumenta Britannica, or Miscellany of British Antiquities*, ed. Fowles, J., annotated Legg, R., 1980, 2 vols (Boston, Toronto: Little Brown and Company, 1980)

_____, *The Natural History and Antiquities of the County of Surrey. Begun in the Year 1673, by JOHN AUBREY, Esq; FRS and continued to the present Time*, ed. Rawlinson, R., 5 vols (originally published London, 1718–19; republished Dorking: Kohler & Coombes, 1975)

_____, *Three Prose Works*, ed. Buchanan-Brown, J. (London: Centaur Press, 1972)

_____, *Remaines of Gentilisme and Judaisme*, ed. Britten, J. (London: W. Satchell, Peyton & Co., 1881)

_____, *Wiltshire: The Topographical Collections of John Aubrey, FRS, AD 1659–70, with illustrations, corrected and enlarged by John Edward Jackson, MA, FSA, of Brasenose College, Oxford, Rector of Leigh Delamere, Vicar of Norton, and Hon. Canon of Bristol*, ed. Jackson, J. E. (The Wiltshire Archaeological and Natural History Society, Devizes: Henry Bull, 1862)

_____, *The Natural History of Wiltshire; by John Aubrey FRS (written between 1656 and 1691), edited and elucidated by notes, by John Britton, FRA*, ed. Britton, J. (The Wiltshire Topographical Society, London: J. B. Nichols and Son, 1847; republished, with an introduction by Ponting, K. G., Trowbridge, Wiltshire: Redwood Press Limited, 1969)

_____, *Aubrey on Education, a hitherto unpublished manuscript by the author of Brief Lives*, ed. Stephens, J. E. (London: Routledge and K. Paul, 1972)

Bacon, F., *The remaines of the Right Honorable Francis, Lord Verulam, Viscount of St Albanes, sometimes Lord Chancellour of England being essayes and severall letters to severall great personages, and other pieces of various and high concernment not heretofore published: a table whereof for the readers more ease is adjoined*, Bacon, Francis, 1561–1626, Bodley, Thomas, 1545–1613, Palmer, Herbert, 1601–47 (London: printed by B. Alsop for Lawrence Chapman, and are to be sold at his shop . . ., 1648)

_____, *The Philosophical Works of Francis Bacon*, ed., Robertson, J. M. (London: Routledge, 2013)

Balme, M., ed., *Two Antiquaries: a selection from the correspondence of John Aubrey and Anthony Wood* (Edinburgh: Durham Academic Press, 2001)

Bennett, K., 'John Aubrey and the rhapsodic book', *Renaissance Studies*, vol. 28, no. 2 (2014), pp.317–32,'

_____,'John Aubrey and the "Lives of Our English Mathematical Writers"', in Eleanor Robson and Jacqueline Stedall, eds, *The Oxford Handbook of the History of Mathematics* (Oxford: Oxford University Press, 2009), pp.301–29

_____, 'John Aubrey, Hint-Keeper: Life-Writing and the Encouragement of Natural Philosophy in the pre-Newtonian Seventeenth Century', *The Seventeenth Century*, 22 (2007), pp.358–80

_____, 'John Aubrey and the Circulation of Edmund Waller's Of a Tree Cut in Paper', *Notes and Queries*, 49 (2002), pp.344–5

_____, 'John Aubrey, William and Judith Dobson and the 8th Earl of Pembroke: the Provenance of William Dobson's Executioner with John the Baptist's Head', *Notes and Queries*, 49 (2002), pp.352–5

_____, 'John Aubrey's Collections and the Early-Modern Museum', *Bodleian Library Record*, 17 (2001), pp.213–45

_____, 'Editing Aubrey', in Joe Bray, Miriam Handley, and Anne C. Henry, eds, *Ma(r)king the Text* (Aldershot: Ashgate, 2000)

_____, 'Shakespeare's Monument at Stratford: A New Seventeenth-Century Account', *Notes and Queries*, 47 (2000), p.464

_____, 'John Aubrey's Oxfordshire Collections: An Edition of Aubrey's Annotations to his Presentation Copy of Robert Plot's Natural History of Oxfordshire', MS Ashmole 1722, *Oxoniensia*, 64 (1999), pp.59–86

_____, 'John Aubrey, Joseph Barnes's Print-Shop and a Sham Newsletter', *The Library*, 21 (1999), pp.50–8

_____, 'A New Anthony Wood Manuscript Paper', *Notes and Queries*, 45 (1998), pp.184–6

Birch, T., *The History of the Royal Society*, 4 vols (London, 1756–7)

Bobrick, B., *The Fated Sky: Astrology in History* (London: Simon and Schuster, 2006)

Boyle, R., *Correspondence of Robert Boyle 1636–1691*, eds Hunter, M., Clericuzio, A., and Principe, L. M., 6 vols (London, Pickering & Chatto, 2001)

_____, *The Works of the Honorable Robert Boyle in Six Volumes*, ed. Rivington, J. and F. (London, 1772)

Bradley, S., and Pevsner, N., *London: The City Churches* (New Haven: Yale University Press, 1998)

Britton, J., *Memoir of John Aubrey, FRS* (London: Wiltshire Topographical Society, 1845)

Browne, T., *Hydriotaphia, urne-buriall : or, A discourse of the sepulchrall urnes lately found in Norfolk; Together with The garden of Cyrus: or The quincunciall, lozenge, or net-work plantations of the ancients, artificially, naturally, mystically considered. With sundry observations* (London: printed for Hen. Brome, 1658)

Buchanan-Brown, J., 'The Books Presented to the Royal Society by John Aubrey, FRS', *Notes and Records of the Royal Society of London*, 28 (1974), p.167

Burl, A., *John Aubrey & Stone Circles: Britain's first archaeologist, from Avebury to Stonehenge* (Stroud: Amberley, 2010)

Camden, W., *Camden's Britannia, 1695*: a facsimile of the 1695 edition published by Edmund Gibson [translated from the Latin], with an introduction by Piggott, S., and a bibliographical note by Walters, G. (Newton Abbott: David and Charles, 1971)

de Castro, P., *A Dictionary of Principal London Taverns since the Restoration*, 4 vols (Salt Lake City, Utah: Genealogical Society of Utah, 1985)

Charleton, W., *Chorea Gigantum* (London: 1663)

Chitty, W., *Historical Account of the Long Family* London: Gilbert and Rivington, 1889).

Clark, A., ed., *The Life and Times of Anthony Wood*, 5 vols (Oxford: 1891–1900)

Colvin, H. M., 'Aubrey's *Chronologia Architectonica*'. In Summerson, J., *Concerning Architecture: essays on architectural writers and writing presented to Nikolaus Pevsner* (London: Allen Lane, the Penguin Press, 1968), pp.1–12

Davies, J. D., 'The Navy, Parliament and Political Crisis in the Reign of Charles II', *The Historical Journal*, vol. 36, issue 02, June 1993, pp.271–88

Douglas, D., *English Scholars 1660–1730* (London: Eyre & Spottiswoode, 1951)

Dragstra, H., '"Before woomen were Readers": how John Aubrey wrote female oral history', in Lamb, M. E., and Bamford, Karen, *Oral Traditions and Gender in Early Modern Literary Texts* (Aldershot: Ashgate, 2008), pp.41–56

Dugdale, W., *The History of St Paul's Cathedral* (London, 1716)

_____, *Monasticon Anglicanum, sive Pandectæ Coenobiorum, Benedictinorum Cluniacensium, Cisterciensium, Carthusianorum, a primordiis ad eorum usque dissolutionem. Ex MSS. Codd . . . digesti per Rogerum Dodsworth [et] Gulielmum Dugdale. [Et Propulaion Johannis Marshami.] 3 voll. [Vol. III. Additamenta quædam . . . necnon fundationes . . . Ecclesiarum Cathedralium ac Collegiatarum continens . . . per Will. Dvgdale.]*, 3 vols (London, vol. 1 1655, vol. 2 1661, vol. 3 1673)

Duncan-Jones, K., *Sir Philip Sidney: Courtier Poet* (London: Hamish Hamilton, 1991)

_____, *Sir Philip Sidney, Selected Poems* (Oxford: Oxford University Press, 1973).

Ellis, M., *The Coffee-house. A Cultural History* (London: Weidenfeld & Nicolson, 2004)

Enright, B. J., 'Richard Rawlinson and the Publication of John Aubrey's Natural History and Antiquities of Surrey', *Surrey Archaeological Collections*, 54 (1956), p.124

Evelyn, J., *The Diary of John Evelyn*, ed. de Beer, E. S., 6 vols (Oxford: Clarendon Press, 1955)

Foskett, D., *Samuel Cooper, 1609–1672* (London: Faber, 1974)

Fowles, J., 'The Great Amateur of Archaeology', *Natural History*, August 1982, pp.18–24

Frank, R. G., 'John Aubrey, FRS, John Lydall, and Science at Commonwealth Oxford', *Notes and Records of the Royal Society of London*, 27 (1973), pp.193–217

_____, *Harvey and the Oxford Physiologists: A Study of Scientific Ideas and Social Interaction* (Berkeley / Los Angeles: University of California Press, 1981)

Garland, P., *Brief Lives, by John Aubrey; a play in two acts for one player* (London: Faber, 1967)

Gaskill, M., 'Witchcraft, Politics and Memory in Seventeenth-Century England', *The Historical Journal*, 50, 2 (2007), pp.289–308

Gregg, R., *Harvey and the Oxford Physiologists: A study of scientific ideas* (Berkeley/Los Angeles: University of California Press, 1980)

Grew, N., *Musæm Regalis Societatis* (London: 1681)

Gunther, R. T., *The Old Ashmolean: the Oldest Museum for the History of the Natural Sciences and Medicine* (Oxford: Oxford University Press, 1933)

_____, 'The Library of John Aubrey, FRS', *Bodleian Quarterly Record*, 6 (1931), pp.230–6

_____, 'The Ashmolean Copy of Plot's Natural History', *Bodleian Library Quarterly*, 6 (1930), pp.165–6

_____, *Early Science in Oxford*, 14 vols. (Oxford: Oxford University Press, 1923–45)

_____, *Historic Instruments for the Advancement of Science: a handbook to the Oxford Collections*, (Oxford: Oxford University Press, 1925)

Hartmann, C. H., *Faringdon in the Civil War*, http://www.faringdon. org/hycivilwarHartmann.htm

Harvey, W., *Exercitationes de Generatione Animalium, quibus accedunt quaedam de Partû, de Membranis ac Tumoribus Uteri, et de Conceptione* (1651)

_____, *De motu cordis* ('Anatomical Exercises Concerning the Motion of the Heart and Blood in Living Creatures') (1628)

Haycock, D. B., *William Stukeley: Science, Religion and Archaeology in Eighteenth Century England* (Woodbridge: Boydell Press, 2002)

Hearne, T., *Hearne's Remarks and Collections*, vol. 7 (Oxford: Oxford Historical Society, 1906)

_____, *The Remains of Thomas Hearne: Reliquiae Hearnianae; being extracts from his MS diaries*, compiled by Dr John Bliss, revised by John Buchanan-Brown (London, Fontwell: Centaur Press, 1966).

Hobbes, T., *Leviathan*, ed. Malcolm, N., 3 vols (Oxford: Clarendon Press, 2012)

_____, *The Correspondence of Thomas Hobbes*, ed. Malcolm, N., 2 vols (Oxford: Oxford University Press, 1994)

Hooke, R., *The Diary of Robert Hooke, 1672–1680*, transcribed from the original in the possession of the Corporation of the City of London (Guildhall library), eds Robinson, H. W., and Adams, W. (London: Taylor & Francis, 1935)

_____, *Cometa, Containing Observations of the Comet in April, 1677* (London: J. Martyn, 1678).

Hopkins, C., *Trinity: 450 Years of an Oxford College Community* (Oxford: Oxford University Press, 2005)

Horsfall Turner, O., '"The Windows of this Church are of several Fashions": architectural form and historical method in John Aubrey's "Chronologia Architectonica"', *Architectural History*, 54 (2011), pp.171–93

Hunter, M., ed., *Printed Images in Early Modern Britain: Essays in Interpretation* (Aldershot: Ashgate, 2010)

_____, *Boyle: between God and Science* (New Haven, London: Yale University Press, 2009)

_____, *Robert Boyle Reconsidered* (Cambridge: Cambridge University Press, 1994)

_____, *Robert Boyle (1627–91): Scrupulosity and Science* (Woodbridge, Suffolk: Boydell Press, 2000)

_____, *Science and the Shape of Orthodoxy: Intellectual Change in Late Seventeenth-Century Britain* (Woodbridge, Suffolk: Boydell Press, 1995)

_____, *The Royal Society and Its Fellows, 1660–1700: The Morphology of an Early Scientific Institution*, BSHS monographs, 4 (Chalfont St Giles, Bucks.: British Society for the History of Science, 1994)

_____, *Establishing the New Science: The Experience of the Early Royal Society* (Woodbridge, Suffolk: Boydell Press, 1989)

_____, *Science and Society in Restoration England* (Cambridge: Cambridge University Press, 1981)

_____, *John Aubrey and the Realm of Learning* (London: Duckworth, 1975)

_____, 'The Bibliography of John Aubrey's Brief Lives', *Antiquarian Book Monthly Review*, 1 (1974), p.6ff.

_____, 'The Royal Society and the Origins of British Archaeology', *Antiquity*, 65 (1971), pp.113–21, 187–92

_____, and Knight, Harriet, 'Print, Manuscript and the Impact of Baconianism in Seventeenth-Century Medical Science', *Medical History*, 51(2) (1 April 2007), pp.145–64

_____, and S. Schaffer, eds, *Robert Hooke: New Studies* (Woodbridge, Suffolk: Boydell Press, 1989)

Hutton, R., *The Restoration: A Political and Religious History of England and Wales 1658–1667* (Oxford: Oxford University Press, 1985)

Jackson, J. E., 'Aubrey's Wiltshire Antiquities', *Notes and Queries*, 2nd ser., 8 (1859), pp.467–8

Jardine, L., *The Curious Life of Robert Hooke: the Man who Measured London* (London: HarperCollins, 2003)

Jeffrey, E. (ed.), *The Antiquarian repertory: a miscellaneous assemblage of topography, history, biography, customs, and manners; intended to illustrate and preserve several valuable remains of old times*, 4 vols (London, 1808)

Kemp, M., *The Chapel of Trinity College, Oxford* (Oxford: Scala Arts and Heritage, 2014)

Keynes, G., *A Bibliography of Sir Thomas Browne* (Oxford: Clarendon Press, 1968)

Kircher, A., *Ars magna lucis et umbrae* (Rome, 1646)

Leland, J., *The Itinerary of John Leland the Antiquary*, published by Thomas Hearne (Oxford: James Fletcher, 1770)

Lennard, R., 'English Agriculture under Charles II: The Evidence of the Royal Society's "Enquiries"', *The Economic History Review*, vol. 4, no. 1 (Oct. 1932), pp.23–45

Lewis, R., *Language, Mind and Nature: Artificial Languages in England from Bacon to Locke* (Cambridge: Cambridge University Press, 2007)

———, 'The Efforts of the Aubrey Correspondence Group to Revise John Wilkins's Essay (1668) and their Context', *Historiographia Linguistica*, 28 (2001), pp.333–66.

Lodwick, F., *Writings on Language, Theology, and Utopia*, ed. Henderson, F., and Poole, W. (Oxford University Press: Oxford, 2011)

Macaulay, T. B., *The History of England from the Accession of James II to the death of William the Third*, 5 vols, (London: Chatto & Windus, 1905)

MacGregor, A., ed., *Tradescant's Rarities, Essays on the Foundation of the Ashmolean Museum 1683, with a catalogue of the surviving early collections* (Clarendon Press: Oxford, 1983)

Malcolm, N., *Aspects of Hobbes* (Oxford: Oxford University Press, 2002)

Manning, P., 'Bringing in the Fly', *Folklore: A Quarterly Review*, vol. 25 (1914)

McMains, H. F., *The Death of Oliver Cromwell* (Lexington: University of Kentucky Press, 2000)

Mortimer, S., *Reason and Religion in the English Revolution: The Challenge of Socinianism* (Cambridge: Cambridge University Press, 2010)

Mydorgius, C., *Sectiones Conicas* (Paris, 1639)

Ogilby, J., trans., *Homer his Odysses translated, adorn'd with sculpture, and illustrated with annotations, by John Ogilby* (London: printed by Thomas Roycroft for the author, 1665)

———, *Queries in order to the description of Britannia* (London, 1673)

Ovenell, R. F., *The Ashmolean Museum 1683–1894* (Oxford: Clarendon Press, 1986)

Parry, G., *The Arch Conjurer – John Dee* (New Haven and London: Yale University Press, 2012)

Pell, J., *Idea of Mathematics* (1650)

Pepys, S., *The Diary of Samuel Pepys*, ed. Latham, R., and Matthews, W., 11 vols (London, 1970–83)

Plot, R., *The Natural History of Oxfordshire* (Oxford, 1667)

Poole, W., *John Aubrey and the Advancement of Learning* (Oxford: Bodleian Library Publishing, 2010)

———, *The World-Makers: Scientists of the Restoration and the Search for the Origins of the Earth* (Oxford: Peter Lang, 2010)

———, 'The Genesis Narrative in the Circle of Robert Hooke and Francis Lodwick', in *Scripture and Scholarship in Early Modern England*, ed. A. Hessayon, and N. Keene, (Aldershot: Ashgate, 2006), pp.41–57

Powell, A., *John Aubrey and his Friends* (London: Eyre & Spottiswoode, 1948; new and rev. edn, London: Heinemann, 1963)

———, 'John Aubrey's Books I, II', *Times Literary Supplement*, 13 (20 Jan. 1950), pp.32–48

Purdon, J. J., 'Aubrey's Discourse in Paper', *Essays in Criticism*, 55 (2005), pp.226–47

Raymond, J., *Pamphlets and Pamphleteering in Early Modern Britain* (Cambridge: Cambridge University Press, 2006)

———, *The Invention of the Newspaper, English Newsbooks, 1641–1649* (Oxford: Clarendon Press, 1996)

Rumsey, W., *Organon Salutis. An Instrument to Cleanse the Stomach. As also divers new Experiments of the virtue of Tobacco and Coffee: how much they conduce to preserve humane health* (London: Daniel Pakeman, 1657)

Salmon, V., *The Study of Language in 17th Century England* (Amsterdam, Philadelphia: John Benjamins Publishing, 1988)

Sharpe, K., and Zwicker, S. N., *Writing Lives: Biography and Textuality, Identity and Representation in Early Modern England* (Oxford: Oxford University Press, 2008)

Short, T., *An essay towards a natural, experimental, and medicinal history of the principle mineral waters: of Cumberland, Northumberland, Westmoreland, Bishop-prick of Durham, Lancashire, Cheshire, Staffordshire, Shropshire, Worcestershire, Glocestershire, Warwickshire, Northamptonshire, Leicestershire, and Nottinghamshire, particularly those* of Neville Holt, Cheltenham, Weatherslack, Hartlepool, Astrope, Cartmall &c. Wherein they are carefully examined and compared, their mineral contents are discovered and separated, their uses shewn and explained [et]c. To which is added, a short discourse on cold and tepid bathing, and a table of the temperature of all the warm waters in England, and most of the cold baths, from Carlisle to Glocester and Oxford. Being the second volume of The mineral waters of England (Sheffield: John Garnet, 1740)

Somner, W., A treatise of the Roman ports and forts in Kent, by William Somner, Publish'd by James Brome. To which is prefixt the life of Mr Somner, ed. W. Kennett (Oxford: printed at the Theater, 1693)

Stevenson, C., The City and the King: Architecture and Politics in Restoration London (New Haven and London: Yale University Press, 2013)

Stukeley, W., Stonehenge, a Temple restor'd to the British Druids (London, 1740)

Turnbull, G. H., 'Samuel Hartlib's Acquaintance with John Aubrey', Notes and Queries, 195 (1950), pp.31–3

Turner, J. W., 'A Talent for Friendship, Edmund Wyld of Houghton Conquest', Bedfordshire Biographies, XII, Bedfordshire Magazine, vol. 3, no. 19 (1951–2)

Uglow, J., A Gambling Man: Charles II and the Restoration (London: Faber, 2009)

Virgil, Eclogues, Georgics, Aeneid 1–6; trans. H. Rushton Fairclough, 2 vols (Cambridge, Mass., London: Harvard University Press, 1999–2000).

Virgil, The Works of Virgil, trans. John Dryden (London: J. Walker, 1818).

Wase, C., Grati Falisci Cynegeticon, Or, A Poem of Hunting By Gratius the Faliscian, trans. Christopher Wase (London: printed for Charles Adams, 1654)

_____, Considerations Concerning Free Schools, as settled in England (Oxford, 1678)

Wattie, M., 'Robert Hooke on his Literary Contemporaries', The Review of English Studies, vol. XIII, no. 50 (April 1937)

Westfall, R. S., Science and Religion in Seventeenth-Century England (New Haven, London: Yale University Press, 1958)

Wilkins, J., Mathematical Magick (London, 1648)

Williams, K. J., 'Training the Virtuoso: John Aubrey's Education and

Early Life', *The Seventeenth Century*, vol. 27, no. 2 (Summer 2012), pp.157–82

_____, John Aubrey's antiquarian scholarship: a study in the seventeenth-century Republic of Letters, DPhil., University of Oxford (2012)

Willman, R., 'Hobbes on the Law of Heresy', *Journal of the History of Ideas*, 31 (1970), pp.607–13

Willmoth, F., *Sir Jonas Moore: Practical Mathematics and Restoration Science* (Woodbridge, Suffolk: Boydell Press, 1993)

Wood, A., *Athenae Oxonienses : an exact history of all the writers and bishops who have had their education in the most ancient and famous University of Oxford, from the fifteenth year of King Henry the Seventh, Dom. 1500, to the end of the year 1690 representing the birth, fortune, preferment, and death of all those authors and prelates, the great accidents of their lives, and the fate and character of their writings : to which are added, the Fasti, or, Annals, of the said university, for the same time*, 2 vols (London: printed for Tho. Bennet, 1691–2)

_____, *Historia et Antiquitates Universitatis Oxoniensis*, 2 vols (Oxford: e Theatro Sheldoniano, 1674)

Worden, B., *The English Civil Wars 1640–1660* (London: Phoenix, 2010)

_____, *Literature and Politics in Cromwellian England: John Milton, Andrew Marvell, Marchamont Nedham* (Oxford: Oxford University Press, 2007)

_____, *Roundhead Reputations: the English Civil Wars and the passions of posterity* (London: Penguin, 2001)

_____, *The Rump Parliament 1648–53* (Cambridge: Cambridge University Press, 1977)

Index